Through Baca's Vale

J C Philpot

Arranged
By
Noel Pogson

All rights reserved; no part of this publication may be reproduced, stored in a retrieval system, or transmitted by any means, electronic, mechanical, photocopying, or otherwise without the prior permission

First published in Great Britain in 2018 by Balbardie Press

First edition April 2018

Copyright ©

ISBN - 978-0-9933801-5-0

Printed and bound in the country of purchase

This edition of

J C Philpot's Baca's Vale

is dedicated to

Theo N

whom God brought across

my path to revive

my soul when

I was weary

Feeling, as we do, our own miserable helplessness, sinking under the pressure of our daily weakness, mourning over our continual failures, and grieving on account of our perpetual backslidings; encompassed by foes and distressed by fears; how strengthening it is to our faith, thus tried to the uttermost, to believe that he who has purposed has power to perform.

J C Philpot

"Blessed is the man whose strength is in thee; in whose heart are the ways of them; who passing through the valley of Baca make it a well; the rain also filleth the pools."

Psalm 84:5-6

Original Preface

Some years ago, as is well known to most of our readers, we published a series of extracts in the form of Daily Portions from the works of our late dear Father, J. C. Philpot, which received a welcome far, far more cordial than we had ventured to hope or expect. Indeed, the numerous testimonies that have reached us again and again, from various quarters, of the blessing of God richly attending the perusal of these Portions have made our hearts burn within us, and the thought that He should condescend to put His seal of approbation upon our labours may well excite the deepest humility and gratitude.

Now, with mixed feelings of pleasure and regret, we find the edition is rapidly coming to an end, and as several friends have expressed a wish for another series of Portions culled from the same source, we thought, as there still remained sufficient material to draw upon, that we should prefer to bring out another book rather than merely reprint the former. That the present volume is larger and contains more matter will be seen at a glance: the fact is, all the suitable short pieces were selected for the earlier one, consequently, these in most cases are longer, which, under the circumstances, was unavoidable, but we trust that even the busiest may be able to spare a few minutes to read the portion for the day. If it is a little long, may it be found proportionately seasonable and weighty, refreshing to a weary spirit – a word of encouragement or exhortation to pilgrims journeying Zionwards.

As a frontispiece, a collotype portrait has been added, copied from the most pleasing photograph we possess of our dear Father. This we thought would be valued, not only by those who knew him personally, but by a new generation, who would doubtless like to have some idea of the outward form and features of one whom, though they never saw him in the flesh, they love and esteem for his works' sake.

It may be observed in this as in the former volume that some of the pieces begin and end rather abruptly, but it must be remembered that they were not written for the purpose to which they are now applied, as was the case with Mason's and Hawker's Portions, but are merely extracts gathered, as the title of the earlier work suggested, from those sheaves which have been garnered for the use and edification of the Household of Faith.

In conclusion, we can only express our earnest desire and prayer that the Lord God of Sabaoth may again be graciously pleased to smile upon our efforts, and continue to bless the words of His late dear servant, who "being dead, yet speaketh," to the souls of His living family, and His name shall have all the praise.

S. & D. M. Philpot
Croydon, 1893

Foreword

The writings of J.C. Philpot have been a source of blessing to many people over many years. His sound expositions of Holy Scripture, his simple explanations of the truths therein, and his practical applications of the same to people's lives has made his written works a treasure trove of spiritual wealth for every seeking sinner, and every battling believer, in every generation.

Joseph Charles Philpot M.A. is the best remembered of all the Strict Baptist preachers of Victorian times. He was born in Kent in 1802 to Charles Philpot, a Church of England rector, and his wife Maria. Having been educated at home by his father, he received a scholarship to Worchester College in Oxford where he graduated with a First in Classics in 1824. Remaining at Oxford for a further year, he secured a fellowship at the College, afterwards moving to Ireland where he earned a living as a tutor to the two sons of a wealthy lawyer. During that time, he fell in love with the eldest daughter of the family, but was refused permission to marry her. However, his heartbreak was soothed by the joy that he found after he had been brought to saving faith in Jesus Christ.

On his return to England, he became the curate of the parishes of Stadhampton and Chiselhampton in Oxfordshire. There he immersed himself in Christian ministry for seven years, and large crowds attended his services eager to hear him preach. At this time, he became acquainted with William Tiptaft, the vicar of a neighbouring parish, and as they studied the Bible together, they began to understand the blessed Doctrines of Grace.

Disillusioned with the unbiblical teachings and practices of the Church of England, Tiptaft became a Baptist and founded a church in Abingdon. Though unwilling to leave his own congregation, Philpot resigned in 1835 convinced that Baptist principles agreed with Scripture. Six months later in a Baptist Chapel at Allington, he was baptised by John Warburton, a Strict Baptist pastor from Trowbridge.

J.C. Philpot became the Strict Baptist Pastor of churches in Stamford and Oakham in 1836. Preaching to one congregation one Lord's Day and the other the next, crowds packed in to hear him. In 1864, almost 30 years of faithful and fruitful ministry ended due to ill-health.

However, Philpot's ministry was not limited to the pastorate, but found a greater audience through the printed word. Though he had helped with 'The Gospel Standard Magazine' since its inception in 1835, from 1840 until his death he was its editor. His contributions to this magazine have ensured that '...he being dead yet speaketh.' (Hebrews 11:4)

Ian Loughrin
Pastor of Benhar Evangelical Church
April 2018

Arranger's Preface

This edition of 'Through Baca's Vale' has been arranged to meet the need for a very lightly updated version of this classic work which is more accessible to 21st Century readers. Whilst remaining wholly true to the original in content and message, it carefully updates some of the more complex 19th Century language and grammar, which for many these days proves to be a barrier. This light editing is generally restricted to splitting up many of the very lengthy paragraphs and carefully restructuring some of the extremely long sentences, whilst leaving the full original sense and language essentially unchanged.

The King James Version of Scripture is used throughout, both for the opening text of each devotion and for the many hundreds of quotes Philpot marshals to expound the Word. As a further enhancement to earlier editions, references have been embedded within the text to enable the reader to more easily find and review the passages of Scripture from which Philpot draws. Philpot himself often paraphrased, tending to follow the pattern of the Geneva Bible of 1560, so where odd words differ from the King James Version in the body of his text, this may well be the cause and origin.

Readers should also bear in mind that scientific knowledge was somewhat more limited in the 19th Century, and therefore some of the similes used then might not pass scientific scrutiny in our 21st century. However, they have been left largely unchanged, as has Philpot's original choice of words, some of which may no longer be deemed 'politically correct' in the strange days in which we live.

In only one case has a noun been changed in order to avoid wording which would now be seen as offensive, although in Philpot's day, and even up until the late 20th Century, it would have seemed rational and normal.

I trust that you will find these devotions as encouraging and challenging in their new form as I do, and that they will strengthen your faith as they have done for many thousands of Christian readers over the years since they were originally published. The truth contained within them is as precious and real today as it was then, and remains fresh and pertinent with repeated study. You will be able to read this volume many times during your life and will always be surprised to find something new which you missed first time around.

Noel Pogson
April 2018

January

January 1st

"Hold up my goings in thy paths, that my footsteps slip not."
Psalm 17:5

Without scrupulously or superstitiously observing "days, and months, and times, and years," (Gal. 4:10), few of us altogether pass by so marked an epoch as the dawning of another year upon our path without some acknowledgment of it both to God and man. When we open our eyes on the first morning of the year, we almost instinctively say, 'This is New-year's day'. Nor is this, at least this should not be, all the notice we take of it, or all the acknowledgment we make of that opening year of which we may not see the close.

When we bend our knees before the throne of grace, we mingle with thankful acknowledgment for the mercies of the past year, both in providence and in grace, earnest petitions for similar mercies to be experienced and enjoyed through the present. Last evening witnessed our confessions of the many, many grievous sins, wanderings, backslidings, and departings from the living God during the year now gone; this morning witnesses our supplications for grace to hold up our goings in his paths, that our footsteps slip not through the year just come.

Tears are most suitable at the burial of the dead; hopes and desires at the birth of the living. The past year was the departed father, worn out with age and infirmity; the present year is the new-born babe in the arms of the smiling mother. It is still, however, mid-winter. Today, the first of the new year differs little in outward appearance from yesterday, the last of the old, yet the thoughtful, prayerful mind takes little notice of wintry skies. It feels that the old, worn-out year has sunk into its grave, with all its trials and afflictions, and that a new year has come in its place, with its new hopes and new mercies. If it brings new trials, the promise still stands that new strength will be given to meet and overcome them.

Refreshed and strengthened at the throne by such or similar communings with the God of all our mercies, we go down to meet our families, and are at once greeted on all sides with, "I wish you a happy New Year," a greeting which we warmly and affectionately return. Almost every friend, and well-near every acquaintance that we meet with in the course of the day, greets us with the same kind wish.

Now in all this there may be a great deal of formality, lip-service, and traditional usage; but there may be also a good deal of sincerity, kindness, and affection. We are not, surely, so shut up in miserable self as to have no desire for the health and happiness, the temporal and spiritual welfare, of our families, our friends, or even our acquaintances. And if we desire their good, we need not be backward or unwilling to express it in a few words of friendly greeting.

"Be ye kind one to another, tender-hearted," (Eph. 4:32); "Be pitiful, be courteous," (1Pet. 3:8); "If it be possible, as much as lieth in you, live peaceably with all men," (Rom. 12:18). These are all precepts imbued with the spirit of the gospel, and may be, indeed, should be, attended to without the least sacrifice of that faithfulness which becomes those who would daily walk in the fear of the Lord.

There may be a form of kind words as well as a "form of sound words," (2Tim. 1:13), and as we use the latter in perfect harmony with the doctrines of the gospel, so we may use the former in perfect harmony with the spirit of the gospel.

2nd

"But grow in grace, and in the knowledge of our Lord and Saviour Jesus Christ. To him be glory both now and for ever. Amen."
2Peter 3:18

Growth is the sure mark of life. We see this in vegetation, in the animal creation, in the growth of our own bodies, and of every other thing in which there is life. Where, then, there is the life of God in the soul, there will be a growth in that life. Paul says to the Thessalonian Church, "We are bound to thank God always for you, brethren, as it is meet, because that your faith groweth exceedingly," (2Thes. 1:3), and Peter says, "But grow in grace, and in the knowledge of our Lord and Saviour Jesus Christ." There is also "an increasing in the knowledge of God," (Col. 1:10), and a coming "in the unity of the faith, and of the knowledge of the Son of God, unto a perfect man, unto the measure of the stature of the fullness of Christ," (Eph. 4:13).

It was for this increasing knowledge of the Son of God that Paul stretched every desire of his soul when he followed after, if that he might apprehend that for which also he was apprehended of Christ Jesus. Thus, reaching forth unto those things which were before, he pressed toward the mark, for the prize of the high calling of God in Christ Jesus, (Phil. 3:13-14).

This is not what is nowadays called 'progressive sanctification', as if the flesh got holier and holier, for the flesh will ever be "the old man, which is corrupt according to the deceitful lusts," (Eph. 4:22).

This is a growth of that "new man, which after God is created in righteousness and true holiness," (Eph. 4:24).

We should ever be striving after the growth in grace of the new man, this closer conformity to the image of Christ, with all the powers of our soul. We should not be satisfied with a low and lean state before God, but with unceasing prayer and supplication we should be begging of the Lord that we might be "filled with the knowledge of his will in all wisdom and spiritual understanding; that [we] might walk worthy of the Lord unto all pleasing, being fruitful in every good work, and increasing in the knowledge of God," (Col. 1:9-10).

3rd

"I will sing of the mercies of the Lord forever."
Psalm 89:1

We are surrounded on every side with mercies for the body and mercies for the soul, yet there are times and seasons when the mercies of God, both in providence and grace, seem hidden from our eyes. Days when the workings of sin, rebellion, and unbelief hide his face, and weeks or months when the difficulties of a thorny path in this world, and a rough and trying road in the soul hide the mercies of God from us, though they ever compass us about. As with Elisha's servant, though the mountain is surrounded by horses and chariots of fire, and the angels of God are round about us, yet are our eyes blind and we cannot see them. At the very moment when God is showering mercies upon us, and preparing others in reserve, through some trying dispensation we are filled with murmuring and rebellion, and cry, 'Is his mercy clean gone forever, will he be favourable no more?'

This is our infirmity and weakness, but it no more arrests the shower of God's mercies than the parched field arrests the falling rain. The mercies of God, like himself, are infinite, and he pours them in profusion upon his Church and people. They come freely as the beams of the sun shining in the sky; as the breezes of the air we breathe; as the river that never ceases to flow. Everything testifies of the mercy of God to those whose eyes are anointed to see it, and who are interested in it. To them all things in nature, in providence, and in grace proclaim with one united harmonious voice, 'The mercy of the Lord endureth forever'.

Now, as these mercies of God are sensibly felt in the soul, they soften, meeken, and subdue the spirit. They melt it into the obedience of faith, and raise up in it the tenderness of love. By this we are prepared to enter into the beauty and blessedness of the precept as an integral part of the gospel. If I take a review of the mercies of God and feel no saving interest in them, or if they are not personally and individually mine, I slight or perhaps even rebel against the precept as too hard and severe. The yoke is too heavy for my neck to bear. My Jewish mind, my stiff-necked disposition, shrinks from obedience to God's word.

But let my soul be favoured with a sweet discovery of the mercies of God; let them reach my heart and soften and subdue my spirit, then there is no cross too heavy to bear, no trial too hard to be endured, no path of suffering and sorrow in which we cannot patiently, if not gladly, walk. The reason why the precepts are not obeyed is because the mercies of God are not felt. Love and obedience attend each other as the shadow waits upon the sun.

4th

"Confirming the souls of the disciples, and exhorting them to continue in the faith, and that we must through much tribulation enter into the kingdom of God."
Acts 14:22

The word "confirming" implies that the souls of Christ's disciples need strengthening and upholding. Yet if no temptation tried them, no sharp sorrows grieved them, and no painful afflictions distressed them, where would be the need for confirming? If there were no sensible weakness of soul, no sinking of heart, no despondency of spirit, no giving way of faith and hope, and no doubt or fear in the mind, how could the souls of the disciples be strengthened and encouraged?

The souls of God's people are not made of cast iron against which arrow after arrow may be discharged and leave no dent, or make any impression. The hearts of the Lord's people are, in a measure, conformed to the heart of Christ, and what do we read of his heart? "My heart," he says, "is like wax; it is melted in the midst of my bowels," (Psa. 22:14).

Thus the Lord's people, who carry in their bosom broken hearts and contrite spirits, made so by grace, are often sinking, often shaken, often cast down through the many trials they have to encounter. It is for this reason that they need confirming, supporting, and strengthening, and that the Lord himself would lay his everlasting arms underneath them, lift them into his bosom, and make his strength perfect in their weakness.

Is not this the gospel way? Can I, by dint of creature exertion, brace up my soul to a certain pitch and confirm myself? If trouble comes, am I like a patient sometimes under the keen knife of the surgeon to brace up my nerves to bear the operation more unflinchingly? This is nature, flesh and reason; not grace. The Lord does not require this of his people. He dealt not so with his beloved apostle, according to the letter Paul wrote to the Corinthian church. What did the Lord speak into his heart, under trial and temptation, that he might proclaim it upon Zion's walls to the Church of the living God? "My grace is sufficient for thee: for my strength is made perfect in weakness," (2Cor. 12:9). To which he adds, "Most gladly therefore will I rather glory in my infirmities, that the power of Christ may rest upon me."

Yet it is very painful to the Lord's people to find no strength when they need it most, no faith when they have the greatest want of it, and no help when it is most required. To pass through this experience baffles and disconcerts many of the living family of God. However, the Lord is often pleased in a mysterious way to communicate his own strength and make it perfect in weakness. He then deals with his family as he did with the worthies of old, who "out of weakness were made strong," then can they bless the Lord for their very weakness, and, like Paul, glory in their infirmities, because the power of Christ rests upon them.

5th

"Through the tender mercy of our God; whereby the dayspring from on high hath visited us, to give light to them that sit in darkness and in the shadow of death, to guide our feet into the way of peace."
Luke 1:78-79

There is a way of peace, and that is the Lord Jesus Christ, for in scripture he is referred to as both 'our peace' and 'the way'. He has made peace through the blood of his cross, (Col. 1:20), having slain the enmity thereby, and came and preached peace to those who were afar off, sitting "in darkness and the shadow of death," and to those who were near, (Eph. 2:16-17). The dayspring, then, breaking in upon the soul, shines upon the way of peace, and guides the feet into it. The light shines upon the way lined with blood; the way of salvation through the finished work, atoning blood, and meritorious sufferings of the Son of God. As, then, the light shines upon the way, and it is seen as a way of peace, a way of pardon and reconciliation, a way of access and acceptance, a way of grace and glory, a way of life and happiness, the feet of faith move towards it, enter upon it, and walk in it.

This is a peace that passes all understanding, a peace which the world cannot give or take away, or even understand. It is a holy calm, a gracious subduing of all rebellion. That power, which once said to the boiling waves and howling winds, "Peace, be still!" is the power that does it all. How great the change! Instead of being at war with God, being at peace with Him and seeing by the eye of faith that the whole way from earth to heaven, as revealed in the Person and work of the Son of God, is peace from first to last. How settling to know that as long as the feet are moving in that path, they are walking in a way of peace. What yearning there is to know, feel, and enjoy more of this peace, the peace of which Jesus said, "Peace I leave with you, my peace I give unto you," (John 14:27).

The only true peace is peace in believing, peace through atoning blood, and peace by walking in sweet communion with Father, Son, and Holy Spirit. Nor are we left ignorant how it is to be attained and maintained; "Be careful for nothing; but in every thing by prayer and supplication with thanksgiving let your requests be made known unto God; and the peace of God, which passeth all understanding, shall keep your hearts and minds through Christ Jesus," (Phil. 4:6-7).

6th

"O God, thou art my God; early will I seek thee: my soul thirsteth for thee, my flesh longeth for thee in a dry and thirsty land, where no water is;"
Psalm 63:1

David here speaks of seeking God for what he is in himself as distinct from what God has to give. Partaking of his gifts is one thing, but receiving God himself is quite another. Therefore he says, "O God, thou art my God; early will I seek *thee*," as distinct from seeking his gifts. The bride may value her bridegroom's wealth, but what counts the gold apart from the bridegroom himself? In like manner the Church highly prizes her royal Husband's gifts and blessings; but what are these compared to Him who, in her admiring eyes, is the chief among ten thousand and altogether lovely? Thus, as seen by the eye of faith, there is that in his most blessed Majesty which alone can satisfy the soul taught by his Spirit and influenced by his grace.

The soul was made for him, and it was gifted with immortality by him. Powers and faculties were given to it that might be expanded

January

into an infinite capacity to know and to enjoy him. So that being created for God, nothing but God can really satisfy its cravings and desires. Yet in him, as revealed to a believing heart, there is that which can satisfy. His favour is life; his presence is heaven begun; his love is a foretaste of eternal bliss. Thus in seeking the blessings he has to bestow, we do not seek them independent of the Giver. We love the gift, but we prize the Giver more. Without the Giver, the gift would be worthless. The bridal ring is the pledge of union, but what purpose a bride and a ring without a bridegroom? It would be mockery, and so it is with the Lord. If he gave all the favours and blessings which he has to bestow but withheld himself, it would merely mock us, but when he gives them, he gives us also himself.

As when the bridegroom puts the ring on the finger of his betrothed he gives himself with the gift; so also, when the Lord seals a sense of his espousal upon the heart of his beloved one, in giving his love he gives himself. Nothing else can satisfy the desires of an awakened soul.

'It is Jesus that I want;' says the soul. 'Without him, heaven itself would be hell. Without him life would not be life, glory would not be glory, and immortality would not be immortality!'

Without the sun, our verdant earth could not exist, and without Christ, his living Church could not exist. In the absence of the sun, no amount of candles could take the place of heaven's own glorious light, and in like manner no amount of righteousness, however bright, if kindled by human hands, could make up to the Church for the absence of the Sun of righteousness.

He must be our all. In having him, we have everything, and in not having him we have nothing. May the Lord the Spirit write that truth deeply upon your heart that you may take it wherever you go, and make it ever your bosom companion. If you have Christ, then you have everything; if you have not him, you have nothing. This continual feeling of happiness in and with him, and of misery out of and without him, as maintained in your breast by the power of the blessed Spirit, will be leading you to seek him perpetually.

This is what made David say, "Early will I seek thee."

7th

"Let us lift up our heart with our hands unto God in the heavens."
Lamentations 3:41

January

When the Lord lays judgment to the line and righteousness to the plummet, when he makes the living man complain on account of his deserved chastisement for sin and thus brings him to search and try his own ways, he raises up an earnest cry in that man's soul.

"Let us lift up our heart with our hands," says the prophet, first noting the lifting up of the heart. There is no mere bended knee, nor a simple outward appearance with a grave and solemn countenance, that easiest and most frequent cover of hypocrisy. There are to be no empty hands raised aloft accompanying empty recited prayers, that idol of this age, but only a genuine and honest lifting up of the heart first, followed by the hands.

This is the only true prayer, when the heart is poured out before the throne of grace, the Spirit interceding for us and within us, with groanings that cannot be uttered. "God is a Spirit; and they that worship him must worship him in spirit and in truth," (John 4:24). A contrite heart and a broken spirit, the inward panting of the soul after his manifested presence, the heaving sigh and penitential tear will only be regarded by him when we turn away from mere lip-service and bodily exercise.

But there is also much here implied in the words, "God in the heavens." This expression represents him as seated far *above* all heavens, enthroned in light, majesty, and glory unspeakable, and yet sitting on his throne of mercy and grace to bless the soul that waits upon him. He is still accessible, full of love and compassion for the poor and needy one that lifts up his heart together with the hand, that he may receive pardon and peace out of Jesus' fullness, and pants with unutterable longings that the Lord himself would graciously smile and beam love and favour into his soul.

This lifting up of the heart – the only true and acceptable prayer – no man can create in himself. God, who works all things after the counsel of his own will, can alone work in us thus "to will and to do of his good pleasure," (Phil. 2:13). Nature cannot, with all her efforts, and all her counterfeit imitations of vital godliness, accomplish this spiritual sacrifice. She may cut her flesh liberally with lancets, and cry, "Baal, hear us," from morning until evening, but she cannot bring down the holy fire from heaven, (1Kings 18:26).

She can lift the hand, but she cannot lift up the heart. Depend upon it that in this spiritual communion with the living God, out of the sight and out of the reach of the most refined hypocrite and self-deceiver, much of the power of vital godliness lies. This lifting up of the heart when no eye sees and no ear hears, in the daily and hourly transactions of life, in the lonely chamber and on the midnight bed, at the workplace and in the field, surrounded by the world and yet separated from it, this is a secret known only to the living family of God.

January 8th

"And I will pray the Father, and he shall give you another Comforter, that he may abide with you for ever; even the Spirit of truth; whom the world cannot receive, because it seeth him not, neither knoweth him: but ye know him; for he dwelleth with you, and shall be in you"
John 14:16-17

The holy Comforter and most gracious Spirit does not take up a merely temporary abode in the heart of the Lord's people. When he once takes up his dwelling there, he forever abides and lives in that heart, as our text says, "He shall give you another Comforter, that he may abide with you forever."

Oh, the blessing, for where once that holy Dove alights, there that Dove abides! He does not visit the soul with his grace and then leave it to perish under the wrath of God, or allow his work to wither, droop, and die unloved. Where he has once come into the soul with power, there he fixes his continual habitation, for he makes the bodies of the saints his temple. He consecrates them to the service of God. He takes up his dwelling in their hearts, and there he lives, there he moves, there he works and sanctifies body and soul to the honour and glory of the Lord God Almighty.

What a blessing it is to have received such a gracious and heavenly Teacher as the Spirit of truth! If this be your happy case, you know the truth for yourself, and the truth is dear to your soul. It has been ingrafted by a divine witness in your heart, and inlaid by the power of God in your conscience. The truth as it is in Jesus is very, very precious to you. You cannot part with it; it is your very life. Sooner than part with God's truth and your saving interest therein, you would be willing in favoured moments to lay down your life itself.

What is it therefore that makes you love God's truth? What has given you a heart to embrace it and delight in it? When you have come to the house of prayer, maybe with a fainting body and a troubled mind, what has yet supported your weary steps and brought you on? And when you have gone home from hearing the word, what has cheered your heart, in the dark and gloomy night as you have lain upon your bed, and drawn your affections up to the Lord Jesus Christ? The Comforter, the Spirit of truth. He, and he alone, could give God's truth so firm and enduring a place in your heart, conscience, and affections.

Then live that truth as well as love it, and proclaim its power and efficacy in your life and conversation. If the Spirit has written his truth upon your heart, he will bring forth that truth in your lips and in your

January

life. He will make it manifest that you are "children that cannot lie." You will show forth the power of truth in the sincerity of your speech, in the uprightness of your movements, in your family, in the Church, in your business, in your general character and deportment, and in everything which displays the reality of religion and the power of vital godliness.

9th

"Knowing this first, that no prophecy of the scripture is of any private interpretation. For the prophecy came not in old time by the will of man - but holy men of God spoke as they were moved by the Holy Spirit."
2Peter 1:20-21

The Bible is put into our hands as a revelation from God. As such, we have received it from our fathers. As such, and as such only, does it claim our attention and our obedience. If it is not the word of God – we speak with reverence – it is an imposture.

Now, if we can but firmly establish the necessity of a revelation from God, we have laid a strong foundation for a belief that the Bible is that revelation, and that no other is worth a moment's examination. This argument from necessity, then, is very strong - stronger, perhaps, than it at first appears, and as extensive in application as firm in strength. To feel the force of this argument, cast your eyes for a few moments over creation, and see what a provision has been made everywhere by its All-wise and All-powerful Creator for necessity. From man, at the head of creation, down to the lowest organised structure, there is not a necessity for which provision has not been made, and that in exact proportion to its needs. You yourself came into this world a poor, naked, helpless infant, full of necessities, and must have perished from the womb had not provision been made for them. Who filled for you your mother's breast with milk and her heart with love to care for you? Who ensures these miracles of providence are meted out to all creatures as well as to man?

But you have a soul as well as a body, and it is no less naked and no less necessitous. Shall the body have its necessities and these be provided for, but the soul have its necessities and these not be provided for? Is there no nourishing milk for the soul as well as for the body? Is there no "sincere milk of the word" that it may grow thereby, (1Pet. 2:2)?

The craving after God felt by every new-born soul and the eagerness with which it flies at once to get comfort and instruction from the Word is very telling. The holy joy with which it hails every ray of heavenly light that shines on its dark path evidently shows how deep the necessity of a divine revelation is as laid down in the relationship between man and his Maker. And to meet that necessity, that divine Maker has provided the soul with a never ending supply meats all securely stored up in his word.

10th

"Bless the LORD, O my soul: and all that is within me, bless his holy name."
Psalm 103:1

As the Son has glorified the Father and the Father has glorified the Son, so there is a people in whom both the Father and the Son will be glorified. Jesus therefore said, "And the glory which thou gavest me I have given them; that they may be one, even as we are one," (John 17:22); and again, "All mine are thine, and thine are mine; and I am glorified in them," (John 17:10).

When God's goodness and mercy in the face of Jesus Christ is revealed to this group of people, (whom he has formed for himself in order that they might show forth his praise), they reflect his glory straight back unto him. How is this done? By their praising and blessing his holy name for the manifestation of his goodness and mercy to their soul. We thus see in what a blessed circle this glory runs. The Father glorifies the Son; the Son glorifies the Father; both unite in glorifying his chosen and redeemed people; and they glorify Father and Son by giving them the glory due to their name.

We therefore read that the gentiles "glorify God for his mercy," (Rom. 15:9), but how? "Rejoice, ye Gentiles, with his people. And again, Praise the Lord, all ye Gentiles; and laud him, all ye people," (Rom. 15:10-11).

This is beautifully developed in Psalm 103. It begins with blessing and praising God. "Bless the Lord, O my soul: and all that is within me, bless his holy name. Bless the Lord, O my soul, and forget not all his benefits." Why was it that David called upon his soul to bless the Lord, and even appealed to every faculty within him to unite in blessing his holy name? Why did he charge it upon his soul not to forget all God's benefits, but bear them in perpetual remembrance?

For this reason – that he might render unto God a tribute of thankful praise. Now by this God is glorified, for whoever offers praise glorifies him. We cannot add to his glory; for his glory is above the heavens. It is infinite, eternal, ineffable. No creature therefore can add to it or take from it; but he does permit poor worms of earth to

January

glorify him by giving him a tribute of thankful praise. But this we can only do by believing in his dear Son, receiving of his fullness grace for grace, and blessing and praising his holy name for the manifestation of his goodness, mercy, and love, as brought into our soul by his own divine power.

11th

"To them that are sanctified by God the Father, and preserved in Jesus Christ, and called:"
Jude 1

What a mercy it is for God's people that before their vital union with Christ, before they are grafted experimentally into him during this life, they have an eternal, immanent union with him which began before all worlds. It is by this eternal union that they are brought into this world of time. It is by virtue of this eternal union that they come into the world at such a time, at such a place, from such parents, under such circumstances, as God has appointed. It is because of this eternal union that the circumstances of their time-state are ordained.

Further, by the workings of this eternal union, they are preserved in Christ before they are called and they cannot die until God has brought them into a vital union with Christ. Whatever sickness they may pass through, whatever injuries they may be exposed to, whatever perils assault them on sea or on land, die they will not, and die they cannot, until God's purposes are completed by bringing them into that fore-ordained and vital union with the Son of his love.

This eternal union watched over every circumstance of their birth, watched over their childhood, watched over their manhood, and watched over every detail of their life. It preserved and cared for them until the appointed time and place when "the God of all grace," according to his eternal purpose, was pleased to quicken their souls, and thus bring about their experimental union with the Lord of life and glory.

12th

"But we are bound to give thanks alway to God for you, brethren beloved of the Lord, because God hath from the beginning chosen you to salvation through sanctification of the Spirit and belief of the truth."
2Thessalonians 2:13

January

There is an impartation of righteousness as well as an imputation of it, and the impartation of it is the communication of a divine nature to the soul. Have I one grain of holiness in myself? No, not a one. Can all the religious men in the world, by all their united exertions, raise up a single grain of spiritual holiness in their hearts? No, not an atom, with all their efforts. If all the preachers in the world were to unite together for the purpose of working just one grain of holiness in one man's soul they might strive to all eternity, but they could no more by their preaching create holiness, than by their preaching could they create a lump of gold.

Yet because, by a gracious act of God the Father, Jesus is made unto his people sanctification, he imparts a measure of his own holiness to them. He works in them to will and to do of his own good pleasure, (Phil. 2:13), and he sends the Holy Spirit to raise up holy desires. In short, he communicates or gives to us a nature which is perfectly holy, and which therefore loves holiness and has communion with a holy God. We receive a heavenly, spiritual, and divine nature, which bathes in eternal things as its element, and enjoys spiritual things as sweet and precious. It may indeed be small in measure, and he that has it is often exercised and troubled because he has so little of it, yet he has just enough to know what it is.

Has not your soul, though you feel to be a defiled wretch, though every iniquity is at times working in your heart, though every worm of obscenity and corruption is too often trailing its filthy slime upon your carnal mind – has your soul not felt and does it still not sometimes feel a measure of holiness Godwards? Do you never feel a breathing forth of your soul into the bosom of a holy God? Heavenly desires, pure affections, singleness of eye, simplicity of purpose, a heart that longs to have the mind, image, and likeness of Jesus stamped upon it – this is holiness such as the Lord of life and glory imparts out of his fullness to his poor and needy family.

13th

"The LORD bless thee, and keep thee."
Numbers 6:24

The key to the words, "The Lord bless thee," is, I believe, to be found in Ephesians 1:3, "Blessed be the God and Father of our Lord Jesus Christ, who hath blessed us with all spiritual blessings in heavenly places in Christ." The blessings prayed for in our text would seem to be chiefly spiritual blessings, not that we are to think

January

lightly of temporal favours. They are left-hand blessings, if not right-hand mercies; they are gifts to be thankful for on earth, if not graces that take us to heaven. They are provision for the perishing body, if not food for the immortal soul. Among these are health, and strength, and such a measure of worldly goods as shall keep the wolf from the door and enable us to owe no man anything but love. One might also include children growing up to be a comfort to their parents; a kind and affectionate partner; warm and faithful friends and an untarnished name. When we get to the end of our lives, enough set aside to make provision for those dear and near to us, that their tears over our body may not be doubly embittered by poverty and dependence. Who shall say that these are not blessings for which God is to be praised? Viewed by the eye of faith, blessings in providence come down from heaven steeped in mercy.

And yet how short, oh, how infinitely far short do these temporal blessings, which perish in the using, fall of spiritual blessings which endure for evermore! A striking proof of this is that when we are privileged to draw near to the throne of grace with some measure of faith and feeling, the heart's desire is wholly towards spiritual blessings. At such times the eye of the soul is so wholly and solely fixed upon them, that there is scarcely left place either in the heart or on the lip to ask or desire any other.

Now look again at our text and see the person for whom the blessing is asked. "The Lord bless THEE." Thee is the singular form, yet when the high priest pronounced the blessing he did not fix his eye upon, nor did he address his speech to, any one individual. It was spoken to the whole assembly of the congregation of Israel, and yet the words were so framed as to make the blessing apply to each individual. Such often are God's blessings – personal and individual. Gracious souls, when they have heard the word preached with any particular sweetness or power, often say, 'It was all for me'. Well it might have been, but are you the only 'me' in the place? Might not someone sitting by your side say also 'It was all for me'? Our God takes the same words spoken and individually applies them to each heart, tailoring the blessing to the need. Don't think that only one is to be blessed, and the others excluded. There is enough for each, and there is enough for all.

There is something so singularly appropriating in the mercy of God when brought into the heart that it often seems as though it were for me and for me alone. Yet here is the blessedness of the mercies of God, here are the riches of his grace and glory – that one having a part does not exclude the other. It is not like a natural family, where each successive child seems to withdraw a portion of the inheritance from the others, so that, if they had the covetous feelings of grown-up people, the elder might well say to the new-born babe, 'We don't want you, you little robber! Why are you come to take portions with us?'

It does not narrow the heavenly inheritance that there are so many to enjoy it. We do not get a smaller part because it is shared with millions. If such were the case it would narrow God himself, for God is the inheritance, and in God is enough to satisfy to the full and beyond myriads of elect angels as well as myriads of ransomed men! There need be no envy in the things of God. Such feeling is excluded by the freeness, fullness, and richness of God's love, and the true child rejoices to see the gifts of the Father given in abundance to their siblings.

14th

"The LORD bless thee, and keep thee."
Numbers 6:24

How we need the Lord to keep us! We stand upon slippery places. Snares and traps are laid for us in every direction. Every employment, every profession in life, from the highest to the lowest, has its special temptations. Snares are spread for the feet of the most illiterate as well as the most highly cultivated minds; nor is there anyone, whatever his position in life may be, who has not a snare laid for him, and such a snare as will surely prove his downfall if God does not keep him.

When Elisha sat upon the mountain and his servant was distressed lest his master should be taken away by violence, the prophet prayed the Lord to open his servant's eyes. What did the man then see? Chariots and horses of fire all around about the mountain guarding the prophet, (2Kings:6:17). Perhaps if the Lord were to open our eyes to see spiritual things as he opened the eyes of Elisha's servant, we might see devils where he saw angels, or see ourselves surrounded by Beelzebub and his legions, as the eyes of the servant saw Michael with the flaming hosts of heaven.

Well, then, may it be the desire of our soul, 'Lord keep me' – keep me in thy providence, keep me by thy grace. Keep me by planting thy fear deep within my soul and maintaining that fear alive and effectual in my heart. Keep me when waking, keep me when sleeping, keep me by night and keep me by day. Keep me at home and keep me abroad; keep me with my family and keep me with my friends; keep me in the world and keep me in the Church. Lord keep me according to thy promise, every moment of every day, keep me by thy Spirit and grace with all the tenderness implied in thy words, "Keep me as the apple of thine eye," (Psa. 17:8).

My friends, you can know little of your own heart, little of Satan's devices, little of the snares spread for your feet, unless you feel how deeply you need this blessing, "The Lord keep thee." We need not doubt that he will, for we read of the righteous that they are "kept by the power of God through faith unto salvation," (1Pet. 1:5), and that "He will keep the feet of his saints," (1Sam. 2:9).

15th

"The Lord make his face shine upon thee."
Numbers 6:25

The allusion here seems, to my mind, to be of the sun. When the natural sun has not risen, the world must needs be dark if the sun is still beneath the horizon. So with many gracious souls, it is darkness with them, midnight darkness, Egyptian darkness, darkness to be felt, because at present neither the Day-star has appeared, nor the Sun of righteousness risen upon them with healing in his wings. It will and must be dark with them until the Sun rises.

Sometimes even after the sun has risen we see not his face, for clouds, deep, dark clouds, may obscure the face of that bright luminary throughout the whole day, and we may not get a single ray from him through the whole period that he is above the visible horizon. So, many of the Lord's family, after the Sun has risen upon them in the morning of their spiritual life, may pass much of their subsequent time under shadowy clouds, until perhaps at evening tide there is light, and a departing ray gilds the dying pillow.

At other time there are days when mists drive rapidly across the face of the bright orb of day, and yet occasionally he peeps through the breaking clouds. Is not this in some measure an emblem of the way in which the Sun of righteousness is continually obscured by the mists and fogs which spring up out of our unbelieving heart? Hidden from view by the doubts and fears that, like the vapours of the valley, spread themselves, to our view, over his beauteous face.

Yet there are times when he gleams through the clouds and disperses the mists. When the Lord is pleased to bless the soul and shine upon it with any sweet manifestation, then he breaks in through the dark clouds, but soon they gather again. It is not in Christian experience to have one bright endless summer day. We do not live in a spiritual Australia or Peru, where clouds and mists

January

less often obscure the face of the sun. Our spiritual climate is humid, and our inward latitude is the chilling north.

See from our text who is the instigator. "The LORD make his face shine upon thee." It is the Lord who is sovereign in these matters. We cannot lift up our hand and remove the cloud. We have as much power to stretch forth our hand and sweep away the mists that obscure the Sun of righteousness, as we have power with the same hand to sweep away a London fog.

How this puts the creature into his rightful place, and the creature is only in his rightful place when he sees that he is nothing, and that God is all in all. How blessed to see the face of the Father, and to see it shine not as a result of our chasing after him, but of his own delight! How blessed to see his face not covered with lowering clouds of justly-merited displeasure, as sometimes we see in the natural sky an obscured sun looking angrily down, presaging wind and storm.

It is indeed true that, when we have brought guilt into our consciences, the face of God is seen to lower with anger. We have brought his just displeasure upon our heads, and although not angry with the persons of his people, yet is he justly angry with our sins. A sense of this in our soul covers his smiling face with clouds. "Thou hast covered thyself with a cloud, that our prayer should not pass through," (Lam. 3:44).

"The Lord make his face shine upon thee," and if he makes his face shine upon thee, he will make thy face shine too. It was so with Moses was it not when he was in the mount and was holding sweet communion with God? When he came down amongst the people, the skin of his face shone! The glory of God was there reflected upon it, and if the Lord makes his face shine upon you, it will make your face not unlike the face of Moses when you go among the people of God.

16th

"And be gracious unto thee."
Numbers 6:25

How sweet the gospel is, but what is it that makes the gospel sweet? That one word which sheds a perfume throughout the whole – grace.

Take grace out of the gospel and you destroy it. Without grace you nullify and overthrow it, and it is the gospel no more. Grace

January

pervades every part and every branch of the blessed gospel. It is the life of the gospel, and is in short the gospel itself.

So, what of our text, which asks that God "Be gracious unto thee?" In what way then is God to be gracious? Can he be gracious to thee in a broken law? What does the law know of grace? Maybe in resolutions of amendment, or creature performances, or outworked human righteousness? Can the Lord, will the Lord show himself gracious in these? I once read of a fanciful project for extracting sunbeams out of cucumbers – we might as well expect to make sunbeams out of cucumbers as to make grace out of the law. It is cold as cucumbers, and there is no sun in it.

Grace, to be grace, must come out of the gospel. It is in the gospel, and out of the gospel alone must it come; and it does come, excluding all creature righteousness, and thereby putting an extinguisher upon all human merit. The apostle sets this forth in his letter to the church at Rome, "And if by grace, then is it no more of works: otherwise grace is no more grace. But if it be of works, then is it no more grace: otherwise work is no more work," (Rom. 11:6).

"The Lord... be gracious unto thee," but how is the Lord gracious? Perhaps you have had occasion, at some time in your life, to go into the presence of someone in worldly rank far your superior, and you went timid, nervous, and trembling; but you experienced what is called a "gracious reception." Did not that enable you to speak and open your petition? So it is in the things of God. A sense of our lowliness and unworthiness may and should make us tremble and feel timid before the face of the Most High. Yet, when he draws us into his presence, and receives us graciously, as king Ahasuerus received the trembling Esther, extending to her the sceptre of his grace, (Est. 5:2), it emboldens the soul to lay its petition at his feet. Nothing emboldens the soul but grace.

Howbeit you feel and often say, 'I am so unworthy'. Let me ask, will you ever be anything else? When do you hope to become worthy? When do you mean to be worthy? If you could be worthy tomorrow, where is your worthiness today? Is the old score from the broken law yet paid? If you venture upon the ground of 'worthiness' you must have the old score rubbed off before you come to the new. Worthiness! Where is it? In man? Never since the day that Adam fell. Man's righteousness fell in Eden. When Adam's hand touched the fruit, worthiness fell to the ground, and never since has it been able to raise its head. I must not, then, go to God upon the ground of my own worthiness.

May I then go on the ground of **un**worthiness? We read of one who did just that, and met with a very gracious reception. "Lord, I am not worthy that thou shouldest come under my roof: but speak the word only, and my servant shall be healed," (Matt. 8:8). What did the Lord say of this man? That he had not found so great faith, no, not in Israel," (Matt. 8:10). There was another who ventured thus; with what words did the returning prodigal couch his confession? "Father... I am no more worthy to be called thy son," (Luke 15:18-19). The response? His father brought out the best robe, a ring of sonship for his hand, and shoes for his battered and worn out feet.

Why? Faith can only dwell with a sense of unworthiness; they are bosom companions; faith in God dwells only in unworthy breasts. If you do not feel unworthy, then by definition you are approaching God on your own merits; you have turned again unto the law and do not feel the need for his grace. If you do feel unworthy, then you are spiritually believing, for it is faith and belief together which give you that sense of unworthiness. You believe you are unworthy, and by the same faith which makes you believe that, you believe and accept God's grace.

"The Lord... be gracious unto thee." Now we understand better why this verse melts the heart whereas law and terrors do but harden it. It is grace that softens, grace that melts, grace that constrains, and grace that produces godly obedience.

17th

"The Lord lift up his countenance upon thee, and give thee peace."
Numbers 6:26

When we offend a person, his face is not toward us as at other times. It was so with Laban towards Jacob, and if we have in any way incurred a friend's or superior's displeasure, we instinctively watch their countenance. Is it down or up? Does it wear a frown or a smile? Is it looking upon us with the eye of affection, or are the eyes averted? We can tell in a moment if we know the countenance. Thus is the blessing asked, "The Lord lift up his countenance upon you," as a kind and affectionate parent upon an obedient child, or as a fond husband upon a loving, devoted wife; for such is God to his children – Father and Husband.

Do we not, as children, often provoke him to look upon us with frowning brow, or rather, not to look upon us at all, to "hide his face," (Mic. 3:4), as we read, "that we cannot see him," (Job 23:9)? The prayer then could be more fully rendered, "The Lord lift up his countenance upon thee," with a smile upon it; free, open, forgiving, merciful, and mild, that you may advance to him.

January

When a disobedient child comes home and sees its father's face not towards it as before, it shrinks away. There is no pressing forward to get upon the knee, no throwing the little arms round the neck and snatching a kiss, only shrinking away through guilt and shame. So it is in the things of God. When conscience tells us how in this and that instance we have disobeyed, been inconsistent, transgressed, and done amiss, when we go into God's presence there is a hanging back, a shrinking away, through fear of an ill reception.

But oh, the change in the child when the frown disappears and the smile comes; when the little one is taken once more into the arms and the tears are kissed away! How much more so in the things of God when he kisses away the tears of the disobedient child, as in the case of the returning prodigal! There are no kisses like those kisses of forgiveness, of mercy, and of restoring grace.

Our text continues, "and give thee peace." Oh, what a blessing is there here! As Deer says, "I will lay me down and sweetly sleep, for I have peace with God." It is this that makes the pillow easy in life, and will alone make the pillow easy in death – peace with God through Jesus Christ, peace through the reconciliation, peace through the blood of sprinkling, "the peace of God which passeth all understanding," (Phil. 4:7).

Others might look for gifts and greatness, but the blessing that the gracious soul most earnestly covets is peace, for this is the sweetest honey-drop in God's cup. It is true that it does not make the heart overflow like joy, nor to dance with exultation like the first beaming in of the rays of hope. Neither does it melt it down like the visits of love, but it is in some respects sweeter than all because it so settles down the soul into sweet assurance. It is the realisation of the Saviour himself, for "he is our peace," and may thus be called the crowning blessing.

18th

"Then will I sprinkle clean water upon you, and ye shall be clean: from all your filthiness, and from all your idols, will I cleanse you."
Ezekiel 36:25

When there are no crosses, temptations, or exercises, a man is sure to go after and cleave unto idols. It matters not what experience he has had, whether of trouble or consolation, distress or enjoyment; if once he ceases to be plagued and exercised, he will be setting up his household gods, (Gen. 35:2), in the secret chambers of imagery. Profit or pleasure, self-indulgence or self-gratification will surely, in one form or another, engross his thoughts, and steal away his heart.

Nor is there anything too trifling or insignificant to become an idol. Whatever is meditated on in preference to God, whatever is desired more than he, whatever more interests us, pleases us, occupies our waking hours, or is more constantly in our mind, becomes an idol and a source of sin.

It is not the magnitude of the idol, but its existence as an object of worship, that constitutes idolatry. I have seen some Burmese idols not much larger than my hand, and I have seen some Egyptian idols weighing many tons, but both were equally idols, and the comparative size had nothing to do with the question. So spiritually, the idol is not to be measured by its size, its relative importance or non-importance. A flower may be as much an idol to one man as a chest full of gold to another. If you watch your heart, you will see idols rising and setting all day long, nearly as thickly as the stars by night.

Now exercises, difficulties, temptations, besetments, losses, trials, afflictions, are all sent to pull down these idols, or rather to pull away our hearts from them. They pull us out of fleshly ease, and prevent us from sitting down contented with a name to live whilst dead. They make us cry for mercy, pull down all rotten props, hunt us out of false refuges, and strip us of vain hopes and delusive expectations.

We do not learn that we are sinners merely by reading it in God's word. It must be wrought, I might say burnt, into us. Nor will any one sincerely and spiritually cry for mercy, or a sense of pardon and reconciliation by the application of atoning blood, until sin in its misery, in its dominion, in its guilt, in its entanglements, in its wiles and allurements, in its filth and pollution, and in its condemnation, is spiritually felt and known.

Where the Holy Spirit works, he kindles sighs, groans, supplications, wrestlings, and pleadings to know Christ, feel his love, taste the efficacy of his atoning blood, and embrace him as all our salvation and all our desire. And though there may, and doubtless will be, much barrenness, hardness, deadness, and apparent carelessness often felt, still that heavenly Teacher will revive his work, though often by painful methods. He will not let the quickened soul rest short of a personal and experimental enjoyment of Christ and his glorious salvation.

January 19th

"For the LORD God is a sun and shield: the LORD will give grace and glory: no good thing will he withhold from them that walk uprightly."
Psalm 84:11

Is not the sun made to shine? It is his nature so to do. So it is with the sun of righteousness; he is made to shine.

Does the natural sun lose any of his light by shining? Why, the more he shines, the more light he seems to have. For all ages he has shone as brightly as now. His beams were as glorious before we had birth or being, and will be as glorious when the eyes which now see him are mouldering in the dust. Thousands of harvests has he ripened, millions and thousands of millions has he fed; but he shows no sign of exhaustion or decay.

Does Jesus lose anything by communicating his light, life, love, and grace? He is all the more glorified thereby; and the more you look to him as the Sun, that as such he might shine into and upon your soul, the more you glorify him as the Sun of righteousness. When in the morning we throw back the shutters or draw up the blinds, it is to receive the sun into the dark room. So the more we are enabled by divine grace to throw back the shutters of doubt and fear, and draw up the blinds of unbelief which hang down over the mind, the more we glorify the Lord Jesus by receiving out of his fullness, and grace for grace, (John 1:16).

O, it is good when our God enables us to look beyond and above doubts, fears, misgivings, and the many things that try the mind. You may pore over your sins and miseries until you fall well-nigh into despair; you may look back upon your wanderings, inconsistencies, and lack of fruitfulness until you are almost ready to sink down without hope and die. To do this is to resemble a person wandering in a dark room, tumbling over the furniture, and at last sitting down saying, 'There is no light' when if he did but throw back the shutters, the sun would shine into the room.

So oft times we sit pondering over our many inconsistencies until we say, 'There is no light in my soul; there never was, and there never will be.' O to be enabled, (when I speak thus, I know well, from soul experience, that it is only God who can do it in us and for us), to throw back the shutters, and look away from those things that so weigh down the mind! Look up, O sinking soul, and see the blessed Sun still shining in the skies of heaven! Why, the very power to do this, the very act of tilting the head, brings with it a felt blessedness.

January

How good it is also to be enabled to make use of Christ as a shield! How often we go into battle without this shield upon our arm, yet depend upon it that the Lord would not have provided such a shield for you unless he knew that your enemies were too many for you. Doubt, fear, darkness, despair, the law, the accusations of a guilty conscience, and the fiery darts of the devil – how can you fight against these enemies without a shield? Why, you would be like a soldier going out against the foe without either sword or musket, and laying his bosom bare to every weapon, without sword or bayonet in his hand to defend himself.

Going into combat against the law, against the accusations of a guilty conscience and a desponding heart, having no blessed Jesus to hold up and hold on to as a shield against these deadly foes would be enough to sink a man into despair. Howbeit if he is enabled to make use of the shield that God has provided, and to hold Christ up against a condemning law, a guilty conscience, an accusing devil, and a desponding mind, he is happy. If he can say to them all, 'Christ has died and died for me', then he receives into the shield all those darts and arrows which would otherwise have sunk into his soul, and they all fall harmless, because they fell on the Lord Jesus, his faithful shield.

20th

"All scripture is given by inspiration of God, and is profitable for doctrine, for reproof, for correction, for instruction in righteousness: that the man of God may be perfect, throughly furnished unto all good works."
2Timothy 3:16-17

On all subjects connected with our most holy faith, it is most desirable to have clear views. Every point of divine truth is laid down with the greatest clarity and precision in God's word. The darkness, the ignorance, and the confusion which prevent us from seeing it are all in us, not in the scripture. Yet as we search the Scriptures, as we meditate upon them, as we by prayer and supplication draw light, life, and wisdom out of Him "in whom are hid all the treasures of wisdom and knowledge," (Col. 2:3), and, above all, as we mix faith with what we read, there is often, if not usually, a gradual breaking-in of light. As we then follow up its heavenly rays, it shines more clearly and broadly, and the truth stands out more fully and prominently before our eyes. This is the only way in which we can be "filled with the knowledge of his will in all wisdom and spiritual understanding," (Col.

January

1:9), and thus be established in the faith, abounding therein with thanksgiving. To understand the scripture, to see in it the mind of the Holy Spirit, to be deeply penetrated with, and inwardly possessed of the heavenly wisdom, holy instruction, and gracious revelation of the counsels and will of God unfolded therein, demands much and continual patient and prayerful study. In business, diligence and industry lead on to prosperity and success, and sloth and idleness are the sure road to ruin. So it is in the greatest, most serious, and important business of all, the concerns of the soul; there is a holy diligence, a heavenly industry, whereby it thrives and grows, and there is a slothful indolence whereby it becomes clothed with rags, (Prov. 23:21).

21st

"A thousand shall fall at thy side, and ten thousand at thy right hand; but it shall not come nigh thee."
Psalm 91:7

When Noah was shut up in the ark, he and the favoured few, you know how they were tossed about, the rains lashing down from heaven and the waters rushing and boiling below. The windows of heaven were opened and the fountains of the great deep were broken up, and whilst they were thus tossed upon the waters, not a drop threatened those who were within. "It shall not come nigh thee." So you see the believer may be surrounded with troubles, and yet they shall not come near him.

And there is something more in the expression used in reference to the making of the ark, "and shalt pitch it within and without with pitch," (Gen. 6:14). Now, it is a most remarkable fact that the word pitch in Hebrew signifies also *atonement*. Now see, the pitch with which the ark was daubed within and without kept every drop of water out. This very expression for pitch in the Hebrew signifies also atonement; and is it not the atonement that keeps out the water? Can anything but the atonement keep the soul from the waters of God's wrath and from the floods of vengeance that shall sweep away the world with the ungodly? There is nothing but the atonement, and that bears up the soul, and keeps out every drop of rain. "It shall not come nigh thee."

"Many sorrows shall be to the wicked: but he that trusteth in the LORD, mercy shall compass him about," (Psa. 32:10). "And not only so, but we also joy in God through our Lord Jesus Christ, by whom we have now received the atonement," (Rom. 5:11).

January

"By whom we have now received the atonement." This is it, to have the "atonement." God cannot twice exact payment for the debt. He is satisfied; he has declared that he is well pleased with the righteousness of his beloved Son. He exacts no more; his justice demands no more, and, therefore, fury is not in him.

22nd

"For in him dwelleth all the fullness of the Godhead bodily." Colossians 2:9

The temple erected by Solomon in Jerusalem, and the tabernacle set up by Moses in the wilderness were but types of the true temple, the Lord of life and glory. The Lord himself said, "Destroy this temple, and in three days I will raise it up," speaking of his own body. All the beauty and glory of the temple were, therefore, figurative. They typified and shadowed forth the glory of Immanuel, for "in him dwelleth all the fullness of the Godhead bodily."

God the Son has taken to himself a body, according to the words of the fortieth Psalm, and quoted by Paul in his epistle, "a body hast thou prepared me," (Heb. 10:5), and it was a holy, sinless, spotless body. According to the words of the angel to Mary, "that holy thing which shall be born of thee shall be called the Son of God," (Luke 1:35). Neither was it just a holy, sinless, spotless body, for it had united to it a holy, sinless, spotless soul. "He shall see of the travail of his soul, and shall be satisfied," (Isa. 53:11). "My soul is exceeding sorrowful, even unto death," (Matt. 26:38).

This holy sinless body, united with his holy sinless soul, forming his spotless human nature, the Son of God then took into union with himself, and thus became the God-man, Immanuel, God with us.

It is this glorious mystery of godliness that a living soul pants to know. We cannot approach pure Godhead; we cannot understand it; it is a mystery too high and too deep for us, for "Canst thou by searching find out God? Canst thou find out the Almighty unto perfection? It is as high as heaven; what canst thou do? Deeper than hell; what canst thou know?" (Job 11:7-8). Yet when God would make himself known to the children of men, he made himself known by his only begotten Son, the second Person in the glorious Trinity, taking into union with himself the flesh and blood of the children. Thus, so far as the Lord gives us faith, we can approach unto an invisible God through the visible God-man.

As John says, "We beheld his glory, the glory as of the only begotten of the Father, full of grace and truth," (John 1:14), and again, "No man hath seen God at any time; the only begotten Son, which is in the bosom of the Father, he hath declared him," (John 1:18).

Therefore, when Philip said to him, (John 14:8), "Lord, shew us the Father, and it sufficeth us," Jesus replied "Have I been so long time with you, and yet hast thou not known me, Philip? he that hath seen me hath seen the Father; and how sayest thou then, Shew us the Father?" (John 14:9). And why? Because, as he says in John 10:30, "I and my Father are one."

The desire, then, of every living soul, (I am sure it is my desire when the Lord is pleased to work it in my heart), is to be led by the Spirit of God into an acquaintance with the God-man. It is to behold the glory of God in Jesus Christ; to see the Godhead shining through the manhood, and yet to see the manhood veiling and yet deriving glory from the Godhead. Thus we come to Jesus as unto a high priest that is able to save to the uttermost all that come unto God by him. We feel nearness of access to the Father by approaching him through the Son of his love, and thus enjoy sweet communion with Immanuel, God with us, God in our nature, God making himself known by taking our flesh and blood into union with himself.

23rd

"So that we ourselves glory in you in the churches of God for your patience and faith in all your persecutions and tribulations that ye endure, which is a manifest token of the righteous judgment of God, that ye may be counted worthy of the kingdom of God, for which ye also suffer."
2Thessalonians 1:4-5

The Lord has chosen that his people should pass through deep and cutting afflictions, for it is through much, or many tribulations, as the word really signifies, "through many tribulations" they are to enter the kingdom of God above, and into the sweetness and power of the kingdom of God below, (Acts 14:22). Howbeit every man will resent this doctrine except God has experimentally led him into it. It is such a rough and rugged path; it is so contrary to flesh and blood; it is so inexplicable to nature and reason, that man, proud, rebellious man, whether he be in a profession or whether he be out of a profession, will never believe that he must through much tribulation enter into the kingdom. This is the reason why so many find, or seek to find, a smoother way to glory than the Lord has appointed his saints to walk in, but shall the Head travel in one path, and the members in another? Shall the Bridegroom walk and wade through seas of sorrow, and the bride never so much as wet her feet with the water? Shall the Bridegroom be crucified in weakness and suffering, and there be no inward crucifixion for the dearly-beloved of his heart? Shall the Head suffer, grieve, agonise, groan, and die, and the members dance down a flowery road, without inward sorrow or outward suffering?

"Bastards may escape the rod,
Sunk in earthly, vain delight;
But the true-born child of God
Must not, would not, if he might."

Yet, perhaps, there are some who say in their heart, 'I am well convinced of this, but my coward flesh shrinks from it. I know if I am to reach the Canaan above, I must pass through the appointed portion of tribulation, but my flesh shrinks back.'

It does! Oh it does! Who would willingly bring trials upon himself? Therefore, the Lord does not leave these trials in our hands, but he himself appoints a certain measure of tribulation for each of his people to pass through. They will come soon enough, you need not anticipate them or wish for them. God will bring them, in his own time and in his own way. What is more, God will not merely bring you into them, but God will bring you through them, and He will bring you out of them. In Zechariah 13:9, the prophet talks of God's judgement cutting many off, howbeit the third part was not so much brought into the fire, but was brought *through* the fire to cause them to call upon his name.

What, then, will be our mercy? It will be our mercy if we are enabled to ask the Lord to bless us with faith and patience under tribulation. It will be our mercy to ask the Lord to give us strength to bear the storm and to lie as clay in his hands, and ask the Lord to conform us to the image of his Son, to guide us through this valley of tears below, and eventually to take us to be with him above.

24th

"Always bearing about in the body the dying of the Lord Jesus."
2Corinthians 4:10

The two aspects, if I may use the expression, of our gracious Lord in which are wrapped up all our faith, hope, and love, are a dying Jesus and a risen Jesus – Christ in his sufferings and death, and Christ in his resurrection and life. This is the Christ of God. This is the Son of God, in whom we believe unto life eternal, as he is presented to our view in the Scriptures of truth and by the inward teaching and testimony of the Holy Spirit. If you do not believe in a dying Christ and in a risen Christ, your faith is not the faith of a Christian. Now just see how this bears upon our text.

Why do we bear about in our own bodies the *dying* of the Lord Jesus? It is that the *life* of Jesus might be made manifest in us. As we bear about the dying of the Lord Jesus, as we suffer with him, die with him, and enter by faith into the mystery of his crucifixion, thereby being mystically and spiritually crucified with him, we rise out of this death into union with the risen, living Christ. We derive life, strength, grace, and power out of his glorious fullness for he is risen from the dead. He is no more in the tomb into which he sank in all the weakness of death, but is risen again and was thus "declared to be the Son of God with power," (Rom. 1:4).

Yes, he has gone up on high, and now sits at the right hand of God in the highest heavens. He is gone within the veil, to be the High Priest over the house of God; there, also, he rules and reigns as King in Zion; and there he ever lives as our glorified and risen Head. As, then, we bear about in the body the dying of the Lord Jesus, as crucified with him and conformed to his death, so as "risen with him," there is even now in our body a manifestation of his risen life.

25th

"That the life also of Jesus might be made manifest in our body."
2Corinthians 4:10

It is in this earthen vessel, our poor mortal body, that both the death of Jesus and the life of Jesus are made manifest. In the trouble, the perplexity, the being cast down, is the dying of Jesus. In not being distressed, in not being in despair, in not being forsaken, in not being destroyed, is the life of Jesus. Thus in the same body there is a dying Christ and a living Christ, Christ in his cross in his weakness - and Christ at the right hand of God in his power. To know these two things is to know the power of Christ's resurrection, and the fellowship of his sufferings, those two divine blessings which the soul of Paul so longed to realise and experience.

In the knowledge then, the experimental knowledge I mean, for all other knowledge is of no avail, of Christ crucified and Christ risen, consists the spiritual life of a child of God. Living this life is to live a life of faith in the Son of God. It is to be baptised into that Spirit

January

which Paul was baptised with when he said, "I am crucified with Christ: nevertheless I live; yet not I, but Christ liveth in me: and the life which I now live in the flesh I live by the faith of the Son of God, who loved me, and gave himself for me," (Gal. 2:20).

The present life of Christ at the right hand of God the Father, is the source and foundation of all our present life. "Because I live, ye shall live also," was his gracious promise when here below; and he has gone up on high, to fulfil that promise and make it effectual. He is "our life", and this life must be made manifest in our mortal flesh, both to ourselves and to others. It is made manifest to ourselves by the communication of light, life, liberty, and love, and made manifest to others by the fruits of a life and conversation adorning the gospel, and by walking in all holy obedience to its precepts.

26th

"For there is one God, and one mediator between God and men, the man Christ Jesus."
1Timothy 2:5

No sooner has living faith embraced the Person of Jesus, (and that is the first object on which faith lays hold), than it embraces him as the divinely-appointed Mediator. And how sweet and suitable is such a Mediator to a poor, sinful, crawling reptile, a wretch defiled, morning, noon, and night, with everything foul and filthy, who has broken the law of God a million times, and cannot keep it a single moment! 'How can I,' argues the soul, 'so full of sin and depravity, how can I approach with acceptance the great, glorious, and holy Jehovah? I cannot, I dare not!'

Yet the eye of faith ever is ever drawn to the divinely-appointed Mediator, the glorious Intercessor, the great High Priest over the house of God. It sees One that has shed his blood to put away sin, One who has righteousness to justify, one that has a fullness of grace and glory to give to the poor, needy, and naked. When the soul sees this one as faith sees, as hope embraces, and as love enjoys, there *is* a coming to God through this divine Mediator.

As the Apostle says, "Who through him [we] have access by one Spirit unto the Father," (Eph. 2:8), and, "Who by him do believe in God, who raised him up from the dead, and gave him glory; that your faith and hope might be in God," (1Pet. 1:21). Our only access to God is through the Mediator whom he has appointed. All your prayers, tears, sighs, and groans; all your religious thoughts, acts,

January

and words are worthless, utterly worthless, unless perfumed by the intercession of the only-begotten Son of God.

See to this point. I would, in all affection, charge it upon your conscience, that you look well how you approach the Father. Do you approach him through the Son of his love? Is there a solemn feeling in your heart, when you draw near to the throne, that you approach only through Jesus? Is there a believing reception of his atoning blood into your conscience as the only sacrifice that purges away sin, and of his justifying righteousness as the only robe of acceptance before God? See to it well. Examine your conscience thoroughly upon the matter, for it is vital ground. See that you approach the Father through the Son of his love, and through him alone; for depend upon it, if you approach Him in any other way, you are but a presumptuous professor; there is no holy fire burning on the altar of your soul; nor will any answer come down but through this divinely-appointed way.

27th

"The eyes of all wait upon thee; and thou givest them their meat in due season."
Psalm 145:15

The Lord will bring all his children sooner or later, each in their measure, to 'wait upon him'. Whatever trouble they are in, "the eyes of all wait upon thee." Whatever temptations they have to pass through, "the eyes of all wait upon thee." Whatever difficulty in temporal things, whatever conflict in spiritual things, whatever hardship in providence, whatever exercise in grace be their lot, the Lord will bring all his children at one time or another into this experience, "the eyes of all wait upon thee."

"Wait upon thee" for deliverance or for a manifestation; for the lifting up of the light of thy countenance and for a soft word spoken by thy mouth to the soul; for a smile of thine approving face and for one testimony of thine everlasting favour.

Do you know what it is to 'wait upon God' in this manner? Do you wait upon him by night and by day as he works within you? Do you wait upon him on your bed or behind the counter? Do you wait upon him in the solitary fields or in the crowded streets? He who knows not this 'waiting upon God' lacks that evidence, lacks that divine feature, which the Holy Spirit has stamped here upon all his living family.

"And thou givest them their meat in due season." There is meat, then, or provision that they are waiting upon God for; that they are to

January

receive at his hands, and it is called *"their* meat." It belongs to them. All the elect of God have such provision laid up for them in Christ, "for it pleased the Father that in him should all fullness dwell," (Col. 1:19), and he promised to "abundantly bless her provision," and "satisfy her poor with bread," (Psa. 132:15). Though none of God's quickened family ever dare *claim* the blessing at God's hands, yet the Lord has so stored up blessings in Christ, that they are actually and eternally theirs, for as the Apostle says, "all things are yours," (1Cor. 3:21).

It is "their meat." That is, provision specially set aside for the elect of God. Blood shed for their sins, but for their sins only; righteousness brought in for them, but for them only; love bestowed upon them, but upon them only; and promises revealed for their comfort, but for their comfort only. It is an eternal inheritance, "incorruptible and undefiled, and that fadeth not away, reserved in heaven" for them, (1Pet. 1:4), and for them only. It is *their* meat, because it is theirs in Christ, being lodged in Christ for their benefit.

It is theirs also in another sense; and that is, they are the only people who hunger after it, who have an appetite for it, who have a mouth to feed upon it, and who have a stomach to digest it. They are the only ones whose eyes are truly open to see what the "food" is. Others feed upon shadows of religion; they know nothing of the savoury food of the gospel. As the Lord said to his disciples, "I have meat to eat that ye know not of," (John 4:32). His food was the hidden communications of God's love, the visitations of his Father's presence, the divine communion that he enjoyed with his Father whilst the disciples were gone away. As he said unto them, "My meat is to do the will of him that sent me, and to finish his work," (John 4:34).

So, for the children of God, there is food in Christ, and the Lord gives them a hunger after this food. He not only sets before their eyes what the food is, but he kindles inexpressible longings in their soul to be fed therewith. God's people cannot feed upon husks, nor upon ashes, nor upon chaff, nor upon the east wind, nor upon grapes of gall and the bitter clusters of Gomorrah, (Deut. 32:32). They must have meat, savoury strengthening food such as their soul loves, that which God himself communicates, and which his hand alone can bring down, and give unto them, so that they may receive it from him as their soul-satisfying portion.

28th

"The fire shall test every man's work of what sort it is."
1Corinthians 3:13

How careful and anxious we should be to have two points well secured in our hearts. First, to be right concerning the foundation. "Do I believe in the Son of God? Have I clear views of the Sonship, the Deity, and the pure humanity of Christ? Have I drunk in no secret error? Am I hiding in my bosom no corrupt doctrine? Is my creed sound? Is the word of God received by me, as God has revealed it, into a believing heart?" How many are wrong as to the foundation itself!

Then comes, "Am I *upon* the foundation? Did God himself put me there? Did I see its suitability to my lost and undone soul? Did the blessed Spirit take of the things of Christ and reveal them to me in the hour of need? Was the Son of God made precious to my soul by an act of faith? Am I looking to him, cleaving to him, longing for him, hanging upon him, and trusting wholly to his Person and work? How stands the foundation? Am I on it?"

The next important question is, "How stands the building? Has the Holy Spirit wrought anything with a divine power in my soul? The faith I profess, is it of God? The hope I enjoy, do I believe it came from the Lord himself to support my soul in the trying storm? My repentance, is it genuine? My profession, is it sincere? My walk, is it consistent? My conscience, is it tender? My desires, are they spiritual? My prayers, are they fervent? My heart, is it honest? My soul, is it right before God? What am I looking to as the foundation, and what am I looking to as the building? Do I hang all my hopes upon Christ as the Rock, and all my religion upon the work of the Holy Spirit in my heart?"

If you can answer these questions as in the sight of God, "Yes, yes, ten times yes;" then you are right, you are right. If you stand upon the foundation that God has laid in Zion, you are right; you are right if God the Spirit has wrought a living faith in your heart. But you are wrong, you are wrong if you stand not upon God's foundation; you are wrong, you are wrong, and that for eternity, unless the Holy Spirit is at work upon your conscience.

29th

"Fight the good fight of faith, lay hold on eternal life, whereunto thou art also called."
1Timothy 6:12

The main office of the hand is to take hold of and grasp an object. The human hand is a masterpiece of anatomy, the fingers and the strong opposing thumb being expressly constructed by their Divine

January

Craftsman to seize and retain objects; and therefore every muscle, artery, vein, and nerve conspire together to fulfil this destined office.

Is there not in the office of faith something analogous to and corresponding with this? What saith the Lord? "Let him take hold of my strength, that he may make peace with me; and he shall make peace with me," (Isa. 27:5). There is a taking hold, then, of God's strength. Is not this by faith? Is there any other grace of the Spirit which takes hold of the Lord, as Jacob took hold of the wrestling angel, or as sinking Peter laid hold of Jesus hand?

"Lay hold on eternal life," is Paul's charge to Timothy. But how is eternal life, and especially Jesus, "the Life," laid hold of, except by faith? "He that believeth on me," says Jesus, "hath everlasting life." We lay hold of eternal life by believing on Christ.

So we read also of fleeing "for refuge to lay hold upon the hope set before us," (Heb. 6:18). As the manslayer fled for refuge to the appointed city, and when his hand grasped the gates was safe, so guilty sinners flee for refuge to the Lord Jesus, and by faith lay hold upon the hope set before them in the gospel of the grace of God.

30th

"Let us run with patience the race that is set before us." Hebrews 12:1

None can run this race but the saints of God, for the ground itself is holy ground of which we read that 'no unclean beast is to be found therein.' None but the redeemed walk there, and none have ever won that prize but those who have run this heavenly race as redeemed by precious blood.

Now no sooner do we see by faith the race set before us than we begin to run; and, like Christian in the "Pilgrim's Progress," we run from the City of Destruction, our steps being winged with fear and apprehension. All this, especially in the outset, implies energy, movement, activity, and pressing forward. We are running, as it were, for our life; escaping as Lot to the mountain; fleeing, and as the prophet speaks, "like as ye fled from before the earthquake in the days of Uzziah king of Judah," (Zech. 14:5), or as the manslayer fled to the city of refuge from the avenger of blood.

As, then, the runner stretches forward hands, feet, and head, intent only on being first to reach the goal, so in the spiritual race there is a stretching forth of the faculties of the new-born soul to win the heavenly prize. There is a stretching forth of the spiritual *understanding* to become possessed of clear views of heavenly

January

truth. There is a stretching forth of the *desires* of the heart to experience the love of God, to feel acceptance with him through the blood of sprinkling, and to know the way of salvation for ourselves, having clear evidences that our feet are in it. We long for tokens of good, manifestations of the pardoning love of God, and to walk in his fear, live to his praise, and enjoy union and communion with our blessed Lord.

There is a stretching forth of the *affections* of the heart after Jesus and the truth as it is in Jesus, with many longings, breathings, earnest cries, and fervent wrestlings at the throne of grace that we may know the truth and by the truth may be sanctified and made free. So, when you look at the word "race" as emblematic of a Christian's path, you see that it is not intended to mean any outward movement of the body, what the Apostle calls "bodily exercise," (1Tim. 4:8). It is an inward movement of the soul, or rather of the grace that God has lodged in your bosom, and to which are communicated spiritual faculties, whereby it moves forward in the ways of God, under the influences of the blessed Spirit.

31st

"Howbeit when he, the Spirit of truth, is come, he will guide you into all truth: for he shall not speak of himself; but whatsoever he shall hear, that shall he speak: and he will shew you things to come."
John 16:13

"He shall not speak of himself." There is something peculiarly gracious in this feature of the Holy Spirit, that, if we may use the expression, he does not glorify himself by speaking of himself in the same direct, personal manner as the Father and the Son speak of themselves. Thus the Father speaks of himself all through the word; and the Son speaks of himself in Scripture after Scripture; but the Holy Spirit, though he speaks in the Scripture, for by his divine inspiration the whole was written, yet does not speak of himself in a positive, direct manner, nor call upon us in a clear, personal way to believe in, worship, and adore him.

But his office and work are to testify to our conscience and bear witness to our spirit of both the Father and the Son. Thus as a Spirit of adoption he enables the soul to cry, "Abba, Father," and so testifies of the Father. As a Spirit of revelation he manifests to the soul the glorious Person of Christ, and thus testifies of the Son. But he does not in a personal manner manifest himself, or testify of himself.

How, then, do we know him? By his operations, his influences, his teachings, his consolations, his sealings, his softenings, his meltings and humblings, his waterings, enlargings, openings, liberatings, strengthenings, and enablings. The Lord therefore said unto his disciples, "but ye know him; for he dwelleth with you, and shall be in you," (John 14:17). Thus we know his indwelling by the light he gives to see our evidences clear and bright, by the life which he diffuses into the soul to renew and revive our drooping graces, and by the submission which he imparts in affliction and tribulation to the sovereign will of God. The meekness which he bestows under the chastening rod is further proof, as is the gracious confidence which he will not allow us to cast away, the holy boldness which he grants before the enemies of truth, and the zeal for that truth which he kindles in the heart as it is in Jesus, for the glory of God. Lastly, his indwelling provides the suitable words which he brings to the mind in defence of the gospel, and the power which he gives to speak them forth with an authority which silences, even if it does not convince, the adversary.

Thus, though the blessed Spirit does not speak of himself, he makes himself effectually known by his indwelling power and grace.

'O blessed Teacher, holy Comforter, gracious Intercessor, and heavenly Witness, come and take up thy abode in our heart. Reveal there and form Jesus, the hope of glory, and shed abroad the love of God. There bear thy divine testimony to our sonship, and cry "Abba, Father." There teach, sanctify and bless, that we and all in whom thou hast wrought thy work of grace might be filled "with all joy and peace in believing, that we may abound in hope, through the power of the Holy Ghost," (Rom. 13:15).

February

February

1st

"And if children, then heirs; heirs of God, and joint-heirs with Christ; if so be that we suffer with him, that we may be also glorified together"
Romans 8:17

This is the especial blessedness of being a child of God; that death, which puts a final extinguisher on all the hopes and happiness of all the unregenerate, gives him the fulfilment of all his hopes and the consummation of all his happiness. It places him in possession of "an inheritance incorruptible, and undefiled, and that fadeth not away, reserved in heaven for you, who are kept by the power of God through faith unto salvation ready to be revealed in the last time," (1Pet. 1:4-5).

In this present earthly life, we have sometimes sips and tastes of sonship, feeble indeed and interrupted, so that it is with us as one said; 'Though you here receive but little, scarce enough for the proof of your proper title, yet are they so far pledges of an inheritance to come. But this life is only an introduction to a better. In this life we are but children, heirs indeed, but heirs in their minority; but in the life to come, if indeed we are what we profess to be, sons and daughters of the Lord Almighty, we shall be put into full possession of the eternal inheritance.

And what is this? Nothing less than God himself. "Heirs of God," says the Apostle. For as the Lord said to Abraham, "I am thy shield and exceeding great reward;" as he said to the Levites, "I am their inheritance," so God himself is the inheritance of his people; yes, he himself in all his glorious perfections. All the love of God, the goodness of God, the holiness of God, all his happiness, bliss, and blessedness, all his might, majesty, and glory, as shining forth in the Person of his dear Son in all the blaze of one eternal, unclouded day - this is the saint's inheritance. Let us not then be weary in well-doing, nor faint and tire in running the race set before us with this prize in view, but press on by faith and prayer to win this eternal and glorious crown.

2nd

"They shall ask the way to Zion with their faces thitherward, saying, Come, and let us join ourselves to the LORD in a perpetual covenant that shall not be forgotten."
Jeremiah 50:5

February

Zion is the seat of all gospel blessings. In it is laid "the precious corner-stone," (Isa. 28:16); in it is placed "salvation for Israel," (Isa. 46:13); the Lamb of God stands upon it, (Rev. 14:1); and mercy, redemption, pardon, comfort, strength, deliverance, and glory come out of it. In turning the face then Zionwards, is implied the seeking of gospel blessings. The redeemed are therefore said "to seek the Lord their God," who is only to be found in Zion, his dwelling-place, and where praise waits for him, (Psa. 65:1). But they ask the way to Zion, with their faces there in no light and trifling spirit, and in no presumption that they shall ever arrive there. They have to ask the way step by step, often doubting and fearing whether they be in the way. Having been so often deceived and deluded, they dare no more trust their own hearts; but have to beg of the Lord to show them every inch of the road. They can no longer blindly follow every presumptuous guide, but have to cry to the Lord himself to teach and lead and quicken them in the way, and as they go, they weep.

They mourn over their base backslidings, over the many evils they have committed, over the levity of mind which they have indulged, over the worldliness of spirit, the pride, presumption, hypocrisy, carnality, carelessness, and obstinacy of their heart. They go and weep with a broken heart and softened spirit, not resting in their tears as evidences, but seeking the Lord their God. They seek the secret manifestations of his mercy, the visitations of his favour, and the 'lifting up of the light of his countenance', (Num. 6:26); yearning after a revelation of the love of Jesus and to know him by a spiritual discovery of himself.

In this mind, they seek not to establish their own righteousness; they seek not the applause of the world, nor the good opinion of professors; they seek not the smiles of saints, nor to make themselves Christians by their own exertions, but "they seek the Lord their God." They seek his face day and night, seek his favour, seek his mercy, seek his grace, seek his love, seek his glory, seek the sweet visitations of his presence and power, seek him wrestling with him until they find him to be their covenant God, who heals all their backslidings.

3rd

"The sacrifices of God are a broken spirit: a broken and a contrite heart, O God, thou wilt not despise."
Psalm 51:17

February

The heart that feels the burden of sin, that suffers under temptation, that groans beneath Satan's fiery assaults, that bleeds under the wounds inflicted by committed evil, and is broken and contrite.

This brokenness of heart and contrition of spirit is a thing which a child of God alone can feel. However hard his heart at times may seem to be, there will be seasons of spiritual reviving. However he may seem steeled against any sense of love and mercy, or even of misery and guilt, from time to time when he is least expecting and looking for it, there will be a breaking down of his soul before the Lord. There will be a bewailing of himself, a turning from the world to seek the Lord's favour, and a casting himself as a sinner once more on undeserved mercy. Tears will flow down his cheeks, sighs burst from his bosom, and he will lie humble at the Saviour's feet.

If your soul has ever felt this, you have a better thing than any gift; for this brokenness of spirit is a thing that accompanies salvation, and is a sacrifice that God will not despise.

4th

"Woe to them that are at ease in Zion."
Amos 6:1

Bunyan says, in his plain, homely language, "A Christian man is never long at ease; when one fright's gone, another doth him seize."

Sin will never let him rest long, nor Satan let him rest long, nor God let him rest long, nor his own fears let him rest long. He cannot be at ease until his conscience is purged with the blood of sprinkling; until his soul has been blessed with a feeling sense and enjoyment of the love of God; until he has sweet manifestations of pardoning mercy, blessed revelations of Christ to his soul, with the voice and witness of the Spirit in his breast. This is not the ease of Moab, who "hath been at ease from his youth, and [is] settled on his lees," (Jer. 48:11), but the ease of which the Psalmist speaks when he says, "His soul shall dwell at ease," (Psa. 25:13).

All ease but this is the sleep of the sluggard; it is carnal ease as opposed to spiritual. If then he drops into carnal ease, and for a time sin does not seem to plague, nor Satan tempt, nor the world persecute, the Christian man feels that he is getting wrong. He has lost a burden, but not in the right way, and would rather have the burden back than be left to have his portion among those who are at ease in Zion.

February 5th

"For my people have committed two evils; they have forsaken me the fountain of living waters, and hewed them out cisterns, broken cisterns, that can hold no water."
Jeremiah 2:13

There is nothing so piercing as the remembrance of backsliding against a good and holy God. There is nothing so wounding to a tender conscience as having sinned against manifested mercy and revealed salvation. It seems almost like doing despite to the Spirit of grace; almost like trampling underfoot the blood of the covenant whereby we were sanctified, and treating our best Friend worse than his very enemies treated him. And as these things are brought to mind, and laid upon the conscience with weight and power, they will sometimes sink us very low into despondency and gloom so as almost to take away our very hope.

Yet the Lord is very merciful and compassionate to those who fear his name. He regards the prayer of the destitute, and will not despise their cry. He listens to the sighs and confessions of the penitent heart, and broken, contrite spirit; and thus, though he will ever abase him that is high, he will exalt him that is low. He will never give up his rightful claim to his people. If he has bought us with his precious blood, he will never allow that purchase to be annulled by the malice of Satan or by the wickedness of our own nature.

How striking are the words of the prophet, "but thou hast played the harlot with many lovers; yet return again to me, saith the LORD," (Jer. 3:1). "Turn, O backsliding children, saith the LORD; for I am married unto you: and I will take you one of a city, and two of a family, and I will bring you to Zion," (Jer. 3:14). "Return, ye backsliding children, and I will heal your backslidings," (Jer. 3:22), and shall we not answer, as did the prophet of old? "Behold, we come unto thee; for thou art the LORD our God. Truly in vain is salvation hoped for from the hills, and from the multitude of mountains: truly in the LORD our God is the salvation of Israel," (Jer. 3:22-23).

6th

"And the LORD will create upon every dwelling place of mount Zion, and upon her assemblies, a cloud and smoke by day, and the shining of a flaming fire by night."
Isaiah 4:5

February

There is an allusion here to the cloudy pillar which rested upon the tabernacle. It was as a cloud by day, but as a pillar of fire by night. The reason of this is evident. By day, the cloud and the smoke were sufficiently visible; but not so in the night season. In the night, therefore, it was a pillar of fire, that the presence of the Lord might be distinctly seen. Spiritually viewed, this night may signify dark seasons in the soul; for there is night as well as day in the experience of God's saints. Now when they are in these dark seasons, they need clearer and brighter manifestations of the Lord's presence than when they are walking in the light of day. Thus this "shining of a flaming fire by night" may represent the shining in of the Lord's clearer, fuller, and more manifested presence, the livelier and more powerful application of his word to the heart; the brighter evidences and clearer marks that he gives of his favour, which, compared with the cloud, are as the shining of a flaming fire. It is the same presence of God, and the same glory, as was the case with the cloudy pillar; but that presence and that glory are seen in a more conspicuous manner as giving light in seasons of darkness.

The shining of a flaming fire by night may also represent the shining light of the word of truth which is spoken of as "a light that shineth in a dark place," (2Pet. 1:19). How often when the mind is dark, and evidences obscured, there is little else seen but the clear shining of the word of truth to which the soul turns its eyes as its only guiding light. "Your word," says David, "is a lamp unto my feet, and a light unto my path." We often get into spots where we have to look outside of ourselves to the clear shining of truth in the word of God, for there is darkness everywhere else. To that light we have to look and wait, and sometimes at a great distance and for a long season, until that word comes near and begins to shine into the heart.

Yet with that shining light, as it draws near and gives forth its comforting rays and beams, comes in due time the presence and glory of God. So to fix our heart upon the word of promise, and wait for its fulfilment, is to walk by faith and not by sight. Thus to Abraham the word of promise was by day a cloud; but when "a horror of great darkness fell upon him," the same word of promise, as the word of a covenant God, was as a burning lamp that passed between the pieces of the offered sacrifices, (Gen. 15:17).

7th

"A cloud and smoke by day, and the shining of a flaming fire by night: for upon all the glory shall be a defence."
Isaiah 4:5

February

The glory of the Lord is his presence in the soul, for that is represented by the cloud, as it was when his glory filled the house of God, which Solomon built. Now this glory of the Lord in the cloud and smoke by day, and in the shining of a flaming fire by night, is to be a defence, both upon every dwelling-place of mount Zion and upon her assemblies. A defence against what? Chiefly against four things.

First, it is a defence against error. No person can embrace error who knows anything of the presence and power of God in his soul, or has ever seen anything of the glory of God in the face of Jesus Christ; for all error is opposed not only to God's truth, as revealed in the word, but to God's presence as revealed in the heart. What is more, this is true both as regards individuals and churches. God will never sanction error as held by either. He will never bless with his manifested presence any erroneous man, be he minister or private individual, for he never honours or blesses anything but his own truth, and those only who believe and hold it. As the prophet says, "for them that honour me I will honour," (1Sam. 2:30).

This is a very important point; for you will often hear erroneous men speak as if they knew spiritual things by divine teaching and by divine testimony, and will often boast confidently of their comforts and enjoyments, as if they had gotten their views from God himself, though they turn the truth of God into a lie.

Be not deceived by these men or their false pretensions. They have only kindled a fire to compass themselves about with sparks, that they may walk in the light of their fire, and in the sparks which they have kindled. The Spirit of truth guides into all truth, and cannot and will not countenance or bless error. The Lord's own prayer to his heavenly Father for his disciples was, "Sanctify them through thy truth: thy word is truth," (John 17:17). The soul never was divinely sanctified by a lie, nor the regenerate heart comforted by error.

Second, this glory will also be a defence against all evil, for nothing makes sin so to be seen and abhorred as sin as the presence of the Lord. He is known and felt at such moments to be infinitely pure and holy, and a holy God must needs hate sin. If, then, his presence be felt in the soul as a cloud in which he manifests his glory in the face of Jesus Christ, it will be a defence against all the sins in which you might be entangled, when there is no such sensible presence to make you revere and adore his great and glorious Majesty.

Third it is, therefore, also a defence against all temptations which would lead us into anything contrary to God and godliness.

Fourth it will be a defence too against all enemies. You may have many enemies, both without and within; but all their attempts to injure you will be unsuccessful if you have the cloud of the Lord's presence in your soul and his glory in your midst. No enemy can hurt you if the Lord is your defence. He will watch very jealously over

February

what he himself has communicated by his Spirit and grace to your heart, and his presence will be your best defence against every foe and against every fear.

8th

"And for their sakes I sanctify myself, that they also might be sanctified through the truth."
John 17:19

Christ is made to his people sanctification, (1Cor. 1:30). What am I? What are you? Are we not filthy, polluted, and defiled? Do not some of us, more or less, daily feel altogether as an unclean thing? Is not every thought of our heart altogether vile? Does any holiness, any spirituality, any heavenly-mindedness, any purity, any resemblance to the divine image dwell in our hearts by nature? Not a grain! Not an atom! How then can I, a polluted sinner, ever see the face of a holy God? How can I, a worm of earth, corrupted within and without by indwelling and committed sin, ever hope to see a holy God without shrinking into destruction?

I cannot see him, except so far as the Lord of life and glory is made sanctification to me. Why should men start so at "imputed sanctification?" Why should not Christ's holiness be imputed to his people as well as Christ's righteousness? Why should they not stand sanctified in him, as well as justified? Why not? Is there anything in Jesus, as God-man Mediator, which he has not for his people? Has he any perfection, any attribute, any gift, any blessing, which is not for their use? Did he not sanctify himself that they might be sanctified by the truth? Is he not the holy Lamb of God, that they might be "holy, and without blame before him in love?" What is my holiness, even such as God may be pleased to impart to me? Is it not, to say the least, scanty? Is it not, to say the least, but little in measure? But when we view the pure and spotless holiness of Jesus imputed to his people, and view them holy in him, pure in him, without spot in him, how it does away with all the wrinkles of the creature, and makes them stand holy and spotless before God.

9th

"Look unto me, and be ye saved, all the ends of the earth: for I am God, and there is none else."
Isaiah 45:22

February

How often we seem not to have any real religion, or enjoy any solid comfort! How often are our evidences obscured and beclouded, and our minds covered with deep darkness! How often does the Lord hide himself, so that we cannot behold him, nor get near to him; and how often the ground on which we thought we stood is cut from under our feet, and we have no firm standing! What a painful path is this to walk in, but how profitable!

When we are reduced to poverty and beggary, we learn to value Christ's glorious riches; the worse opinion we have of our own heart, and the more deceitful and desperately wicked that we find it, the more we put our trust in his faithfulness. The more black we are in our own esteem, the more beautiful and lovely does he appear in our eyes. As we sink, Jesus rises. As we become feeble, he puts forth his strength. As we come into danger, he brings deliverance; as we get into temptation, he breaks the snare. As we are shut up in darkness and obscurity, he causes the light of his countenance to shine. Now it is by being led in this way, and walking in these paths, that we come rightly to know who Jesus is, and to see and feel how suitable and precious such a Saviour is to our undone souls.

We are needy, he has in himself all riches. We are hungry, he is the bread of life. We are thirsty, he says, "If any man thirst, let him come unto me, and drink." We are naked, and he has clothing to bestow. We are fools, and he has wisdom to grant. We are lost, and he speaks, "Look unto me, and be ye saved." Thus, so far from our misery shutting us out from God's mercy, it is the only requisite for it. So far from our guilt excluding his pardon, it is the only thing needful for it, and so far from our helplessness ruining our souls, it is the needful preparation for the manifestation of his power in our weakness. We cannot heal our own wounds and sores; that is the very reason why he should stretch forth his own arm.

It is because there is no salvation in ourselves, or in any other creature, that he says, "Look unto me... *for I am God,* and there is none else."

10th

"For the word of God is quick and powerful, and sharper than any two-edged sword."
Hebrews 4:12

What is meant by the word of God being "quick?" That it moves with swiftness and velocity? It is certainly said of God's word that it "runneth very swiftly," (Psa. 147:15), but that is not the meaning of the word "quick" in our text. It here means 'living', and corresponds with the expression, "lively oracles," (Acts 7:38). It is an old English word and we find it again in the expression, "who shall judge the quick and the dead," (2Tim. 4:1), that is, the living and the dead. So we read of Korah, Dathan, and Abiram that they went down quick, (that is, alive), into the pit, (Num. 16:30). So also the Lord is said to have quickened, (made spiritually alive), those who were previously dead in trespasses and sins, (Eph. 2:1). The word 'quick', then, does not mean moving with velocity, but living, or rather communicating life, and thus distinguished from the dead letter.

Truth, as it stands in the naked word of God, is lifeless and dead; and as such, has no power to communicate what it has not in itself, that is, life and power to the hearts of God's people. It stands there in so many letters and syllables, as lifeless as the types by which they were printed. But when the incarnate Word takes of the written word, and speaks it home into the heart and conscience of a vessel of mercy, whether in letter or substance, then he endues it with divine life, and it enters into the soul, communicating to it a life that can never die.

James tells us that, "Of his own will begat he us with the word of truth," (Jas. 1:18), and Peter says, "Being born again, not of corruptible seed, but of incorruptible, by the word of God, which liveth and abideth for ever," (1Pet. 1:23).

Eternal realities are brought into the soul, fixed and fastened by an Almighty hand. The conscience is made alive in the fear of God; and the soul is raised up from a death in sin, or a death in profession, to a life heavenly, new, and supernatural.

11th

"Not as though I had already attained, either were already perfect: but I follow after, if that I may apprehend that for which also I am apprehended of Christ Jesus."
Philippians 3:12

The Apostle Paul, perhaps the greatest saint that ever lived upon earth, had to confess that even he had not attained. There was that in Christ more than he had ever seen, ever known, ever felt, ever tasted, ever handled, ever realised. There were heights in his glory, depths in his love, in his sufferings, in his bitter agonies in the garden and on the cross, which passed all apprehension and comprehension. Therefore he says, "Not as though I had already attained." I am a child still, a learner still, as weak as ever, as helpless as ever to obtain what I need. Though I follow on; though I forget the things which are behind and reach forward to the things before; though I know what I am aiming at, what I am seeking; though my eye is single, my heart earnest, yet it is not with me as if I had already attained.

Now just put yourself in that scale; and to measure yourself aright, look at these things. Are you following after? Do you see that there is something which is to be tasted, handled, felt, and realised of the precious things of God? Have you ever had any sips, tastes, drops, foretastes? Has your heart ever been melted, softened, warmed by the goodness and mercy of God, by the love of Christ? Did you ever feel that there was a sweetness, blessedness, and happiness in the things of God to which nothing else could be compared? Has your heart ever been opened and enlarged by the love of God, so that you felt that spirituality of mind which is life and peace; and could you have continued in that spot it would have been to you all that you needed to make you look death calmly in the face?

Now it is these sips, tastes, and drops, these sweet discoveries of what the Lord is to believing souls, which draw forth the desires of the heart and enable it to follow after.

Except that darkness intervenes - the Lord withdraws himself, sin works, Satan tempts, trials perplex your mind, unbelief rises up and begins to question everything. Then there is no following on, everything looks so dark and gloomy and divine things are so out of sight. Doubts and fears so possess the mind and it seems as if we came so short, so very short, that the question arises whether we may not come short at last; whether we may not have deceived ourselves; whether all we have felt may not have been a dreadful delusion.

Yet see how this darkness works. How it stirs the mind up; how it makes us seek again and again to possess realities. Look how it seems to open the eyes afresh to understand true religion, and that it consists in the teachings and operations of the Holy Spirit upon the heart. Thus our very short-comings, our deficiencies, and our complaints are blessedly overruled and made to work graciously to stir us up to run again the race set before us.

Yet depend upon it, the most highly-favoured saint upon earth will have reason to say with Paul, "Not as though I had already attained, either were already perfect," that is, matured and ripened. Not perfect in understanding, nor perfect in heart, nor perfect in lip, nor perfect in life. Every saint of God will have to confess imperfection - imperfection stamped upon all that he has and is - imperfection, imperfection upon everything but the work of the Son of God upon the cross and the work of God the Holy Spirit in the soul.

February 12th

"I drew them with cords of a man, with bands of love."
Hosea 11:4

When God draws his people near unto himself, it is not done in a mechanical way. They are drawn, not with cords of iron, but with the cords of a man; the idea being of something feeling, human, tender, touching; not as if God laid an iron arm upon his people to drag them to himself, whether they wished to come or not. This would not be grace nor would it be the work of the Spirit upon the heart. God does not so act in a way of mechanical force. We therefore read, "Thy people shall be willing in the day of thy power," (Psa. 110:3). He touches their heart with his gracious finger, like the band of men whom he thus inclined to follow Saul, (1Sam. 10:26). He communicates to their soul both faith and feeling, and he melts, softens, and humbles their hearts by a sense of his goodness and mercy. For it is his goodness, as experimentally felt and realised, which leads to repentance.

If you have ever felt any secret and sacred drawing of your soul upward to heaven, it was not compulsion, not violence, not a mechanical constraint, but an arm of pity and compassion let down into your very heart, which, touching your inmost spirit, drew it up into the bosom of God. It was some such gracious touch as that spoken of in the Song of Solomon, "My beloved put in his hand by the hole of the door, and my bowels were moved for him," (Song 5:4). It was some view of his goodness, mercy, and love in the face of a Mediator, with some dropping into your spirit of his pity and compassion towards you, which softened, broke, and melted your heart. You were not driven onward by being flogged and scourged, but blessedly drawn with the cords of a man, which seemed to touch every tender feeling and enter into the very depths of your soul.

Why is this? Because it is as man that our blessed Lord is the Mediator; it is the man Christ Jesus, the man who groaned and sighed in the garden, the man that hung upon the cross, the man who lay in the sepulchre, the man who is now at the right hand of the Father, and yet the God-man. For it is through his humanity that we draw near unto God.

His blood was the blood of humanity. His sufferings were the sufferings of humanity. His sacrifice was the sacrifice of humanity, and his death was as the death of the humanity. As these are opened up with divine power, they form, so to speak, a medium whereby we may draw near unto God, without terror and without alarm, because God in Christ manifests himself as altogether love.

February

13th

"Who gave himself for us, that he might redeem us from all iniquity, and purify unto himself a peculiar people, zealous of good works."
Titus 2:14

How can anyone who knows anything of the blessedness of atoning blood , of redeeming love, and of the sanctifying influences of the Holy Spirit continue in sin that grace may abound? Doctrinal professors may do these things, for a mere 'letter knowledge' of the truth brings with it no deliverance from the power of sin.

Can a living soul, one in whom the God of all grace is carrying on his gracious work, can such an one trample underfoot the cross of the suffering Son of God? It is impossible that a man who knows the redeeming efficacy of Christ's atoning blood, and whose conscience is made tender in the fear of God, can, whilst under the sweet influence of that love, deliberately load more sin onto his crucified Lord.

Only if there is a falling under the power of sin and temptation, as with David and Peter, but there will not be a wilful sinning against him when the blessed Spirit is bringing near his blood, grace and love. May we never forget that the suffering Son of God gave himself to purify unto himself a peculiar people. They are a people whose thoughts are peculiar, for their thoughts are the thoughts of God, having the mind of Christ. Their affections are peculiar, for they are fixed only on things above. Their prayers are peculiar, for they are wrought on in their heart by the Spirit of grace and supplication. Their sorrows are peculiar, because they spring from a spiritual source. Their joys are peculiar, for they are joys which the stranger cannot understand. Their hopes are peculiar, for they are anchored within the veil, and their expectations are peculiar, for they expect not to reap a crop of happiness in this marred world, but look for happiness in the kingdom of rest and peace in the bosom of God.

If they are peculiar inwardly, they should be peculiar outwardly. They should make it manifest that they are a peculiar people by walking in the footsteps of the Lord the Lamb, taking up the cross, denying themselves, and living to the honour, praise, and glory of God.

14th

"Jesus answered and said unto her, If thou knewest the gift of God, and who it is that saith to thee, Give me to

February

drink; thou wouldest have asked of him, and he would have given thee living water."
John 4:10

How blessed a thing is vital godliness! That is the thing I always wish to contend for. Not for forms and ceremonies, or doctrines floating in the brain, but for the life of God in the soul; the only thing worth knowing; the only thing to live by, and I am sure the only thing to die by. How different is vital godliness received into the heart and conscience, by the operation of God the Spirit, out of the fullness of Christ - how different is this fountain of living water from the stagnant, dead water of lip-service, formality, and hypocrisy!

And sure I am, if our souls have ever been baptised into a spiritual knowledge of this heavenly secret; if ever we have tasted the sweetness, felt the power, and experienced a measure of the enjoyment of vital godliness in the heart and conscience, we shall desire no other but living water. No, in all that we do for the Lord, or for those that fear his name, in every prayer, in every ordinance, we shall be, more or less, looking out for living water.

Are we, who profess to be in the wilderness, like the thirsty traveller in the deserts of Arabia, panting after the wells and the palm trees? Do we know what it is, after long seasons of drought, when the living water has sunk well-near out of sight, to find its streams again springing up in the conscience? How living souls thirst after these revivings! We cannot now be satisfied with lip religion, pharisaical religion, doctrinal religion, a name to live whilst dead, the form of godliness without the power. A living soul can no more satisfy his thirst with mere forms and ceremonies, than a man naturally thirsty can drink out of a pond of sand. He must have living water, something given by the Lord himself, springing up in his soul.

Yet, does not the Lord say, that he will give it to those that ask it? Shall we not ask, then, and seek for it? And will he deny us? Has he denied us in time past? Will he deny us in time to come? Has he not the same loving and compassionate heart now, as beat in his bosom towards this poor sinner at the well of Samaria? He still emboldens us to ask. He is now seated upon the throne of grace and mercy as the Mediator between God and man. And if, through mercy, we know something of the gift of God; and if, through divine teaching, we know something of the glorious Person of Jesus, and have enjoyed a measure of its sweetness in our heart, sure I am, we shall ask, and our souls will receive the testimony of God in our conscience, that he will not deny us, but give unto us "living water."

February 15th

"And I heard a loud voice saying in heaven, Now is come salvation, and strength, and the kingdom of our God, and the power of his Christ: for the accuser of our brethren is cast down, which accused them before our God day and night."
Revelation 12:10

Salvation. What salvation? Salvation by grace, salvation full and free; salvation without any intermixture of creature righteousness; salvation gushing from the bosom of God; salvation flowing wholly and solely through the blood of the Lamb. However, salvation can only be tasted after a previous foretaste of condemnation. Heaven can never be looked up into before there has been a looking down into the pit of hell. There must have been an experience of guilt, before there can be the enjoyment of pardon.

"Now is come salvation." Salvation from what? Salvation from the accusations of Satan, from the curses of the law, from the fear of death, from the terrors of hell, and from the sentence of damnation.

How does such salvation come? Whilst the battle is going on, whilst the issue is doubtful, whilst hand to hand, foot to foot, and shoulder to shoulder, Satan and the soul are engaged in deadly strife, there is no felt experience of salvation. There may be hope, enabling the soldier to stand his ground, but there is no shout of victory until the enemy is put to flight, but when Satan is defeated, when his accusations are silenced, and when the soul is liberated, then "is come salvation."

The sweetest song that heaven ever proclaimed, the most blessed note that ever melted the soul, is salvation! Saved from death and hell, saved from 'the worm which dieth not and the fire which is not quenched' (Mark 9:44), saved from the sulphurous flames of the bottomless pit. Saved from the companionship of tormenting fiends and all the foul wretches under which earth has ever groaned, saved from blaspheming God in unutterable woe and saved from an eternity of misery without hope. Saved into heaven – the sight of Jesus as he is, perfect holiness and happiness, the blissful company of holy angels and glorified saints, and all this during the countless ages of a blessed eternity!

What tongue of men or angels can describe the millionth part of what is contained in the glorious word "salvation!"

February 16th

"Shew me thy ways, O LORD; teach me thy paths."
Psalm 25:4

    To lie with a broken heart and contrite spirit at the footstool of mercy beseeching God to teach us, is indeed a blessed spot to be in. It is the evidence of a childlike spirit, and shows such simplicity, reality, and genuineness that it bears stamped upon it the indubitable marks of true discipleship. Wherever we see such a coming out of SELF, with a renunciation of our own wisdom, strength, and righteousness, such a putting aside of all creature religion, and such a real spirit of humility before God, we must receive it as something beyond and above nature. Nothing but the power of God seems able to bring a soul so completely out of the shell and crust of self-righteousness, and so to lay open its spiritual nakedness before him.
    Naturally there is something very sweet in seeing a docile, teachable disposition, and on the other hand, few things are more offensive than the pride of ignorance, the abominable conceit of people who think they know everything when really they know nothing, but are too proud to be taught.
    The only road to knowledge is to possess a meek, teachable, inquiring spirit, a willingness to learn springing out of a consciousness of ignorance. This spirit is what we see sometimes in children, nor is there a more pleasant sight for parent or instructor than to see a child docile; earnestly seeking information, and glad to receive instruction. If anything can open the mouth to teach, it is finding such a disposition to learn.
    So in grace; where there is a humble, quiet, docile spirit, it seems to draw forth out of the Lord's heart and mouth these secrets of heavenly wisdom which he hides from others; as he spoke in the days of his flesh, "I thank thee, O Father, Lord of heaven and earth, because thou hast hid these things from the wise and prudent, and hast revealed them unto babes." The babes are those who are teachable and childlike, and to whom as such God reveals the treasures of his heavenly wisdom.

February 17th

"And there I will meet with thee, and I will commune with thee from above the mercy seat."
Exodus 25:22

After a child of God has enjoyed something of the goodness and mercy of God revealed in the face of his dear Son, he may wander from his mercies, stray away from these choice gospel pastures, and get into a waste-howling wilderness where there is neither food nor water; and yet, though half-starved for poverty, has in himself no power to return. So what has brought him for the most part into this state? Forgetfulness of the mercy seat; and as the Lord meets his people only there, a gradual estrangement from him.

But in due time the Lord seeks out this wandering sheep, and the first place he brings him to is the mercy seat, confessing his sins and seeking mercy. Faithful to his own word, once more the Lord meets him there, and O what a meeting! A penitent backslider and a forgiving God! O what a meeting! A guilty wretch drowned in tears, and a loving Father falling upon his neck and kissing him! O what a meeting for a poor, self-condemned wretch, who can never mourn too deeply over his sins, and yet finds grace super-abounding over all its aboundings, and the love of God bursting through the cloud, like the sun upon an April day, and melting his heart into contrition and love!

But this is not all. The Lord is pleased sometimes to show his dear people the evils of their heart, to remove by his Spirit and grace that veil of pride and self-righteousness which hides so much of sinful self from our eyes, and to discover what is really in us - the deep corruptions which lurk in our depraved nature, the filth and folly which is part and parcel of ourselves, the unutterable baseness and vileness so involved in our very being.

Now by itself this would drive us from the throne of grace. 'Can God dwell here?' is the sinner's question. 'Can I be possessed of the fear of God when such thoughts and feelings overflow my mind, and seem to fill me as if with the very dregs of hell?' Yet still he is drawn from time to time to the throne of grace to confess these sins before the mercy seat, for he cannot, dare not, stay away from it; and again God is true to his word, "There I will meet with thee." There once more he reveals a sense of his mercy and goodness, and once more shows that, whatever the sinner be in himself, he is faithful to his own promise.

18th

"But speaking the truth in love."
Ephesians 4:15

February

There is a marginal reference in our bibles giving an alternative meaning of 'sincerity' underlying this verse. Sincerity lies at the root of all gracious profession. If a man is not sincere he is nothing. God makes a man sincere by planting his truth in his heart; and whenever God does make a man sincere, the truth which he has implanted will grow. Truth does not lie in a man's soul dead and motionless, like a stone in the street; it is a living, active, expansive principle. If the truth is in the soul, it will be ever pushing out error, because the two principles cannot exist together; and as Isaac thrust out Ishmael, and Jacob proved stronger than Esau, so will simplicity and godly sincerity be ever mightier than craft and deception.

The truth of God in the heart will not wither and die, but will be shined upon by the Sun of righteousness, and sunned into fruitfulness by the smiles of God; and as truth becomes day by day more and more precious, so will error and evil become day by day more and more hateful. A sincere soul stands "girt about with truth;" and truth forms its shield and buckler, (Psa. 91:4).

But how does this Christian sincerity prove the soul's safeguard from error? By putting it ever on the watch tower, looking out and looking up for the teaching of God and the light of his countenance. A soul made spiritually sincere takes nothing upon trust; it requires the seal of God on all it receives, and the witness of the Spirit to all that it feels. He who is sincere sees the rocks ahead on which others concerning faith make shipwreck; and being well ballasted with temptations, afflictions, and trials, he is not easily tossed to and fro with every wind of doctrine. His desire to be right keeps him right; his fear to be wrong preserves him from wrong. The light of God in his soul makes him see; the life of God in his heart makes him feel; the fear of God in his conscience makes him honest; the love of God in his affections makes him love; and all this gives truth such a firm place in him that there is no room for error.

The Apostle adds, therefore, "in love." It is not enough to be "sincere;" we must be "sincere in love." Mark that. It is not receiving God's truth as a certain orderly system; it is not furnishing our heads with a sound doctrinal creed and well-ordered Calvinistic scheme which will avail us in the trying hour. It is to have the truth of God brought into our soul by a divine power, and realising such unutterable sweetness in it as communicates a firm abiding love, both to the truth itself, and to Him of whom it testifies and from whom it comes. It is thus we are made "sincere in love."

The fear of God creates the sincerity, the application of the truth with power creates the love to it. And when we are thus made "sincere in love" we are brought out of the childish state in which we are carried about with every wind of doctrine, and in danger of

February

being entrapped by the cunning craft of every deceiver. We know the truth, love the truth, and become established in the truth.

19th

"Thou openest thine hand, and satisfiest the desire of every living thing."
Psalm 145:16

That word has oft been sweet to me, "every living thing." How comprehensive it is, and how low it descends! How it comes down to the weakest and lowest and least of God's family, if he is only a "thing," only a "living thing," if he cannot see himself a man in Christ, nor see himself a child of God. No, nor even see himself a new-born babe! If he cannot see in himself even the features of a child, yet he can't deny to be "a living thing!"

Now, perhaps, if you cannot trace the spiritual features of a grown-up man stamped upon your being, and are exercised with distressing doubts as to whether your experience even amounts to that of a new-born babe, you may yet come in here, as being "a living thing," a nondescript. If you are the sort of person that cannot make yourself out, having an experience which you think nobody can fathom, having exercises which nobody else seems to be harassed with, and walking in a path where no other child of God seems ever to have walked before you, you are still a living thing.

Did not one say of old, (and have not you and I echoed his words), that he was "as a beast before you," (Psa. 73:22), and not a man? For "surely I am more brutish than any man, and have not the understanding of a man," (Prov. 30:2), but I am possessed of life still, and breathing after God still, with that in the soul which cannot rest satisfied short of the manifestation and the presence of God.

But here is the mark of the "living thing" – the desire. "Thou satisfiest *the desire* of every living thing." Not natural desires; not "the desire of the sluggard, which has nothing," that is, nothing spiritual in the desire, or in the answer; but the spiritual desires that the Holy Spirit himself has kindled; desires after God, "as the hart panteth after the water brooks, so panteth my soul after thee, O God." These are desires to know Christ by some sweet revelation of his glory, desires to be brought to the foot of the cross and to have his image stamped upon our soul, desires to be led into the length and breadth and depth and height of that love of his which passeth knowledge. This is a desire to walk before God accepted in the Beloved, a desire to feel that in our souls which shall sweetly satisfy us that we are eternally His.

February

This "living thing," though a nondescript in his own feelings, has that which marks the existence of life in him. He has a host of living desires towards the living God, he goes about breathing affections after Jesus, he has a restless, dissatisfied heart, discontented with the things of time and sense. He feels no pleasure in what the world presents, sighing to the Lord for the discoveries of his grace and his love.

20th

**"Where the Spirit of the Lord is, there is liberty."
2Corinthians 3:17**

The gospel is "the perfect law of liberty," (Jas. 1:25), therefore the very perfection of liberty, and thus thoroughly and entirely free from the least taint of bondage, and the slightest tincture of servitude. It is this perfect freedom which distinguishes it from the law which "works wrath," (Rom. 4:15), and "gendereth to bondage," (Gal. 4:24).

It is, therefore, a freedom from sin. Freedom from its guilt, as having the heart "sprinkled from an evil conscience," (Heb. 10:22). Freedom from its filth by "the washing of regeneration and renewing of the Holy Ghost," (Titus 3:5). Freedom from its love, because "the love of God is shed abroad in our hearts by the Holy Ghost," (Rom. 5:5). Freedom from its dominion for "ye are not under the law, but under grace," (Rom. 6:14), and freedom from its *practice*, because by becoming "servants to God, ye have your fruit unto holiness, and the end everlasting life," (Rom. 6:22).

How, then, can this pure, holy, and precious gospel be condemned as leading to licentiousness? It is because its power, its preciousness, its happy, holy, heavenly liberty have never been experimentally known by some who, like the Galatians, do all they can to "frustrate the grace of God," by "turning again to the weak and beggarly elements whereunto they desire to be in bondage," (Gal. 4:9). Others, like those monsters of wickedness whom Jude and Peter denounce with such burning words, pervert and abuse the liberty of the gospel unto licentiousness, "sporting themselves with their own deceivings," and, "while they promise others liberty, are themselves the servants of corruption," (2Pet. 2:19)."

Now the liberty of the gospel, as revealed in the Scriptures, and made experimentally known to the soul, steers, so to speak, between these two extremes, and is as perfectly free from the least intermixture of legal bondage as from the least taint of Antinomian licentiousness. It is, indeed, this holy liberty, heavenly power, and gracious influence of the precious gospel, under the teaching and testimony of the Holy Spirit, which makes it so suitable to our case and state when first convinced of sin, and cast into prison under guilt and condemnation.

What release but a perfect release would suit our deplorable case as prisoners in the pit where there is no water, shut up under wrath and guilty fear through a condemning law and an accusing conscience? This pure and precious gospel, therefore, comes down to our pitiable state and condition as a message of pure mercy, revealing pardon and peace through a Saviour's blood. If and when, by grace, we can receive, embrace, and entertain that gospel as a word from God to us, it proclaims liberty as with a jubilee trumpet through every court and ward of the soul.

What were we before this precious gospel reached our ears and hearts? Were we not bondslaves to sin, serving diverse lusts and pleasures, taken and led captive by Satan at his will? Whilst we talked about enjoying life, were we not, through the fear of death, subject to bondage? When we saw the saints of God not daring to do what we did greedily, we thought that *they* were the slaves, and that *we* were the free men, not knowing that "to whom we yield ourselves servants to obey, his servants we are, whether of sin unto death, or of obedience unto righteousness." We had no knowledge that "whosoever committeth sin is the servant of sin," (John 8:34), and that our boasted freedom was real servitude, whilst their apparent bondage was real freedom, for they had a saving interest in that precious declaration of Christ, "If the Son, therefore, shall make you free, ye shall be free indeed.

21st

"I kill, and I make alive; I wound, and I heal."
Deuteronomy 32:39

The work of grace in the soul, in its very beginnings, penetrates deeply into its inmost substance. It wounds and lays open the conscience to the eye of infinite Purity and Holiness. "The entrance of thy words giveth light; it giveth understanding unto the simple," (Psa. 119:130). "For the word of God is quick, and powerful, and sharper than any two-edged sword, piercing even to the dividing asunder of soul and spirit, and of the joints and marrow, and is a discerner of the thoughts and intents of the heart," (Heb. 4:12).

February

All conviction, to be true conviction, must be thorough. The field must be ploughed, broken up, and furrowed, before the seed can find a home, it must become a seedbed for the seed to fall into so as to germinate and grow. There is much to be done in a sinner's heart before Christ can dwell in him by faith, or be formed in him the hope of glory. The heart is naturally very hard. Thorns, thistles, and briars overspread its surface, and the noxious weeds of pride and lust have taken deep root. Much grubbing up of these bosom sins, our inbred self-righteousness and fleshly holiness, our creature strength and self-sufficiency is needed to prepare us to receive a free grace salvation, separate us from the world and false professors, embitter to us the loved things of time and sense, and lay us suing for mercy at the foot of the cross.

The first work, therefore, of conviction must be deep, or at least thorough, in order to make room for Christ and his salvation. So it is with any manifestation or discovery of the Lord Jesus Christ, any application of his blood, any visitation of his presence, or any shedding abroad of his love. These divine realities do not float upon the surface, but sink deep, and penetrate into his heart of hearts, into a man's inmost and deepest soul.

How soon is all lost and forgotten, but what the blessed Spirit writes himself in the heart! People say, "How well we have heard!" but all is lost and dropped before they get home from the house of prayer. They read a chapter, close the Bible, and with it, all they have read is closed too. Many have passing pangs of conviction, and passing desires, who give little proof of living under the Spirit's anointings. That divine Spirit does not let the saints of God off so easily. He holds them fast and firm to the work of conviction until he has slain them outright; and when he blesses he heals as deep as he wounds, and reveals the gospel as powerfully as he applies the law.

22nd

"But when the Comforter is come, whom I will send unto you from the Father, even the Spirit of truth, which proceedeth from the Father, he shall testify of me."
John 15:26

The special work and office of the Holy Spirit is to testify of Jesus, to glorify him, to take of the things that are his, and to show them to the soul. It follows therefore that without these teachings and testimonies of the Holy Spirit we have no true, no saving knowledge of Christ, no living faith in him, no sweet communion with him, no tender and affectionate love toward him. Are not these the marks which peculiarly distinguish the living family of God from those dead in sin, and those dead in profession?

A bare knowledge of the letter of truth can communicate no such gracious affections as will warm, soften, melt, and animate the soul of a child of God, under the felt power and influence of the Holy Spirit. Bare knowledge can create no such faith as gives him manifest union with Jesus and can inspire no such hope as carries every desire of his heart within the veil. Neither can it produce such godly sorrow for sin as makes him loathe and abhor himself in dust and ashes, or shed abroad such love as makes him love the Lord with a pure heart fervently.

But the same blessed and holy Teacher who takes of the things that are Christ's and reveals them to the soul, thus raising up faith, hope, and love, and bringing into living exercise every other spiritual gift and grace, first prepares the heart to receive him in all his gracious characters and covenant relationships by deeply and powerfully convincing us of our need of him as our all in all.

Is he a Priest? We need his atoning blood and his all-prevailing intercession that we may have peace with God, and that our prayers and supplications may rise up with acceptance into his ears.

Is he a Prophet? We need his heavenly instruction, that we may sit at his feet and hear his word, so as to believe his promises and obey his precepts.

Is he a King? We need his powerful and peaceful sceptre to subdue every foe, calm every fear, subdue every lust, crucify the whole body of sin, and bring into captivity every thought to the obedience of Christ.

23rd

"Forasmuch then as the children are partakers of flesh and blood, he also himself likewise took part of the same; that through death he might destroy him that had the power of death, that is, the devil."
Hebrews 2:14

By his sufferings, blood shedding and death, our gracious Lord made a complete atonement for sin and fulfilled every demand of the law. Not only did he wash his people from all their iniquities in the fountain of his precious blood, wrought out and brought in a perfect and everlasting righteousness for their justification, but "through

February

death [he destroyed] him that had the power of death, that is, *the devil.*" It was by his death on the cross that our gracious Lord "spoiled principalities and powers, and made a show of them openly, triumphing over them in it," (Col. 2:15).

It is a point little considered, though one of much importance, that the Lord Jesus had, as if personally, to grapple with and overcome the prince of the power of the air, to hurl Satan from his usurped throne, to destroy his works, and overthrow his kingdom. He didn't do this not by an act of omnipotent power, but by an act of the lowest weakness, for "he was crucified through weakness," (2Cor. 13:4),

According to our simple views, we might think that all that was needed to overthrow Satan was an act of omnipotent power. But this was not God's way. The king over all the children of pride, in the depths of infinite wisdom, was to be dethroned by an act of the deepest humility, of the most meek and submissive obedience, of the intensest suffering of God's own beloved Son, as standing in the place of those over whom Satan and death had triumphed through sin.

We read that "the Son of God was manifested that he might destroy, (literally, 'loosen' or 'untie'), the works of the devil," (1John 3:8). Thus, he came to untie and release all that Satan had fastened up by traversing, as it were, the whole ground, from the very first entrance of sin and death. By a course of holy and meritorious obedience, he came to repair the wreck and ruin produced by the primary author of all disobedience, but also, as the final stroke, he came to destroy and put down the disobedient and rebellious prince of darkness himself.

24th

"Thus saith the LORD; I remember thee, the kindness of thy youth, the love of thine espousals, when thou wentest after me in the wilderness, in a land that was not sown." Jeremiah 2:2

Salvation is a gift, the choicest and richest gift which the hands of a Triune God, whose name is Love, can bestow. It is a portion, an inheritance, an estate, a treasure, an eternal reality. The full possession, the entire enjoyment, the complete acquisition of this predestinated weight of glory is indeed reserved until a future state, but the pledges, the firstfruits, the early ripe clusters, the first dewdrops of this eternal inheritance, are given to the elect whilst here upon earth.

February

The everlasting enjoyment of the presence and glory of Christ is often compared in Scripture to a wedding. Thus we read of "the Lamb's wife," (Rev. 19:7), and of "the marriage of the Lamb." So the Church is said to be "brought unto the king in raiment of needlework," (Psa. 45:14), as the bride in Eastern countries was brought by the father to the bridegroom.

Howbeit, we read also of 'espousals', which always preceded the celebration of marriage. "I remember thee, the kindness of thy youth, the love of thine espousals," and as the Paul spoke to the church at Corinth, "I have espoused you to one husband, that I may present you as a chaste virgin to Christ," (2Cor. 11:2). In like manner, "Mary was espoused to Joseph, before they came together," (Matt. 1:8), that is, before they knew each other as man and wife. Now this espousal was a necessary prelude to marriage, though it was not the same thing, and, therefore, a betrothed virgin was punished as a fornicator by the Levitical law if she was unfaithful to her espoused husband. To be betrothed had the nature of marriage in it, though it was not the same thing as the marriage; the parties did not yet live together and were not put in possession of each other.

Thus, it is in our life here on earth that our spiritual betrothment takes place; the spiritual marriage awaits in the life to come. "I will betroth thee unto me for ever; yea, I will betroth thee unto me in righteousness, and in judgment, and in lovingkindness, and in mercies. I will even betroth thee unto me in faithfulness: and thou shalt know the LORD," (Hos. 2:19-20).

25th

"It is a faithful saying: For if we be dead with him, we shall also live with him: if we suffer, we shall also reign with him: if we deny him, he also will deny us."
2Timothy 2:11-12

To be partakers of Christ's crown, we must be partakers of Christ's cross. Union with him in suffering must precede union with him in glory. This is the express testimony of the Holy Spirit, "if so be that we suffer with him, that we may be also glorified together," (Rom. 8:17). The flesh and the world are to be crucified to us, and we to them; and this can only be by virtue of a living union with a crucified Lord. This is what made the Apostle say, "I am crucified with Christ:

nevertheless I live; yet not I, but Christ liveth in me: and the life which I now live in the flesh I live by the faith of the Son of God, who loved me, and gave himself for me." And again, "But God forbid that I should glory, save in the cross of our Lord Jesus Christ, by whom the world is crucified unto me, and I unto the world," (Gal. 6:14).

An experimental knowledge of crucifixion with his crucified Lord made Paul preach the cross, not only in its power to save, but in its power to sanctify. Through the cross, that is, through union and communion with him who suffered upon it, not only is there a fountain opened for all sin, but for all uncleanness, (Zech. 13:1). Blood and water gushed from the side of Jesus when pierced by the Roman spear.

"This fountain so dear, he'll freely impart;
Unlocked by the spear, it gushed from his heart,
With blood and with water; the first to atone,
To cleanse us the latter; the fountain's but one."

"All my springs are in thee," said the psalmist, the man after God's own heart; and well may we echo his words. All our springs, not only of pardon and peace, acceptance and justification, but of happiness and holiness, of wisdom and strength, of victory over the world, of mortification of this body of sin and death; of every fresh revival and renewal of hope and confidence; of all prayer and praise; of every new budding forth of the soul, as of Aaron's rod, in blossom and fruit; of every gracious feeling, spiritual desire, warm supplication, honest confession, melting contrition, and godly sorrow for sin - all these springs from that life which is hidden with Christ in God, are in a crucified Lord.

Thus Christ crucified is, "to them who are saved, the power of God." And as he "of God is made unto us wisdom, righteousness, sanctification, and redemption," at the cross alone can we be made wise unto salvation, become righteous by a free justification, receive of his Spirit to make us holy, and be redeemed and delivered by blood and power from sin, Satan, death, and hell.

26th

"The dead are raised up."
Matthew 11:5

The "dead" spoken of here are those who by nature are dead in sin. These corpses, then are raised up when life from God visits their souls. They are raised up to faith in Jesus, raised up to hope in his name, raised up to a sense of his dying love to their souls, raised up from doubt and fear, raised up from the depths of despondency to 'look unto him and be saved'.

What a mercy it is that the Lord of life and glory still puts forth the same power in the hearts of his people, that he once put forth in their bodies, and that he raises them up from their state of death and deadness!

Do we not often feel so dead, as though we had not a particle of the grace of God? So dead, that it seems scarcely possible to have a sensation of spiritual life again? So dead, that we almost fear whether the power of God was ever felt in our hearts? Now, the Lord raises up life and feeling in our souls, by putting forth the same power that called Lazarus out of the tomb. And every lifting-up of the heart towards him, every panting desire to know him, every yearning to feel the power of his resurrection, every breathing of tender affection, every sigh, every cry, and every groan, yes, every feeling Godwards, however short and however transient, is a proof that the Lord of life and glory is still putting forth his power in the hearts of his people.

27th

"And Jabez called on the God of Israel, saying, Oh that thou wouldest bless me indeed, and enlarge my coast, and that thine hand might be with me, and that thou wouldest keep me from evil..."
1Chronicles 4:10

An "indeed" blessing is what the soul is seeking after which has ever felt the misery and bitterness of sin, and ever tasted the sweetness of God's salvation. These "indeed" blessings are seen to be spiritual and eternal. Compared with such blessings as these, the soul sees how vain and empty are all earthly things, what vain toys, what idle dreams, what passing shadows. It wonders at the folly of men in hunting after such vain shows, and spending time, health, money, life itself, in a pursuit of nothing but misery and destruction. Every passing funeral bell that such a soul hears and every corpse borne slowly along to the grave that it sees impresses it with solemn feelings as to the state of those who live and die in their sins.

Thus, the awakened soul learns more and more to contrast time with eternity, earth with heaven, sinners with saints, and professors with possessors. By these things is the soul taught, with Baruch, not "to seek great things" for itself, but to seek real things; to seek

February

those things which will outlast time and fit it for eternity. That soul is thus brought to care little for the opinion of men as to what is good or great, but to care much for what God has stamped with his own approbation. A tender conscience, a broken heart, a contrite spirit, a humble mind, a separation from the world and everything worldly, a submission to his holy will, a meek endurance of the cross, a conformity to Christ's suffering image, and a living to God's glory.

As, then, the gracious Lord is pleased to indulge the soul with some discovery of himself, shedding abroad a sweet sense of his goodness and mercy, atoning blood, and dying love, it is made to long more and more for the manifestation of those blessings which alone are to be found in him. For his blessings are not like the mere temporal mercies that we enjoy at his hands, all of which perish in the using, but are forever and ever; and when once given are never taken away. They thus become pledges and foretastes of eternal joys, for they are absolutely irreversible.

When Isaac had once blessed Jacob in God's name, though the blessing had been obtained by deceit, yet having been once given, it could not be recalled.

He said, therefore, to Esau, "[I] have blessed him, yea, and he shall be blessed."

Thus, when the Lord has blessed his people with any of those spiritual blessings that are stored up in his inexhaustible fullness, these blessings have his character, unchanging and unchangeable; for "he is in one mind, and who can turn him?" (Job 23:13), and "Jesus Christ the same yesterday, and today, and for ever," (Heb. 13:8).

28th

"And Jabez called on the God of Israel, saying, Oh that thou wouldest bless me indeed, and enlarge my coast, and that thine hand might be with me, and that thou wouldest keep me from evil...."
1Chronicles 4:10

A coast means a boundary line such as divides one territory from another, or terminates a country, as the sea coast is the boundary of our island. Every quickened soul has a coast; that is, a territory of inward experience, which is limited and bounded by the line that the Holy Spirit has drawn in his conscience. As the Lord divided the tribes to cast their inheritance by line, (Psa. 78:55), so has he cast the lot for every vessel of mercy, and his hand has divided it unto them by line, (Isa. 34:17). This is as it were the tether which fastens down every quickened soul to his own appointed portion of inward experience. Within this tether he may walk, feed, and lie down. It is "the food convenient for him," the strip of pasture allotted him. He cannot, he dare not break this tether, which is fastened round a tender conscience, and every stretching forth beyond his measure to boast in another man's line of things, cuts into and galls this tender conscience.

However, the living soul cannot but earnestly desire to have this coast enlarged. He wants more light, more life, more feeling, more liberty, more knowledge of God in Christ, more faith, hope, and love. He yearns to have his narrow, contracted, shut-up heart enlarged in prayer, in meditation, in communion, and in affection to the people of God. He is not satisfied with the scanty pasture allotted him, but wants a larger measure of heavenly teaching, he longs to be indulged with more filial confidence in and access unto God, and be more delivered from that fear which has tormented him.

"God shall enlarge Japheth, and he shall dwell in the tents of Shem," (Gen. 9:27). "I will run the way of thy commandments, when thou shalt enlarge my heart," (Psa. 119:32).

This enlargement of their border the Lord had sworn to Israel, and to give them all the land which he had promised unto their fathers. Therefore when he had said, "Sing, O barren, thou that did not bear," he added, "Enlarge the place of thy tent, and let them stretch forth the curtains of thine habitations: spare not, lengthen thy cords, and strengthen thy stakes," (Isa. 54:1-2).

Have you any of these fervent desires after light, love, and liberty such that the world, pride, lust, unbelief, covetousness, and carnality may not shut up your heart, but that you may know the love of Christ that passes knowledge, so as to be filled with all the fullness of God?

These are good desires, and very different from rushing presumptuously forward, and chattering about liberty whilst you are slaves of corruption. It is one thing to look through the park gates, and quite another to enjoy the estate; but it is far better to look through the gates with wishful desires, than to break down the fence as a trespasser. To look upon the coffer is not to be put into possession of the writings, but it is better to wait and cry for the key of David than to break it open, and steal the deeds.

He that is kept in the narrow, narrow path between sloth and presumption will be at solemn seasons crying out with Jabez, "Oh that thou wouldest bless me indeed, and enlarge my coast, and that thine hand might be with me, and that thou wouldest keep me from evil, that it may not grieve me!" (1Chr. 4:10).

February

And do you know what was the result if his honest cry? "And God granted him that which he requested."

29th

"Let my soul live, and it shall praise thee; and let thy judgments help me."
Psalm 119:175

When we 'live', we live by faith; as the Apostle says, "The life which I now live in the flesh, I live by the faith of the Son of God," (Gal. 2:20). We live by faith when the Lord is pleased to communicate the precious gift of true faith to the heart. Then indeed we believe.

We believe in Jesus, we believe in his blood, we believe in his righteousness, we believe in his Person, we believe in his dying love; and as faith begins to lift up its drooping head in the soul, as a wilting flower drinks in a refreshing shower, we begin to live a life of faith in the Son of God. As we begin to live, we also begin to love. When we are in darkness, coldness, and barrenness, there is neither love to God nor to man. The very ways of God are a thorough misery to us; the Bible is neglected, and prayer is little attended to; under preaching we are cold, dead, and listless; the company of God's people is forsaken, and the things of eternity seem to fade from our view.

But let the Lord revive his work upon the heart, let him bestow a gracious renewing, let him drop the unction of his Spirit, let the rain and dew of his grace fall, let him manifest himself with life and power; then the whole scene changes. It is like spring after a dreary winter; it is like the outpouring of the rain from heaven after a long season of drought, "thou renewest the face of the earth," (Psa. 104:30). There is a blessed change when the Lord himself is pleased to appear in the soul. That is when it begins to live.

This life will then manifest itself in various ways. Whilst we are dead, prayer is a burden; when we have life, prayer is our very breath. When we are dead, the very thoughts of God are grievous; when we are alive, the thoughts of God are sweet and pleasant. When we are dead, our affections cleave to the things of time and sense; when we are alive, our affections mount up with wings as eagles. When we are dead, the world is our home, though it is but a miserable one; when we are alive, we are looking upward to heaven as the home of the soul when time shall be no more.

March

March

1st

"Take heed therefore... to feed the church of God, which he hath purchased with his own blood."
Acts 20:28

    Atonement for sin stands or falls with the Deity of Christ. If we deny his Deity, we must deny the atonement, for what value or merit can there be in the blood of a mere man that God, for its sake, should pardon millions of sins? This the Socinians clearly see, and therefore deny the atonement altogether. But if there be no atonement, no sacrifice, no atoning sacrifice for sin, where can we look for pardon and peace? Whichever way we turn our eyes there is despair.
    Yet, by the eye of faith, we see the Son of God obeying the law, and by his doing and dying, and acting and suffering, rendering a satisfaction to the violated justice of the Most High and offering a sacrifice for sin. There is in him such a glory and such a value breathing through every thought, word, and action of his suffering humanity, that we embrace him and all that he is and has, with every desire and affection of our regenerated soul. All our religion lies here. All our faith, hope, and love flow unto, and are fixed and concentrated in Jesus Christ and him crucified.
    Without a measure of this in our heart and conscience, we have no religion worth the name, nothing that either saves or sanctifies, nothing that delivers from the guilt, filth, love, power, and practice of sin, nothing that supports in life, comforts in death, or fits us for eternity.
    The way, then, whereby we come to a knowledge of, and a faith in, the Deity of Christ is first by feeling a need of all that he is as a Saviour, and a great one, and then having a manifestation of him by the blessed Spirit to our soul. When he is thus revealed and brought near, we see, by the eye of faith, his pure and perfect humanity and his eternal Deity; and these two distinct natures we see combined, but not intermingled, in one glorious Person, Immanuel, God with us. Until thus favoured we may see the Deity of Christ in the Scriptures, and have so far a belief in it, but we have not that personal appropriating faith whereby, with Thomas, we can say, "My Lord and my God."

2nd

"There are many devices in a man's heart; nevertheless the counsel of the LORD, that shall stand."
Proverbs 19:21

March

A man in his fleshly mind is generally devising some method or other whereby he may escape a practical subjection to the gospel; some way or other whereby he may escape walking in the path of self-denial and mortification of the flesh, and the crucifixion of "the old man with the affections and lusts." He is generally seeking some way or other to indulge the flesh, and yet, at the same time, to stand in gospel liberty, a way to have everything that can gratify his carnal mind, and, at the same time, have a well-grounded hope of eternal life.

The Lord, however, says, "No. These two things are not compatible; he that shall live with Christ must die with Christ; he that shall reign with Christ must suffer with Christ; he that shall wear the crown must carry the cross." So whatever devices there be in a man's heart, or whatever ways and plans he shall undertake to bring his devices to pass, "the counsel of the Lord, that shall stand." Divine sovereignty shall fulfil that which divine sovereignty has appointed, and the purposes of God shall stand upon the ruins of the purposes of the creature.

And it is our mercy, (so far as we are children of the living God), that it should be so. Where would we have been this moment, if the devices in our hearts had succeeded? We would have been in hell. Where would we have been, since the Lord has been pleased, as we trust, to quicken our souls into spiritual life, if all our devices had succeeded? Our eyes would have stood out with fatness, (Psa. 73:7), and we would have had more than heart could wish. We would have been now, if the Lord had left us to our own devices? Indulging in some dreadful temptation, or already have disgraced our name before the Church of God; or, if we had escaped that, we would have only a name to live, whilst our hearts were secretly dead before God. We would have had a form of godliness whilst we inwardly or outwardly denied the power thereof, (2Tim. 3:5).

Therefore it is our mercy that the devices of our hearts should not stand, but that "the counsel of the Lord" should prevail over all the purposes of our base nature. When a man is brought to the right spot, and is in a right mind to trace out the Lord's dealings with him from the first, he sees it was a kind hand which 'blasted his gourds and laid them low'.

It was a kind hand that swept away his worldly prospects, which reduced him to natural as well as to spiritual poverty, which led him into exercises, trials, sorrows, griefs, and tribulations; because, in those trials he has found the Lord, more or less, experimentally precious. Jacob found it so; he blessed the Lord for the path in which he had been led. Though his days had been few and evil, he could see how the Lord had 'fed him all his life long unto that day', amid all the changing vicissitudes through which he had passed in body and soul; and he blessed that hand which had guided him through that difficult way, and yet brought him to a "city of habitation."

3rd

"For we which live are alway delivered unto death for Jesus' sake, that the life also of Jesus might be made manifest in our mortal flesh."
2Corinthians 4:11

What is meant by the expression, "our mortal flesh?" It does not mean the carnal mind, but our earthly tabernacle; and the expression is similar to another in this chapter, "We have this treasure in *earthen vessels,* that the excellency of the power may be of God, and not of us," (2Cor. 4:7). It is, then, in this poor body, compassed with infirmities, that the life of Jesus is made manifest. This divine life will often spring up in fervent breathings after God, in the actings of living faith, in the sweet communion the people of God have with one another, in reading the Scriptures, in the application of precious promises, and under the preached word. From time to time it bubbles up like a spring from its source. Sometimes indeed it runs underground, buried as it were under the load of "our mortal flesh;" but again and again it reappears, drawn up by the Sun of righteousness. "Spring up, O well."

Its risings are, however, proportionate to its sinkings. Thus in proportion as we cease to pray naturally, do we pray spiritually; as we cease to hope in the flesh, do we hope in the Lord; as we cease to believe with the head, do we believe with the heart. When we see an end of all perfection in self, then we begin to find perfection in Christ, and when we see nothing in our hearts but sin, misery, and wretchedness, then we begin to taste spiritual consolation. Thus in proportion as nature sinks, the life of Jesus rises, and is made manifest in our mortal flesh.

Is the soul, then, longing to have sweet manifestations of the life of Jesus? Where must it go to get them? What does the word of God say? "Whence then cometh wisdom? and where is the place of understanding? Seeing it is hid from the eyes of all living, and kept close from the fowls of the air. Destruction and death say, We have heard the fame thereof with our ears," (Job 28:20-22).

Until, then, we get to "destruction and death," the destruction of fleshly hopes and the death of creature religion, we do not so much as ever hear the fame of true wisdom with our ears. Thus, when we get into darkness, then light springs up; when we get into despondency, hope arises; when we are tempted with unbelief and infidelity, faith appears. Thus those are the wisest in whom creature wisdom has most ceased; those are the strongest who have learned most experimentally their own weakness; those are the holiest who have known most of their own filthiness; those are the most religious in a true sense who have least religion of their own. So that just in proportion as we are delivered unto death, and execution takes place on what the creature loves, so does the life of Jesus begin to rise and make itself blessedly manifest.

4th

"Bind the sacrifice with cords, even unto the horns of the altar."
Psalm 118:27

Are you a poor broken-hearted child of the living God? Is there any measure of the Spirit of Christ in you? Is there any faint resemblance of his meekness and holy image stamped upon you? Then you feel yourself bound with cords to the horns of the altar. You feel the strong ties of necessity, and you feel the strong ties of affection binding you there. But with this, you feel also that you are a struggling victim; that you would gladly escape the troubles and trials that being bound to the horns of the altar brings upon you. You would gladly get into an easier path if you could, or if you dared, would willingly set up some altar yourself, made after the pattern of Damascus, (2Kings 16:10). You would even, like the Roman Catholic, worship with your body a material cross, instead of worshiping in your soul the adorable God-man who hung and bled there. You would gladly, if you could, step out of a self-loathing, exercised, tried, harassed, and tempted path, to get into the flowery meadow of doctrine and speculation, and there walk at ease without one pang in your conscience, or one trial in your soul.

But the Lord has said, "Bind the sacrifice with cords, even unto the horns of the altar." You are so bound. From those horns you cannot escape. You may fume, fret, and rebel against all or any of these cords, but you cannot break them. In your strugglings you may even stretch these cords to their utmost extent, but they are too firmly fastened round your tender conscience, and too strongly wreathed round your broken heart, for you to burst them. They would sooner cut your heart in two, than you could break them, or escape from them.

March

In your right mind, you would not be otherwise than bound with these cords. In your right mind, you want the cords tightened, and so to be drawn nearer and nearer unto it, and to have the blood that was shed upon it sprinkled upon your conscience. In your right mind, you want to see with the eye of faith the Victim that once lay bleeding and writhing there; and as you look upon him, you want to drink into his image, and to feel the melting power and softening efficacy of that sight.

But connected with it are such trials, such temptations, and such sacrifices, that you, in your fits of rebellion or flesh-pleasing ease, would at times as gladly get away, as at other times, you would gladly get near.

Vile wretches that we are, who would often prefer to serve the flesh and the world and take our chance, as men speak, for eternity, than suffer trials and temptations as the followers of Christ! But it is our mercy that we can neither make nor unmake, do nor undo, bind nor break any one cord of eternal love, but that, in spite of the creature, God will "fulfil all the good pleasure of his goodness, and the work of faith with power," (2Thes. 1:11).

5th

"And what is the exceeding greatness of his power to us who believe, according to the working of his mighty power, which he wrought in Christ, when he raised him from the dead."
Ephesians 1:19-20

Man needs to be roused by a mighty and effectual power out of his state of sleep and death. It is not a little pull, a gentle snatch at his coat, a slight tug of his sleeve, which will pull him out of his sins. He must be snatched from them as a person would be snatched out of bed when the house is on fire, or pulled out of a river when sinking for the last time. Let us never think that the work of grace upon the heart is a slight or superficial one. Indeed, there needs a mighty work of grace upon a sinner's heart to deliver him from his destructions. We always, therefore, find the work of grace to begin by a spiritual sight and sense of our ruined condition before God. But this alone will not suffice to make us true-hearted disciples of Jesus. It is a preparation, a most needful preparation for a sight of the King in his beauty, but it is not the same thing as to see and believe in the Son of God unto eternal life. We must have something far beyond any convictions of sin or any sense of our lost and ruined condition. We must have by faith a view of the blessed Lord more or less manifested to our souls by that Holy Spirit whose office it is to take of the things of Christ and to reveal them to the heart so as to see his suitability, his grace, his glory, his work, his blood, and his obedience. We need to see these divine and blessed realities by the eye of faith, to know and feel for ourselves that they are exactly adapted to our case and state and that they are the very things we require to save us from the wrath to come. We must be settled in our minds that so far as we have a saving interest in them we are saved from the floods of destruction.

Wherever this believing sight of Christ is given to the soul, it creates and maintains a faith that works by love. Thus wherever there is a view of Jesus by the eye of faith, wherever he manifests and makes himself in any measure precious to the soul, love is the certain fruit of it, for we love him because he first loved us. As a result, when we begin to love the Lord, love gives us a binding tie which creates union and communion with him, and he then unveils his lovely face. As he discovers more and more of his beauty and blessedness unto us, it gives him a firm place in the heart's warmest, tenderest affections, and then he comes and takes up his abode in the soul and rules there as its rightful Lord.

The following things therefore are indispensably necessary to true discipleship; first, a spiritual sense of our lost, ruined condition; then a knowledge of Christ by a gracious discovery of his suitability, beauty, and blessedness; and thirdly, a faith in him that works by love and purifies the heart, overcomes the world, and delivers from death and hell.

6th

"Therefore it is of faith, that it might be by grace."
Romans 4:16

Of faith, we read expressly that, "It is the gift of God." This is the grand master-grace of the soul; it is the grand wheel which moves every other wheel in the heart; it is the eye, the ear, the hand of the new man of grace. Only so far as we have faith, and the Lord draws out this faith in exercise, have we any true spiritual feeling.

But what makes me prize the gift of faith? It is knowing so much and so painfully the indwelling and inworking of unbelief. Is not this the case naturally? What makes me prize health? It is having a poor, weakly body. What makes me prize rest? Fatigue. What makes me prize ease? It is pain. What makes me prize food? It is hunger. What makes me prize the cup of cold water? It is thirst. By these feelings, I not only know the reality by the lack of it, but also enjoy the blessing when communicated.

It is just so spiritually, as naturally. What can I know of faith, except I am exercised, (and exercised I am almost daily), by the workings of unbelief, infidelity, questionings of the reasoning mind, and all the spawn of an unbelieving heart? As the soul is tossed up and down, (and it is often tossed up and down on this sea of unbelief), it learns to prize the harbour of faith. When the Lord mercifully communicates a little faith to the soul, and faith begins to realise, feel, experience, and feed upon the truth as it is in Jesus, then we know what faith is by the possession of it.

What a mercy it is that the Lord has the gift of faith to bestow! Here are poor souls toiling, troubling, labouring, groaning, sighing, oppressed with unbelief – that great giant in the heart, who has slain his thousands and tens of thousands. How our souls sometimes sink down under this wretched unbelief! But how we prize the faith all the more when it comes! How all the sinkings make the risings higher, and all the sadness makes the change more blessed! As the tossings to and fro of the sailor upon the sea, with all the perils and sufferings of the voyage, make the calm harbour so pleasant, so all the tossings up and down of unbelief endears the holy calm of living faith to the soul.

7th

"Beautiful for situation, the joy of the whole earth, is mount Zion, on the sides of the north, the city of the great King."
Psalm 48:2

We have sometimes thought that the reason why Zion typically represents the royal throne of Jesus is not well understood by many. Mount Zion, literally, was a steep hill of Jerusalem, so steep and inaccessible that for generations after the children of Israel had gained possession of the land, it still remained, like a little Gibraltar, in the hands of the Jebusites, the original inhabitants of the place. "As for the Jebusites the inhabitants of Jerusalem, the children of Judah could not drive them out: but the Jebusites dwell with the children of Judah at Jerusalem unto this day," (Jos. 15:63).

When David was anointed king over Israel, and had reigned at Hebron seven years and six months, he cast his eyes toward Jerusalem, as a preferable metropolis, and a more suitable seat of his extended empire. However, as long as the hill of Zion was occupied by the warlike Jebusites, they would retain their command of the lower city. His first step, therefore, was, with the help of God, to dispossess the Jebusites of their stronghold. So strong was this hill-fort by nature and fortification that the Jebusites ridiculed all his attempts to capture it, putting on the ramparts "the blind and the lame," those we would call the worn-out invalids of the army, as if these, who could neither see nor walk, were amply sufficient to baffle all David's attempts at its capture, (2Sam. 5:6-8).

Joab, however, as a prize set before him, for which he was to be David's chief captain, mounted the hill, smote the lame and the blind on the wall, and the Jebusites behind the wall, and won possession of the coveted spot, (1Chr. 11:6). There David henceforward dwelt, as its conqueror, as in a castle. There he fixed his royal abode, and thence he swayed his sceptre over the whole land of Israel, from Dan to Beersheba.

Its very name was typical, for it signifies literally, "sunny," or "shine upon," as facing the south, and ever basking in the rays of the warm sun. Thus the sunny hill of Zion, as a hill of conquest, and as the royal seat of David, became a suitable type of the throne of Jesus in the courts above, won by lawful conquest, (Rev. 3:21), where is now located his royal palace, and where he rules and reigns as the anointed King of heaven and earth. Thus mount Zion typically represents not the cross, but the crown; not the law, but the gospel; not the battle, but the victory.

8th

"O LORD, be gracious unto us; we have waited for thee: be thou their arm every morning, our salvation also in the time of trouble."
Isaiah 33:2

Israel often has to pass through times of sorrow and trouble, and deep temporal and spiritual trouble is the allotted portion of many, if not of most of the people of God. But having found that the Lord is a Saviour, and the only Saviour who can support in trouble and deliver out of trouble, there is this conviction deeply implanted and firmly written upon their heart that he is a Saviour in the time of trouble.

It is the purpose of God to hunt us out of all lying refuges, that we may believe in Jesus to the saving of our soul. That we may prove that he is able to save to the uttermost all who come unto God by him; that we may learn what salvation is, and that we may know it for ourselves as a divine and blessed reality.

Thus, though he is always a Saviour, yet he is not experimentally a Saviour in times of worldly ease, carnal prosperity, and seasons of carelessness. But in times of trouble, when none can do us any good or stretch forth a healing hand but the Lord alone, then to come to his gracious Majesty and find there and then how he can and does save in trouble and out of trouble, this is that which endears such a Saviour to believing hearts.

Observe also the expression, "time of trouble," and how it includes not only every trouble which may befall us temporally or spiritually, but clearly intimates that there is not a single season or time when trouble comes that the Lord is not able and willing to save us out of it. How well this corresponds with those gracious words and that sweet promise, "Call upon me in the day of trouble: I will deliver thee, and thou shalt glorify me," (Psa. 50:15).

9th

"But God be thanked, that ye were the servants of sin, but ye have obeyed from the heart that form of doctrine which was delivered you."
Romans 6:17

How great reason we have to thank God that he so instructed his Apostle to set forth how a sinner is justified! For how could we have attained to the knowledge of this mystery without divine revelation? How could we know in what way God could be just and yet the justifier of the ungodly? How could we otherwise see all the perfections of God harmonising in the Person and work of Jesus Christ? Or how could we see therein his law maintained in all its rigid purity and strictest justice, and yet mercy, grace, and love still be allowed to have full play in a sinner's salvation?

It was the Spirit of God which led Paul deeply into this blessed subject; and especially in the Epistle to the Romans does he trace out this grand foundation truth with such clearness, weight, and power, that the Church of God can never be sufficiently thankful for this portion of divine revelation. His grand object is to show how God justifies the ungodly by the blood and obedience of his dear Son so that "as by one man's disobedience many were made sinners, so by the obedience of one shall many be made righteous," (Rom. 5:19).

He declares that "the righteousness of God... is by faith of Jesus Christ unto all and upon all that believe," (Rom. 3:22). Further, that, "through the redemption that is in Christ Jesus, Whom God hath set forth to be a propitiation through faith in his blood," he pardons the sinner, justifies the ungodly, and views him as righteous in the Son of his love.

In opening up this subject, the Apostle, in Romans 5, traces up this justification to the union of the Church with her covenant Head. He shows us her standing in Christ as well as in Adam; and that all the miseries which she derives from her standing in the latter are overbalanced by the mercies that flow from her standing in the former. He winds up with that heart-reviving truth, that "where sin abounded, grace did much more abound; that as sin has reigned unto death, even so might grace reign through righteousness unto eternal life."

This then is the form of doctrine, or mould of teaching, into which the soul is delivered when it is brought into a heart-felt reception of, and a feeling acquaintance with it. By being led more or less into the experimental enjoyment of the doctrine, the soul is favoured with a solemn acquiescence in, and a filial submission to the doctrine, as all its salvation and all its desire. And as the mould impresses its image upon the moist plaster or melted metal poured into it, so the heart, softened and melted by the blessed Spirit's teaching, receives the impress of this glorious truth with filial confidence. It feels its sweetness and power, and is filled with a holy admiration of it as the only way in which God can justify an ungodly wretch, not only without sacrificing any one attribute of his holy character, but rather magnifying thereby the purity of his nature, and the demands of his unbending justice.

10th

"For I am not ashamed of the gospel of Christ: for it is the power of God unto salvation to every one that believeth; to the Jew first, and also to the Greek."
Romans 1:16

What is meant here by the word power? It is a term much used in the New Testament. "The kingdom of God," it is declared, "is not in word, but in power;" and true faith is said to "stand not in the wisdom of men, but in the power of God." What, then, is power? It is a divine operation that God himself puts forth in the soul. It cannot be described in words, nor explained so as to be understood by our mental capacity. It must be felt to be known; and must be realised in a man's own soul before he can have any spiritual conception of it. "Thy people," we read, "shall be willing in the day of thy power," (Psa. 110:3).

When the gospel does come to the soul by the application of the blessed Spirit, and a divine power accompanies it, though the power itself cannot be described even by the person himself, it is made known by the effects which follow it. For instance, here is a poor wretch condemned by the law, and in his apprehensions lying forever under its fearful curse. He may, perhaps, see there is salvation in Christ, and know in his judgment there is salvation in no other; but he cannot lay hold of Christ, nor get from under the condemnation he feels. Why? Because the gospel has not been made the power of God unto salvation to his soul. See how he begs, cries, prays, and supplicates God to have mercy on him, though. Continually he is endeavouring to seek God, and beseech him to have mercy on his soul, but he cannot get peace to his conscience; he is still in trouble and distress, bowed down with bondage, guilt, and fear. Here is a man longing to see the "power of God" displayed.

Now, when the Lord is pleased to apply some portion of his blessed word to this soul, or to speak home some particular promise, the power which accompanies this raises up a special faith, whereby that portion of God's holy word, which speaks of Christ, or that particular promise is laid hold of. Here, then, is power communicated with the gospel. The gospel has now come not unto him, "in word only," (1Thes. 1:5), as it might often have done before, leaving him all the while in guilt and fear, but with "power;" and, by the faith thus raised up, he believes in Jesus to the saving of his soul.

He could not believe in him before, for his faith, such as it was, being devoid of power, left him where it found him, as forlorn and helpless as the man who fell among thieves. No. He might as well attempt to create a world, as to believe in the Son of God unto deliverance.

But no sooner does he believe what the Holy Spirit applies, than a sweet and sacred power comes into his soul. A power which takes away his doubts and fears, dispels guilt from his conscience and banishes the mists and fogs that for months have hung over his soul. It reveals in him a precious Jesus; makes the promises of the gospel to glitter before his eyes like dew-drops in autumn; and gives him an unspeakable nearness to God, through the Person, blood, and righteousness of Christ, such as he never knew until the gospel came with power, and faith was raised up in his soul.

March 11th

"Let thy mercies come also unto me, O LORD, even thy salvation, according to thy word. So shall I have wherewith to answer him that reproacheth me: for I trust in thy word."
Psalm 119:41-42

A living soul wants to return an answer to the one who reproaches him, but he cannot do it of himself, for he has not a word to speak in self-justification; that is utterly cut off, and therefore he needs to have that which shall furnish him with an answer to these reproaches. What is it alone that can furnish him with an answer? The mercies of God in his soul.

'Lord, give to me thy mercies, the salvation which thou hast promised me. Then will I have an answer for those who reproach me, for I trust in thy word.' The coming in of mercies into the soul, and the manifestation of salvation to the heart afford an answer for those who reproach.

If you will observe, the word mercies is in the plural, there being many mercies; but salvation is in the singular, there being only one salvation. In what way, then, did the Psalmist want these mercies? Merely as standing in the letter of the word? Only as recorded in the inspired word of truth? As things to look at, as objects hung up, as it were, in a picture, merely for the eye to gaze upon? No indeed. He wanted them in his heart, to "come to him," to visit him, to be breathed into him, to be made part and parcel of him, to be the life-blood that should circulate in his veins, to be the very kingdom of God set up with power in his soul.

And why did he want internal mercies? Because he had internal reproaches. Why did he need mercies in his soul? Because condemnation was in his soul. It was there the sentence of death was written; it was there the sentence of acquittal needed to be recorded. It was there that reproach was felt; it was there the answer to reproach was to be given.

If the reproach were merely outward, the answer might be outward also; but the reproof being inward, in the heart, in the conscience, in the feelings, it was needed that the answer should be in the same place. It needed to be written in the same spot, engraved in the same tablets, and brought home with the same or far greater power, so as to be a sufficient answer to the reproaches of him that reproached him.

March 12th

"Such as sit in darkness and in the shadow of death, being bound in affliction and iron."
Psalm 107:10

What a blessed thing is light, the light of life, the light of God's countenance, the light of the glorious gospel, the light of Jesus' face! "Truly the light is sweet, and a pleasant thing it is for the eyes to behold the sun," (Ec. 11:7). To whom is it pleasant? To those who sit in darkness and the shadow of death. How such hail the first rays of light! If you were shipwrecked, cast by night upon a deserted rock, how you would welcome the first beams of the morning light to show you where you were, and what hopes there were of final escape. So, similarly, how a sense of danger, magnified by the darkness, makes a shipwrecked soul welcome that first beam of spiritual light that he may see the way of escape from hell to heaven. How sweet to such it is to have any divine light dawn upon the mind, to have any breaking in of the goodness and mercy, grace and glory, of the blessed Jesus.

The more we sit in darkness, the more we prize light. Many high professors despise all this, and run up against it a building built upon frames and feelings, making a 'Christ' out of our experience. Poor souls! Their light is not worth having; and their religion, it is to be feared, is but a fire of their own kindling, the light of which will never light them to heaven. Why then do they despise the light of heaven? Because they never sat in darkness and because they never felt the shadow of death. Therefore, truly, what is their light? A will-o'-the-wisp, a gas-lamp, a meteor, a falling star, anything and everything but the dayspring from on high, for the Sun of righteousness is hid from their eyes.

The Lord's people cannot be guiled with a gas-lamp or a will-o'-the-wisp. They must have Jesus. They must have his blood upon their consciences, his grace in their hearts, his presence in their souls. They crave sweet discoveries of his Person and work, the whispers of his love, the touch of his finger, and the smiles of his face. They must have Jesus for themselves. 'Give me Christ, or else I die,' is their feeling.

What therefore makes them break forth with these earnest sighs and cries? Their spiritual eyes are open, they have life, but they are sitting in darkness and in the shadow of death. Were they otherwise, they would be content to remain as they naturally are; dark and dead. Feeling their state, however, they long for those beams of heavenly sunlight, and when it breaks in upon their soul, they welcome it with joy and embrace it, because it comes from and leads to God.

March 13th

"But he knoweth the way that I take: when he hath tried me, I shall come forth as gold."
Job 23:10

What a purifying effect experience of trial produces; what a separation it makes of the dross from the ore! If a man has a grain of faith in his soul, trial will discover it; if he has a particle of living hope, temptation will bring it to light; if he has a grain of love, trial will extract it from the ore. If he has any patience, any humility, any fear of God, any desire to be right, any dread to be wrong, any honesty, any sincerity, or any integrity it will surface under trial. If he has any vital power in his soul, anything of the grace of God in his heart, trial will reveal it as surely as the hot flame under the crucible manifests the gold by breaking up its alliance with the dross.

You scarcely know whether you are a believer or an unbeliever until you pass through trial. The nature of faith as a divine gift and spiritual grace is unknown unless you have passed through this fiery trial. The worthlessness of creature religion, the emptiness of everything in self is hidden before you drop into this furnace.

We are tempted sometimes, perhaps, to doubt the truth of the Scriptures, the Deity of Christ, the efficacy of his atonement, and many things which I will not even hint at in your ears lest I unwittingly sow infidel seeds in your heart. Now when we are thus exercised, trial as a fire burns up everything that stands in the wisdom and strength of the creature, and brings us to the point where nothing but that which is of God in the soul can live in the flame.

If we find something in our heart which lives in the flame, if we find there a faith which trial cannot burn up, a hope it cannot destroy, a love it cannot consume, a fear of God which it cannot conquer, then we see in our heart that which is like pure gold in the midst of the dross. We can say in some measure with Job, "when he hath tried me, I shall come forth as gold."

14th

"Is there no balm in Gilead? is there no physician there?"
Jeremiah 8:22

There is balm in Gilead, and there is a physician there. This is, and must ever be, our only hope. If there were no balm in Gilead, what could we do but lie down in despair and die? For our sins are so great, our backslidings so repeated, our minds so dark, our hearts so hard, our affections so cold, our souls so wavering and wandering, that if there were no balm in Gilead, no precious blood, no sweet promises, no sovereign grace, and if there were no physician there, no risen Jesus, no great High Priest over the house of God, what well-grounded hope could we entertain? Not a ray. Our own obedience and consistency? These are a bed too short and a covering too narrow.

When there is some application of the balm in Gilead, it softens, melts, humbles, and at the same time thoroughly heals. No, this balm strengthens every nerve and sinew, heals blindness, remedies deafness, cures paralysis, makes the lame man leap as a deer and the tongue of the dumb to sing, and thus produces gospel sight, gospel hearing, gospel strength, and a gospel walk.

When the spirit is melted, and the heart touched by a sense of God's goodness, mercy, and love to such base, undeserving wretches, it produces gospel obedience, a humble obedience. This is not that proud obedience which those manifest who are trusting to their own goodness and seeking to scale the battlements of heaven by the ladder of self-righteousness, but an obedience of gratitude, love, and submission - willingly, cheerfully rendered, and therefore acceptable to God, because it is flowing from his own Spirit and grace. It is the application of this divine balm which purifies the heart, makes sin hateful, and Jesus precious, and not only dissolves the soul in sweet gratitude, but fills it with earnest desires to live to God's honour and glory.

This is the mysterious way the Lord takes to get honour to himself. As he opens up the depth of the fall, as he makes the burden of sin felt and shows the sinner how his iniquities have abounded, he brings the proud heart down, and lays the head low in the dust. As he then makes him sigh and cry, and grieve and groan, he applies his sovereign balm to the soul, brings the blood of sprinkling into the conscience, sheds abroad his mercy and love, and thus constrains the feet to walk in cheerful and willing obedience unto him.

This is obeying the precept from right motives, right views, right influences, under right feelings, and to right ends. This is the true Christian obedience, obedience "in the spirit and not in the letter," an obedience which glorifies God, and is attended by every fruit and grace of the Spirit.

15th

"Foolishness is bound in the heart of a child; but the rod of correction shall drive it far from him."
Proverbs 22:15

March

We profess to believe in an Almighty, All-present, All-seeing God; and we would be highly offended if a person said to us, 'You do not believe that God sees everything, that he is everywhere present, that he is an Almighty Jehovah.' We would almost think that he was taking us for an atheist, and yet practical atheists we daily prove ourselves to be.

For instance, we profess to believe that God sees everything, and yet we are plotting and planning as though he saw nothing. We profess to know that God can do everything, and yet we are always cutting out schemes, and carving out contrivances, as though he were like the gods of the heathen, simply looking on and taking no notice. We profess to believe that God is everywhere present to relieve every difficulty and bring his people out of every trial, and yet when we get into the difficulty and into the trial, we speak, think, and act as though there were no such omnipresent God! We forget that he knows the circumstances of the case and can stretch forth his hand to bring us out of it.

Thus the Lord is obliged, (I speak with all reverence), to thrust us into trials and afflictions because we are such blind fools that we cannot learn what a God we have to deal with. Only when we come experimentally into those spots of difficulty and trial, out of which none but such a God can deliver us, will we understand.

This, then, is one reason why the Lord often plunges his people so deeply into a sense of sin. It is to show them what a wonderful salvation from the guilt, filth, and power of sin there is in the Person, blood, and righteousness of the Lord Jesus Christ. For the same reason they walk in such scenes of temptation, in order to show them what a wonder-working God he is in bringing them out.

This, also, is the reason why many of his people are so harassed and plagued. It is that they might not live and act as though there were no God to go to, no almighty friend to consult, no loving Jesus to rest their weary heads upon. It is in order to teach them experimentally and inwardly those lessons of grace and truth which they never would know until the Lord, as it were, thus compelled them to learn, and actually forced them to believe what they profess to believe.

Such pains is he obliged to take with us, for such poor scholars, such dull creatures we are. He has to teach us what a God he is, and what a merciful and compassionate High Priest we have. In order to open up the heights, and depths, and lengths, and breadths of his love, he is compelled at times to treat his people very roughly, and handle them very sharply. He is obliged to make very great use of his rod, because he sees that foolishness is so bound up in the hearts of his children that nothing but the repeated rod of correction will ever drive it far from them.

March
16th

"Now therefore ye are no more strangers and foreigners, but fellow citizens with the saints, and of the household of God."
Ephesians 2:19

If grace has touched your heart, and if the love of God has come into your soul, it has placed you among the saints of the Most High, and given you every privilege which God ever did or could give to that blessed company.

What are their privileges?

To be washed in the atoning blood of the suffering Son of God, to be clothed in the justifying righteousness of his perfect and meritorious obedience, to be consecrated by the indwelling of the Holy Spirit, the Comforter. To have the love of God as their enduring portion, to have peace in believing and supplies of grace as needed, to have support and strength as they pass through this valley of tears, to receive comforts abounding in proportion to the abundance of afflictions. To feel the everlasting arms beneath in death, to gain a mansion of eternal bliss for the soul when the body drops into the grave, and to be renewed with a glorious resurrection of the body at the appearance of Christ in glory.

All that the love of God can give, all that the blood of Christ has been a channel for communicating, and all that the Spirit of God can reveal to any heart, or has ever brought with power into the soul of any saint. All these things become ours when we become fellow-citizens with the saints of God. Our enjoyment of them is not indeed always or often, although we get sips and tastes, and drops and crumbs, but as Abraham was given possession of Canaan when he had nothing to set his foot on, yet was it his as much by promise as it became his children's by strength of hand.

Does not the Apostle declare this, in the broadest and clearest language, where he says, "For all things are yours; whether Paul, or Apollos, or Cephas, or the world, or life, or death, or things present, or things to come; all are yours," (1Cor. 2:21-22). Why is it that are all things yours? For "ye are Christ's; and Christ is God's," (1Cor. 3:23).

17th

"I and my Father are one."
John 10:30

March

There is a great deal of cavilling in some men's minds about the expression, 'the blood of God'. 'How could the Godhead bleed? How could the Godhead suffer?' they say, but if it is not the blood of Him who was God, I might just as well rely for salvation on the blood of one of the thieves that were crucified with him.

What is Christ's human nature? That is the rock on which many gallant ships have struck. It is not a person, having a distinct existence apart from the Deity of Christ; but it is a nature – what the Holy Spirit calls a "Holy Thing," (Luke 1:35). His nature was and is a body that God prepared for him, (Heb. 10:5), taken into intimate, mysterious, and inexplicable union with the Person of the Son of God. So that, whatever that human nature did and suffered, from its intimacy and union with the Son of God, the Son of God did and suffered. Did that nature bleed? It bled as having union with Deity; it being, so to speak, the instrument that Deity made use of.

To use an illustration - as my soul touches an object through my hand, or speaks its thoughts by my tongue; so Deity not being itself able to bleed, bled through the humanity. Did that nature suffer? It was not the mere suffering of a human person, as a man might suffer; but it was the suffering of a holy nature in intimate union with the Person of the Son of God. Did that nature obey? The Son of God obeyed through and with that nature.

So that, to cavil at the expression, "the blood of God" is nothing less than to strike a blow at a great fundamental truth. We might object, on the same ground, to the expression, "God our righteousness," as the Prophet speaks, "And this is the name whereby he shall be called, The Lord our righteousness," that is, "Jehovah our righteousness," (Jer. 23:6). Who is our righteousness but the Son of God? What was that righteousness but the obedience of his human nature, for Godhead could no more obey than suffer and bleed; and yet Jehovah is our righteousness. And if we do not object to the expression, "the righteousness of God," why should we cavil at the expression, "the blood of God?"

Now this is the grand mystery which faith embraces, and which is dear to the heart of every God-taught soul. What a power and efficacy, as the veil is taken off the heart, does faith see in that sacrifice! What an atoning sacrifice does it see made for sin by the blood of the Son of God! Faith does not view it as the blood of a man! Can the blood of a man put away sin? But when we see it as the blood of the Son of God, oh, what value, efficacy, power, and glory shine forth in it! But until the veil is taken off the heart we cannot see it; nor can we, until the Spirit makes it experimentally known, learn what a divine reality there is in this blood to purge the guilty conscience.

March 18th

"We have also a more sure word of prophecy; whereunto ye do well that ye take heed, as unto a light that shineth in a dark place, until the day dawn, and the day star arise in your hearts."
2Peter 1:19

The "sure word of prophecy" is the mind of God revealed in the Scripture of truth. This is compared to "a light that shineth in a dark place." This "dark place" is the heart of man, and a dark place it is; and the light shining in the dark place is when the Spirit of God pours his own heavenly light into the dark heart. The Spirit of God works by the word of God. He makes use of the Scriptures of truth, and by means of these blessed Scriptures he communicates light. There is no light in the Scriptures themselves; they cannot teach a man to profit, that being God's prerogative. They are a dead letter, nothing but a collection of words and syllables; there is no light in them, no, not a particle. It is when the Spirit of God gives understanding and throws light upon them that he shines through them into the heart.

I might compare the Scriptures to the moon - the moon has no light in herself, but she borrows all her light from the sun - blot out the sun from the sky, and the moon would cease to shine. I might compare the Scriptures to what James compares them, "If any be a hearer of the word, and not a doer, he is like unto a man beholding his natural face in a glass," (Jas. 1:23). Here the Scriptures are compared to a mirror, or a looking-glass, but light must still shine upon the face and the glass. Of what use is a looking-glass on a dark night? It reflects no image; it presents to you no likeness; you discern not your features therein; it might be nothing else but a naked board, as far as any reflection it gives of your face. But let light come into the room, or let the sun rise and shine upon it, and your countenance is reflected therein.

So it is with the word of God. It is utterly ineffectual until the Spirit shines upon it, but when he shines upon it, he casts at the same time a ray of light into your heart. As he shines with this twofold ray, first upon the word, and then into your soul, he reflects from the word your very image, and you see yourself just as you are, most clearly portrayed. Now this is the light shining in a dark place. This is the light of God's truth shining into the darkness of your heart. This becomes a "sure word" to you. Faith is raised up in your heart to credit what God has revealed. The shining in of this light into your dark heart causes you to believe, and believing, you receive the word of prophecy as a sure word.

March

19th

"That which is born of the flesh is flesh; and that which is born of the Spirit is spirit."
John 3:6

There is no promise made in scripture that we shall be set free in this life from the indwelling and the inworking of sin. Many think that they are to become progressively holier and holier, that sin after sin is to be gradually removed out of the heart, until at last they are almost made perfect in the flesh. This is but an idle dream, and one which, sooner or later in the case of God's people, will rudely and roughly be broken to pieces. Nature will ever remain the same, and we shall ever find that the flesh will lust against the spirit. Our Adamic nature is corrupt to its very core. It cannot be mended, it cannot be sanctified, it will be at the last what it was at the first, inherently evil, and as such will never cease to be corrupt until we put off mortality, and with it we put off the body of sin and death.

What we *can* hope for, long after, expect and pray for, is that this evil nature may be subdued, kept down, mortified, crucified, and held in subjection under the power of grace. As to any such change passing upon it or taking place in it as to make it holy is but a pharisaic delusion. Such thinking promises holiness in the flesh, but leaves us still under the power of sin. It opposes with deadly enmity that true sanctification of the new man of grace, which is wrought by a divine power, and is utterly distinct from any fancied holiness in the flesh, or any vain dream of its progressive sanctification.

20th

"For whom he did foreknow, he also did predestinate to be conformed to the image of his Son, that he might be the firstborn among many brethren."
Romans 8:29

The risen body of Christ is the type to which the risen bodies of the saints are to be conformed, for "as we have borne the image of the earthy, we shall also bear the image of the heavenly," (1Cor. 15:49). This is that glorious image to which all the saints are to be conformed, although fully retaining all the essential characteristics of humanity, otherwise such a body would cease to be manhood in conjunction with Godhead. So unspeakably glorious is this risen body of the blessed Lord, to the image of which the risen saints will be conformed, that whilst on earth we can form neither a concept of its surpassing glory, nor the inferior degree of glory which will clothe the bodies of the saints at the resurrection. "Beloved, now are we the sons of God, and it doth not yet appear what we shall be: but we know that, when he shall appear, we shall be like him; for we shall see him as he is," (1John 3:2).

Of this we may be sure, that there will always be an essential and unapproachable distinction between the glory of Christ's humanity and that of his saints. His humanity, being in eternal union with his Deity, derives thence a glory which is distinct from all other, and to which there can be no approach, and with which there can be no comparison. The glory of the moon never can be the glory of the sun, though she shines with his reflected light. He "shall change our vile body, that it may be fashioned like unto his glorious body," (Phil. 3:21), but though alike, it will not be the same.

It will be the saints' eternal happiness to see him as he is, and to be made like unto him; but it will be their everlasting joy that he should ever have that pre-eminence of glory which is his birthright, and to adore him which will ever be their supreme delight. To have a body free from all sin, sickness, and sorrow, filled to its utmost capacity of holiness and happiness, able to see him as he is without dying under the sight, and to be re-united to its once suffering but now equally glorified companion, an immortal soul, expanded to its fullest powers of joy and bliss - if this be not sufficient, what more can God give?

21st

"In whom the god of this world hath blinded the minds of them which believe not, lest the light of the glorious gospel of Christ, who is the image of God, should shine unto them."
2Corinthians 4:4

Oh! What beauty and blessedness shine forth in the gospel, when we view it connected with the Person and work of the Son of God! Take the doctrines of grace isolated from the Person of Christ and they are but scattered limbs, there is no beauty within them. View the truths of the gospel in connection with the Person and work of the Son of God, and what a heavenly light, what a divine glory is cast upon every truth connected with his sacred Person, with his atoning blood, his finished work, and his dying love! This is the way to receive the gospel. Not as a thing of shreds and patches, a mere collection or scheme of certain doctrines floating up and down God's word as waifs and strays from a stranded ship; but as one harmonious gospel, full of grace, mercy, and truth, impregnated with divine blessedness, and all connected with, and springing out of the Person of the God-man.

How it seems to lift us up for a time, whilst the feeling lasts, above sin, misery, and wretchedness to view our completeness in Christ, and to see our saving interest in his finished work. How heartening to behold ourselves members of his mystical body, to triumph in his holy triumphs, to rejoice in his victories, and to ascend with him above the smoke and stir of this dim spot that men call earth. As one might rise out of a London fog into a pure atmosphere, and bask on some mountain-top in the bright beams of the sun, so the dear saint of God, when he is privileged to read his title clear, see his name in the book of life, feel the love of God in his heart, and rejoice in Christ, is lifted up above the fog and smoke of this dim spot, and sitting with Christ in heavenly places, he feels a sweet victory over every foe internal, external, and infernal.

There is also no other way whereby we *can* get out of it. Like a man in that London fog, struggling on with impenetrable cloud in the east, west, north, and south, and smoke all around, so it is whilst we are struggling onward with sin and self. North, south, east, and west, there is nothing but fog, deep and dense. We must be raised out of it to the mountaintop, and this only can be by being lifted up with a sweet testimony of saving interest in the blood and love of the Son of God.

This lifts up, and this lifts out. It gives strength and alone will give victory. When we fall short of realising these precious things, we grope for the wall like the blind, and stumble in desolate places like dead men. It is true that the saints of God usually see only little of these blessed things, just from time to time brought in and taken away, but sufficient to taste their sweetness, to know their beauty and see their glory. Sufficient, while they last, to help them onward in their course and keep them pressing forward until they reach that eternal glory.

22nd

"Elect according to the foreknowledge of God the Father."
1Peter 1:2

Foreknowledge of the persons of the elect in the divine economy precedes election. "For whom he did foreknow he also did predestinated to be conformed to the image of his Son," (Rom. 8:29). This foreknowledge was not any eternal foreview of their faith or love in time, as if *that* were the ground of God's choice of them. It implies, first, that thorough knowledge which God had of them, of all that should concern them, and of all the depths of sin and rebellion, disobedience and ungodliness of which they were guilty *before* being called by grace. It is a knowledge of all their grievous backslidings, slips, and falls, with all the base returns that they should make for his goodness and mercy toward them *after* he had touched their hearts by his finger.

Then secondly and chiefly, it signifies the good will and pleasure, together with that everlasting love of God the Father, whereby he foreknew them with a holy approbation of them, a divine affection toward them, and a holy and unalterable delight in them as viewed in his dear Son, chosen in him and "accepted in the Beloved," (Eph. 1:6). Thus election is not, if we may use the expression without irreverence, a dry choice of them in Christ. It is a choice of them as foreknowing, with a holy approbation, each of his elect family personally and individually. However they might differ among themselves in the infinite variety whereby one man varies both naturally and spiritually from another, his approving knowledge of each and all of them in Christ Jesus was in sweet harmony with his determinate choice. To realise this in soul feeling is very sweet and precious.

We do not really know ourselves. We may have seen a little into our fallen state by nature, and may know something of the dreadful evils that lurk and work within; we may have had some passing skirmishes, or even some hot battles with our proud, rebellious, unbelieving, infidel, and desperately wicked heart, but we do not *know* ourselves as God knows us. Even though we may cry, "Search me, O God, and know my heart; try me, and know my thoughts," (Psa. 139:23), yet how shallow for the most part and how superficial is the request, let alone that true knowledge and experience of ourselves! How little do we measure our sinfulness by the holiness of God, or look down into the depths of our nature as they lie naked and open before the eyes of him with whom we have to do!

When, then, we think that he who knew from the beginning all that we ever should be in the depths of the Adamic fall, and notwithstanding that still chose us by determinate decree in his dear Son unto eternal life, what a blessed lift does it give to the soul out of all those sinkings into which a sight and sense of sin is continually casting it.

March 23rd

"For the LORD God is a sun and shield: the LORD will give grace and glory: no good thing will he withhold from them that walk uprightly."
Psalm 84:11

Wherever the Lord gives grace, he, in and with that grace, gives glory. We, therefore, read, "Moreover whom he did predestinate, them he also called: and whom he called, them he also justified: and whom he justified, them he also glorified," (Rom. 8:29). Thus he has already made them, even while on earth, partakers of his glory; and this by making them partakers of his grace; for as in the bud is the bloom, and in the bloom the fruit. So in budding grace is the bloom of glory - grace being but glory begun, and glory being but grace finished.

Yet what is "glory?" Viewed as future, in its full consummation, it is to be with Jesus in realms of eternal bliss, where tears are wiped from off all faces. Glory is to see him as he is; to be conformed to his glorious likeness; to be delivered from all sin and sorrow; to be perfectly free from all temptations, trials, burdens, and exercises. It is to dwell forever in that happy land, "the inhabitants [of which] shall not say, I am sick," (Isa. 33:24). It is where a weary body, a burdened conscience, a troubled heart, and a faint and weary mind, are utterly and forever unknown.

It is having a glorified body re-united to a glorified soul, and for both to be filled with as much happiness and holiness, bliss and blessedness, as an immortal spirit can hold and an immortal frame can endure. It is to be drinking in to the full, with unutterable satisfaction but without satiety, the pleasures that are at God's right hand for evermore.

Now, no human heart can conceive, nor human tongue unfold in what the nature and fullness of this glory consists; "for it is written, eye hath not seen, nor ear heard, neither have entered into the heart of man, the things which God hath prepared for them that love him," (1Cor. 2:9).

Yet all this glory shall the Lord give to those upon whom he has already bestowed his grace. He gives them grace now, to bring them through this wilderness world, this valley of tears, this scene of temptation, sin, and sorrow; and when he lands them on that happy shore, he gives them there the fullness of his glory. Then will be fully accomplished the Redeemer's prayer, "Father, I will that they also, whom thou hast given me, be with me where I am; that they may behold my glory, which thou hast given me: for thou lovedst me before the foundation of the world," (John 17:24).

Their right and title to the enjoyment of this predestinated inheritance is securely lodged in the hands of their covenant Head who is living at God's right hand to save them to the uttermost. All their temptations, enemies, sins, and sorrows can never hinder them from reaching the shore on which God has decreed they shall safely land. Satan may spread a thousand snares to entangle their feet, and not a day or scarcely an hour may pass that they are not burdened with indwelling sin. A myriad of lusts may start up in arms from the depths of their carnal mind; and many a pang of guilt, and the chill of despair may seem at times wholly to cut them off from eternal life.

Yet, where the Lord has given grace he will give glory, for when he gives grace with the left hand, he gives glory with the right. We might even say that with both hands he gives at once both grace and glory, for as grace and glory flow out of the same loving heart, and are given by the same loving God, they may be said to be given by both hands at one and the same time.

A portion or foretaste of this glory is given on earth in every discovery of the glory of Christ; as the Lord speaks, "And the glory which thou gavest me I have given them," (John 17:22). This he did when "he manifested forth his glory, and his disciples believed on him," (John 2:11).

24th

"And he led them forth by the right way, that they might go to a city of habitation."
Psalm 107:7

Wherever the Lord leads, we can safely follow. Though the path may be rough, if the Lord upholds us, we can walk in it without stumbling. Whatever the Lord bids, we can do if we have but his presence; whatever he calls upon us to suffer, we can bear if we have but the approbation of a good conscience and his approving smile. Oh, the wonders of sovereign grace! The cross is no cross if the Lord gives strength to bear it; affliction is no affliction if the Lord supports under it; trial is no trial if sweetened by his smile, and sorrow no grief if lightened by his love. It is our fretfulness, unbelief, carnal reasoning, rebellion, and self-pity which make a rough way a wrong way; but grace in its all-conquering power, not only subdues every difficulty without, but its greater triumph is to subdue every difficulty within.

It is, and ever must be, one of the strongest principles of our faith, that every way must, in the end, be a right way if it be God's way. Is it not, according to the verdict of our own conscience, a right way to lead us forth out of the world, out of sin, out of self, out of pride and self-righteousness, and out of evil in every form? Is it not a right way to lead us into everything which is good, holy, gracious, acceptable, saving, and sanctifying? It is not a right way to do everything that can conform us to the image of Christ, who was a man of sorrows and acquainted with grief, and make us fit for the inheritance of the saints in light?

And what is the end of all this leading and guiding? "That they might go to a city of habitation," it is to lead us to the new Jerusalem, the glorious city which has foundations, whose builder and maker is God. There, some of our friends have gone before; there they dwell as citizens of that blessed city which is all of pure gold, like unto clear glass; a city which has no need of the sun, neither of the moon to shine in it, for the glory of the Lord enlightens it, and the Lamb is the light thereof. This is the city of habitation where the saints will forever dwell; and the Lord is leading forth each and all of his wilderness wanderers by the right way, that he may bring them in the same way into his eternal presence, and to the enjoyment of those pleasures which are at his right hand for evermore.

25th

"Who in the days of his flesh... offered up prayers and supplications with strong crying and tears unto him that was able to save him from death..."
Hebrews 5:7

The Apostle says that Christ was "crucified through weakness," (2Cor. 13:4). We must remember, however, that weakness was not imperfection in him, though it is imperfection in us; for when we speak of the weakness of Christ's human nature, we mean its weakness as compared with the strength and power of his divine nature. Our Lord felt the weakness of his humanity, for though in union with his eternal Deity, though most blessedly upheld and supported by the power and strength and consolation of the Holy Spirit, yet it was inherently weak, and an experience of its weakness was a part of the sufferings that he endured.

Having, then, to bear as laid upon this weakness the whole weight of imputed sin, the whole curse of the law, the whole indignation of the Almighty, our Lord was brought to a spot where he needed special support. It was to be brought through that work safely, honourably, successfully, agreeably to the will of God and in the fullest harmony with the eternal purposes that our suffering Lord directed his prayers and supplications. This was the solemn conflict which our gracious Lord had to endure in the garden in its beginning, and upon the cross in its finishing.

We know what he felt – at least the Holy Spirit has given us an account of that solemn agony in the garden when he said, as in a moment of weakness, "Let this cup pass from me," (Matt. 26:39). It was so bitter in contemplation and so full of unmitigated wrath, and the ingredients were so mingled with the anger of the Almighty against sin and the manifestation of his displeasure against everyone who was chargeable with it, that his own strength to carry it must have failed. Standing there as our substitute, to endure in our place what we must have endured without him, and to bear the whole weight of eternal wrath and indignation which must have sunk us and all the millions with us to a deserved hell, he needed the special interposition of the help of God to hold him up and sustain him as he drank it to the very dregs.

It was to obtain this help that he offered up prayers and supplications with strong crying and tears. It was the vehemency of the conflict which made blood fall from his brow and tears drop from his eyes, and engaged his whole soul in an agony of mingled grief and horror, fear and supplication, each increasing and stimulating the other. The whole simply poured forth with prayers, cries, weeping, and supplications unto him that was able to save him from death; not from the death that he came to die, but to save him from everything connected with the original sentence of death, as involving in it the wrath of God and its consequences.

26th

"...and was heard in that he feared."
Hebrews 5:7

There is something in my mind extremely mysterious and yet divinely blessed in the expression, "in that he feared," and it is right to mention that there is some little difficulty as to the correct rendering of the expression. The word means in the original not so much fear as indicating dread or apprehension, but a holy reverence and a tender cautiousness. It means literally the great care with which we handle brittle vessels, and, as used in the New Testament, signifies a reverential fear of God. It is used, for instance, of Noah, where he is said to be "moved with fear," (Heb. 11:7), and is translated "godly fear" in those words, "whereby we may serve God acceptably with reverence and godly fear," (Heb. 12:28).

It does not, therefore, mean fear in any such sense of the word as would imply a servile dread. It does not mean that our gracious Lord was possessed with that servile dread of the Almighty which reprobates feel and those who never were partakers of the grace of God. Rather our Lord, as an exemplar of every grace of the Spirit, was possessed of that holy reverence and godly fear in its abundant measure of which we have but a small portion. Now just in proportion to the depth of the grace that was in him, the power of God that rested upon him, and the operations and influence of the Holy Spirit in his soul, so was the measure of holy reverence and godly fear which dwelt in his sacred humanity.

Contemplating, therefore, the greatness of the work, he had before his eyes not so much the bodily sufferings of the cross as all the mental agonies. Writ large was the distress of soul, the conflict with the law in its load and curse, the indignation of the Almighty against sin in the Person of the Surety, the hidings of his Father's face, and the withdrawal of the light of his countenance.

Foreseeing all these dolorous sufferings of the cross, and tasting the first drops of that shower which was so soon to fall upon his sacred head, it seemed as if his holy soul was filled with the most solemn reverence and deep apprehension of the majesty of God.

This is the fear of which our text speaks. It is in the bible's margin "his piety," but reverence, godly fear, holy apprehension, and tender awe convey the meaning of the word much better than the expression "piety."

It was prophesied of him that "the spirit of the LORD shall rest upon him, the spirit of wisdom and understanding, the spirit of counsel and might, the spirit of knowledge and of the fear of the LORD," (Isa. 11:2). Thus his prayers, his cries, his supplications, and his tears rose up with sweet acceptance into the ears of his Father. They came out of a heart filled with reverence and godly fear under the promptings and influences of that eternal Spirit who wrought in him every grace both in its possession and its exercise, and through whom he offered himself without spot to God.

27th

"Is anything too hard for the Lord?"
Genesis 18:14

March

The Lord will make us feel that though his arm is not shortened that it cannot save, nor his ear heavy that it cannot hear, yet he is still to be enquired of. He is indeed a God that works wonders; apparent impossibilities are nothing with him; he has but to speak and it is done. However, he causes us to know his power by making us feel our weakness.

He will often keep at a great distance, and for a long time, in order to make us value his presence. He will make us sink very low that he may lift us very high. He will make us taste the bitterness of the gall and wormwood of sin that we may know the sweetness of manifested pardon. He will teach us to abhor ourselves in our own sight, and loathe ourselves for our abominations, before we shall see and know ourselves washed in his blood, clothed in his righteousness, and to stand before him without spot or wrinkle or any such thing.

The Lord in one sense is easy of access upon his throne of grace, but in another very hard to be got at. He invites his dear people to come and spread their needs before him; he encourages them with a thousand promises; he says in our text, "Is anything too hard for the Lord?" Yet he will make us set a due value upon his visitations; they shall not be given to us very easily or very frequently so that we may not hold them cheap. It is not 'ask and have immediately'. We have to learn what sin cost our dear Redeemer; we have to see the holiness and majesty of God; we have to learn that though mercy is free, and grace superabounds over rampant sin, yet it must be got at after many a struggle. It may only be had after many a cry, many a sigh and groan, and many a fervent petition; that though all fullness dwells in the Lord the Lamb, and he invites us to come and take of the water of life freely, yet it is guarded on every side by many things that would drive back the false professor.

Thus he teaches us to put due value upon his grace, upon the visitations of his countenance and the words of his lips. They cost the dear Redeemer the deepest agonies of body and soul, and sufferings of which no finite mind can conceive. Therefore they are not to be given out without teaching us to know through what channel they came, nor what it cost the blessed Son of God to give out of his fullness those supplies of grace by which he enriches our need.

28th

"For thou wilt not leave my soul in hell; neither wilt thou suffer thine Holy One to see corruption."
Psalm 16:10

March

When the adorable Lord by a voluntary act laid down his life, the last words that he spoke were, "Father, into thy hands I commend my spirit," (Luke 23:46). By his 'spirit' we are to understand his human soul which at once went into paradise, into the immediate presence of God, as he intimated in the words, "And now come I to thee," (John 17:13). Nor did he go there that day alone. A trophy was soon to follow him; the soul of that repenting, believing malefactor, who, a partner with him in suffering, had become by his sovereign grace a partner with him in glory.

There was, then, an actual separation of the Redeemer's body and soul; but this did not destroy or affect the union of his Deity with his humanity. That union remained entire, as his holy soul went into paradise in union with his Deity, and thus he was still God-man as much in paradise as he was at the tomb of Lazarus, or at the Last Supper. Yet his sacred body, though life was gone out of it by the act of death, still remained 'that holy thing'. Death did not taint that sacred body in the tomb in the same manner as sin did not taint it in the virgin's womb Virgin. The promise was, therefore, "thou wilt not leave my soul in hell, neither wilt thou suffer thine Holy One to see corruption."

This holy body was essentially incorruptible, as being begotten of the Holy Spirit by special and supernatural generation, and of the flesh of the Virgin; and as in all other acts of the sacred Trinity, Father, Son, and Holy Spirit were all engaged that no taint of corruption should assail it in death. The Father promised, and as God that cannot lie, by his almighty, superintending power he therefore performed. The Son, by the same innate, active, divine energy with which he assumed his body in the womb, preserved it untainted and uncorrupted in the grave. The Holy Spirit who formed that body in its first conception, breathed over it his holy influence to maintain it, in spite of death and the tomb, as pure and as incorruptible as when he first created it.

These things are indeed difficult to understand or indeed conceive; but they are heavenly mysteries, which faith receives and holds fast in spite of sense, reason, and unbelief. For see the tremendous consequences of allowing any taint of corruption to assail that blessed body. Could a tainted body be resumed at the resurrection? Corruption would have marred it as it will mar ours; and how could a corrupt body have been again the habitation of the Son of God? We are often instrumentally preserved from error not only by knowing and feeling the sweetness and power of truth, but by seeing, as at a glance, the tremendous consequences which a denial of vital, fundamental truths involves.

March 29th

"For by one offering he hath perfected for ever them that are sanctified."
Hebrews 10:14

To be sanctified is to be made a partaker of that holiness, without which no man shall see the Lord. It is to be made a new creature, to "put on the new man, which after God is created in righteousness and true holiness," (Eph. 4:24). In short, to be "made partakers of the divine nature," (2Pet. 1:4), and thus have the holiness of God breathed into and communicated to the soul. Without this inward sanctification, none can enter the gates of heaven. To be made fit, therefore, for the heavenly inheritance, you must have a heavenly heart and a praising, adoring, loving spirit; you must delight yourself in the Lord as being so holy and yet so gracious, so pure and yet so loving, so bright and glorious and yet so condescending and sympathising.

Now this fitness for the holiness, happiness, and employments of heaven is communicated at regeneration, in which the new man of grace, though weak, is still perfect. Look at the thief upon the cross – what an instance is he of how the Spirit of God can, in a moment, make a man fit for heaven! Here was a vile malefactor, whose life had been spent in robbery and murder, brought at last to suffer the just punishment of his crimes. Yet further, as we are told that "they who were crucified with him reviled him," we have reason to believe that at first he joined his fellow malefactor in blaspheming the Redeemer when he was himself but hours from death.

Then, unsought and unrequested, sovereign grace touched his heart. It brought him to see and feel what he was as a ruined sinner and opened his eyes to view the Son of God bleeding before him. It raised up faith in his soul to believe in his name, and created a spirit of prayer that the Lord of heaven and earth would remember him when he came into his kingdom. That was perhaps the greatest act of faith we have recorded in all Scripture, almost equal if not superior to the faith of Abraham when he offered up Isaac on the altar.

The dying Redeemer heard and answered the man's cry, and said unto him, "Today shalt thou be with me in paradise," (Luke 23:43). Spirit and life accompanied the words, and raised up at once in his soul a fitness for the inheritance, and before the shadows of night fell, his happy spirit passed into paradise, where he is now singing the praises of God and of the Lamb.

Many a poor child of God has gone on almost to his last hours here on earth without a manifestation of pardoning love and the application of atoning blood, but no child of God has ever been allowed to die without the Holy Spirit revealing salvation to his soul. No child of God has failed to experience that heavenly tuning of his heart to sing the immortal anthems of the glorified spirits before the throne. No child of God has left this world before he was sanctified, before he put on the new man, or before he became a partaker of the divine nature.

30th

"The eternal God is thy refuge."
Deuteronomy 33:27

Who is this eternal God? He is the great and glorious Jehovah, eternal in his Trinity of Persons and in the Unity of his Essence. See what a depth of blessedness there is in this God being an eternal God; and that in and of this eternity, each Person of the Godhead has an equal share.

Look at the *love* of God, and how it stretches into eternity. Not being a thing of time, it was not fixed upon us when we were first brought into being. It did not first issue from his bosom when we were quickened into divine life. It was a love which existed in eternity past, as being the love of an eternal God. "I have loved thee with an everlasting love: therefore with lovingkindness have I drawn thee," (Jer. 31:3).

See how eternal are the *thoughts* of God, those thoughts which were of good, not of evil. They were eternal thoughts of peace to the Church; eternal thoughts of mercy to his beloved family; eternal thoughts of manifesting his grace in the Person and work of his dear Son. They were thoughts of goodness and love flowing forth to those whom he had chosen in Christ, that they might be one with him, members of that glorious body of which his dear Son should be the Head.

Consider also the eternal *purposes* of God that nothing could defeat, that all the waves of time could not break through. See also his eternal *wisdom* to devise, and eternal *power* to accomplish.

Oh, this eternal God! We look back and we see what a God he was from all eternity, and then we look forward and see what he will be to all eternity. We see him unchanging and unchangeable, resting in his love without variableness or the shadow of a turn, whether in eternity past, or in eternity to come. We think of the spirits of just men of old made perfect. We follow in faith and hope the souls of dear departed friends, and view them drinking the pleasures which are at his right hand forever. So it will be for all eternity, his children free from sin, ever delighting in the smiles of an eternal God, ever living in his favour, ever conformed to the glorious image of his eternal Son, and ever drinking fresh draughts of love and bliss in his eternal presence.

Oh, this eternal Father, and the depths of his fatherly love in the gift of his dear Son! Oh, the love, condescension, and tenderness of this eternal Son in the depths of his mercy, sacrifice, and grace in suffering, bleeding, and dying for poor, guilty sinners!

Oh, the wisdom, power, grace, and blessedness of this eternal Spirit, in taking of the things of Christ, unfolding the Person of Jesus, bringing him near, revealing him to the soul, sprinkling the conscience with his blood, and making him known and precious!

What a depth of gratitude is everlastingly due from the redeemed Church of God, to all the three sacred Persons of the glorious and undivided Trinity, and that both in his Trinity of Persons and his Unity of Essence the eternal God should be their refuge!

31st

"Neither doth God respect any person: yet doth he devise means, that his banished be not expelled from him."
2Samuel 14:14

The promise to God's children runs, "I will seek that which was lost, and bring again that which was driven away," (Ez. 34:16). Guilt, temptation, Satan, doubts, and fears have driven them away from the shelter of the tabernacle. Yet the Lord has respect unto these also. He says he will "bring again", but how?

By nothing but a sense of mercy. It is not by frowns, but by smiles. "I drew them," says the Lord, "with cords of a man" (that is, the tender feelings that are bound up in the human heart), "with bands of love," (Hos. 11:4). You may thunder, you may lightning, you may take the whip and flog a poor backslider - but you can never flog him home. He must be drawn by mercy, by the goodness of God, which leads to repentance.

How was Peter brought back? By the look which Jesus gave him as he stood in the hall of the high priest; that look of mingled love and reproach. It was this that made Peter go out and weep bitterly. A frown would have driven him into despair, and made him hang himself by the side of Judas; but that look of mingled reproof and love both wounded and healed. It filled heart and eyes with the deepest grief and sorrow, yet it did not drive him away. It poured such a healing balm into his mourning soul that when Jesus was risen from the dead, and by his angel sent him a special message that he would see him again in Galilee, he leaped into the sea to meet his Lord as he stood on the shore.

Without that look and without that message, he would rather have sunk to the bottom of the sea with self-reproach, than leaped to the shore with love and affection. Thus was brought again poor driven-away Peter, and thus too, by the voice of pardon, was brought again poor driven-away David. And why? Because the Lord devises means that his banished be not expelled from him.

April

April
1st

"O Israel, thou hast destroyed thyself; but in me is thine help."
Hosea 13:9

God is all-wise, and therefore he makes no rash act or takes any precipitate steps. Because the original plan of salvation was devised by infinite wisdom, so all the successive steps in the execution of that plan are directed by the same boundless wisdom. "Wherein he hath abounded toward us in all wisdom and prudence," says Paul, (Eph. 1:8). Thus, in his dealings with his people, God does not put them at once into possession of all the blessings which he has laid up for them.

For example, he has pardoned their sins, but he does not immediately put them into possession of this blessing when he calls them by his grace. He first has to teach them their need of the pardon. He has to prepare their heart for the right reception of it. Such pardon is no common gift, and he has to teach them how to value it. By it they are saved from wrath and eternal misery, and from his dreadful displeasure and ever-burning indignation against sin. They have need to be shown, and made deeply to feel, both *from* what they are saved and *to* what they are saved. An oak does not grow to its full stature in a day. It needs years of sunshine and storm, of beating winds and howling tempests to give it strength and constancy, a deep and wide root, and a lofty, branching stem. It is so with God's children who need months and years of trial and temptation that they may push a deep root downwards, and grow healthy and vigorously upwards.

Thus, before the soul can know anything about salvation, it must learn deeply and experimentally the nature of sin, and of itself, as stained and polluted thereby. It is proud and needs to be humbled. It is careless and needs to be awakened. It is alive, and needs to be killed. It is full, and requires to be emptied. It is whole, and needs to be wounded. It is clothed, and requires to be stripped. It is, by nature, self-righteous and self-seeking, buried deep in worldliness and carnality. It is utterly blind and ignorant, filled with presumption, arrogance, conceit, and enmity, hating all that is heavenly and spiritual. Sin, in all its various forms, is its natural element and delight.

A man cannot change the colour of his skin, nor the leopard change his spots, and it is so with sin. To make man the direct opposite of what he originally is, to make him love God instead of hating him, to make him fear instead of mock, and obey instead of rebel. To make him tremble at God's terrible majesty instead of running upon the thick bosses of his shield is far beyond the ability of a man. To do this mighty work and to effect this wonderful change requires the implantation of a new nature by the immediate hand of God himself. Only in God can a man's help be found.

2nd

"That your faith should not stand in the wisdom of men, but in the power of God."
1Corinthians 2:5

True faith I may call the *grand tidal wave* of the soul. I will endeavour to explain the expression. We see the river Thames day by day ebbing and flowing. What causes this change? You answer, 'It is produced by the sea in the Channel alternately coming up and retiring'. That is a true explanation, but what makes the sea of the Channel alternately come up and retire? We refer to it as "the grand tidal wave" that comes across the Atlantic Ocean, which, as it ebbs and flows, affects all the minor tides of the neighbouring seas; and thus the tide of the Channel, and that of the river Thames, ebbs and flows in unison with this grand Atlantic tidal wave. Whether that be the best explanation or no, the water surges onwards.

In the same way faith is the tidal wave of the soul; and all the graces and fruits of the Spirit ebb and flow as faith rises or as faith sinks. If faith rises in the soul, all the graces and fruits of the Spirit rise with it. Light increases, life is deepened, the fear of God is strengthened, hope is brightened, and love is augmented. It follows that when faith falls, when our hearts grow cold, all the minor tides of the Spirit's graces fall in unison with it. Thus when the tide of faith recedes , consolation ebbs out altogether, hope recedes to a narrow streamlet, life dwindles to a scanty current, and love is reduced to a shallow channel. As low tide in the Thames reveals muddy banks which the river has forsaken, so when faith sinks to a low ebb in the soul there seems little left but the mud and mire of corruption.

What makes the grand tidal wave move across the Atlantic Ocean? There is a cause for that also. It is drawn up by, and obeys the attractions of the sun and the moon, and is this not true spiritually of the grand tidal wave of faith in the soul? Is it not drawn up by the Sun of righteousness, as the natural sun in part draws up the wave of the ocean, and makes it flow? And when that glorious Sun ceases to draw up faith, does it not ebb and sensibly sink in the soul, as the natural sea sinks when the sun recedes from it?

April 3rd

"In the house of the righteous is much treasure - but in the revenues of the wicked is trouble."
Proverbs 15:6

How different is the estimate that faith makes of riches, honours, and comforts from that made by the world and the flesh! The world has no idea of riches but such as consist in gold and silver, in houses, lands, or other tangible property. It has no thought of honour but such as man has to bestow, and no notion of comfort except in "fulfilling the desires of the flesh and of the mind," (Eph. 2:3).

Howbeit the soul that is anointed by an 'unction from the Holy One', takes a different estimate of these matters. It feels that the only true riches are those of God's grace in the heart, that the only real honour is that which comes from God, and that the only solid comfort is that which is imparted by the Holy Spirit to a broken and contrite spirit. Now, just in proportion as we have the Spirit of God, shall we take faith's estimate of riches, honour, and comfort; and just so much as we are imbued with the spirit of the world, shall we take the world's estimate of these things.

When the eye of the world looked on the Apostles, it viewed them as a company of poor ignorant men, a group of wild enthusiasts who travelled about the country preaching about one Jesus, who, they said, had been crucified, and was risen from the dead. The natural eye saw no beauty, no power, and no glory in the truths they brought forth; nor did it see that the poor perishing tabernacles of these outcast men contained in them a heavenly treasure, and that they would one day shine as the stars forever and ever, while those who despised their word would sink into endless woe. The spirit of the world, and the view that the flesh takes are not altered today. Nature ever remains the same, and can never understand or love the things of eternity; it can only look to, and can only rest upon, the poor perishing things of time and sense.

By this test, therefore, we may in a measure try our own spiritual state. What, for instance, are our daily and hourly feelings about the things of time and sense? What do we think and feel about the things of eternity? Which of the two press with more power on our minds, which occupy more of our thoughts, which are laid up more warmly in our affections?

In the same proportion as the solemn things of eternity or the passing things of time and sense occupy our mind, so is the measure of our faith. In so much as our hearts are fixed upon heaven or earth, and so much as we are living to God or to ourselves, in the same degree can be measured the strength of our faith and the depth of the work of grace upon our conscience.

4th

"But we see Jesus, who was made a little lower than the angels for the suffering of death, crowned with glory and honour; that he by the grace of God should taste death for every man."
Hebrews 2:9

How wondrous it is that he who, as the Son of God, made the angels, should be made inferior to them, and even need and receive their ministering aid and support. Oh the depths of humiliation to which the blessed Redeemer stooped, carrying down into their lowest point that pure, spotless, holy humanity which he had assumed into union with his divine Person as the Son of God!

Now let us ever bear carefully in mind that humiliation is not degradation. Our blessed Lord 'humbled himself' by a voluntary act of surpassing grace. It was no more in the power of men or circumstances to debase him of his glory than of lying witnesses to strip him of his innocency. The spotless purity of his sacred humanity, as in union with his divine nature, and as filled with and upheld by the Holy Spirit, preserved it from degradation in its lowest humiliation. The crown of thorns and the purple robe, the mocking knee of the Roman soldier and the taunting scoff of the Jewish priest, though they called forth the grace, did not tarnish the glory of our suffering Lord. His holy obedience to his Father's will in drinking the bitter cup, his meek dignity amid the worst of insults, and his calm resignation to all the weight of suffering which God or man laid upon him, all shone forth the more conspicuously under every attempt to dishonour him.

It is most sweet and blessed to look down, as it were, into some of those depths of humiliation into which the Redeemer sank, and to see that in the lowest depths of his soul travail, when he was poured out like water, and his heart, broken with grief and sorrow, was melted within him like wax, he was, in the midst of all, the glorious Son of God, though then the suffering Son of man. We see that he was the same Jesus yesterday when hanging on the cross, as he is today at the right hand of his Father, and will be forever in the realms of heavenly bliss.

April 5th

"And the servant abideth not in the house forever - but the son abideth forever."
John 8:35

It is the irreversible blessing of a son that he is never to be turned out of the house, that the union between the Parent and the child can never be broken, and that he is to reign with Christ through the ages of one everlasting day. This is a sweet consolation to God's family that "the son abideth forever." How often is a child of God exercised, whether he shall abide forever, whether he may not draw back to perdition, whether some temptation may not overtake him whereby it shall be made manifest that he is nothing but a deceiver and deceived! Yet the Lord himself says, "the son abideth forever." Let him be but a babe, let him have but the first beginning of spiritual life in his soul, yet he "abideth forever." He has the same interest in the affections of the Father, is a fellow-heir with Christ, and has a title to the same inheritance as those who are of longer standing, and those who are much his elders in age.

Howbeit, sometimes the son may get tired of the restraint of his Father's house. God is a wise Parent as well as a kind one. He will treat his children with the most tender kindness and intimacy, but he will never allow them to be guilty of disrespect towards him. Sometimes, then, the sons get weary of their Father's house; they are like the younger son in the parable, when he asked his father to give him his portion, and when he had gotten it, he went away into a far country, away from his father's house, from under his father's roof, and wasted it in riotous living. This is where many of God's children get. There is a restraint in God's house, where the soul is not really blessed with the personal and present enjoyment of gospel truth, and restraint being ever irksome, the vain, idolatrous heart thinks it can derive some pleasure from the world which is not to be found under the roof of the Father. Therefore, he gradually withdraws his steps from his Father's house, seeks to derive some pleasure from the things of time and sense, erects some idol, and falls down to worship it.

Even so, notwithstanding all this, "the son abideth forever." The Father of all his people in Christ does not disinherit his dear children; and though earthly parents may disinherit theirs, God's family are never cast out of the inheritance. The true-born Israelite who had waxed poor and sold himself unto the stranger was to obtain his freedom in the year of jubilee, (Lev. 25:47, 54), and to return to his own house and his own estate. So the son who has departed from his Father's house, and sold himself under sin, and become a slave to that cruel taskmaster, when the year of jubilee comes, the year of restoration, and the silver trumpet is sounded, shakes off his shackles and fetters. He casts aside the livery of servitude, returns to his Father's house, and is received with joy beneath his Father's roof. O what a meeting! The forgiving Parent, and the disobedient child! The Father dissolved in tears of affection; the child dissolved in tears of contrition!

Whatever, then, be our wanderings of heart, our alienation of affection, and our backsliding of soul; however we may depart from God, so far as we are sons, we shall abide in the house forever. We shall possess an "inheritance incorruptible and undefiled, which fadeth not away, reserved in heaven for [those] who are kept by the power of God through faith unto salvation," (1Pet. 1:4-5).

It will be our mercy then to abide in the house below as members of the family, without departing from it, until reunited to the family above, "general assembly and church of the firstborn, which are written in heaven," (Heb. 12:23).

6th

"And shall not God avenge his own elect, which cry day and night unto him, though he bear long with them?"
Luke 18:7

"Behold, he prayeth," (Acts 9:11), was the word of the Lord to Ananias to convince him that the dreaded persecutor, Saul of Tarsus, had been quickened by the Spirit. And what a mercy it is for the quickened soul that the blessed Spirit thus helps his sinking, trembling spirit, puts life and energy into his cries and sighs, holds him up and keeps him steadfast at the throne. What a blessing that the Spirit thus enables him to persevere with his earnest suings for mercy, mingles faith with his petitions, and himself most graciously and kindly intercedes within him and for him with groanings which cannot be uttered. This is "praying with the spirit," (1Cor. 14:15), and praying "in the Holy Spirit," (Jude 20). This is pouring out the heart before God, (Psa. 62:8), and pouring out the soul before the Lord, (1Sam. 1:15). By this free discharge of the contents of an almost bursting heart, sensible relief is given to the burdened spirit.

By this special mark, the convictions of a quickened soul are distinguished from the pangs of guilt and remorse, which are sometimes aroused in the natural conscience. Cain said, "My punishment is greater than I can bear," but there was neither

April

repentance nor prayer in his heart for "he went out from the presence of the Lord," (Gen. 4:16), the very presence which the living soul is seeking to reach and be found in, and into which the Spirit brings him, (Eph. 2:18).

Saul was "sore distressed," when God answered him, "neither by dreams, nor by Urim, nor by prophets," but he goes to the witch of Endor, and in the end falls upon his own sword. Judas repented of his accursed treachery, but went and hanged himself. No prayer, no supplication was in either of their hearts. So it is prophesied that men shall gnaw their tongues for pain, and yet shall blaspheme the God of heaven because of their pains and their sores, and not repent of their deeds, (Rev. 16:10-11). It is not so with the elect who cry day and night unto God. Their prayers, perfumed with the incense of their all-prevailing Intercessor at the right hand of the Father, enter into the ears of the Lord of Sabbath.

7th

"But we all, with open face beholding as in a glass the glory of the Lord, are changed into the same image from glory to glory, even as by the Spirit of the Lord."
2Corinthians 3:18

A view of Christ's glory, and a foretaste of the bliss and blessedness it communicates, has a transforming effect upon the soul. We are naturally proud, covetous, and worldly, often led aside by, and grievously entangled in, various lusts and passions, prone to evil, averse to good, easily elated by prosperity, soon dejected by adversity, peevish under trials, rebellious under heavy strokes, unthankful for daily mercies of food and clothing, and in other ways ever manifesting our vile origin. To be brought from under the power of these abounding evils, and be made "fit for the inheritance of the saints in light," we need to be "transformed by the renewing of our mind," and conformed to the image of Christ.

Now this can only be by beholding his glory by faith, as the Apostle speaks, "But we all, with open face beholding as in a glass the glory of the Lord, are changed into the same image from glory to glory, even as by the Spirit of the Lord." It is this believing view of the glory of Christ that supports us under heavy trials, producing meekness and resignation to the will of God. We are therefore bidden to "consider him that endured such contradiction of sinners against himself, lest ye be wearied and faint in your minds," (Heb.

12:3), and to "run with patience the race that is set before us, looking unto Jesus," (Heb. 12:1).

Sickness also sometimes befalls us, and then we need special support. The sands of our time are fast running out, and there is no turning the glass. Our days have "passed away as the swift ships: as the eagle that hasteth to the prey," (Job 9:26), and death and eternity are fast hastening on. When the body sinks under a load of pain and disease, and all sources of happiness and enjoyment from health and strength are cut off; when flesh and heart fail, and the eye-strings are breaking in death, what can support the soul or bear it safe through Jordan's swelling flood, but those discoveries of the glory of Christ? That shall make it sick of earth, sin and self, and willing to lay the poor body in the grave, that it may be forever ravished with his glory and his love.

Thus we see how the glory of Christ is not only in heaven the unspeakable delight of the saints, whose glorified souls and bodies will then bear "an exceeding and eternal weight of glory", but here on earth, in their days of tribulation and sorrow. This same glory, as revealed to their hearts, supports and upholds their steps, draws them out of the world, delivers them from the power of sin, gives them union and communion with Christ, conforms them to his image, comforts them in death, and lands them on that heavenly shore.

We thus see Christ, like the sun, not only illuminating all heaven with his glory, the delight of the Father, the joy of the spirits of just men made perfect, and the adoration of all the angelic host, but irradiating also the path of the just on earth. We see him casting his blessed beams on all their troubles and sorrows, and lighting up the way wherein they follow their Lord from the suffering cross to the triumphant crown.

8th

"Praying always with all prayer and supplication in the Spirit, and watching thereunto with all perseverance and supplication for all saints."
Ephesians 6:18

If we do not continually "pray in the Spirit," our limbs will, so to speak, shrink, and our armour will drop off. The knights of old exercised every day in their full armour, or they could not have borne it, nor used their weapons with dexterity and strength. So must the Christian warrior, by prayer and supplication, "exercise [himself] unto godliness," (1Tim. 4:7). To this daily exercise must be added, "watching thereunto". Watching for the answer to those prayers; waiting for the appearing of the Lord "more than they that watch for the morning," (Psa. 130:6). This watching must also be done, "with all perseverance," (Eph. 6:18), never giving it up, taking no denial, begging of the Lord again and again, and wrestling with him until he appears to bless, visit, and shine upon the soul.

O how this heavenly recipe keeps every part of the armour bright, and the soldier active and expert in its use! The armour of itself, as being from heaven, gets neither dull nor rusty. It is we who get sluggish in its use, but, to our apprehension, exercising faith and prayer make it glitter more brightly. See how the prayer of faith brightens up the belt of truth and makes it glitter and shine! See how it burnishes the breastplate of righteousness and makes it fit tightly round the bosom! See how it causes the helmet of salvation to glitter in the sun, and its noble plumes to wave in all their native lustre! See how it beats out every dent that the shield of faith may have received from the fiery darts of the evil one, and fits it for fresh encounters! And oh, how it sharpens the sword of the Spirit, how it gives it a brighter polish and nerves the arm to wield it with renewed activity and vigour!

This is the secret of all true victory! All must be well when we are in a prayerful, meditative, watching state. All is ill, though, when this heavenly recipe is neglected, when the hands droop, and the knees faint, and prayer seems dead and motionless in the breast. Let there be in the soul an abiding spirit of prayer, and victory is sure. Satan has little power against the soul that has such an abiding spirit of prayer, and is "watching thereunto with all perseverance." Yet without this spirit of prayer, we are a prey to all his temptations, and can neither take, wear, nor use the only armour against them.

9th

"Let your light so shine before men, that they may see your good works, and glorify your Father which is in heaven."
Matthew 5:16

To glorify God is the highest ambition of angels. The brightest seraph before the throne has no higher aim, no greater happiness, than to bring glory to his name. Howbeit a poor sinner on earth may glorify God as much, and in some way more, than the brightest

April

angel in the courts of eternal bliss. What different views the eyes of God and the eyes of men take of events passing on the earth. What glory is brought to God by all the victories gained by one country over another? I have thought sometimes that a poor old man, or feeble, decrepit woman, lying on a workhouse pallet, fighting with sin, self and Satan, yet enabled amid all to look to the Lord Jesus, and by a word from his lips overcoming death and hell, though when dead thrust into an cheap coffin, to rot in a pauper's grave, brings more glory to God than all the exploits of Nelson or Wellington, and that such victories are more glorious than those of Waterloo or Trafalgar.

It is true that the parish officers will not proclaim such a victory; nor will bells ring or cannons roar at such exploits; but the God of heaven and earth will get more glory from such a despised creature, than from all the generals and admirals who have ever drawn up armies in battle or sunk hostile fleets beneath the wave. Truly does the Lord say, "My thoughts are not your thoughts, neither are your ways my ways, saith the LORD," (Isa. 55:8).

It is indeed astonishing that glory should be brought to his great name by what his people do and suffer upon earth; that their feeble attempts to believe, to love, and to hope in him; to speak well of his name; and to adorn his doctrine in their life and conversation, should redound to his honour and praise. Wondrous indeed is it that a poor, insignificant worm, whom perhaps his fellow-mortal will scarcely deign to look at, or will pass by with a shrug of contempt, should add glory to the great God that inhabits eternity, before whom the highest angels and brightest seraphs bow with holy adoration!

Well may we say, 'What are all the glorious exploits that men are so proud of, compared with the tribute of glory rendered to God by his suffering saints?' You may feel yourself one of the poorest, vilest, neediest worms of earth; and yet if you believe in the Lord Jesus Christ with a living faith, hope in his mercy, love his dear name, and in your vocation adorn his doctrine by a godly, consistent life, you are privileged above princes and nobles, yes, even above crowned heads, and all the glory of man, because you are bringing glory to God.

It matters not what may be your station in life. You may be a servant, master, wife, husband, child, and your rank and station may be high or low, but whatever it be, still in it you may bring glory to God. If a servant, by obedience, cleanliness, industry, and attention to the directions of your master or mistress. If a master or mistress, by kindness and liberality to your dependents, and doing all that you can to render the yoke of servitude light. There is not a single Christian who may not glorify God, though in worldly circumstances he be, or seem to be, totally insignificant. Glory is brought to God by those who live and walk in his fear, and more sometimes by the poor than by the rich. Only adorn the doctrine of God in all things, and you will bring glory to God in all things.

10th

"Verily, verily, I say unto you, He that entereth not by the door into the sheepfold, but climbeth up some other way, the same is a thief and a robber."
John 10:1

Here are three marks whereby you may know whether you have entered by faith into the sheepfold. First, have you any evidence of being saved in the Lord Jesus Christ with an everlasting salvation? Secondly, have you felt any blessed and holy freedom and liberty of going in and coming out of the heavenly sheepfold? Thirdly, have you found pasture? Sometimes finding pasture in the ordinances of God's house; sometimes in the sacred truths of the gospel, as you read or hear the word of truth; and especially in partaking by faith of the flesh and blood of the Lamb.

If you can say yes, then good, but there may be those who are in this spot. They see plainly that Christ is the door, and they are fully convinced that there is no other way of entrance into the fold but by him; and yet they do not feel to have entered personally and experimentally in, so as to enjoy for themselves its privileges and blessings.

Yet have not such entered in by hope and expectation? If I am talking of you, how could you have entered in by expectation unless something in you, which you could not give yourself, were expecting a blessing from God? You could only enter by expectation if you possessed a principle of living faith, whereby, though at present weak and feeble, you yet realise the sweetness of the blessings held forth in the gospel?

How different is this state of soul experience from climbing daringly and presumptuously over the wall, or taking the ladder of self-righteousness, and thus helping yourself in by some other way than the door. How much better to be lying in humility at the gate, looking to Jesus and longing to enter in, begging of him to open the door and give you admission, rather than to make yourself a daring and rash intruder. How different is this humble, dependent, and self-abased state of soul from self-righteousness on the one hand, and bold presumption on the other.

April

There is everything to encourage the weak and feeble part of the flock who long to enter into the fold. To them Jesus opens his arms wide, and says in their heart and ears, "I am the door," (John 10:7). 'Enter through me, and by no other way. There is access to God by me, for I am the way, the truth, and the life. If you enter in by me, you shall be saved from all you justly dread and fear, both as regards this life and the life to come. You shall go freely in and freely out, and find pasture; lying down and feeding on my divine Person, flesh, and blood on earth, as the prelude and foretaste of enjoying me forever in the blissful courts of heaven above.'

11th

"Behold, a virgin shall conceive, and bear a son, and shall call his name Immanuel."
Isaiah 7:14

The Deity of the Son of God shines all through the sacred page. It is the grand cardinal point, on which all the doctrines of grace turn; and he that is unsound there, is unsound everywhere. The Godhead of Christ does not rest upon a few texts of Scripture, but it shines all through the Scripture; it is the light of the Scripture, and it is the life of the Scripture. Take away the Deity of Jesus from Scripture, and you would do the same thing spiritually as though you blotted the sun out of the sky naturally. The sacred page would be one black darkness.

However, the Person of Jesus is not Deity only. No man can see God and live, so we could not bear to look upon him if he were pure Deity. Therefore the Son of God has taken into union with himself our nature, he has 'taken upon him the seed of Abraham' (Heb. 2:16). That "holy One" who was begotten by the Holy Spirit in the womb of the Virgin Mary is there united to the second Person of the glorious Trinity, that Godhead and manhood might form one glorious Person, Immanuel, God with us.

Now to the eye of faith there is the greatest beauty and glory in Christ's humanity. The enlightened soul views Deity shining through the manhood; and when it sees Jesus "going about, doing good," when it hears the words that dropped from his gracious lips, when it views him by the eye of faith, bleeding, suffering, agonising, and dying, it sees the Godhead in all these acts, upholding and shining through the manhood. It is this union of the two natures in one glorious Person that fills every heart which receives it in the faith of it and in the love of it, with a measure of pure affection.

April

Here, then, the Church has a view of the glorious Person of Jesus; and she falls in love with him. There is something in supernatural beauty which kindles spiritual affection, as there is something in natural beauty which kindles natural affection. When the quickened soul sees supernatural beauty, it immediately falls in love with it. The spiritual affections centre in spiritual beauty. And thus, when the redeemed and regenerated soul sees the glorious Person of Christ, God-man, Immanuel, God with us, and has a taste and sense of his love, the blessed Spirit thereby kindles in it spiritual affection, and attracts it with these 'cords of love and bands of a man.'

12th

"As the truth is in Jesus."
Ephesians 4:21

Without truth there is no regeneration; for it is by "the word of truth" that we are begotten and born again, (James 1:18; 1Peter 1:23). Without truth there is no justification; for we are justified by faith, which faith consists in crediting God's truth, and so gives peace with God. Without the truth there is no sanctification; for the Lord himself says, "Sanctify them through thy truth - thy word is truth," (John 17:17). Without the truth there is no salvation; for "God hath from the beginning chosen you to salvation through sanctification of the Spirit and belief of the truth," (2Thes. 2:13).

As the truth is the instrumental cause of all these blessings, the divinely-appointed means whereby they become manifested mercies, so truth enters into and is received by all the graces of the Spirit as they come forth into living exercise. Thus, without the truth, there is no faith; for the work of faith is to believe the truth. What is all the difference between faith and delusion? That faith believes God's truth, and delusion credits Satan's lies. "And for this cause God shall send them strong delusion, that they should believe a lie, that they all might be damned who believed not the truth, but had pleasure in unrighteousness," (2Thes. 2:11-12).

Without truth there is no hope; for the province of hope is to anchor in the truth. "That by two immutable things, in which it was impossible for God to lie, we might have a strong consolation, who have fled for refuge to lay hold upon the hope set before us; which hope we have as an anchor of the soul, both sure and steadfast, and which entereth into that within the veil," (Heb. 6:18-19). The two immutable things in which hope anchors are God's word and God's

April

truth; in other words, the pledged veracity and faithfulness of him who cannot lie.

This made King David say, "I have hoped in thy word," (Psa. 119:74). It caused King Hezekiah to affirm that, "Those who go down to the pit cannot hope for thy truth," for, as the prophet said, "The living, the living, he shall praise thee, as I do this day," (Isa. 38:18-19). The apostle Paul confirmed, "that we, through patience and comfort of the scriptures might have hope," (Rom. 15:4), that is, the consolation which the truth of God revealed in the Scriptures affords us hope.

Without truth there is no love, for it is by "the love of the truth" that the saved are distinguished from the lost. Those that are lost perish "because they received not the love of the truth, that they might be saved," (2Thes. 2:10). It is only as we speak the truth in love that we "grow up into him in all things, which is the head, even Christ," (Eph. 4:15). Thus "the fruit of the Spirit is in all goodness, and righteousness, and truth," (Eph. 5:9), and this in the Person of the Son of God, for "grace and truth came by Jesus Christ," (John 1:17).

13th

"The lips of the righteous feed many: but fools die for want of wisdom."
Proverbs 10:21

There is such a connection between true wisdom, which is "a knowledge of the holy," (Prov. 30:3), and the fear of the Lord; and between ignorance of the Lord and sin, that saved saints are called "wise," and lost sinners are called "fools," not only in the Old Testament, as continually in the Proverbs, but also in the New.

Many of the Lord's people look with suspicion upon knowledge, from not seeing clearly the vast distinction between the spiritual, experimental knowledge for which we are now contending, and what is called "head knowledge." They see that a man may have a well-furnished head and a graceless heart, that he may understand "all mysteries and all knowledge," and yet be "nothing," (1Cor. 13:2); and as some of these all-knowing professors are the basest characters that can infest the churches of truth, those who really fear the Lord stand not only in doubt of them, but of all the knowledge possessed by them.

Yet, put the same truth in a different form, and ask the people of God whether there is not such a divine reality, such a heavenly blessing, as being "taught of God," (John 6:45), and having "an unction from the Holy One, whereby we know all things," (1John 2:20), and they will quickly aver the truth of it. Ask them whether knowing the truth for oneself, and finding that it makes them free, (John 8:32), or whether there is not a "counting of all things but loss for the excellency of the knowledge of Christ Jesus our Lord," and they will not hesitate to concur.

What of a stretching forth of the desires of the soul to "know him, and the power of his resurrection, and the fellowship of his sufferings," (Phil. 3:10), and whether there is not "a knowledge of salvation by the remission of sins," (Luke 1:77)? Without doubt, will be the response.

Is there "a knowledge of the glory of God in the face of Jesus Christ," (2Cor. 4:6), and a being "filled with the knowledge of his will," (Col. 1:9)? Is there an "increasing in the knowledge of God," (Col. 1:10), and "a growing in grace and in the knowledge of the Lord and Saviour Jesus Christ," (2Pet. 3:18)?

Ask the living family of God whether there be not knowledge such as this, and if such knowledge is not the very pith and marrow, the very sum and substance of vital godliness, and they will with one voice exclaim, "It is!"

14th

"Now ye are clean through the word which I have spoken unto you."
John 15:3

What God does, he does by the word of his grace and the influences which accompany that word. Forever bear in mind that God does nothing but by his word. The sanctifying, cleansing effects therefore which attend the word of his grace under the operations of the Spirit are spoken of as "the washing of water by the word," (Eph. 5:26). 'The word' is the written Scripture; the 'water' is the power of the Holy Spirit, and the 'washing' is the cleansing effect of the application of the word.

Let me ask you this question, if you doubt my word. How are we to get the burden and guilt of our sins off our conscience? How is the defilement of mind which sin produces to be removed? How can the bondage of spirit which sin creates be undone, and the fears and alarms of the soul which sin works be calmed?

You will say, "By believing in Jesus Christ, for being justified by faith we have peace with God."

That is true, but how can we believe in Jesus Christ, so as to find this peace? By the word of his grace, accompanied by the special influence, unction, and dew of the Holy Spirit revealing and making known pardon and acceptance with God, which is therefore spoken of as "the washing of water by the word," (Eph. 5:26). For as water washes the body, so the word of truth washes the soul. It washes away the guilt and filth and defilement of sin.

As the blessed Lord said, "Ye shall know the truth, and the truth shall make you free," (John 8:32), and again, "He that is washed needeth not save to wash his feet, but is clean every whit," (John 13:10). Thus as water when applied cleanses the body from natural filth, so does the word of promise, the word of truth, the word of salvation revealing and making known the Saviour's precious blood, cleanse the conscience from the guilt, filth, and defilement of sin.

15th

"But all things that are reproved are made manifest by the light: for whatsoever doth make manifest is light."
Ephesians 5:13

Feeling is the first evidence of supernatural life; a feeling compounded of two distinct sensations, one referring to God, and the other referring to self. The same ray of light has manifested two opposite things, "for whatsoever doth make manifest is light," and the sinner sees at one and the same moment God and self, justice and guilt, power and helplessness, a holy law and a broken commandment, eternity and time, the purity of the Creator and the filthiness of the creature. These things he sees, not merely as declared in the Bible, but as revealed in himself as personal realities, involving all his happiness or all his misery in time and in eternity.

Thus it is with him as though a new existence had been communicated, and as if for the first time he had found there was a God. One ray of supernatural light, penetrating through the veil spread over the heart, has revealed that dreadful secret - a just God, who will by no means clear the guilty. This piercing ray has torn away the bed too short, and stripped off the covering too narrow. A sudden, peculiar conviction has rushed into the soul. One absorbing feeling has seized fast hold of it, and well-near banished every other. 'There is a God, and I am a sinner before him,' is written upon the heart by the same divine finger that traced those fatal letters on the palace wall of the king of Babylon, which

April

made the joints of his loins to be loosed, and his knees to smite one against another, (Dan. 5:5-6).

"What shall I do? Where shall I go? What will become of me? Mercy, O God! Mercy, mercy! I am lost, ruined, undone! Fool, madman, wretch, monster that I have been! I have ruined my soul. O my sins, my sins! O eternity, eternity!' Such and similar cries and groans, though differing in depth and intensity, go up out of the new-born soul well-near day and night at the first discovery of God and of itself. These feelings have taken such complete possession of the heart that it can find no rest except in calling upon God. This is the first pushing of the young bud through the bark, the first formation of the green shoot, wrapped up as yet in its leaves, and not opened to view. These are the first pangs and throes of the new birth, before the tidings are brought, "A man-child is born."

"What shall I do to be saved?" cried the jailer. "God be merciful to me a sinner!" exclaimed the tax-collector. "Woe is me, for I am undone!" burst forth from the lips of Isaiah.

16th

"Shall iron break the northern iron and the steel?"
Jeremiah 15:12

You see that the Lord, when he is pointing out the trials his people are passing through, compares them to iron. He does not diminish their weight; he does not at all lower their oppressive tendency. Howbeit, in order to administer a suitable remedy to Jeremiah's soul, he brings forward something stronger. "Shall iron," he says, "break the northern iron and the steel?" The inference is clear. Surely the "northern iron and the steel" is by far the stronger. The common iron never can break through the northern iron, which is a metal of such a far superior nature, and still less prevail against that keen well-tempered steel which can cut through everything it touches.

Now if your hearts are exercised with iron sorrows, temptations, trials, and perplexities, I am sure you will want the almighty power of God in your souls to cut them asunder. Take heart, God can do it. Are you a poor persecuted believer? God can cut down in a moment that enemy who is persecuting you. Are you tempted of Satan? He in a moment can cut his fiery darts asunder. Are you passing through a severe trial? By the application of some precious promise the Lord can in a moment cut the trial asunder. Are you entangled in some grievous snare that you feel and cry out under night and day, and yet are unable to extricate yourself? The Lord

April

can in a moment, by the application of his precious word to your soul, cut that snare asunder. He has but to bring against it "the northern iron and the steel," and it is done in a moment.

How was it with Jeremiah? Did not he say, "Thy words were found, and I did eat them; and thy word was unto me the joy and rejoicing of mine heart," (Jer. 15:16). Why? Because keen persecutions, sharp trials, severe temptations had given him an appetite; *that* was the reason why the "word was found." He fell upon it as a hungry man upon a crust. It was sweet to his soul, because it brought with it a precious deliverance from the temptations and the sorrows his soul was groaning under.

Thus, we see that in proportion as we feel the iron nature of trials and sorrows, shall we experience "the northern iron and the steel" of God's almighty power and grace to deliver. Happy are the people that are in such a case! Happy the people that have this Lord for their manifested God!

17th

"Lead me in thy truth, and teach me: for thou art the God of my salvation;"
Psalm 25:5

By what steps do we usually embrace the truth as it is in Jesus? First of all, for the most part, we receive it as a doctrine; the judgment being more or less informed and the eyes of our understanding being enlightened to see it in the word. The doctrine for some time may be floating in our mind; but after a time, as the Lord leads us more into a knowledge of our own hearts, and into a deeper feeling of our necessities, he lets down the truth from our head into the heart, and it then becomes a truth. It is very sweet to have a doctrine turned into a truth.

Then, after a time, we need something more than a truth; we need it as a blessing. When we are brought into pressing straits and severe trials, we need the doctrines, which we first received into our minds as truths, now to be blessed by a divine application to our souls. Thus, what we first knew in our judgments as a doctrine, is afterwards received in our conscience as a truth, and then is applied to our heart of hearts as a blessing. We find God's word and we eat it, to the joy and rejoicing of our souls.

Thus it is with respect to Christ's ascension. We receive it first as a doctrine, as a great and glorious part of the scheme of salvation. Later we begin to see, as we are led into a deeper knowledge of it, what a wonderful truth it is to have a Mediator at the right hand of God. What a consolation to have an Intercessor pleading by the efficacy of his atoning blood and justifying righteousness, for poor, needy, guilty souls. This draws out faith, hope, and love from our heart to this ascended and interceding Mediator. Then later, as the Spirit reveals the virtue and efficacy of this glorious Mediator in the guilty conscience, the truth becomes a rich, unctuous, and savoury blessing.

Experience therefore, far from casting out the doctrines of grace, only leads the soul into a vital acquaintance with them. We might as well think of saving our lives by drawing bones out of our body as of blessing our souls by casting out the doctrines of grace. Yes, we daily feel more deeply the need of the doctrines being brought into our heart by divine power; we feel them more to be the stay and support of our soul, as my arm when raised is stayed and supported by the bones which God has placed there.

18th

"Of his own will begat he us with the word of truth, that we should be a kind of firstfruits of his creatures."
James 1:18

If we look at the work of the Spirit on the heart, we shall see how, in all his sacred dealings and gracious movements, he invariably employs truth as his grand instrument.

Does he pierce and wound? It is by the truth, for the sword of the Spirit is the word of God, and that we know is the word of truth. If he mercifully heals, if he kindly blesses, it is also by means of truth, for the promise is, "Howbeit, when he, the Spirit of truth has come, he will guide you into all truth," (John 16:13). And when he thus comes, it is as a Comforter, according to those gracious words, "But when the Comforter is come, whom I will send unto you from the Father, even the Spirit of truth, which proceedeth from the Father, he shall testify of me," (John 15:26).

In fact, if we look at the new man of grace that the blessed Spirit begets and brings forth in the heart, we shall see that all his members and faculties are formed and adapted to a living reception of the truth. As the eye is adapted to light; as the ear to sound; as the lungs to the pure air that fills them with every breath; as the heart to the vital blood which it propels through every bounding artery, so is the new man of grace fitted and adapted to the truth of God. In the same way that these vital organs perform their peculiar

April

functions only as they encounter these external agents, so the organs of the new man of grace only act as truth is impressed upon them by the power of the blessed Spirit.

Has, then, the new man of grace eyes? Yes indeed, for to see the truth, (Eph. 1:18-19). Has he ears? Of a certainty, for to hear the truth, (Isa. 55:3 and Luke 9:44). Has he hands? For sure, to lay hold of and embrace the truth, (Prov. 4:13, Isa. 27:5 and Heb. 6:18). Has he feet? It is that he may walk in the truth, (Psa. 119:45, Luke 1:6, 3John 4). Has he a mouth? Oh yes, it is that he may feed upon the truth, the living truth, yes, upon His flesh who is truth itself, (John 6:35, 14:6). "Open thy mouth wide, and I will fill it," says the Lord to the Psalmist, (Psa. 81:10).

19th

"[I] have poured out my soul before the Lord."
1Samuel 1:15

How much there is in that expression pouring out the soul before the Lord! Shall I use a familiar figure to illustrate it, as sometimes familiar figures are best adapted to that purpose? Look at a sack of corn; you know, when the mouth of the sack is tied up, there is no pouring out its contents; but let the sack be opened and thrown down, and then its contents are immediately spilled, and the rich grain falls upon the floor. Our hearts are sometimes like the sack with the mouth tied. There are desires, pantings, and longings; there are needs which are urgently felt, but we cannot give them utterance. As we read, "I opened my mouth and panted," (Psa. 119:131). We seem to be tied up tight, unable to utter what is within, but the Lord in mercy, at times, opens the mouth; and then when the mouth is opened, the heart can pour out its desires, just as the rich grain is poured out of a sack when the mouth is untied.

Howbeit, the sack be full before the grain is poured out. If there are but a few grains at the bottom, or only half-a-pint of wheat in one corner, though you open the mouth, there is no pouring out of the rich grain. So it is with our hearts. If the heart be not full; if there be no vehement desires struggling for utterance, we may open the mouth, but there is no pouring it out in pantings and longings.

If you want a scriptural instance of what it means to pour out the soul before the Lord, read the first chapter of the first book of Samuel. There you will find that gracious woman Hannah, so agitated, and so discovering the state of her mind by the convulsive movements of her frame, that the high priest charged her with being drunken. Yet, though her heart was so full that her lips quivered, and her very features betrayed what was passing within, yet she meekly replied to his chiding speech, when he bade her to put away her wine.

"No, my Lord; I am a woman of a sorrowful spirit; I have drunk neither wine nor strong drink, but have poured out my soul before the Lord," (1Sam. 1:15).

That was something like prayer, and we know what a blessed answer the Lord gave her, and how the Holy Spirit has recorded her triumphal song.

20th

"O our God, wilt thou not judge them? for we have no might against this great company that cometh against us; neither know we what to do: but our eyes are upon thee."
2Chronicles 20:12

Jehoshaphat did not know what to do; he was all but at his wit's end, and yet he took the wisest course a man could take. This is the beauty of it; that when we are fools, then we are wise; when we are weak, then we are strong; when we know not what to do, then we do the only right thing. Had Jehoshaphat taken any other course, had he collected an army, had he sent throughout Judah and raised troops, and forged swords and spears, he would certainly have been defeated! Howbeit, in not knowing what to do, he did the very thing he should do.

"Our eyes are upon thee," said the king in resignation. 'Thou must fight our battles; thou must take the matter into thine own hands. Our eyes are upon thee, waiting upon thee, looking up, and hoping in thee; believing in thy holy name, expecting help from thee, from whom alone all help can come.'

It is painful work to be brought to this point, to the place where we know not "what to do, but our eyes are upon thee," implying there is no use looking to any other quarter. It assumes that the soul has looked, and looked, and looked elsewhere in vain, and then fixed its eyes upon God as knowing that from him alone all help must come.

This I believe to be the distinctive mark of a Christian, that his eyes are upon God. On his bed by night; in his room by day; in his business or at the market; when his soul is in trouble, cast down, and perplexed, his eyes are ever upon God. From him alone all help must come for none else can reach his case. All other but the help of God is ineffectual; it leaves him where it found him; it does him no good.

We are never safe except our eyes are upon God. Let our eyes be upon him, we can walk safely; let our eyes be upon the creature, we are pretty sure to slip and stumble.

21st

"But of him are ye in Christ Jesus, who of God is made unto us wisdom, and righteousness, and sanctification, and redemption; that, according as it is written, He that glorieth, let him glory in the Lord."
1Corinthians 1:30-31

Wisdom, righteousness, sanctification, and redemption. God has made Christ all these things to his people. He has set him up as their eternal Head, made him the Bridegroom of their souls, that out of his fullness they may all receive. Then, just in proportion as they learn these two lessons – what they are, and what he is – they receive him into their hearts; and they receive what he is to them in the purpose of God.

Am I a fool? Do I feel it and know it? Have I had painful experience of it, so that all my creature wisdom is turned into one mass of foolishness? Do I catch by the eye of faith a view of the risen Mediator, "Immanuel, God with us," and see what he is made of God to us? The moment my eye sees him as "wisdom," that moment a measure of divine wisdom flows into my conscience.

Am I polluted and defiled throughout? Have I no righteousness of my own? Is all my obedience imperfect? Am I unable to fulfil the requirement of God's holy law? If once I catch by the eye of faith this glorious truth, through him who is the truth, that Jesus Christ is of God made unto me "righteousness", the moment I see that by the eye of faith, a measure of imparted righteousness flows into my heart.

Am I an unholy, depraved, filthy wretch? Does corruption work in my heart? The moment I catch by the eye of faith Jesus made unto me of God "sanctification," that moment a measure of sanctification comes into my heart, drawing up holy affections, casting out the love of the world, curbing my reigning lusts, and bringing my soul into submission at his footstool.

Am I a poor captive, entangled by Satan, by the world, and my own evil heart? Can I catch this glorious view that Jesus Christ, at the right hand of the Father, is made unto me "redemption"? If I can believe that he is made such for me, that I have a standing in him, and a union with him, so that he is my redemption, then that moment a measure of deliverance comes into my soul, and redemption imputed becomes redemption imparted; the soul receives then internally what Christ has done externally.

In short, when Christ is received as "wisdom, righteousness, sanctification, and redemption," he becomes all these in vital manifestation.

22nd

"Beloved, now are we the sons of God, and it doth not yet appear what we shall be: but we know that, when he shall appear, we shall be like him; for we shall see him as he is." 1John 3:2

What Christ is to the Church and what the Church is to Christ can never be really known until time gives place to eternity, faith to sight, and hope to enjoyment. Nor even then, however far beyond all present conception the powers and faculties of the glorified souls and bodies of the saints may be expanded, will we fully know. However conformed we are to the glorious image of Christ, or however ravished we become with the discoveries of his glory and the sight of him as he is in one unclouded day, the depth of the relationship will still be hidden. Not even then will the utmost stretch of creature love, or the highest refinement of creature intellect, wholly embrace or fully comprehend that love of Christ, which, as in time so in eternity, "passeth knowledge," as being in itself essentially incomprehensible, because it is infinite and divine.

Who can calculate the amount of light and heat that dwell in and are given forth by the sun that shines so gloriously in the noonday sky? We see, we feel, we enjoy its bright beams; but who can number the millions of millions of rays that it casts forth upon all the surface of the earth, diffusing light, heat, and fertility to every part? If the creature and the creation be so great, glorious and incomprehensible, how much greater, more glorious and more incomprehensible must be its divine Creator!

The Scriptures testify of the saints in glory that when Christ shall appear, they shall be like him, for they shall see him as he is, (1John 3:2). They shall also see the Lord face to face, and know even as they are known, (1Cor. 13:12). Their vile body shall be fashioned like unto his glorious body, (Phil. 3:21), they shall be conformed to his image, (Rom. 8:29), and be satisfied when they awake with his likeness. They shall be before the throne of God, and serve him day and night in his temple, (Rev. 7:15), and their sun shall no more go down, for the Lord shall be their everlasting light, (Isa. 60:20). They shall have an exceeding and eternal weight of glory, (2Cor. 4:17), and shall shine as the brightness of the firmament, and as the stars forever and ever, (Dan. 12:13).

But to bestow all this unspeakable bliss and glory, there must be in infinite Deity unfathomable depths which no creature, however highly exalted, can ever sound. There must be heights which no finite, dependent being can ever scan.

God became man, but man can never become God. He fully knows us, but we can never fully know him, for even in eternity, as in time, it may be said to the creature, "Canst thou by searching find out God? Canst thou find out the Almighty unto perfection? It is as high as heaven; what canst thou do? Deeper than hell; what canst thou know? The measure thereof is longer than the earth, and broader than the sea," (Job 11:7-9).

But if, as we believe, eternity itself can never fully or entirely reveal the heights and depths of the love of a Triune God, how little can be known of it in this state of time! Yet that little at times seems overwhelming, and is the only true balm for all sorrow, the only foundation of solid rest and peace.

23rd

"A friend loveth at all times, and a brother is born for adversity."
Proverbs 17:17

If I may use the expression, we do not need a dead but a living Jesus. We do not need an absent, but a present Jesus, nor a once, but a now Jesus. We need a friend at the right hand of God at the present moment. We need an omniscient, omnipresent, omnipotent and yet pitiful and loving Mediator between God and us. We need an interceding High Priest and a Surety, and we need a Representative bearing our nature in the courts of heaven, who can show mercy and compassion to us now upon earth, 'Whose heart is made of tenderness, Whose affections melt with love.'

Our needs make us feel this. Our sins and sorrows give us perpetual errands to the throne. This valley of tears is ever before our eyes, and thorns and briars are perpetually springing up in it, that rend and tear our flesh. We need a real friend. Have you not sometimes tossed to and fro upon your weary couch, and almost cried aloud, "O that I had a friend!" You may have received cruel blows from one whom you regarded as a real friend; but you have been cruelly deceived. You feel now you have no one to take care of you or love you, and whom you can love again; and your heart sighs for a friend who shall be a friend indeed. The widow, the orphan, the friendless, the deserted one, all keenly and deeply feel this. But if grace has touched your heart, you feel that though all men forsake you, there is the Friend of sinners, a Brother born for adversity, a Friend who loves at all times, who will never leave or forsake you.

But we need this friend to be almighty, for no other can suit our case - he must be a divine Friend. For who but God can see us wherever we are? What but a divine eye can read our thoughts? What but a divine ear can hear our petitions? What but a divine hand can stretch itself forth and deliver? Thus, the Deity of Christ is no dry, barren speculation, no mere Bible truth, but an experience wrought powerfully into a believer's inmost soul. Happy soul! Happy season when you can say with the Church of God, "This is my beloved, and this is my friend, O daughters of Jerusalem," (Song 5:16).

Thus the very needs of the soul instinctively teach us that a friend, to be a friend, must be a heavenly friend; that his heart and hand must be divine, or they are not the heart and hand of a friend for us.

This Friend, who's bitterest reproach here on earth was that he "was the Friend of sinners," is the blessed Jesus, our great High Priest in the courts above, and such a reproach on earth is his highest glory in heaven. We find him at times to be very merciful, very pitiful, and very compassionate. I am sure that we need all the compassion that is in his loving breast; for we are continually in states of mind when nothing but his pure mercy can suit, when nothing but his rich and boundless compassion is adapted to our case.

24th

"Yet a little while, and the world seeth me no more; but ye see me: because I live, ye shall live also."
John 14:19

Communion with Christ rests on three things – seeing him by faith, living upon his life, and experiencing his manifested presence, and yet all these three depend on his resurrection and a knowledge of its power. As risen from the dead, the saints see him; as risen from the dead, they live a life of faith upon him; as risen from the dead, he manifests himself unto them; and as life and feeling spring up in their souls from sweet communion with him, the power of his resurrection becomes manifest in them.

This communion therefore, with the Lord Jesus as a risen Head, all the reconciled and justified saints of God are pressing after, according to the measure of their grace and the life and power of God in their soul. It is indeed often sadly interrupted and grievously broken through by the sin that dwells in us. Yet the principle is there, for that principle is life; and life is the privilege, the possession, and the distinction of the children of God. You need none to assure you that Jesus is risen from the dead if he manifests himself to your soul. You need no evidence that you are one of his sheep if you have heard and know his voice. So you may say, "Jesus is risen, for I have seen him; Jesus is risen, for I have heard him; Jesus is risen, for I live upon him."

Communion with Jesus is the life of true religion, and indeed without it religion is but an empty name. Without him, we can do nothing. He is our life, our risen covenant Head, our Advocate with the Father, our Husband, our Friend, and our Brother. How are we to draw sap out of his fullness, as the branch from the vine, or how can we know him personally and experimentally in any one of his endearing relationships, unless by continual communion with him on his throne of grace?

This is the grand distinguishing point between the living and the dead, between the true child of God and the mere professor, that the one has real union and communion with a risen Jesus, and the other is satisfied with a form of godliness. Every quickened soul is made to feel after the power of God after communion from above, after pardon and peace, and after visitations of mercy and grace. When he has had a view of Christ by faith, and some revelation of his Person and work, and grace and glory, nothing afterwards can ever really satisfy him but that inward communion of spirit with Jesus whereby the Lord and he become one.

"He that is joined unto the Lord is one spirit," (1Cor. 6:17).

25th

"Then said I, Woe is me! for I am undone; because I am a man of unclean lips, and I dwell in the midst of a people of unclean lips: for mine eyes have seen the King, the LORD of hosts."
Isaiah 6:5

April

God has described his Zion as full of "wounds, and bruises, and putrefying sores," (Isa. 1:6). When the Church of God fell in Adam, she fell with a mighty crash, which broke every bone and bruised her flesh with wounds that are now ulcerated from top to toe. Her understanding, her conscience, and her affections were all fearfully maimed. Her understanding was blinded; her conscience stupified, and her affections alienated. Every mental faculty thus became perverted and distorted.

As in a shipwrecked vessel the water runs in through every hole, so when Adam fell upon the lee shore of sin and temptation, and made shipwreck of the image of God in which he was created, sin rushed into every faculty of body and soul, and penetrated into the inmost recesses of his being.

Or to use another figure; as when a man is bitten by a poisonous serpent, the venom courses through every artery and vein, and he dies a corrupted mass from head to foot, so did the poison fang of sin penetrate into Adam's inmost soul and body, and infect him with its venom from the sole to the crown.

Howbeit, the fearful havoc which sin has made is never seen nor felt until the soul is quickened into spiritual life. Oh, what work does sin then make in the conscience, when it is opened up by the Spirit of God! Whatever superficial or shallow views we may have had of sin before, it is only as its desperate and malignant character is revealed by the Holy Spirit that it is really seen, felt, grieved under, and mourned over as indeed a most dreadful and fearful reality. It is this sword of the Spirit which cuts and wounds; it is this entrance of life and light that gashes the conscience; it is this divine work which lacerates the heart and inflicts those deep wounds which nothing but the "balm in Gilead" can heal.

And not only is a poor convinced sinner cut in his conscience, inwardly lacerated and gashed by sin as thus opened up by the Spirit of God, but, as the prophet speaks, "the whole head is sick, and the whole heart faint," (Isa. 1:5). He is thus labouring under a complication of diseases. Every thought, word, and action is polluted by sin. Every mental faculty is depraved. The will chooses evil; the affections cleave to earthly things; the memory, like a broken sieve, retains the bad and lets fall the good; the judgment, like a bribed or drunken juryman, pronounces heedless or wrong decisions; and the conscience, like an opium-eater, lies asleep and drugged in stupified silence.

This miserable state, brought upon us and into us by the fall, all the people of God must in some measure feel. It is of no use mincing the matter and saying that a person can be saved by the grace of God and the blood of Christ, without knowing anything of the depth of misery and wretchedness into which he is sunk as the fallen child of a fallen father. We must go down into the depths of the fall to know what our hearts are, and what they are truly capable of. We must have the keen knife of God to cut deep gashes in our conscience and lay bare the evil that lies so deeply imbedded in our carnal mind, before we can enter into and experience the beauty and blessedness of salvation by grace.

26th

"We having the same spirit of faith, according as it is written, I believed, and therefore have I spoken; we also believe, and therefore speak."
2Corinthians 4:13

There is a distinction to be made between faith and the spirit of faith. The spirit of faith is faith in exercise. Faith sometimes is like a day in which there is no wind blowing. It is so calm, that there scarcely appears to be any air stirring to move a leaf, but, after a time, a gentle breeze comes and blows over the earth. Thus it is with faith and the spirit of faith.

Faith in repose is like the calm air of a summer's day, when there is nothing moving or stirring; faith acting, faith in exercise, is like the same air in the gentle breeze which makes itself sensibly felt. If God has given me faith, that faith is never lost out of my breast. If once a believer, I always am a believer; for if I could cease to believe, I would cease to be a child of God; I should lose salvation out of my heart, for I am saved by grace through faith.

Yet there may be many times and seasons when I may not have much of the spirit of faith. Faith may be very inactive, I will not say stagnant, for that would almost imply death, but still, quiet, calm, sleeping like a bird with its head under its wing, but in due time there is a stirring, a movement, a gracious blowing of the Spirit.

"Awake, O north wind, and come, O south wind; blow upon my garden," (Song 4:16). "Come from the four winds, O breath," (Ezek. 37:9). This heavenly breath of the Holy Spirit acts upon faith, awakens it, revives and reanimates it, and draws it forth into lively operation. It thus becomes a spirit of faith, acting spiritually and energetically according to its measure. John was "in the Spirit on the Lord's day," (Rev. 1:10). He was not always in the Spirit by lively action, though he was never out of the Spirit by his extinction. So faith is sometimes, so to speak, in the Spirit; and then its eyes are open, like the eyes of John, to see spiritually what he saw visibly, the Person of Christ, and its ear open to hear inwardly what he heard outwardly, the words of Christ.

April 27th

"For there are three that bear record in heaven, the Father, the Word, and the Holy Ghost: and these three are one."
1John 5:7

All God's people are led into a knowledge of the Trinity, and not by metaphysical reasoning or subtle arguments addressed to the understanding. The Spirit teaches them by the power and dew of divine truth resting upon the heart, not by reasoning addressed to the head. God's true children learn the doctrine of the Trinity in that inner man, the soul.

Under divine teaching, they learn the authority, justice, majesty, and holiness, and in due time feel the love, of God the Father.

They learn the Godhead of Christ in their souls, by seeing and feeling the power of his blood as the blood of God, (Acts 20:28), and his righteousness as the "righteousness of God," (Rom. 3:22).

They learn the Deity and Personality of the Holy Spirit by feeling the divine power of his operations on their hearts. They learn also that he is God, by perceiving how he scrutinises all their actions, brings to light every secret thought, and applies passages of Scripture to their souls, which none but God could produce, or so suitably apply.

When they are thus led by divine teaching into the Three Persons of the Godhead, they are brought to know and feel in the depths of conscience that there are Three Persons, equal in power, will, essence, and glory, and but one Jehovah. No man can learn these truths in a saving manner except by this special teaching. He may know all this, and much more than this, in his understanding and judgment, but such knowledge remains in his head. A sensible realisation of the power of these things in the conscience, a divine melting of the heart under them, with an enlargement of soul, and an experimental enjoyment of them, is the alone fruit of God's teaching resting on him, so as to make him "a new creature" in Christ.

28th

"That by two immutable things, in which it was impossible for God to lie, we might have a strong consolation, who have fled for refuge to lay hold upon the hope set before us."
Hebrews 6:18

It is utterly impossible for God to lie. The earth may be dissolved, and all creation reduced to chaos, and still he would be truth. He would cease to be God if the faintest breath of a change, or the mere shadow of a turning should pass over the glorious Godhead, but it is impossible for God to lie. Therefore this holds out strong consolation for those that have fled for refuge to lay hold of the hope set before them.

What is the ground of this strong consolation? This is the ground, that God has eternally determined and sworn by himself - that he will save and bless those who have fled for refuge and lay hold of the hope that is set before them in the gospel. This is the foundation of their consolation, this is the ground of their hope, that God has made such and such promises, and confirmed such and such promises by his solemn oath. Those who flee for refuge, and lay hold upon this hope, have a saving interest in and title to them, and have a manifest assurance of being "heirs of promise," (Heb. 6:17).

Now, did you ever in your life feel spiritual consolation? If ever you did, it was by laying hold of the hope set before you in the gospel. There was no consolation ever got by looking at fallen self. If ever there was any true consolation, any hope raised up in the heart, any solid comfort, it came out of the actings of living faith, embracing the blood and righteousness of Christ, tasting a measure of his preciousness, seeing his glory and beauty, and feeling the heart in some measure dissolved into nothingness at his footstool.

Not looking at ourselves, but receiving as empty-sinners out of his fullness; not trusting to ourselves, or our own attainments, but going to Jesus, and receiving something into our hearts out of him. Nothing but this can give us consolation; and the more it is felt, the more it will give us a "strong consolation."

29th

"The God of all grace."
1Peter 5:10

All we have and are, everything we know and feel, comes from "the God of all grace." We have nothing spiritually good in ourselves; all therefore that we have is the free gift of his hand, and comes from the ever-flowing Fountain of mercy and truth. It will be our mercy, then, as the Lord may enable us, to be ever looking unto him. Not looking to books and not looking to ministers, for these are only instruments, and in themselves but poor instruments. The soul must look through all and above all to "the God of all grace."

The Lord enable you to examine every truth as it is brought before you by the light of God's Spirit in your heart, to "prove all things, and hold fast that which is good," (1Thes. 5:21).

However deeply you may feel the vileness of your heart, remember there is "the God of all grace" to turn to. If you feel yourself the vilest of sinners, he suits you the more as "the God of all grace." If you feel dark, stupid, and barren, it is the greater reason that you should call on "the God of *all* grace" to revive your drooping soul. If any have lost past enjoyments, and are now "walking in darkness" that may be felt, it is the more reason they should seek "the God of all grace," that he may supply their needs out of Christ's fullness, as the covenant Head.

Yes, whatever trials, perplexities, and temptations may harass your soul, it is only to open the way for "the God of all grace" to appear. In whatever affliction you may be, it will be your wisdom, as it will be your mercy, to be looking up unto him, that he may comfort your soul; and, turning from man, as Hezekiah turned his face to the wall, commit your case to him.

30th

"For I was alive without the law once; but when the commandment came, sin revived, and I died."
Romans 7:9

The Apostle describes in his own case how men are affected toward the law before it enters as a condemning sentence into their heart. "I was alive without the law once." The law was hanging over him as a condemning sentence, as a minister of death, as a messenger of wrath, as a consuming fire, but he felt it not. As with a thunderstorm in the remote distance, he might hear the low mutterings of the thunder which once rolled over Sinai's fiery mount, or he might see from far the play of those lightnings which scorched its top, but the storm was in the distance. He went about without thinking, or feeling, or fearing, or caring whether the law was his friend or enemy. In his own case he rather viewed it as his friend, for he was using it as a friendly help to build up his own righteousness. He had gone to it, but it had not come to him; he knew its letter, but not its spirit; its outward commands, but not its inward demands. He therefore speaks of himself as being "alive without the law," that is, without any knowledge of what it was as a ministration of condemnation and death.

April

Then, in God's own appointed time and way, "the commandment came;" that is, it came with power into his conscience. He found that he could keep every one of the commandments but the tenth; for according to his apprehension and his interpretation of them, they did not extend beyond an external obedience. But the tenth commandment, "You shall not covet," struck into the very depth of his conscience, for it was a prohibition from the mouth of God of the inward lusts of the heart, and that prohibition attended with a dreadful curse.

Under this stroke sin, which before lay seemingly dead in his breast, revived like a sleeping serpent; and what was the consequence? It stung him to death, for he says, "and I died;" for the commandment which was ordained unto life he found to be unto death! Sin could not brook to be thwarted or opposed; it therefore rose up in enmity against God, took advantage of the commandment to rebel against the authority of Jehovah, and its guilt in consequence falling upon his conscience, made tender in the fear of God, slew him.

It would not have done so had there been no life in his soul; but there being light to see and life to feel the anger of God revealed in the commandment, when the law came into his conscience as a sentence from a just and holy Jehovah, the effect was to produce a sentence of death in himself. This experience, which the Apostle describes as his own, is what the law does and ever must do when applied to the conscience by the power of God. It kills. It slays the condemned sinner, and is a sentence of death in a man's own conscience, which awaits only the hour of death and the day of judgment to be carried into execution.

May

May

1st

"Wherefore in all things it behoved him to be made like unto his brethren, that he might be a merciful and faithful high priest in things pertaining to God, to make reconciliation for the sins of the people."
Hebrews 2:17

God gave the persons of the elect into the hands of his dear Son, as Jacob committed Benjamin into the hands of Judah; and as Judah accepted Benjamin, so Christ accepted the Church and undertook to bring it unto God, or he himself would bear the blame forever. Oh how this faithfulness was tried! Men tried it; devils tried it; God tried it; but it came gloriously through all. Yet what loads were laid upon it! How the very knees of Jesus, so to speak, staggered beneath it! How, as Deer says, he had "Strength enough, and none to spare!"

How he had to sustain the curse of the law and the load of imputed sin! How he had to drink up a very hell of inward torment! How he had to be agonised in body, and more than agonised in soul! What bloody sweat in the garden, what tears, what sore amazement, what heaviness of spirit, what sorrowfulness even unto death; what pangs of body upon the cross, what grief of mind, what distress of soul, did the Holy Lamb endure in being faithful unto God! How he might have prayed, and his Father would have sent him twelve legions of angels! He had but to speak, and he might have soared to heaven and left the cross and all its shame and suffering behind.

But no, he was faithful to God and to the work which he had undertaken. Six weary hours he hung upon the cross. Six weary hours he endured the wrath of God, and that most cutting stroke of all, reserved to the last as the bitterest drop in the whole cup, the hiding of his Father's face, which wrung from his bosom that cry, such as neither earth nor heaven have heard before, "My God, my God, why hast thou forsaken me?" Yet not until he had finished the work did he give up his spirit, and so he was faithful "in [all] things pertaining to God."

He is faithful also in all things pertaining to man. He could say to the Father, "Those that thou gavest me I have kept, and none of them is lost, but the son of perdition," John 17:12). He had no charge to save Judas from death and hell; but of all the others whom he had received as his Father's gift, he could say, "none of them is lost," (John 17:12). Thus he was faithful whilst he was on earth, and how faithful he is now!

May

The high priest under the law had two offices to execute; he had to offer sacrifice for the people, and to offer prayer and intercession for them. Throughout his life upon earth Jesus fulfilled the first in many ways, not just upon the cross; now in heaven he fulfils the second, as there making by virtue of his presence continual intercession for us.

"It is Christ that died, yea rather, that is risen again, who is even at the right hand of God, who also maketh intercession for us," (Rom. 8:34).

2nd

"Watch and pray, that ye enter not into temptation."
Matthew 26:41

The entering into temptation is a different thing from temptation itself. The instruction here is to enter not into temptation.

A temptation presents itself and draws near to us, but do we draw near to it? If conscience sounds an alarm, and we keep, so to speak, to the windward of temptation, we are for the present safe. Temptation is a pleasant shore which invites the unwary, but upon which the squall blows fiercely and without warning; it is a coast strewn with ten thousand wrecks and with the bleached bones of innumerable drowned mariners. Keep the ship's head to windward, and she may weather the point; neglect sail and helm, and she will go ashore.

David and Joseph sailed this coast and were exposed to a similar temptation. David entered into it, and fell; Joseph was kept from entering into it, and stood. In the country, you often see a footpath across a field; if we keep in it we are safe, but we may be tempted by various objects to diverge a little, to gather a flower, or saunter upon the banks of the river, or make a shortcut across the corner. Whilst we are in the footpath, temptation may be very near, but we have not yet entered into it. We are upon the borders of it, it has presented itself to our minds, but we have not yet entered into its territory.

Few, if any, enter into temptation without falling by it. The fly hovers around the spider's web, but only on touching does it enter into it. The bird flies around the fowler's snare, but only on pecking the bait is the trap sprung. The moth flutters around the candle, but only by entering the flame will it burn its wings.

The Lord's words were not, "watch and pray against temptation," but "watch and pray that ye enter not into temptation." Few come out of temptation as they entered into it. How clearly James has described the difference between enduring temptation and falling by temptation. He does not say, "Blessed is the man who is free from temptation," but "who endureth temptation," (Jas. 1:12). Blessed is the man who is kept in the path, who sees temptation on every side, but endures it and is not drawn out of the path by it, for "when he is tried, he shall receive the crown of life," (Jas. 1:12). He has fought the good fight, won the battle, and shall receive the crown.

He adds, "Let no man say when he is tempted, I am tempted of God," (Jas. 1:13). He must not say that the Lord presents temptation to him and is therefore chargeable with it if he falls, for "God cannot be tempted with evil, neither tempteth he any man, but every man is tempted, when he is drawn away of his own lust, and enticed."

There is no sin in temptation, for our Lord "was in all points tempted like as we are, yet without sin," (Heb. 4:15). Nor in lust is there practical, though there is speculative sin. It is when the two meet and embrace, when the will consents to the act, silencing the voice of God and conscience, that sin is produced.

Following the giving in to lust, following the consented act comes the fearful and fatal fruit, "and sin, when it is finished, bringeth forth death," (Jas. 1:15). That is, as I understand it, death in the conscience, guilt, condemnation, and misery, and the deadening of all the fruits and graces of the blessed Spirit.

3rd

"In that day shall the Branch of the Lord be beautiful and glorious."
Isaiah 4:2

Where in heaven or on earth can there be found such a lovely Object as the Son of God? "What is thy beloved more than another beloved?" (Song 5:9), ask the companions of the Bride. She has a ready answer, "My beloved is white and ruddy, the chiefest among ten thousand," (Song 5:10).

If, then, you have never seen any beauty in Jesus, you have never seen Jesus; he has never revealed himself to you; you never had a glimpse of his lovely face, nor a sense of his presence, nor a word from his lips, nor a touch from his hand. Howbeit if you have seen him by the eye of faith, and he has revealed himself to you even in a small measure, you have seen a beauty in him beyond all other beauties, for it is a holy beauty, a divine beauty, the beauty of his heavenly grace, the beauty of his uncreated and eternal glory. No earthly countenance can wear this beauty, no man or woman, not Adam, in all his unfallen innocency, nor his fair partner Eve, with all her virtue, grace, and dignity, for it is the beauty of the glorious Son of God, which he forever wears as the Son of the Father in truth and love."

And as he is "beautiful," so is he "glorious." Oh, what a glory does faith see sometimes in his eternal Deity, in his divine Sonship, in what he is in himself as the brightness of the Father's glory and the express image of his Person, and in what he is as made unto us wisdom and righteousness, sanctification and redemption! How glorious does he show himself to be in his atoning blood and dying love. Even as sweating great drops of blood in Gethsemane's gloomy garden, and as hanging in torture and agony upon Calvary's cross, faith can see a beauty in the glorious Redeemer, even in the lowest depths of ignominy and shame. Was there not a glory in his meek obedience, in his suffering patience, in his submission to his Father's holy will, in his uncomplaining resignation to the heaviest strokes of vindictive justice, in bearing our sins in his own body on the tree, and thus putting away sin by the sacrifice of himself? Yet more especially does faith see him glorious as rising from the dead and going up on high, and sitting down at the right hand of the Father, crowned with glory and honour and with all things put under his feet.

4th

"And the fruit of the earth shall be excellent and comely for those who are escaped of Israel."
Isaiah 4:2

By "the fruit of the earth" we may understand that gracious and holy fruit which grew upon the Branch for his church – and it seems to be called "the fruit of the earth," because it appeared on earth when our Lord was there. All his words, works, and ways are in view, together with all the parables, doctrines, precepts, and promises uttered by his mouth during the days of his flesh, but this is not all. We think also of the benefits and blessings that spring in the way of redemption out of his complex Person, and which grow as an holy fruit out of him, being the Branch, such as his atoning blood, his glorious righteousness, his dying love, his resurrection and ascension, and his power to save to the uttermost all that come unto God by him. These may all be considered as "the fruit of the earth," because they were wrought by him in and upon the earth, and done in the days of his flesh when his gracious feet were upon this earthly ball.

This fruit is "excellent" to the escaped of Israel. There is seen in it a divine excellency. Therefore, there is not a shadow of a fault to be found with it. It is perfect in all its parts; complete to the very centre, and therefore seen to be excellent, as so glorifying to God, and so adapted to every need and woe of those that are left in Zion and remain in Jerusalem.

It is "comely" too. In his sufferings, in his blood shedding, obedience, holy life and expiatory death, there is a surpassing comeliness, because in them shine forth a divine glory and a heavenly beauty. It is indeed the same word as is translated "beauty" in the holy garments made for Aaron by Moses, (Ex. 28:2), and clothed in which he ministered before the Lord when he went into the holy place. Even so our great High Priest now ministers within the veil in the holiness and beauty of his glorified humanity; and as this is seen and apprehended by faith, the Church sings,

"I sat down under his shadow with great delight, and his fruit was sweet to my taste," (Song 2:3).

"His glory is great in thy salvation - honour and majesty hast thou laid upon him," (Psa. 21:5).

5th

"Then shall we know, if we follow on to know the Lord." Hosea 6:3

We gather from these words that there is such a thing in soul experience as "a following on to know the Lord;" and indeed there is no obtaining the blessings which are laid up for the righteous, unless there is this following on. "To know the Lord" is the desire of every living soul; that is, to know him by his own divine manifestations, by the gracious revelation of his grace, his love, his presence, and his glory.

The expression, "follow on," implies that there are many difficulties, obstacles, and hindrances in a man's way, which keep him back from "knowing the Lord." Now the work of the Spirit in his soul is to carry him on in spite of all these obstacles. Nature, and all the work of nature, and all the power of Satan working on nature, is to draw the man back; but the work of the Spirit on the soul is to lead him forward. It is the work of the Spirit to keep alive in him the fear of God, to strengthen him from time to time with strength in his inner man, to give him those enlargements, to drop in those hopes, to communicate that inward grace, and to gird up the loins of his mind, so that in spite of sense, reason, and nature, he is compelled to follow on.

Sometimes he seems driven, and sometimes drawn, sometimes led, and sometimes carried, but in one way or another, the Spirit of God so works upon him that, though he scarcely knows how, he still "follows on." His burdens make him groan for deliverance; his temptations cause him to cry for help; the very difficulty and ruggedness of the road make him want to be carried every step, and he is compelled to cry out for a guide because of the intricacy of the path. In such a way, the Lord the Spirit working in the midst of, under, and through every difficulty and discouragement, still bears him forward, and carries him on; and thus brings him through every trial and trouble, every temptation and obstacle, until he sets him before the Lord in glory.

It is astonishing to me how our souls are kept alive. A living man is a marvel to himself, but a saint is a marvel to all. Carried on, and yet so secretly; worked upon, and yet so mysteriously; and led on, guided, and supported through so many difficulties and obstacles, that he is a miracle of mercy.

As the Apostle says, he is "a spectacle unto the world, and to angels, and to men," (1Cor. 4:9). The world wonders, the angels admire, and men stand astonished at how the quickened soul is carried on amid all its difficulties, obstacles, trials, and temptations, and yet in spite of all "following on."

To what end, then, is this "following on?" It is "To know the Lord," as the sum and substance of all religion, as the very marrow of vital godliness. It is to know Jesus, so as by faith to enter into his beauty and loveliness, and feel ourselves one spirit with him, according to those words, "He that is joined unto the Lord is one spirit," (1Cor. 6:17).

6th

"Brethren, I count not myself to have apprehended: but this one thing I do, forgetting those things which are behind, and reaching forth unto those things which are before, I press toward the mark for the prize of the high calling of God in Christ Jesus."
Philippians 3:13-14

Faith that rests short of believing in, laying hold of, and resting upon the Son of God in his finished work, will not be the work of faith that God will own and crown with his approbation. Likewise, love that never labours for an entrance into the mysteries of his dying love, will be found more a love in lip and tongue than in heart and life. It follows that hope which anchors anywhere short of the finished work of the Son of God, hangs upon a brittle cable which will snap asunder, or a rotten piece of iron which will part in the first heavy storm.

Do not rest in the knowledge of a few doctrines in the letter of truth. Do not take up with a few passing thoughts and feelings, and do not be satisfied with a few fleeting convictions or a few transient desires. Press on to know the blessed mysteries of the gospel as the food of your soul. Press on to know the Son of God, not only as a crucified man, not only as sweating blood in dark Gethsemane's garden, and agonising on Calvary's tree; but press on to know him as the exalted God-man.

Know him as the Mediator at the right hand of the Father, ever living to make intercession, and able to save to the uttermost all that come unto God by him. Press on to enjoy him as your living Head, distilling into you as a living member of his mystical body what the Psalmist calls, "the dew of his youth;" that is, the fruits of his resurrection, ascension and glorification, as manifested by the gifts and graces of the Holy Spirit.

Press onward to know the power of the precious gospel you profess, to enjoy it more in your soul, and to manifest its reality more in your conduct, your conversation, and your life.

7th

"For to be carnally-minded is death; but to be spiritually minded is life and peace."
Romans 8:6

One of the most blessed marks of regenerating grace, and one of the surest fruits of the love of God shed abroad in a renewed heart, is that spiritual-mindedness of which Paul declares it is "life and peace."

To be "spiritually-minded," to live and walk under the blessed power and influence of the Holy Spirit, to have the heart and affections drawn up from this poor, vain scene, to where Jesus sits at the right hand of God, this is the life of which Paul speaks. This is the life of God in the soul, with all its present blessedness and future glory, and all its 'peace'; for peace and rest are alone to be found in this path of union and communion with a glorified Redeemer.

In this sweet spirituality of mind, in these heavenly affections, and in this communion with the Lord at his own throne of grace, the life and power of godliness much consist. We trust we know, from what we have felt in our own bosom, what this sweet spiritual-mindedness is, and what are its blessed effects?

May

It is a key to unlock the Scriptures, for then we read them under the same sacred influence, and by the same divine teaching by which they were written. It is a door of prayer, for under these calm and peaceful emotions the soul, as if instinctively and necessarily, seeks communion with God. It is the fruitful parent of sweet meditation, for the truth of God is then thought over, fed upon, and found to be bread from heaven. It is the secret of all life and power in preaching, for unless the heart of the preacher be engaged in, melted by, and softened by the truth delivered, there will be a hardness in its delivery which will make itself sensibly felt by the living hearer.

It is furthermore the power of all spiritual conversation, for how can we talk with any unction or profit unless we are spiritually-minded and in that frame of soul wherein the things of God are our chief element, where they are the language of our lips because they are the delight of our soul?

But to be otherwise – to be carnally-minded on our knees, with the Bible open before our eyes, in the house of prayer, at the Lord's table, in the company of the family of God – what a burden to our spirit! What a condemnation to our conscience, what a parent of doubt and fear whether matters can be right between God and our own soul, when there is such a distance between him and us!

It is true that the most eminent saints and servants of God have their dead and dark seasons. Periods when the life of God seems sunk to so low an ebb as to be hardly visible, so hidden is the stream by the mud-banks of their fallen nature. Still it glides onward, round them, if not through them; and sometimes a beam of light falls upon it from above, as it threads its way toward the ocean of eternal love, which manifests not only its existence but its course, and that it gives back to heaven the ray it receives from heaven.

By these very dark and dead seasons, the saints and servants of God are instructed. They see and feel what the flesh really is, and how alienated from the life of God it must be. They learn in whom all their strength and sufficiency lies, and are taught that in them, that is, in their flesh, dwells no good thing. They discover that no exertions of their own can maintain in strength and vigour the life of God. They find that all they are and have, all that they believe, know, feel, and enjoy, with all their ability, usefulness, gifts, and grace, flows from pure sovereign grace, from the rich, free, undeserved, and yet unceasing goodness and mercy of God.

In this hard school of painful experience they learn of their emptiness and nothingness, and that without Christ indeed they can do nothing. Thus they become clothed with humility, that lovely, becoming garb; they cease from their own strength and wisdom, and learn experimentally that Christ is, and ever must be, all in all to them, and all in all in them.

May

8th

"For we have not an high priest which cannot be touched with the feeling of our infirmities; but was in all points tempted like as we are, yet without sin."
Hebrews 4:15

Our gracious Lord experienced temptation in every shape and form, for the word of truth declares that he was "in all points tempted like as we are, yet without sin." I wish to speak very cautiously upon this subject, for upon a point so difficult and so mysterious there is great risk of speaking amiss. So long as we keep strictly within the language of the Scripture we are safe, but the moment that we draw inferences from the word without special guidance by the Spirit of truth, we may greatly err.

You may think then, sometimes, that your temptations are such as our gracious Lord could never have been tempted by; but that word of the Apostle decides the question, "in all points tempted like as we are, yet without sin."

It is a solemn mystery which I cannot explain, how temptation in every point, shape, and form could assail the holy soul of the immaculate Redeemer. I fully believe that it is so. I see the grace and wisdom of it, and my faith acquiesces in it as a most blessed truth, but I cannot understand it.

I know also and believe, from the testimony of the word and that of my own conscience, that whatever temptations he was assailed with, not one of them could or did sully, stain, or spot his holy humanity. That humanity remained absolutely and perfectly a pure, unfallen, immortal nature, able to die by a voluntary act, but having in itself no seeds of sickness, mortality, or death. Even so, I read that, though thus possessed of a holy, pure, and spotless humanity, in everlasting union with his own eternal Deity, in all points he was tempted like as we are.

I cannot explain the mystery, and I do not wish to do so. I receive it as a mystery, in the same way as I receive that great mystery of godliness, "God manifested in the flesh," (1Tim. 3:16). Howbeit I still bless God that he was tempted in all points like as we are, for it makes him such a sympathising High Priest with his poor, exercised, tried, and tempted family here below.

I have sometimes compared the temptations which beat upon the soul of the Lord to the waves of the sea that dash themselves against a pure, white marble rock. The rock may feel the shock of the wave; but it is neither moved by it nor sullied. It may at times be all but buried by the fury of the sea, but it still stands unmoved, immovable in all its original firmness. When the tide recedes and the sun breaks forth upon its face, it still shines in all the brightness of the pure, glittering marble of which it is made. So none of the temptations with which the Lord was assailed moved the Rock of ages, or sullied the purity, holiness, and perfection of the spotless Lamb of God. They but made his beauty sparkle and shine ever brighter in the sea of sin.

9th

"And they shall call his name Emmanuel, which being interpreted is, God with us."
Matthew 1:23

We must never, even in thought, separate the human nature of our adorable Redeemer from his divine. Even when his sacred body lay in the grave, and was thus for a small space of time severed from his pure and holy soul by death and the tomb, there was no separation of the two natures. His human soul, after he had once become incarnate in the womb of the Virgin, never was parted from his Deity, but went into paradise in indissoluble union with it.

It is a fundamental article of our most holy faith that the human nature of the Lord Jesus Christ had no existence independent of his divine. In the Virgin's womb, in the lowly manger, in the lonely wilderness, on the holy mount of transfiguration, in the gloomy garden of Gethsemane, in Pilate's judgment hall, on the cross, and in the tomb, Jesus was still Immanuel, God with us. So ineffably close and intimate is the conjunction of the human nature with the divine, that the actings of each nature, though separable, cannot and must not be separated from each other.

Thus, the human hands of Jesus broke the seven loaves and the fish; but it was God-man who multiplied them so as to feed therewith four thousand men, besides women and children. The human feet of Jesus walked on the Sea of Galilee; but it was the Son of God who walked over the waves to the ship. The human lips of Jesus uttered those words which are "spirit and life," (John 6:63), but it was the Son of the living God who spoke them, (John 6:69). The human hands and feet of Jesus were nailed to the cross; but the blood shed by them was indeed divine, for all the virtue and validity of Deity were stamped upon it, (Acts 20:28).

May
10th

"And now, Lord, what wait I for? my hope is in thee."
Psalm 39:7

True religion is a very simple thing. Simplicity is stamped upon all the works of God, and especially upon the work of grace. The more genuine, therefore, our religion is, the more simple it will be. To be simple is to be child-like, and to be child-like is to have that mind and spirit without which no man can enter into the kingdom of heaven.

Can we, then, with this child-like simplicity, walk step by step here with David, and follow him throughout? Can we put our seal to these things, and say, "Lord, what wait I for?" Is your religion brought into this narrow point? "Truly my soul waiteth upon God: from him cometh my salvation," (Psa. 62:1). "My soul, wait thou only upon God; for my expectation is from him," (Psa. 62:5).

Such a frame of soul is indeed from the hand of God, for no man ever did, or could bring himself into it, and if we can enter into one part of these heavenly breathings, we shall be able also to enter into the others, and say, "my hope is in thee."

Feeling the weight and burden of sin, we shall be constrained to cry, "Deliver me from all my transgressions," (Psa. 39:8), and feeling our own weakness, and the evil of our hearts, we shall add, as did the psalmist, "make me not the reproach of the foolish," (Psa. 39.8).

If, then, we can sincerely, before God, employ these petitions, may we not ask who produced them? Who wrought this experience in the soul? From whose hands did it come? Surely, surely, the same Lord that taught David must have taught us? The same power that wrought in him must have wrought in us before we could, in sweet experience, enter into this feeling language, and adopt it as our own!

Here, therefore, we see a little of what true religion is. Here we see what are the genuine breathings of a child-like spirit, and what is the experience of a man of God; and it will be our mercy if we can see in David's experience a sweet counterpart of our own.

11th

"Herein is my Father glorified, that ye bear much fruit; so shall ye be my disciples."
John 15:8

When the Lord Jesus Christ was upon earth he was in a suffering state; and to this suffering image all his people must be conformed. In that suffering state he brought glory to God, but afterward was exalted to the right hand of the Father. In the same manner, those who suffer with him will also be glorified with him, and glorious indeed will they be, for they will shine like the stars forever and ever, resplendent in the glorified image of the Son of God. The Apostle therefore writes, "When Christ, who is our life, shall appear, then shall ye also appear with him in glory," (Col. 3:4).

The Lord did not assume angelic nature. He therefore did not adorn or beautify that nature; but by assuming our nature, the flesh and blood of the children into union with his own divine Person, he invested it with surpassing lustre. This is the foundation on which a redeemed sinner brings glory to God, not in himself, but as being a member of Christ, "For we are members of his body, of his flesh, and of his bones," (Eph. 5:30).

What a thought it is, that the lowest believer should actually bring more glory to God than the highest angel; and that the suffering obedience of a saint should be of higher value than the burning obedience of a seraph. To bring glory to God, then, should be our highest aim and most ardent desire. How the Lord urges this upon the consciences of his true disciples, "Herein is my Father glorified, that ye bear much fruit." A little fruit brings but little glory to God. It is in proportion to the amount of rich, ripe fruit that is borne upon the branches of the vine, that the Lord is glorified.

12th

"Ye are they which have continued with me in my temptations."
Luke 22:28

Satan brought all his artillery to bear upon the Son of God. He was permitted to try him to the utmost. It was the purpose of God, that his well-beloved Son should be tempted like as we are; and if you are God's, not a single temptation has beset you which did not beset the Lord of life and glory.

Are we tempted sometimes to doubt a God of providence? The Lord Jesus was similarly tempted, when Satan said to him, "Command that these stones be made bread," (Matt. 4:3).

Are we tempted to vain confidence and presumption? The Lord of life and glory was similarly tempted, when the prince of darkness said to him, "If thou be the Son of God, cast thyself down from hence," (Luke 4:9).

Are we often tempted to disbelieve that we are the children of God, and exercised at times with distressing suspicions and fears lest we have only a profession of religion, without its experimental power in our hearts? Satan repeated the same temptation many times against the Lord, when he said, "If thou be the Son of God;" as Deer says, "O, what an IF was there!"

Are we tempted to turn our backs upon the Lord for the sake of what the world offers? The Lord Jesus was similarly tempted when Satan said that he would give him all that he presented before his eyes when he took him upon the mountain top.

Are we ever tempted to turn from the true God and worship idols? The Lord of life and glory was similarly tempted when Satan with his infernal pride and cursed impudence proposed to the Son of God to worship him. The Son of God worship Satan!

Many, however, see a problem and ask, 'Was Jesus really tempted like I am? How can that be? He was pure, spotless, and holy; but I am full of corruption from the crown of my head to the soles of my feet. The Lord of life and glory had a perfect, unfallen nature, a holy human body, and a holy human soul, taken into union with Deity; but I have a fallen nature, defiled in body and polluted in soul. Can there be a resemblance in our temptations?'

I would ask, what is it in you that feels the burden of temptation when Satan injects his blasphemies into your mind? Is there not a 'something' in you which is grieved, I was going to say tortured, by these fiery darts? Is it the old corrupt nature, or is it not the new nature within you? And if the new nature, is not that nature holy and spotless? Is it not born of God, and therefore as holy as God is holy, and as pure as God is pure?

Thus just in the same way as your pure and holy nature that is born of God is grieved and distressed by the fiery darts of Satan, so was the holy soul of the Lord Jesus ten thousand times more grieved and tortured by the temptations of Satan presented before his pure and spotless mind. The disciples did not forsake their Lord, though so severely buffeted with these temptations; rather, according to the measure of their faith, they partook of them individually and personally, suffering as well as sympathising with him, being wounded, though in a far less degree, by arrows from the same bow.

And thus disciples today continue with Jesus in his temptations by suffering as members with their covenant Head, walking, most of them, in a daily path of trouble and sorrow, tempted mercilessly by Satan, so far as God permits. Tempted by the world and by their own evil hearts; tempted day by day to do everything from which their spiritual nature recoils; day by day tempted to do things which are hateful in the eyes of a pure God, and to them also when in their right mind.

13th

"And I appoint unto you a kingdom, as my Father hath appointed unto me."
Luke 22:29

For whom is this kingdom appointed? Is it for the proud, the presumptuous, the hypocritical, and the self-righteous? No, not for these.

Our Lord said "I appoint unto you," meaning you that "have continued with me in my temptations." It was for you that are tempted and exercised; you that walk in the paths of tribulation; you that follow in the print of the footsteps of a suffering Jesus. It is for you that know the painful exercises of temptation, and yet are strengthened with strength in your inner man, and have "resisted unto blood, striving against sin," (Heb. 12:4), so as not to be carried away or overwhelmed by it.

What kingdom is here being referred to? It is the same kingdom that the Father has given to Jesus. "I appoint unto you a kingdom, as my Father hath appointed unto me."

Now what is the kingdom which God the Father appointed unto his dear Son? Is it to sit upon a throne like an earthly monarch? To wear a diadem, and carry a sceptre?

"My kingdom," said Jesus, "is not of this world," (John 18:36). The kingdom of the Lord of life and glory was to make an end of sin, to abolish death, and "destroy him that had the power of death, that is, the devil," (Heb. 2:14). It is to reign spiritually in the hearts of his chosen; to be King and Lord in Zion, and to rule over the willing affections of his subjects. It is a kingdom of righteousness, peace, and joy in the Holy Spirit; a kingdom of grace set up by the blessed Spirit in the heart; a spiritual kingdom which none can see or enter into but those who are "born of the Spirit," (John 3:6).

His kingdom is a spiritual kingdom, and consists in having a people to see him as he is, a people to glorify him, a people to love him, and a people for him to love. A kingdom cannot be the same to sovereign and subject when it is of an earthly and temporal nature. Were the earthly monarch to impart his kingdom to his subjects, it would cease to be a kingdom, and would become a republic. It is not so with a spiritual kingdom.

Jesus does not diminish his own grace by imparting it to his people, nor does he lessen his own joy by shedding it abroad in their hearts, neither does he sully his own glory by communicating of it to his saints. Our sun has lost no measurable light or warmth by the countless millions of rays that have issued from it since it was created, and in like manner, the glorious Sun of righteousness loses none of the fullness that is in him by communicating of his grace and glory. In him dwells all the fullness of the Godhead bodily, unexhausted, and inexhaustible.

This kingdom then, which he appoints to his tried and tempted disciples, is the kingdom of grace in the heart. It is the kingdom of God in the soul and the presence of Jesus within. It is that kingdom spoken of in Daniel 2:44, as set up on the ruins of all the other kingdoms after they are broken in pieces.

14th

**"Lord, lift up the light of thy countenance upon us."
Psalm 4:6**

The cry of the Church has always been, "Lord, lift up the light of thy countenance upon us."

You may often feel as if immersed in the very shadow of death, and say with Heman, "I am counted with them that go down into the pit: I am as a man that hath no strength," (Psa. 88:4). Howbeit, the very feelings of death, the chill at your heart, and the cold sweat upon your brow, make you long for the appearance of him who is the Resurrection and the Life. They lead you to the one who can in a moment whisper, "Fear not, for I am alive for evermore, and have the keys of hell and of death," (Rev. 1:18).

You may be pressed down at times with the power of unbelief, and think and say there never was a heart like yours, so unable to believe, so doubting at every step. Yet this deep conviction of your wretched unbelief, which is the Spirit's work to show, (John 16:9), only makes you long for that living faith of which Christ himself is not only the Object, but the Author and Finisher.

You may be sunk at times in despondency, as to both your present and future state, but that makes you desire all the more to have a good hope through grace, as an anchor of the soul, both sure and steadfast. You may feel at times the guilt, and not only the guilt, but the dreadful power and prevalence of sin, but that only makes you long the more earnestly for manifestations of pardon and peace, that no sin may have dominion over you.

May

"The mouth of the Lord has spoken it," (Isa. 58:14), that sooner or later you shall have every needful blessing. The valley you now feel to be in shall be exalted; the mountain and hill shall be made low; the crooked shall be made straight, and the rough places plain, and your eye shall see the glory of the Lord. Christ shall be made precious to your heart; he will come sooner or later into your soul, and when he comes he will manifest himself as your Lord and your God.

And so you keep hanging, and hoping, and looking up until he appears; for your heart is still ever saying, 'None but Jesus can do helpless sinners good.'

15th

"And also I have withholden the rain from you, when there were yet three months to the harvest: and I caused it to rain upon one city, and caused it not to rain upon another city: one piece was rained upon, and the piece whereupon it rained not withered."
Amos 4:7

How powerless we are as regards the rain that falls from the sky! Who can go forth when the sun is shining in its brightness and bid the rain to fall? Or when rain is falling, who can go forth and restrain the bottles of heaven? He who gives us rain from heaven and fruitful seasons, filling our hearts with food and gladness, also turns a fruitful land into barrenness for the wickedness of those who dwell therein.

Equally sovereign is the blessing that God gives to the preached gospel. He holds the blessing in his own hand; it is his to give, and his to withhold. If he blesses, it is because he has promised it; but when, where, and to whom it shall come, is at his own sovereign disposal.

Yet what do we naturally desire when the earth is parched up for lack of rain? Knowing that there is rain stored up in the clouds above, and that when it does come it will produce beneficial effects, desires, if not prayers, go up that it may fall. In fact, the earth itself, parched and dried up by heat, the very ground itself, by the fissures and clefts which are made in the soil by a burning sun, silently, mutely, but still imploringly calls upon the rain to fall. Every dried up crack you see in July is as a silent mouth asking the rain to come down. The withered herbage, the cattle lowing in the field, the dried-up ponds and brooks, are all imploring that rain may fall, though not a word is uttered.

So it is in grace. The parched, withered, dried-up feelings of the soul are all so many mute mouths imploring God's blessing to come down. No, the very hardness, barrenness, and sterility felt in our heart when the blessing of God does not rest upon the word, are so many mute appeals to the God of all grace that his blessing would attend the word to our conscience. I say this because you may think sometimes that you are not praying for the blessing of God to rest upon the word because you may not be using vocal prayer, or you are not favoured with a spirit of supplication and grace.

God sees your unexpressed needs, and to those needs he has a kind regard. The babe need not, and indeed cannot ask in so many words for food. The cry of hunger is enough. Or even if too weak to cry, the mother knows the child is hungry by its restless movements; and she is as pleased to give the nutritious food as the babe is to receive it.

So you must not always measure the strength of your prayers by the mere vocal utterance you may give to them. The heart-searching God reads your needs, knows your desolate case, and sees your barren condition. As in the kingdom of his providence, he views from his holy throne the parched ground, and sends down showers because he sees its need; so in the kingdom of his grace he looks upon the parched condition of his people, and gives them spiritual rain because he knows their need.

16th

"In whom all the building fitly framed together groweth unto an holy temple in the Lord."
Ephesians 2:21

The body of Christ is at present scattered, and, if I may so speak fragmentary. Of the members of his mystical body some are now before the throne, "spirits of just men made perfect," and others are still passing through the wilderness. Another portion are yet in the world, alive in body but dead in trespasses and sins, uncalled by grace, destitute of the Spirit, and the final group at present are unborn, still hidden in the womb of time. Howbeit, this earth is the stage whereon ALL the members are from time to time brought into a vital, manifestive union with their living Head.

When I was a boy at school in London, Waterloo Bridge was building; and I and my playmates used to go sometimes to what was then called "The Stone Field," on the other side of the water, where the stones that now make up Waterloo Bridge were being

May

square chiselled. Every vestige of that field, I have no doubt, is gone, and the place covered with buildings; but there stands Waterloo Bridge; and those stones that I used to play upon as a boy now form a part of that beautiful structure which Canova, the great Italian sculptor, said it was alone worth coming to London to see.

Take the idea into spiritual things. The body of Christ is compared in Scripture to a building. "Built upon the foundation of the apostles and prophets, Jesus Christ himself being the chief corner stone; whom all the building fitly framed together groweth unto an holy temple in the Lord." Of this building believers are "living stones," (1Pet. 2:5), and many of them are still in the Stone Field, where they are being hammered and hacked, squared and chiselled by the hand of the great Architect. During this state, like the stones of Solomon's temple, which were hewn and squared at a distance, that "neither hammer nor axe nor any tool of iron [was] heard in the house, while it was in building," (1Kings 6:7), so are these living stones prepared for their future glory. The mallet and the chisel are at work upon them now day by day, that in due time they may fill their designed position in the spiritual building.

I remember well that all the stones which were strewn over the field were marked and numbered; and these figures no doubt denoted their intended position. Every stone so marked was in due time individually transferred to, and now occupies, the exact position that the architect designed for it.

So every living stone is marked and numbered for eternity. It is hewed and squared here in time, and will, in future glory, be placed by the hand of the divine Architect in that place of the spiritual building originally designed for it.

17th

"The statutes of the LORD are right, rejoicing the heart: the commandment of the LORD is pure, enlightening the eyes."
Psalm 19:8

As without a revelation of the doctrine of salvation we would not know how a sinner could be saved, and thus could not glorify God by our faith; so without a revelation of the law we would not know how to serve God, and thus could not glorify him by our obedience. Look at this point, believing child of God. You long to glorify God in your body and in your spirit, which are his, (1Cor. 6:20). You desire, whether you eat or drink, or whatever you do, to do all to the glory of

God, (1Cor. 10:31). There are times and seasons with you when you sigh and mourn over your barren, unprofitable heart and life, and earnestly long to think and speak and act to his honour and glory who has done so much for you in providence and grace. At least, if you have no such desires you are no Christian, and are at the best but a poor, worldly, dead professor.

When and how far do you live to God's glory? Only when and so far as your life, walk, and conduct harmonise with and are guided by the law in the word. For see the connection. We can only glorify God outwardly by doing his will, and we can only know that will, as regards our practical obedience to it, by the express revelation which he has given of it. Where is that revelation? In his word, and chiefly in the preceptive part of it, in the law. It is this which makes it "a lamp unto [our] feet, and a light unto [our] path," (Psa. 119:105).

David therefore cried out, "O that my ways were directed to keep thy statutes!" "Make me to go in the path of thy commandments," and "Order my steps in thy word," (Psa. 119:5, 35, 133), as feeling that it was only by walking in and by the word that he could please God and live to his praise.

We find thousands in this land who think they are doing God service with plans and schemes of their own devising, priding themselves on their good works. To echo what Augustine said of the ancient Roman virtues, these their duties and doings are but "splendid sins", or, to use the language of the Church of England regarding such works, because "they are not done as God has willed and commanded them to be done, we doubt not but they have the nature of sin."

18th

"Hereby know we that we dwell in him, and he in us, because he hath given us of his Spirit."
1John 4:13

A right knowledge and living experience of the Person, graces and operations of the Holy Spirit upon the soul, is a very essential thing. Man is so deeply sunk, so utterly fallen, so unable to bring himself back, that he needs this holy Teacher to lead him into a saving, experimental knowledge of the truth of God; for we know nothing but by his teaching, have nothing but by his giving, and are nothing but through his making. The more clearly, then, that we are led to see, and the more deeply we are taught to feel what we are as fallen sons and daughters of Adam, the more shall we feel our need of and value his blessed operations upon the heart and conscience.

Now, in the case of Aaron, (viewed both as a type of Christ and as personally ministering at the altar of the tabernacle, and thus consecrated to the office of high priesthood), it was not sufficient that he was washed or ceremonially clothed. Aaron had to be anointed by the holy anointing oil before he could stand in the sanctuary of God. So it is with a son of the Most High, one of "the kings and priests" that form "the royal priesthood," (1Pet. 2:9). It is not sufficient for him to be washed in the blood of the Lamb, and clothed in his justifying righteousness; he must be consecrated to God's service by the holy anointing. In other words he must be sanctified, regenerated, and renewed in the spirit of his mind, that, by being made a partaker of the divine nature, (2Peter 1:4), he may enter into a spiritual experience of the truth of God here, and enjoy the eternal pleasures which are at God's right hand hereafter.

From the very nature of the fall, it is impossible for a dead soul to believe in God, know God, or love God. Such a soul must be quickened into spiritual life before it can savingly know the only true God, and Jesus Christ whom he has sent. Thus there lies at the very threshold, and in the very heart and core of the case, the absolute necessity of the regenerating operations of God the Holy Spirit upon the soul. The very completeness and depth of the fall render the regenerating work of the Holy Spirit as necessary, and as indispensable as the redeeming work of the Son of God. The Apostle therefore puts them together, "but ye are washed, but ye are sanctified, but ye are justified in the name of the Lord Jesus, and by the Spirit of our God," (1Cor6:11).

If, therefore, the soul is to enter into eternal glory, it must be prepared for glory by being made a partaker of grace. It must, in this present life, in this time state, be made fit to be a partaker of the inheritance of the saints in light, and be capacitated whilst here below for the eternal fruition of the Triune God. This is achieved by receiving a new and heavenly nature begotten of the Holy Spirit, which as a pure spirit, (for "that which is born of the Spirit is spirit," John 3:6), is capable of seeing, enjoying, and eternally delighting in the open vision of the Deity as manifested in the glorious Person of the God-man.

19th

"And I will betroth thee unto me for ever; yea, I will betroth thee unto me in righteousness, and in judgment, and in lovingkindness, and in mercies."
Hosea 2:19

May

Communion with Christ begins below, in our time state. It is now that the mystery of the marriage union is first made known; now that espousals are entered into; now that the first kiss of betrothed love is given. The 'celebration of the marriage' is to come; but the original betrothal in heaven and the spiritual espousals on earth make Christ and the Church eternally one.

When then the husband becomes united to his wife in marriage, he engages thereby to love her, cherish her, feed her, clothe her, count her interests his interests, her honour his honour, and her happiness his happiness. So too with the blessed Jesus, when in the councils of eternity he betrothed the Church to himself, undertook to be to her and do for her everything that should be for her happiness and honour, perfection and glory.

His own words are, "I will betroth thee unto me forever; yes, I will betroth thee unto me in righteousness, and in judgment, and in loving-kindness, and in mercies. I will even betroth thee unto me in faithfulness; and thou shalt know the Lord," (Hos. 2:20). In the book of Isaiah he says, "For thy Maker is thine husband; the LORD of hosts is his name; and thy Redeemer the Holy One of Israel; The God of the whole earth shall he be called," (Isa. 54:5). And later, "For as a young man marrieth a virgin, so shall thy sons marry thee: and as the bridegroom rejoiceth over the bride, so shall thy God rejoice over thee," (Isa. 62:5).

There must be union before communion, marriage before possession, membership before abiding in Christ and he in us, a being in the vine before a branch issuing from the stem. It is the Spirit that quickens us to feel our need of him; to seek all our supplies in him and from him; to believe in him unto everlasting life, and thus live a life of faith upon him. By his secret teachings, inward touches, gracious smiles, soft whispers, sweet promises, and more especially by manifestations of his glorious Person, finished work, atoning blood, justifying righteousness, agonising sufferings and dying love, he draws the heart up to himself.

He thus wins our affections, and setting himself before our eyes as "the chief among ten thousand and altogether lovely," he draws out that love and affection towards himself which puts the world under our feet. All religion flows from his Spirit and grace, presence and power. He is our sun, and without him all is darkness; he is our life, and without him all is death; he is the beginner and finisher of our faith, the substance of our hope, and the object of our love.

May 20th

"For God, who commanded the light to shine out of darkness, hath shined in our hearts, to give the light of the knowledge of the glory of God in the face of Jesus Christ." 2Corinthians 4:6

When a man walks in the darkness and death of unregeneracy, he has no true light. He may indeed have a false light, as the light of presumption, delusion, or vain-confidence; but all such borrowed light is worse than darkness. As the Lord says, "If therefore the light that is in thee be darkness, how great is that darkness!" (Matt. 6:23).

The only saving light is the light of God shining into the soul, giving us to see and to know "the only true God, and Jesus Christ, whom thou hast sent," (John 17:3). A man may have the clearest light in his judgment, and yet never have the penetrating light of the Spirit producing conviction in his soul. He may have the soundest knowledge of the doctrines of grace, and see the harmonious scheme of salvation, and yet never have seen a holy God by divine teaching, nor have ever felt the spirituality of God's righteous law condemning him as a transgressor. Howbeit "the light of life," as the Lord calls it, is sure to guide its possessor aright. If we have it not, we shall be sure to go astray; we shall be entangled in some error, plunge into some heresy, imbibe some doctrine of devils, drink into some dreadful delusion, or fall into some dreadful sin, and 'concerning faith make shipwreck.'

A false light is something like the lights which pirates hold up to entrap ships to their destruction. It is like the fires, which the "wreckers," those dreadful characters in Cornwall, used to kindle on their coast in order that the mariner might mistake them for some friendly light-house, and run his vessel on the rocks where those heartless wretches plundered it.

A false light will but wreck us on the rocks of presumption or despair, but the light of divine life in the soul is accompanied with all the graces of the Spirit. It is the light of the glory of God, the light of Jesus' countenance, and the light of the Spirit's teaching, and therefore an infallible guide and guard.

As the Apostle says, "Ye have an unction from the Holy One, and ye know all things," (1John 2:20). This infallible pilot will guide the soul that is given to it safe into the harbour of endless rest and peace.

May 21st

"Who his own self bare our sins in his own body on the tree."
1 Peter 2:24

We beg of the Lord, sometimes, to give us a broken heart, a contrite spirit, a tender conscience, and a humble mind. Whilst such is good, it is only a view by faith of what the gracious Redeemer endured upon the cross when he bore our sins in his own body with all their weight and pressure, and with all the anger of God due to them, that can really melt a hard, and break a stony heart. No sight, short of this, can make sin felt to be hateful, can bring tears of godly sorrow out of the eyes, or can make sobs of true repentance wrack the breast. Only this view can draw out the deepest, humblest confessions before God of what dreadful sinners and base backsliders we have been before the eyes of his infinite Purity, Majesty, and Holiness.

What hope is there for our guilty souls; what refuge from the wrath of God so justly our due; what shelter from the curse of a fiery law, except it be in the cross of Jesus? O for a view of him revealed to the eyes of our enlightened understanding, as bearing our sins in his own body on the tree! O to see by the eye of faith, all that dreadful load which has caused us so much inward grief and trouble laid upon him. To see all those fearful backslidings and sad entanglements on which we can but reflect with shame and grief set to his account. O to see by the eye of faith all those words and thoughts and deeds which our conscience testifies against, and all those innumerable evils that we have missed and conscience has forgotten taken off our guilty head and put upon the head of the Lord the Lamb.

Can we get relief from any other source or is a reprieve to be found in any other way? There is no relief anywhere else! Where can you find pardon sealed upon your breast, forgiveness manifested to your soul, or any expectation of winning heaven and escaping hell, except in the cross? From where can you gain some testimony in your own bosom of a saving interest in that precious blood and righteousness, and where glean knowledge that the dear Redeemer bore your sins in his body on the tree?

I know, full well, that it requires special faith, a faith of God's own giving and raising up to believe this, an especial manifestation of salvation by the blood of the Lamb to the soul; a blessed bringing in of the power of Christ crucified to the heart.

I believe I do but speak the inmost conviction of every heart touched by the finger of God when I say, that until this is in some measure done, there is no solid relief and no true peace with God for man. Without such faith being given, there is no firm, abiding foundation on which we can stand as if for eternity, and there is nothing strong enough to banish the fear of death and open the gates of heaven.

22nd

"I have stuck unto thy testimonies: O LORD, put me not to shame."
Psalm 119:31

In whatever state or stage of experience you are, it will be your wisdom and your mercy to hold fast to God's testimony. Has the Lord just begun a work of grace in your heart? Is he showing to you what you are by nature, and bringing before your eyes the sins of your youth, and plunging you in deep convictions? It will be your wisdom, and it will be your mercy, to hold fast to that testimony; not to be driven from your standing into despair, nor pushed forward into fleshly confidence; but to hold fast to that testimony which God himself has implanted.

Has God made you to sigh and cry from the depths of a broken heart - to fall down before his truth? Hold fast to that testimony; he will not put you to shame. Again, if the Lord has done a little more for you, shown you the least glimpse of mercy and favour, and given you some little testimony of your saving interest in the blood of the Lamb, it will be your wisdom, and it will be your mercy, to hold fast to that testimony too. You will meet those who would push you presumptuously forward and those who would drive you despairingly backward. You will find such as would pull you down into the doubts and fears that exercise their own minds, and those who would draw you aside into the vain confidence in which they stand. It will be your wisdom and mercy to abide by the testimony which God himself has revealed. He alone can work in your soul that faith whereby you can and will hold fast to his testimony.

Howbeit some may say, 'How do I know that I am holding fast to God's testimonies?' I would ask, what are the feelings of your hearts towards them? Is there godly fear? Is there holy reverence? Is there trembling awe? Is there any exercise of soul? Any pouring out of the heart before God? Any realising of his presence? Any trembling lest you should offend him? Any desire after him? Any solemn feelings whereby your soul is exercised upon his perfections? Then there is reason to believe there is some testimony of God in your conscience, and that you are holding fast to it.

If your religion be such as leads to vain confidence, to self-righteousness, to presumption, to false security, and to a careless, light, trifling spirit, depend upon it – you are not holding fast to God's testimony, or else you have no testimony from God to hold fast unto. Rather, if the Lord is bringing into your soul some sense of his displeasure; if you have trifled with him, and brought guilt into your soul and trouble into your mind, it will be your wisdom, and it will be your mercy to do as the Lord speaks in Leviticus 26:41, 'accept the punishment of thy iniquity.' Put your mouth in the dust and confess your sin, do not turn aside to presumptuous confidence as though you would blunt the edge of God's sword in your soul, but receive it in your heart, embrace it in your conscience, and cleave to it as the testimony of God himself.

"I have stuck unto thy testimonies." To cleave to everything which God makes known in the conscience, be it judgment, be it mercy, be it a smile or be it a frown, that is our example. Whether it be a testimony for, or a testimony against, whatever it be that comes with power, and is brought to the soul by the application of the Spirit, cleaving to it keeps the soul in a safe and blessed spot.

23rd

"That he would grant unto us, that we being delivered out of the hand of our enemies might serve him without fear, in holiness and righteousness before him, all the days of our life."
Luke 1:74-75

The grand point in all true religion is to be brought by the blessed Spirit into that happy spot where we can serve the living God free from that guilt, bondage, darkness, doubt, and fear which often possess our mind, and are the worst enemies of our soul's peace. Although they are such enemies to all true peace and happiness, yet are they mercifully overruled for our spiritual good. They convince us from whence our help must come, they strip us thoroughly of all creature help and hope, and bring us to the spot where the Lord meets the soul in mercy, sheds abroad his love, and brings near a precious Christ.

We have no reason to thank bondage, guilt and the law, still less sin and Satan, for any work they have done which God has overruled for our good. And yet without some experience of these dead works and the bondage and guilt produced by them, we could not know what it was to have our conscience purged by the blood of sprinkling to serve the living God. There are reasons, therefore, and wise reasons on the part of God, why his children should be thus vexed and plagued.

It is not the 'revealed' will of God that his children should spend so many of their days in darkness, doubt, and fear. He has given us a glorious gospel; he has set before us in Jesus everything for our comfort and relief; he has promised to send his Holy Spirit to testify of Christ, and has filled his word with promises and invitations suited to every case. Howbeit, his 'secret will and purpose' is that we should be thus exercised and tried, and walk in this path of darkness and desolation that we might value more the precious liberty of the gospel, know more of what Christ is, and of what he has done to save us from the depths of the fall. That we might be more deeply indebted to the riches of free and sovereign grace, and come more personally into the blessedness of gospel mercies as made known to our soul by a divine power.

24th

"Surely, shall one say, in the Lord have I righteousness and strength."
Isaiah 45:24

Have you yet learned that you are a sinner in the sight of God? Have you ever felt the length, breadth, and spirituality of his holy law? Do you feel in your very soul that without Christ's righteousness being imputed to you, and his blood being sprinkled upon your conscience, you must die in your sins and never reach the heavenly shore? Has this ever been, or is it still a matter of anxious solicitude to you? Has it ever caused sighs and groans to come out of your heart? Has the spirit of prayer ever been given, to make you plead with the Lord for the forgiveness of your sins, through the merits of a crucified Saviour? And have you any hope but in his blood, righteousness, and finished work?

Now if the Lord has been pleased to exercise your soul in this way, if he has not yet granted the longing desire of your heart, he certainly will in due time reveal his dear Son in you as the God-man who has saved you from death and hell. He will apply his atoning blood to your conscience, bring near his glorious righteousness, shed abroad his dying love, give and strengthen faith, and draw it forth into a blessed assurance of your saving interest in the Son of his love.

Howbeit, if your manifestations should not be very bright and conspicuous, he will give you a good hope through grace, as an anchor of the soul both sure and steadfast; and will draw up your affections to that blessed Lord who sits at the right hand of the Father in power, majesty, and glory. Moreover, as he does this, he enables the believer thus favoured and blessed to take these words into his lips, "In the Lord have I righteousness."

He cannot say it before. He may know that there is no righteousness but in the Lord; he may have utterly renounced his own; he may have sunk very deep into guilt and bondage; but until the Lord the Spirit is pleased to liberate him, he cannot come forth into that liberty. Until he has the witness of the Spirit he cannot cry, "Abba, Father," (Gal. 4:6).

But when the Lord is pleased to bring near his righteousness, to reveal his dying love, and to shed it abroad in his heart by divine power, then he can say, "In the Lord have I righteousness." And when he has this, he wants no other; it is complete, which no other can be. It is acceptable to God; it is available in the courts of heaven; it will bear him up through all the storms of time; it will smooth a dying pillow, and land him safely in a glorious eternity.

25th

"Awake, O north wind; and come, thou south; blow upon my garden, that the spices thereof may flow out. Let my beloved come into his garden, and eat his pleasant fruits."
Song of Solomon 4:16

We are, most of us, so fettered down by the chains of time and sense, the cares of life and daily business, the weakness of our earthly frame, the distracting claims of a family, and the miserable carnality and sensuality of our fallen nature, that we live at best a poor, dragging, dying life.

We can take no pleasure in the world, nor mix with a good conscience in its pursuits and amusements; we are many of us poor, moping, dejected creatures, from a variety of trials and afflictions. We have a daily cross and the continual plague of an evil heart and get little consolation from the family of God or the outward means of grace. We know enough of ourselves to know that in self there is neither help nor hope, and never expect a smoother path, a better,

May

wiser, holier heart, or to be able to do tomorrow what we cannot do today.

As then the weary man seeks rest, the hungry food, the thirsty drink, and the sick health, so do we stretch forth our hearts and arms that we may embrace the Lord Jesus Christ, and sensibly realise union and communion with him. From him come both prayer and answer, both hunger and food, both desire and the tree of life. He discovers the evil and misery of sin that we may seek pardon in his bleeding wounds and pierced side. He makes known to us our nakedness and shame, and, as such, our exposure to God's wrath, that we may hide ourselves under his justifying robe of righteousness. He puts gall and wormwood into the world's choicest draughts, that we may have no sweetness but in and from him, and he keeps us long fasting to endear a crumb, and long waiting to make a word precious.

He wants the whole heart, and will take no less; and as this we cannot give, he takes it to himself by ravishing it with one of his eyes, with one chain of his neck. If we love him, it is because he first loved us; and if we seek communion with him, it is because he will manifest himself to us as he does not unto the world.

Would we see what the Holy Spirit has revealed of the nature of this communion? We shall find it most clearly and experimentally unfolded in the Song of Solomon. From the first verse of that book, "Let him kiss me with the kisses of his mouth," to the last expressed desire of the loving bride, "Make haste, my beloved, and be thou like to a roe or to a young hart upon the mountains of spices," all is a 'song of loves'. All a divine revelation of the communion that is carried on upon earth between Christ and the Church.

She "cometh up from the wilderness, leaning upon her beloved," (Song 8:5), and "his left hand should be under [her] head, and his right hand should embrace [her]," (Song 8:3). She says, "Look not upon me, because I am black," (Song 1:6), but he tells her, "Thou art all fair, my love; there is no spot in thee," (Song 4:7).

At one moment she says, "By night on my bed I sought him whom my soul loveth: I sought him, but I found him not," (Song 3:1), and then she cries again. "It was but a little that I passed from them, but I found him whom my soul loveth: I held him, and would not let him go, until I had brought him into my mother's house, and into the chamber of her that conceived me," (Song 3:4).

Comings and goings; sighs and songs; vain excuses and cutting self-reflections; complaints of self, and praises of him; the breathings of love, and the flames of jealousy; the tender affections of a virgin heart, and the condescending embraces of a royal spouse. Such is the experience of the Christian, in seeking or enjoying communion with Christ as described in this divine book.

May 26th

"Sanctify them through thy truth - thy word is truth."
John 17:17

When the gospel comes 'not in word only, but also in power,' (1Thes. 1:5), it comes "in the Holy Ghost," that is, in and with the teaching and testimony of the Holy Ghost. It is this coming "in the Holy Ghost" which gives the truth in its power such a sanctifying influence upon the heart.

It may be that you ask, 'What is a sanctifying influence?'

It is the communication of holy feelings, heavenly desires, and gracious affections, and the breathing into the soul of that sweet spirituality of mind which is life and peace.

If we are among the people of God, "he hath chosen us in him before the foundation of the world, that we should be holy and without blame before him in love," (Eph. 1:4). If he chastens us in this world, it is "for our profit, that we might be partakers of his holiness," (Heb. 12:10). It is this holiness of heart, this heavenly-mindedness to which I refer when I speak of the sanctifying influence of truth in its power.

Now did truth ever come into your soul with any measure of this sanctifying influence? Did you ever long to get away from the chapel, go home to your room, fall upon your knees, and have blessed fellowship with the Father and his Son Jesus Christ? And were you ever so favoured when you did get home? Or sometimes when alone, in reading, or meditation, or secret prayer, did the word of God ever come into your soul with that sweet unction, savour, and dew that it seemed to make the very room in which you were holy ground?

I remember when God was pleased to reveal his dear Son to my soul in my sick room many years ago, I was afraid almost to go out of my room lest I should lose the sweet, holy feelings and blessed spirituality of mind which I then and there enjoyed. Depend upon it, there is a holiness of heart and affection, an inward holiness, without which no man shall see the Lord. Depend still more upon it, that whenever truth comes into a believer's soul, it comes with that sanctifying influence, which not only gives him a fitness for, but is a blessed foretaste of the inheritance of the saints in light.

May 27th

**"Husbands, love your wives, even as Christ also loved the church, and gave himself for it; that he might sanctify and cleanse it with the washing of water by the word."
Ephesians 5:25-26**

View the Church without the sanctifying operations and influences of regenerating grace, and she is far from Christ. She has no desire towards him, no manifest union or communion with him, no faith in his blood, no hope in his mercy, no love to his name. Were she left always thus, where would be her fitness for heaven?

Yet when the word of truth comes with power, accompanied by the influences of the Holy Spirit to the heart, then there is not only a cleansing of the conscience from the guilt and filth of sin, but there is the communication of a new heart and a new spirit. How plainly is this spoken of by the prophet Ezekiel, where, after the promise, "From all your filthiness, and from all your idols will I cleanse you," it is added, "A new heart also will I give you, and a new spirit will I put within you," (Ezek. 36. 25-26).

We have not only therefore to be washed from our sins in the blood of the Lamb, not only to be pardoned and forgiven and thus have a title to heaven, but we need a fitness for heaven. We need a new heart and a new spirit given to us whereby we may taste, handle, feel, and enjoy the love of Christ as shed abroad in the heart, and through which we may experience the flowings forth of love to him in return. As then the blood cleanses, so the Spirit sanctifies. John therefore says, "This is he that came by water and blood, even Jesus Christ; not by water only, but by water and blood," (1John 5:6). The blood is the blood of the atonement; the water is the sanctifying influences of the Holy Spirit.

Observe in our text the order in which the blessings come. First, is the love of Christ in eternity; secondly, the gift of himself in time; thirdly, the cleansing by blood; fourthly, the sanctifying by the Spirit. Now look at these things for yourselves. Are your sins pardoned? Have you any evidence that you are washed in the blood of the Lamb? Do you believe that you are going to heaven? What does your belief of this, or your hope in it, rest upon? Where are your evidences? Surely not from merely seeing these truths in the Scripture as the bare revelation of God, or believing them from my statements. Such a faith and such a hope, if you have no better, will prove delusive, and will leave you in the hands of him who is a consuming fire.

If your hope of eternal life is well grounded, it is because the word of life has come into your SOUL, and you have been not only cleansed by the application of the blood of sprinkling to your conscience, but sanctified and renewed by the power of the word, through the Holy Spirit, upon your heart.

28th

"That he might present it to himself a glorious church, not having spot, or wrinkle, or any such thing; but that it should be holy and without blemish."
Ephesians 5:27

We do not now see what the Church one day will be, and what she ever was in the eyes of Christ. He looked beyond this world, beyond all the sins and sorrows of our sojourn here, and fixed his eye upon the bridal day, the day when before assembled angels, in the courts of heaven, in the realms of eternal bliss, he should present her to himself a glorious Church, with no spot or wrinkle or any such thing, but holy, and without blemish.

O what a day will that be, when the Son of God shall openly wed his espoused bride; when there shall be heard in heaven, "the voice of a great multitude, and as the voice of many waters, and as the voice of mighty thunderings, saying, Alleluia: for the Lord God omnipotent reigneth. Let us be glad and rejoice, and give honour to him: for the marriage of the Lamb is come, and his wife hath made herself ready," (Rev. 19:6-7).

How cleansed, how sanctified, how washed, how clothed must the Church be in that day when the very eyes of omniscience, which can read the slightest departure, even a wrinkle, from infinite purity, will find in her neither spot nor blemish, so that God himself in all the blaze of his holiness may say of the Church, 'I have viewed her with an omniscient eye; I have looked at every member of the mystical body of my dear Son; I have examined each with all the eyes of Godhead; but there is no spot, there is no wrinkle, no blemish in any one of them; all are complete in him; all stand accepted in the Beloved.'

But you may ask, and this is an inquiry well worth pressing upon your conscience, 'How am I to know that I shall stand at that day without spot or wrinkle?' To answer that inquiry, I ask, what do you know of the cleansing, sanctifying influences of regenerating grace? What do you know of the word of truth laying hold of your conscience, of the word of power coming into your heart, of the blood of Christ being applied, and the love of God shed abroad in your heart by the Holy Spirit?

If, when you are called away from these lower scenes, you have been blessed with a living faith in the Son of God, with the application of his love and blood to your conscience, it will open to you a glorious eternity, forever delivered from all your present sins and sorrows, fears and anxieties. You will be presented at the great day among that glorious Church, which has neither spot nor wrinkle nor any such thing.

But if you live and die without any saving interest in these heavenly blessings, would I be faithful to my commission and to my conscience, if I were to say it will be all well with you? Would it be right to say that you have only on your deathbed to send for a minister to pray by your bedside, to give you the sacrament, and to speak a few comfortable words, and it will be all right with your soul? Would I be faithful to my commission to encourage such a delusion as this, a delusion by which tens of thousands are daily deceived?

I dare not do it. I lift up my voice and cry aloud, 'There is no salvation past, present, or future, but what flows through the precious blood of the Lamb, and is made experimentally known to the soul by the power of the Holy Spirit.'

29th

"Holding faith, and a good conscience; which some having put away concerning faith have made shipwreck."
1Timothy 1:19

We find that, in the Apostle's time, there were people who held faith, or rather what they called faith, and put away "good conscience." He mentions by name, "Hymeneus and Alexander, whom he had delivered unto Satan," that is, excommunicated them out of the Church, as heretics and blasphemers. If to have put good conscience away, stamps a man as unfit for the visible Church of God, it behoves us to search whether we have this weapon at our side, and in our hand.

What then does the Apostle mean by "a good conscience?" I believe he means a conscience alive in God's fear, a spiritual conscience, a tender conscience, what he calls, in another part, "a pure conscience;" "holding faith in a pure conscience," that is, purified from ignorance, from guilt, from the power of sin, "a conscience void of offence toward God and men." Wherever, then, there is living faith in the soul, there will be united with it "a good conscience." The Lord never sends forth a soldier to fight his battles with the weapon of faith only; he puts faith in one hand and "a good conscience" in the other. He that goes forth with what he thinks to be faith, but casts aside "a good conscience," will manifest himself to be one of those characters, who, "concerning faith make shipwreck."

Why is it called "a good conscience?" Because it comes down from God, who is the Author of all good, the Giver of "every good gift, and of every perfect gift," (Jas. 1:17). There is none good but he, and there is nothing good but what he himself implants and communicates. This weapon of a good conscience, with which the Lord arms his soldiers, works with faith, as well as proves the sincerity of faith, and tests its genuineness and reality. Faith, without a good conscience, is dead. It bears upon it the mark of nature, and however high it may rise in confidence, or however it may seem to abound in good works, it is not the faith of God's elect, of which the end is the salvation of the soul.

How therefore does a good conscience work with faith? What is the connection between these two weapons, and how do they mutually support and strengthen each other? In this way. What faith believes, a good conscience feels; what faith receives, a good conscience holds; what faith embraces, a good conscience holds fast. When faith is weak, a good conscience is feeble, but when faith is strong, a good conscience is hard at work. They grow and they wane together, and, like two stems from one root, together do they flourish and fade.

Only he who goes forth with faith in the one hand and 'a good conscience' in the other wars a good warfare. Faith strengthening conscience and conscience strengthening faith, each doing their separate office but still tending to one end; each accomplishing the work which the Lord has appointed, and yet each fighting the Lord's battles, and carrying the soldier safe and victorious over his enemy.

30th

"But my God shall supply all your need according to his riches in glory by Christ Jesus."
Philippians 4:19

If there were no Christ Jesus, then there could be no supplying of our needs. Howling in hell would our miserable souls be, unless there were a Mediator at the right hand of the Father. Lost forever without a blessed Jesus full of love, pity, and power, co-equal and co-eternal in his divine nature with the Father and the Holy Spirit, and yet the God-Man in whom "it pleased the Father that in him should all fullness dwell," (Col. 1:19).

If there were not such a blessed Mediator at the right hand of God, not one drop of spiritual comfort, not one particle of hope, not one grace or fruit of the Spirit to distinguish us from the damned in hell, would ever be our lot or portion. Oh! May we never forget the channel through which these mercies come. May we never, for one moment, think that they could come through any other Person or in any other way, than through God's only begotten Son, now, in our nature, at his right hand as our Advocate, Mediator, and Intercessor with the Father.

And this supply is "according to his riches in glory" which is, I believe, a Hebrew idiom, signifying his glorious riches – riches so great, so unlimited, so unfathomable, raising up the soul to such a height of glory, that they may well be called 'glorious'. And these are "by Christ Jesus." They are stored up in him, locked up in him, and supplied freely out of him, just according to the needs and exercises of God's people.

31st

"For the flesh lusteth against the Spirit, and the Spirit against the flesh: and these are contrary the one to the other: so that ye cannot do the things that ye would."
Galatians 5:17

The Holy Spirit is especially tender of his own work upon the soul. He originally formed it – it is his own spiritual offspring; and as a mother watches over her babe, so the blessed Spirit watches over the spirit of his own creating. It is the counterpart of himself, for it is the spirit that he has raised up in the soul by his own almighty power. He, therefore, acts upon it, breathes into it fresh life and power, and communicates grace out of the inexhaustible fullness of the Son of God, thus enabling the spirit to breathe and act, struggle and fight against the flesh, so that the latter cannot have all its own way, but must submit and yield. For the spirit can fight as well as the flesh. It can act as well as the flesh, and it can desire good as well as the flesh can desire evil.

What a mercy it is that there are those heavenly breathings in our soul of the spirit against the flesh, and those cryings out to God against it. What a mercy it is that the spirit within us thus takes hold of the arm of Omnipotence outside us and seeks help from the Lord God Almighty, and by strength thus communicated fights against the flesh, and gains at times a most blessed victory over it.

For what can the flesh do against the spirit when it is animated by divine power? What are sin, Satan, and the world when they have to oppose a Triune God in arms? This makes the victory sure, that our friends are stronger than our foes, and the work of God upon our soul greater than anything sin, Satan, or the world can bring against it.

This made the Apostle say, after he had been lamenting the inward conflict, "I thank God through Jesus Christ our Lord," (Rom. 7:25). When he had further enumerated the opposition that the Christian has to endure on every side, he cries out, as if in holy triumph, "Nay, in all these things we are more than conquerors through him that loved us," (Rom. 8:37).

June

June 1st

"Who is he that condemneth? It is Christ that died, yea rather, that is risen again, who is even at the right hand of God, who also maketh intercession for us."
Romans 8:34

As the soul is led and taught by the Spirit, it follows the Lord through all the various acts and sufferings of his life. The first spot to which the Holy Spirit takes the poor sinner is the cross of Jesus. That is the first real saving view we get of the Lord of life and glory; the Holy Spirit taking the poor guilty sinner, laden with the weight of ten thousand sins, to the foot of the cross, and opening his eyes to see the Son of God bleeding there as an atoning sacrifice for sin. To be brought there by the power of the Holy Spirit, and receive that blessed mystery of the bleeding, suffering, and agonising Son of God into our hearts and consciences, is the first blessed discovery that God the Spirit favours us with.

Next, we pass on to see Jesus laid dead in the sepulchre; for we have to die ourselves, and we need to see the Forerunner who has entered into the grave for us. We need to feel that we can lie down in the grave, and see that narrow bed in which our body will one day be stretched, in a measure perfumed by Jesus having lain there before us.

Later, when we have travelled from the cross to the sepulchre, we go a step farther to the resurrection of the Lord of life and glory. On the third day, we view him by faith springing out of that earthly tomb in which he lay, rising up in glory and power for our justification, and thus we see in the resurrection of the Lord Jesus the hope of the soul for a blessed immortality.

Yet we do not tarry there. As the Lord the Spirit gives us eyes to see, and moves our heart to feel, we travel on another pace to the ascension of the Lord of life and glory. We tarry not on earth, (for he tarried not here), but mounting up we see him sitting at the right hand of the Father, as the Mediator between God and man, as the divine Intercessor, as the glorious Head of grace. We see him communicating out of his own fullness gifts and graces unto poor and needy souls who are living in daily and hourly bankruptcy. These need to receive perpetual supplies of life, light, and grace out of his fullness to keep them in the way wherein the Lord has set their feet.

We see then that the ascension of the Lord Jesus up on high, and his sitting at the right hand of God, when received into the conscience under the power of the Spirit, is not a dry doctrine. It is not a dead bone of a withered skeleton; but is so connected with all the feelings of our heart, with all our misery and ruin, with all our wretchedness, with all our guilt, with all our daily needs, and with all our hourly necessities, that, when led by the Spirit's teaching to look at this Mediator at the right hand of the Father, it becomes a truth full of blessed sweetness and power to the heaven-taught soul.

2nd

"All that the Father giveth me shall come to me; and him that cometh to me I will in no wise cast out."
John 6:37

Now, poor sinner, upon whose head the beams of a fiery law are darting; now, poor sinner, distressed in your mind, guilty in your conscience, plagued with a thousand temptations, beset by innumerable doubts and fears, can you not look up a little out of your gloom and sadness, and see that the eternal God is your refuge? Do you not cleave to him with the utmost of your power, as being beaten out of every other refuge? Have you not taken hold of his strength that you may make peace with him? Are you not looking to him? He has invited you to, "Look unto me, and be ye saved, all the ends of the earth: for I am God, and there is none else," (Isa. 45. 22). He bids you look at him as Moses bade the Israelites look to the bronze serpent. Poor sinner, groaning under the weight of your transgression, he bids you look to him.

Has the blessed Lord, he into whose lips grace was poured, not said here in our verse, "Him that cometh to me I will in no wise cast out?" Why should you not look? Why should you not come to him? Will he cast *you* out? Do you not feel the secret drawings of his grace, and movements upon your heart, which make you, come often with strong crying and tears, with groans and sighs, earnest, vehement, and continual supplications? What are these but the inward teachings of God, as our Lord said, "It is written in the prophets, And they shall be all taught of God. Every man therefore that hath heard, and hath learned of the Father, cometh unto me," (John 6:45).

The Lord himself said, that no man can come to him except the Father who has sent him draws him. Therefore these comings of your soul in earnest and vehement desire are, according to his own testimony, from the special teachings and gracious drawings of God in you. Having made his dear Son to be the refuge of your soul, he is now drawing you unto him that you may find pardon and peace in him.

Yet perhaps you will say, 'I am so sinful, so guilty, I have been a sinner much worse than you can form any conception of; and it is this which sinks me so low.' Are you lower than brother Jonah when he was in the whale's belly, and, in his own feelings, in the belly of hell? Had he not deliberately turned his back on God and fled from him? What said he in his plight? "Yet I will look again toward thy holy temple," (Jon. 2:4).

Can you not also look again toward the holy temple? Is his mercy clean gone forever? David felt and feared that was his case but it was not so, for "his mercy endureth forever," (Psa. 106, 107, 118, 136 etc.). The psalmist oft repeated that phrase, and it is a long and strong word. Return unto him. Look and live, look and live!

3rd

"In whom also after that ye believed, ye were sealed with that holy Spirit of promise."
Ephesians 1:13

Sealing is subsequent to believing. "In whom also after ye believed, ye were sealed." In legal documents the writing always precedes the sealing. Sealing is the last act, and follows even the signing, putting an attesting stamp on the whole document from the first word to the last signature. So also in grace.

The Spirit begins the work. He writes the first lines of divine truth on the soul; he makes the first impression on the heart of stone, which under his operation becomes a heart of flesh; he writes every truth that he thus makes known on the fleshy tables of the heart. He thus gives faith and hope, and then he comes with his special inward witness, and seals the truth and reality of his own work, so as not only to make it plain and clear, but to ratify and confirm it beyond all doubt and fear, questioning or dispute, either by our self or others.

The work of God on the soul sometimes seems to lie as if dead and dormant; little prayer goes up, and little answer comes down. Then doubts and fears arise whether the work be genuine, and much bondage and darkness sensibly gather over the mind like a dark and gloomy cloud, which much obscures the handwriting of the divine finger. Now the blessed Spirit revives his work by some application of the word with power, some softening and melting of the hard heart by his divine influence, some communication of a spirit of prayer, some discovery of the gracious Lord, some strengthening of faith, a reviving of hope, and a drawing forth of love. He thus puts the seal on his own work, and stamps it as genuine.

Under the sweetness and blessedness of this attesting seal many a poor child of God can look back to this and that testimony, this and that Ebenezer, this and that hill Mizar, this and that deliverance, blessing, manifestation, answer to prayer, special season under the word or on his knees, which were almost lost and buried in unbelief and confusion. The Spirit, especially when he bears witness with our spirit that we are the children of God, and sheds abroad the love of God in our heart, becomes in us the Spirit of adoption whereby we cry, "Abba, Father." In this way is his sealing manifest unto us and complete.

4th

"For all have sinned, and come short of the glory of God." Romans 3:23

What is it to "come short of the glory of God?" It is to act without a view to his glory. Now everything that we have ever done, which has not been done with a single, that is pure eye to God's glory, has the brand of sin stamped upon it. Which of us in an unregenerate state, as the fallen child of a fallen parent, ever had an eye to the glory of God? Did such a thing ever enter into any man's natural heart as to speak to God's glory, act to his glory, consult his glory, and live to his glory? Before ever such a thought or such a desire can enter our breast, we must have seen Him who is invisible; we must have had a view by faith of the glory of the triune God; we must have had a single eye given us by the Holy Spirit to see that glory outshining all creature good.

Every movement, then, of the selfish heart, every desire to gratify, please, and exalt self, is a coming short of the glory of God. This stamps all natural men's religious services with the brand of sin. It leaves the religious in the same dreadful state as the irreligious; it hews down the professing world with the same sword that cuts down the profane world. When men in a state of nature are what is called 'religious,' is their religion's end and aim the glory of God, the glory of free grace, the glory of the Mediator between God and man, the glory of the Holy Spirit, the only Teacher of God's people? Take it in its best, its brightest shape, is it not another form of selfishness, to exalt their own righteousness, and climb to heaven by the ladder of their own doings?

Is not this a coming short of the glory of God? Besides that, the very glory of God requires that every one accepted in his sight should be without spot, speck, stain or blemish. A pure God cannot accept, cannot look upon, cannot be pleased with impurity; and just in proportion to the infinite purity and ineffable holiness of Jehovah, must all impurity, all carnality, all unholiness, and the slightest deviation from absolute perfection be hateful and horrible in his sight.

Now, those of the 'election of grace' are brought more or less to feel all of this. It is the solemn and indispensable preparation of the heart for mercy; it is the introduction by the hand of the Spirit into the antechamber of the King of kings. It is the bringing of the soul to that spot, that only spot, where grace is felt, received, and known. It is, therefore, utterly indispensable for the 'election of grace', for all the ransomed and quickened family of God, to have this felt in their conscience, that they "have sinned, and come short of the glory of God."

5th

"Having therefore, brethren, boldness to enter into the holiest by the blood of Jesus."
Hebrews 10:19

Nothing will satisfy a living soul but coming "into the holiest." He wants to have communion with God, the holy, holy, holy Lord God of hosts. He is not dealing with a God distant and afar off – an idol, a God in whom he has neither faith, nor hope, nor love; who can neither see, nor hear, nor save; a God of his own conception or of some indistinct, traditional opinion. Rather, he feels in his very conscience that he is carrying on a sacred and holy communion with the God of heaven and earth, the God who has made himself in some measure known to his soul as the God and Father of the Lord Jesus Christ. With him he has to do; to him he must come; and with him he must hold holy communion. Before his heart-searching eyes he feels that he stands; into his ever-open ears he pours his petition; to his mercy and pity he appeals; his compassion he craves; his love he seeks; his salvation he longs for; and his presence above all things he earnestly desires. Therefore he must come into the holiest, for there God dwells; and to come unto God is to come there.

The man who thus feels and acts is an Israelite indeed in whom there is no deceit; one of the true circumcision who worship God in the Spirit, rejoice in Christ Jesus, and have no confidence in the flesh. Others are satisfied with the courts of the house, with admiring the external building, or the painted windows, carved pews, and long drawn aisles; with the mere worship of God as so much lip service, but the living soul goes beyond all that into the very heart of the sanctuary itself.

As the high priest on the day of atonement did not tarry among the people in the court, nor with the priests in the holy place, but pressed on, ever pressed on through the thick veil until he got into the holy of holies; so with the saint of God. He does not tarry in the outer court with the profane, nor in the sanctuary with the professor, satisfied only with seeing God with a veil between. He must come into that immediate presence of God, where he may see something of his grace, behold something of his glory, feel something of his mercy, and taste something of his power. It is this desire which makes him press forward into the holiest.

6th

"Go and cry in the ears of Jerusalem, saying, Thus saith the LORD; I remember thee, the kindness of thy youth, the love of thine espousals, when thou wentest after me in the wilderness, in a land that was not sown."
Jeremiah 2:2

If we look at salvation, we shall see that it consists of three parts; salvation past, salvation present, and salvation future. Salvation past consists in having our names written in the Lamb's book of life before the foundation of the world. Salvation present consists in the manifestation of Jesus to the soul, whereby he betroths it to himself. Salvation future consists in the eternal enjoyment of Christ, when the elect shall sit down to the marriage-supper of the Lamb, and be forever with the Lord. Now, none will ever enjoy salvation future who have no saving interest in salvation past, in other words, none will ever be with Christ in eternal glory whose names were not written in the book of life from all eternity. Likewise, none will enjoy salvation future who live and die without enjoying salvation present. In other words, none will live forever with Christ in glory who are not betrothed to him in this life by the manifestations of himself to their soul.

According to the Jewish custom, the man, at the time of betrothing, gave the bride a piece of silver before witnesses, saying to her, 'Receive this piece of silver as a pledge that at such a time you shall become my spouse,' and the parties then exchanged rings.

This meeting of the espoused parties together, who then saw each other for the first time, is a sweet type of the first meeting of the soul with Jesus. The damsel had heard of the youth, but until then had never seen him, as seeking souls hear of Jesus by the hearing of the ear, before their eyes see him. The veil was upon her face, (Gen. 24:65), as the veil is upon the heart, (2Cor. 3:15), until Jesus rends it in twain from the top to the bottom. The bridegroom gave his betrothed a piece of silver, as a pledge that all he had was hers, and thus Christ gives to the soul, whom he betroths to himself by his own manifestations, a pledge, a token, a testimony, which, in itself, is the first-fruits and assurance of eternal glory.

The parties exchanged rings, as pledges of mutual affection and eternal faithfulness. So it is when Christ reveals himself to the soul in his dying love, mutual engagements, mutual promises, mutual assurances and pledges of faithfulness and love pass between the soul and him.

"One shall say, I am the LORD's; and another shall call himself by the name of Jacob; and another shall subscribe with his hand unto the LORD," (Isa. 44:5). At these seasons, 'in the day of the King's espousals,' the language of the soul is, "As the apple tree among the trees of the wood, so is my beloved among the sons. I sat down under his shadow with great delight, and his fruit was sweet to my taste. He brought me to the banqueting house, and his banner over me was love," (Song 2:3-4).

7th

"Hear now, O Joshua the high priest, thou, and thy fellows that sit before thee: for they are men wondered at."
Zechariah 3:8

A saved sinner is a spectacle for angels to contemplate. As the Apostle says, "we are made a spectacle unto the world, and to angels, and to men," (1Cor. 4:9). The ancients used to say that 'a good man struggling with difficulties was a sight for the gods to look at.' We may say, with all Christian truth, that the mysteries of redemption are "things the angels desire to look into," (1Pet. 1:12), and among the mysteries of redemption, what is greater than a redeemed sinner? It is surely a holy wonder that a man who because of original sin and actual sin deserves nothing other than the eternal wrath of God, should be lifted out of perdition justly merited into salvation to which he can have no claim.

That you or I should ever have been fixed on by God's eye of electing love, and should ever have been given to Jesus to redeem is a marvel. That we should ever be quickened by the Spirit to feel our lost, ruined state, and ever blessed with any discovery of the Lord Jesus Christ and of his saving grace – why this is and ever must be a matter of holy astonishment whilst here on earth, and will be a theme for endless praise hereafter.

To see a man so altogether different from what he once was, careless, carnal, ignorant, and unconcerned, is an arresting sight. To see him upon his knees begging for mercy, tears streaming down his face, his bosom heaving with convulsive sighs, his eyes looking upward that pardon may reach him in his desperate state - is not that a man to be looked at with wonder and admiration? To see a man preferring one smile from the face of Jesus, and one word from his peace-speaking lips to all the titles, honours, pleasures, and power that the world can bestow; why, surely if there be a wonder upon earth, that man is one.

Was not this the feeling of the disciples when Saul "preached Christ in the synagogues, that he is the Son of God," (Acts 9:20)? All that heard him "were amazed, and said; Is not this he that destroyed them which called on this name in Jerusalem?" (Acts 9:21).

So we look and wonder, and feel at times a holy joy that he who reigns at God's right hand is ever adding trophies to his immortal crown. Whenever we see any of those near and dear to us in the flesh, be it husband, wife, sister, brother, child, relative, or friend, touched by the finger of this all-conquering Lord, subdued by his grace, and wrought upon by his Spirit, then not only do we look upon such with holy wonder, but with the tenderest affection, mingled with the tears of thankful praise to the God of all our mercies.

8th

"For I am God, and not man; the Holy One in the midst of thee."
Hosea 11:9

We speak sometimes of the attributes of God, and we use the words to help our conception, but God, strictly speaking, has no attributes. His attributes are himself. We speak, for instance, of the love of God, but God is love; of the justice of God, but God is just; of the holiness of God, but God is holy; of the purity of God, but God is

June

pure. As he is all love, so he is all justice, all purity, all holiness. Love, then, is infinite, because God is infinite; his very name, his very character, his very nature, his very essence is infinite love. He would cease to be God if he did not love, and if that love were not as large as himself and as infinite as his own self-existent, incomprehensible essence.

The love of the Son of God, as God the Son, is co-equal and co-eternal with the love of the Father; for the holy Trinity has not three distinct loves, either in date or degree. The Father loves from all eternity, the Son loves from all eternity, and the Holy Spirit loves from all eternity. The love of the Father, of the Son, and of the Holy Spirit, as one, equal, indivisible, infinite Jehovah cannot be otherwise but One. We therefore read of "the love of God," that is the Father, (2Cor. 13:14), of "the love of the Son," (Gal. 2:20), and of "the love of the Spirit," (Rom. 15:30).

This love, being infinite, can bear with all our infirmities, and with all those grievous sins that would, unless that love were boundless, have long ago broken it utterly through. This is beautifully expressed by the prophet Hosea.

"How shall I give thee up, Ephraim? How shall I deliver thee, Israel? How shall I make thee as Admah? How shall I set thee as Zeboim? Mine heart is turned within me, my repentings are kindled together. I will not execute the fierceness of mine anger, I will not return to destroy Ephraim: for I am God, and not man; the Holy One in the midst of thee: and I will not enter into the city," (Hos. 11:8-9).

9th

**"For we which have believed do enter into rest."
Hebrews 4:3**

To rest is usually to 'lean' upon something, or recline against something, is it not? So it is spiritually; we need something upon which to lean. The Lord himself has given us this figure. "Who is this that cometh up from the wilderness, leaning upon her beloved?" (Song 8:5). The figure of "a rock" on which the Church is built, "the foundation" which God has laid in Zion, points to the same idea, that of leaning or dependence. Now when the soul comes to lean upon Jesus, and depend wholly and solely on him, it enters into the sweetness of the invitation.

Have we not leaned upon a thousand things in our lives? And what have they proved to be? They are but broken reeds that have run into our hands and sides, and pierced us through. Our own strength and resolutions, the world and the church, sinners and saints, friends and enemies, have they not all proved to be more or less broken reeds? The more we have leaned upon them, like a man leaning upon a sword, the more have they pierced our souls.

The Lord himself has to wean us from the world, from friends, from enemies, and from self, in order to bring us to lean only upon him. Every prop will he remove, sooner or later, that we may lean wholly and solely upon his Person, his love, his blood, and his righteousness.

Howbeit there is another idea woven into the word 'rest', that of termination. When we are walking, running, or in any way moving, we are still going onwards; we have not got to the end of our journey. When we come to the end of that which we have been doing, when we come to the termination, we rest. So it is spiritually. As long as we are engaged in setting up our own righteousness, in labouring under the law, there is no termination of our labours. Yet when we come to the glorious Person of the Son of God, when we hang upon his atoning blood, dying love, and glorious righteousness, and feel it all sweet, precious, and suitable, then there is rest.

"For we which have believed do enter into rest," says the Apostle. His legal labours are all terminated. His hopes and expectations flow unto, and centre in Jesus. There they end, there they terminate, and such a termination as a river finds in the boundless ocean.

10th

**"The fire shall try every man's work of what sort it is."
1Corinthians 3:13**

The fire which is to try every man's work is not merely God's wrath as manifested at the last day. The word fire here signifies also the fiery trial which takes place in this life, and which God mercifully brings upon his people to burn up their wood, hay, and stubble. It is an inestimable mercy to have all this combustible material burnt up before we come to a death-bed. Fiery trials, such as God sends through afflictions, temptations, distressing feelings, and painful soul exercises, will burn up the wood, hay, and stubble, which his saints are wont to gather up and add to the superstructure during their life. Guilt pressing upon a man's conscience; the terrors of the Almighty in a fiery law; his arrows deeply fixed in the breast and drying up the spirit; fears of death, hell, and judgment; and the terrible consequences of dying under the wrath of God; all these are a part of the fiery trial which burns up the wood, hay, and stubble

June

heaped by Babel builders on the heavenly foundation. All sink into black ashes before this fire, which proves what they are, and what a vain refuge they afford in the day of trouble.

What then stands the fiery trial? God's work upon the soul, the faith that he implants by his own Spirit. It may be weak, but it must be tried. It may seem at times scarcely to exist, and yet being of God, it stands every storm and lives at the last. A good hope through grace, a hope of God's own communicating and maintaining, will stand the storm like a well-tried anchor. Like gold and silver, it will bear the hottest furnace, losing only its dross, but not losing the pure metal, being refined, purified, and manifested all the more as a choice ingot.

So, also, these "precious stones," (1Cor. 3:12), these heavenly visits, sweet manifestations, blessed promises, comforting discoveries, and gracious revelations of the Son of God, with the whispers of his dying, bleeding love - these heavenly jewels can never be lost and never be burnt up. They may be cut and tried, and that keenly and sharply, but being of God's gift and operation, they are essentially indestructible.

11th

"But they that wait upon the LORD shall renew their strength; they shall mount up with wings as eagles; they shall run, and not be weary; and they shall walk, and not faint."
Isaiah 40:31

How different the religion of a living soul is from the religion of a dead professor! The religion of a dead professor begins in self, and ends in self. It begins in his own wisdom, and ends in his own folly. It begins in his own strength, and ends in his own weakness; and being based on his own righteousness it ends in his own damnation! There is in him never any going out of the soul after God, no secret dealings with the Lord, no actings of faith upon the divine perfections.

It is not so with the child of God. Though he is often faint, weary, and exhausted with many difficulties, burdens and sorrows; yet when the Lord does show himself, and renews his strength, he soars aloft, and never ceases to mount up on the wings of faith and love until he penetrates into the very sanctuary of the most High. A living soul never can be satisfied except in living union and communion with the Lord of life and glory. Everything short of that leaves it empty. All the things of time and sense leave a child of God unsatisfied. Nothing but vital union and communion with the Lord of life, to feel his presence, taste his love, enjoy his favour, and see his glory will ever satisfy the desires of ransomed and regenerated souls.

This is then how the Lord indulges his people.

"They shall renew their strength." They shall not be always lying groaning on the ground, not always swooning away through the wounds made by sin, not always chained down by the fetters of the world, not always hunted in their souls like a partridge upon the mountains. There shall be a renewal of their strength; and in their renewal, "they shall mount up with wings as eagles; they shall run, and not be weary; and they shall walk, and not faint."

12th

"I will abundantly bless her provision: I will satisfy her poor with bread."
Psalm 132:15

What a sweetness there is in the word 'satisfy!' This world cannot satisfy the child of God. Have we not tried, some of us perhaps for many years, to get some satisfaction from it? But can wife or husband really "satisfy" us? Can children or relatives genuinely "satisfy" us? Can all that the world calls good or great ever truly "satisfy" us? Can the pleasures of sin "satisfy" us? Is there not in all these an aching void? Do we not reap dissatisfaction and disappointment from everything that is of the creature, and of the flesh? Do we not find that there is little else but sorrow to be reaped from everything in this world?

I am sure I find, and have found for some years, that there is little else to be gathered from the world but disappointment, dissatisfaction, "vanity and vexation of spirit," (Ec. 1:14). The poor soul looks round upon the world and the creature, upon all the occupations, amusements and relations of life, and finds it all one melancholy harvest, reaping only sorrow, perplexity, and dissatisfaction.

Now when a man is brought here, when he sees that all is vanity, then the Spirit is at work. When he wants true satisfaction, genuine happiness, something to permanently fill the aching void, something to bind up broken bones, the bleeding wounds, and leprous sores, then he has an appetite for the truth. After he has studied doctrines, opinions, notions, speculations, forms, rites and ceremonies in religion; after he has looked at the world with all its charms and works and found them empty; after he has looked at himself with all his empty workings and struggles; when he has found nothing but bitterness of spirit, vexation and trouble in all he sees; when he is, at the last, utterly sunk down a miserable wretch, then, when the Lord opens to him something of the bread of life, he finds a satisfaction which he could never gain from any other quarter.

It is for this reason that the Lord so afflicts his people. This is why some carry with them such weak, suffering tabernacles, why some have so many family troubles, why others are so deeply steeped in poverty, why others have such rebellious children, and why others are so exercised with spiritual sorrows that they scarcely know what will be the end. It is all for one purpose, to make them miserable out of Christ, dissatisfied except with gospel food; to render them so wretched and uncomfortable that God alone can make them happy, and alone can speak consolation to their troubled minds.

13th

"That Christ may dwell in your hearts by faith."
Ephesians 3:17

God bade Moses receive from the people oil for the light, and to set up a candlestick with seven lamps, ever burning with this oil, to illuminate the holy place. This light was no doubt typical of the Holy Spirit, but as it is only by his own gracious light that the Lord Jesus is made known, we may still say, that as Christ dwells in the heart by faith, faith giving him a place in the bosom, he dwells in the enlightened understanding of his saints in the gracious light of his own manifestations.

Have you not seen at times wondrous beauty in the gospel? Has not a sacred light shone, from time to time, upon the holy page when it testified of Christ? Have you not seen wondrous glory in a free gospel, a gospel that saves the sinner, and yet magnifies and glorifies the justice of God; a gospel that reconciles every apparently jarring attribute, brings justice and mercy to kiss each other, and makes God to be just, and yet the justifier of him who believes in Jesus? Now that light whereby you saw the glory of God in the face of Jesus Christ, was gospel light; and as Christ came into the heart in the glory of that light, he may be said to dwell in the shining light of his own grace.

You may complain, and often bitterly complain, of the darkness of your mind, and it may seem at times as if you never had any true light to shine into your soul. However, I would have you carefully observe these two things; first, that the very cause of the darkness which you feel is the presence of light. The Apostle, therefore, says, "All things that are reproved are made manifest by the light: for whatsoever doth make manifest is light," (Eph. 5:13).

Apply these words to your case. Is there not something in you that discovers to you your darkness, and not only discovers it, but reproves it, and makes it manifest as a thing to be condemned? This 'something' is the light, for "for whatsoever doth make manifest is light," (Eph. 5:13). As you not only see it, but feel and mourn under it, it is "the light of life" which the Lord promised to those who follow him.

Observe, secondly, that whenever a little light dawns in again upon your soul, in that light you again see the same grace and glory in Christ which you saw in him before. Now, what a proof this is that Christ dwells in the heart by faith, and that the light in which we see him, is the light with which he has enlightened our understanding, and in which he dwells.

14th

"Again, they are minished and brought low through oppression, affliction, and sorrow."
Psalm 107:39

Oppression is the exercise of strength against weakness, the triumph of power over helplessness, so that poverty literally opens the door for oppression. So it was with Hezekiah. When he was laid on his bed of sickness and death stared him in the face, he expected to be cut off and cast into perdition. This opened the door for oppression; says he, "Lord, I am oppressed; undertake for me," (Isa. 38:14). The cold damps of death stood upon his forehead, and despair pressed upon his soul. All his fleshly religion vanished in a moment, and he had but just enough faith and strength to cry out under the gripe of the oppressor's hand at his throat, "Undertake for me," (Isa. 38:14).

Oppression then is a weight and a burden superadded to poverty. It is not the same thing as poverty, but it is an additional infliction to poverty. A man may be poor without being oppressed; but when he is poor and oppressed too, it makes the poverty tenfold greater than before. Thus the Lord, in his dealings with his people in order to bring them down, first strips them and makes them poor; and when he has made them poor, and brought them into the depths of soul-destitution, then he causes burdens to lie on them as heavy loads, as though they would sink them into a never-ending hell.

Yet this groaning, panting, sighing, and crying of the soul under the burden is the mark of life. The dead in sin feel nothing; the hypocrites in Zion feel nothing; and those that are at ease in a fleshly religion feel nothing. They may have powerful temptations; they may have alarming fears of going to hell; but as to any heavings up of a quickened conscience under the weight of oppression, as to any pouring out of the heart before God, or any giving vent to the distresses of the soul in sighs and cries unto the Lord to have mercy, to speak peace, and bring in a sweet manifestation of pardon and love, and to keep at this day after day, and night after night until the Lord appears; these are exercises unknown to the dead, and peculiar to the living family.

A man may "cry for sorrow of heart, and shall howl for vexation of spirit," (Isa. 65:14), but as the prophet speaks, "they have not cried unto me with their heart, when they howled upon their beds," (Hos. 7:14).

To breathe and pant after the Lord, to groan and sigh because of oppression, to wrestle with the Saviour and give him no rest until he appears in the soul – this inward work is known only to the elect. It is out of the reach of all who have a name to live whilst they are dead. It is the fruit of the pouring out of the spirit of grace and supplications into their soul; it is the work of the Holy Spirit in the heart, helping its infirmities, and making intercession in it with groanings which cannot be uttered.

15th

"A time to kill, and a time to heal."
Ecclesiastes 3:3

All through the Christian's life there will be "a time to kill, and a time to heal."

We sometimes read in books, and hear in conversation, an experience of this kind. The work of grace commences with very powerful convictions of sin, bringing the soul to the very brink of hell, and then a wonderful revelation of Jesus Christ follows with a powerful application of his atoning blood to the conscience and a blessed manifestation of God's love to the soul.

What follows this experience? Does the Christian possess an unwavering assurance during the remainder of their sojourn upon earth? Do sin and Satan never distress nor wound them? Does the flesh lie calm and tranquil, like the summer sea, never lashed up by angry gusts into a storm of fretfulness and rebellion? Do the sea birds of doubt and fear never flit with screams around them, as harbingers of a tempest, but instead the gale of divine favour gently fills their sail, and wafts them along until they reach the harbour of endless rest?

Is this consistent with the Scriptures of truth? Does not the word of God set forth the path of a Christian as one of trial and temptation? Can a living soul pass through many scenes without ever being killed experimentally in his feelings as one of "the flock of slaughter?" (Zech. 11:7). Does not a chequered experience run through the whole of a Christian's life? Does the Scripture ever afford us the least warrant to believe that a man can be walking in the footsteps of a tempted, suffering Lord, who continues for months and years together at ease in Zion, without any trouble, exercise, grief, or distress in his soul?

David never was there. Jeremiah never was there. Paul never was there. Heman never was there. Asaph never was there. You will find that no saints of God, whose experience is left on record in the Bible, ever were there. Their path was one of change and vicissitude; sometimes down, sometimes up, sometimes mourning, sometimes rejoicing, but never long together in one unvaried spot.

The Spirit of the Lord, in carrying on this grand work in the hearts of God's people, will be continually operating in two distinct ways upon their souls. Jeremiah was a prophet of the Lord, and he was "set over the nations and over the kingdoms to root out, and to pull down, and to destroy, and to throw down" – thus ran one part of his commission.

"To build and to plant" was the second part of his office. These two distinct operations were to run through the whole of his mission; they were "the burden of the Lord," laid upon him at his first call to the prophetical office, and they continued during the whole of his ministry, a space of more than forty years.

Did he, then, merely on one occasion pull down, and on one occasion build up? Was not the whole of his ministration, as evidenced in the prophecies that are contained in the book that bears his name, a continual pulling down with one hand, and building up with the other? So is it then with the ministry of the Spirit of the Lord in a vessel of mercy. He is continually killing, continually healing, continually casting down, continually raising up, now laying the soul low in the dust of self-abasement, and now building it up sweetly in Christ.

June 16th

"In those days, and in that time, saith the LORD, the iniquity of Israel shall be sought for, and there shall be none; and the sins of Judah, and they shall not be found: for I will pardon them whom I reserve"
Jeremiah 50:20

Some have feared lest in the great day their sins should be brought to light, and they put to shame by the exposure of their crimes to open view; but that will not be the case with the dear family of God. We read indeed that "many of them that sleep in the dust of the earth shall awake, some to everlasting life, and some to shame and everlasting contempt," (Dan. 12:2), because their sins will be remembered and brought against them as evidences of their just condemnation.

Howbeit, the wise, who "shall shine as the brightness of the firmament," (Dan. 12:3), will rise to glory and honour and immortality, and not one of their sins will be remembered, be charged, or be brought against them. They will stand arrayed in Christ's perfect righteousness and washed in his blood, and will appear before the throne of God without spot or blemish.

We can scarcely bear the recollection of our sins now, but what would become of us if the spirit of one unburied sin could flit before our eyes in the day when the Lord makes up his jewels? If any one sin of the Lamb's wife could be remembered or brought against her, where would be the voice which John heard in Revelation, as "the voice of a great multitude, and as the voice of many waters, and as the voice of mighty thunderings, saying, Alleluia: for the Lord God omnipotent reigneth," (Rev. 19:6).

Now what sayeth this voice? "Let us be glad and rejoice, and give honour to him: for the marriage of the Lamb is come, and his wife hath made herself ready. And to her was granted that she should be arrayed in fine linen, clean and white: for the fine linen is the righteousness of saints," (Rev. 19:7-8).

Suppose that any of the past transgressions of the Lamb's wife could be brought against her on that marriage day, one instance of unfaithfulness to her plighted troth, would it not be sufficient to prevent the marriage, mar the wedding supper, and drive the bride away for very shame? No, there is no truth in God's word more certain than the complete forgiveness of sins, and the presentation of the Church to Christ at the great day, "faultless before the presence of his glory with exceeding joy," (Jude 24).

June 17th

"And it shall come to pass in that day, that the great trumpet shall be blown, and they shall come which were ready to perish in the land of Assyria, and the outcasts in the land of Egypt, and shall worship the LORD in the holy mount at Jerusalem."
Isaiah 27:13

Called by the sounding of the great trumpet, the perishing and outcasts "come." And what do they do when they come? Do they trifle with sin, mock their God, and abuse his grace? We do not read so. They "worship the Lord in the holy mount at Jerusalem."

They worship him in spirit and in truth, and they worship him in the beauty of holiness. With purified hearts, purged consciences, and spiritual affections, they fall down before him, and their souls are impressed with a sense of the greatness of his love. They had no such heavenly feelings beforehand, and therefore they could not worship the Three-In-One God in the holy mount, nor at Jerusalem. The great trumpet had not yet been blown, the jubilee had not yet come, the chains had not yet been knocked off nor the shackles loosed, and the prison-gates had not been thrown open; they could not therefore worship God freely, fully and calmly, with liberty of access and freedom of spirit.

Note that they worship him in the holy mount. The holy mount we may understand to signify spiritually Mount Zion, the place where Jesus sits in glory. This is the ancient declaration of the Father, "Yet have I set my king upon my holy hill of Zion," (Psa. 2:6). Here Jesus ever sits with love in his heart, grace on his lips, and the gospel in his hands. He sits on that holy hill, sways a holy sceptre, and rules in the hearts of a holy people. Men talk much of holiness; and indeed they may well talk of it, for it is a most solemn declaration that without holiness "no man shall see the Lord," (Heb. 12:14).

However, what sort of holiness are most men seeking after? A holiness of the flesh, a sanctity of the creature. They must do this and abstain from that; and if they so manage to mortify the flesh then they are holy. A certain number of prayers must be said, a certain number of chapters read, and a list of duties done. This is a Popish holiness, the sanctified austerity of a St. Dominic, but it is not that holiness without which no man shall see the Lord.

Biblical holiness is of a very different nature; different in source, manner, means, and end. True holiness is that which is produced by the Spirit of God in the soul. There is no other source.

June

How then does the Holy Spirit produce such holiness? Is it by the law or by the gospel? By the gospel, certainly.

When the great trumpet of jubilee sounds in the soul, when it listens to the notes, and comes obedient to its call, it is to worship the Lord in his holy mount at Jerusalem. True holiness is then produced in the soul, for then there are given spiritual desires, spiritual affections, spiritual views, spiritual feelings, and spiritual hearts. This is the holiness which is wrought in the soul by the Spirit of God, and without which no man shall see the Lord.

18th

"But, beloved, we are persuaded better things of you, and things that accompany salvation, though we thus speak." Hebrews 6:9

What is "salvation?" In looking at salvation, we must consider it in two points of view; salvation wrought out for us, and salvation wrought out in us. Salvation was wrought out for the Church by the finished work of the Son of God, when he cried with his expiring breath, "It is finished," (John 19:30). The salvation of the "remnant according to the election of grace," (Ro. 11:5), was at that moment completely accomplished, so that nothing could be added to, or taken from it. "For by one offering he hath perfected for ever them that are sanctified," (Heb. 10:14), and thus the Church stands complete in Christ, without "spot, or wrinkle, or any such thing," (Eph. 5:27).

But there is a salvation which is wrought out in the soul, which is the manifestation and application of that salvation which Jesus wrought out by his sufferings, blood-shedding, and death. This salvation we can only know experimentally so far as the blessed Spirit brings it into our hearts, and seals it there with holy unction and heavenly savour.

But all the people of God cannot feel sure they have this salvation as an experimental reality. Doubts, fears, darkness, and temptations becloud their path and Satan hurls his fiery darts into their souls. As a result they are often unable to realise their saving interest in the Lord Jesus Christ and his salvation. They do not doubt that the Lord Jesus is the Saviour of those who believe, and they know that there is no other refuge for their guilty souls than the blood of the Lamb. They are effectually stripped from cleaving to a covenant of works and they are not running after things that cannot profit them, nor hiding their heads in lying refuges. From all these things they are effectually cut off by a work of grace on their souls.

Yet, through the unbelief of their hearts, the deadness of their frames, the barrenness of their souls, and the various temptations with which they are exercised, they fear they have not the marks of God's family, and are not able to realise their saving interest in the love and blood of the Lamb.

The Apostle, therefore, speaks of "things that accompany salvation;" that is, certain marks and signs, certain clear and indubitable tokens of the work of grace on the soul. And, speaking to the Hebrews, he says for their comfort and encouragement, "We are persuaded," whatever be your doubts and fears, whatever the darkness of your mind, however exercised with sharp and severe temptations, "we are persuaded" that you are in possession of those "better things," of those "things that accompany salvation;" and that this salvation is therefore eternally yours.

19th

"But as many as received him, to them gave he power to become the sons of God, even to them that believe on his name."
John 1:12

Wherever faith is given to the soul to "receive" Christ, there will be mingled with this faith, and blessedly accompanying it, love to the Lord of life and glory. Sometimes we may know the existence of faith when we cannot see it by discerning the secret workings and actings of love towards that Saviour, in whom God has enabled us to believe. There will be, from time to time, in living souls a flowing forth of affection towards Jesus. From time to time, he gives the soul a glimpse of his Person; he shows himself, as the Scripture speaks, "through the lattice," (Song 2:9). Perhaps he passes hastily by, but he gives us a transient glimpse of the beauty of his Person, the excellency of his finished work, dying love, and atoning blood, as ravishes the heart. He secretly draws forth every affection of the soul, so that there is a following hard after him, and a going out of the desires of the soul towards him.

Thus, sometimes as we lie upon our bed, as we are engaged in our business, as we are occupied in our several pursuits of life the Lord is pleased secretly to work in the heart. It might happen under the word, or reading the Scripture, but there is a melting down at the feet of Jesus, or a secret, soft, gentle going forth of love and affection towards him, whereby the soul prefers him before thousands of gold and silver, and desires nothing so much as the inward manifestations of his love, grace, and blood.

Thus a living soul receives Christ not just as driven by necessity, but also as drawn by affection. The soul does not receive Christ merely as a way of escape from "the wrath to come," or merely as something to save it from "the worm that dieth not, and the fire [that] is not quenched," (Mark 9:44). The receiving is certainly mingled with necessity, sweetly and powerfully combined with it, and intimately and intricately working with it, but there is also the flowing forth of genuine affection and sincere love that goes out to him as the only object worthy of our heart's affection, of our spirit's worship, and of our soul's desire.

We cannot say that less than this comes up to the meaning of the scriptural expression to receive Christ.

20th

"As ye have therefore received Christ Jesus the Lord, so walk ye in him; rooted and built up in him, and stablished in the faith, as ye have been taught, abounding therein with thanksgiving."
Colossians 2:6-7

It is a goodly sight to see a noble tree, and we may gather from the strength of the tree the strength of the soil, for only in deep and good soil will such trees grow.

Now look at the trees of righteousness, the planting of the Lord, that he may be glorified! What depth and richness there is in the heavenly soil in which they are planted! View the true, real, and eternal Sonship, the glorious Deity of Jesus, and view that Deity in union with his suffering humanity! What soil is there! What breadth to hold thousands and thousands of noble trees! What depth for them to root in! What fertility to clothe them with verdure and load them with fruit! The most fertile natural soils may one day be exhausted, but this is inexhaustible. For can Deity ever be exhausted? Is it not its very nature to be infinite? And when we view what our most blessed Lord now is at the right hand of God, what a perfect and complete Saviour he is for the soul to lay hold of!

Again, as a tree spreads its roots more deeply and widely into the soil, the more nourishment and moisture does it suck up. So it is with a believing heart. The more Christ is laid hold of by faith, the more the soul roots into him, the more heavenly nourishment it draws out of his fullness. The firmer hold it takes of him, and the more deeply it roots into him, the stronger it stands. This is being "rooted" in Christ.

A religion must always be a shallow, deceptive, and ruinous religion if it has not Christ to root in, for then it must be rooted in self. If, however, it is planted and rooted in Christ, then there is a sufficiency, a suitability, a glorious fullness in him in which the soul may take the deepest root. That root is not only for time but for eternity; for such a faith can never be confounded, such a love can never perish, and such a hope can never be put to shame.

21st

"Thy word is a lamp unto my feet, and a light unto my path."
Psalm 119:105

O what a change takes place in the soul's feelings toward the word of God when God is pleased to quicken it into divine life! Nor need we wonder why there is such a marked revolution in our feelings toward it, for it is by the power of God's word upon the heart that this wondrous change is effected. "Of his own will begat he us with the word of truth," (Jas. 1:18). Other books may instruct and amuse; they may cultivate the mind, feed the intellect, and charm the imagination, but what more can they do? I do not mean by this to despise or set aside every other book but the Bible, for without books society itself, as at present constituted, could not exist; and to burn every book would be to throw us back into the barbarism of the Middle Ages. Let, then, books have their place as regards this life; but what can they do for us as regards the life to come? What can our renowned authors, our choice classics, our learned historians, our great dramatists, or our eloquent poets do for the soul in seasons of affliction and distress?

How powerless are all human writings in these circumstances. Is it not as Deer well says–

"What balm could wretches ever find
In wit, to heal affliction?
Or who can cure a troubled mind
With all the pomp of diction?"

Now here is the blessedness of the word of God, that when everything else fails, it comes to our aid under all circumstances, so that we can never sink so low as to get beyond the reach of some promise in the word of truth. We may come, and most probably shall come, to a spot where everything else will fail and give way except the word of God, which forever is settled in heaven. Then the word of grace and truth which reaches down to the lowest case, the word of promise upon which the Lord causes the soul to hope, will still turn towards us a friendly smile. It will still encourage us under all circumstances to call upon the name of the Lord, and to hang upon his faithfulness who has said, "Heaven and earth shall pass away, but my words shall not pass away," (Matt. 24:35).

Thus, under circumstances the most trying to flesh and blood, where nature stands aghast and reason fails, there the word of God will come in as a counsellor to drop in friendly advice, and as a companion to cheer and support the mind by its tender sympathy. It will come as a friend to speak to the heart with a loving, affectionate voice. We need not wonder, then, how the word of God has been prized in all ages by the family of God; for it is written with such infinite wisdom, that it meets every case, suits every circumstance, fills up every aching void, and is adapted to every condition of life and every state both of body and soul.

22nd

"He found him in a desert land, and in the waste howling wilderness; he led him about, he instructed him, he kept him as the apple of his eye."
Deuteronomy 32:10

How true it is that God led his people 'about'. What a circuitous, tangled, backward and forward route was that of the children of Israel in the wilderness! Yet every step was under God's direction, for they never moved until the cloudy pillar led the way.

How then does the Lord lead about in grace? By leading his Israel into a path of which they do not see the end. One turn of the road hides the next. I have read that you may make a road with a curve at every quarter of a mile, and yet in a hundred miles the distance will not be so much as a mile more than a perfectly straight line. So it is with grace. The length of the road swallows up the turnings.

Yet all these turnings make the road seem more round about than it really is. All before us is hidden. For instance, when the Lord begins a work of grace, he brings convictions of sin, opens up the spirituality of the law, makes the soul feel guilty, guilty, guilty in every thought, word, and deed, but does a man in that condition know what the Lord is doing? Can he clearly trace out the work of God upon his soul? Is he able to say, "This, this is the work of God upon my heart?"

For the most part, he knows not what is the matter with him and why he is so distressed, nor why he can take no rest and why the things of eternity keep rolling in upon his soul. He cannot see why he stands in continual dread of the wrath to come nor why his mind is so exercised with thoughts upon God and why he feels condemnation, bondage, and misery.

Nor even when the Lord is pleased to raise him up to some hope, to apply some sweet promise to his soul, to encourage him in various ways under the ministry of the word, can he often take the full comfort of it. He may for a time, but it is soon gone, and he can scarcely believe it to have been real. Unbelief suggests that it did not come exactly in the right way, or did not last long enough, or did not go deep enough, or was not just such as he has heard others speak of, and in this way he is filled with doubts, fears, and anxieties whether it was really from the Lord.

Yet when God leads him on a step further, when he opens up the gospel and reveals Christ, and drops into his heart some sweet testimony, his fears abate. When God gives him some blessed discovery of his saving interest in the Lord Jesus, and seals it with a divine witness in his heart, this banishes all his doubts and fears, and fills his soul with joy and peace. Then a day later, after this great comfort, when the sweet feeling is gone, he will sink again very low, and may question the reality of the revelation he has enjoyed.

All this is being "led about," for one turn of the road always hides the next.

23rd

"Blessed is the man whose strength is in thee; in whose heart are the ways of them; who passing through the valley of Baca make it a well; the rain also filleth the pools."
Psalm 84:5-6

David casts a glimpse here at those pilgrims who were taking their upward journey to worship God in Zion. He marks their road, and takes occasion to spiritualise it, for he says that the ways of these pilgrims Zionward are 'in their hearts'. Their pilgrimage is heartfelt.

What are these ways? It is this; that "passing through the valley of Baca, they make it a well." This valley of Baca appears to have been a very perilous pass, through which pilgrims journeyed toward Jerusalem; and on account of the difficulties, dangers, and sufferings that they met with, it was named "the valley of Baca," or "the valley of weeping," "the valley of tears."

Yet the Psalmist says, "Blessed" is the man whose heart is in this pilgrimage, and who passing through this vale of tears makes it a well of blessing, not a desert of despair. Here is the distinctive character of the true pilgrim. He is not merely journeying through the "valley of Baca" with his eyes drowned in tears, his heart filled with sorrows, his soul cut with temptations and his mind tried by suffering. His distinctive feature is that, no matter what befalls, he "makes it a well." This the ungodly know nothing of; this the professing world, for the most part, are entirely unacquainted with; this is the secret "which no fowl knoweth, and which the vulture's eye hath not seen," (Job 28:7).

A feature of the valley of Baca was that when the pilgrims travelled, the burning sun above and the parched ground beneath made the whole valley arid, dry and scorching, and yet they 'made it a well'. Wells had been dug in this valley of Baca for the pilgrims to slake their thirst at, and David, looking at these wells, applies them spiritually to the refreshment that the Lord's people meet with in their course Zionward. "Make it a well;" that is, there are from time to time sweet refreshments in this valley of tears; there are bubblings up of divine consolation; there are fountains of living waters, streams of heavenly pleasures. Yet there is further spiritual significance here in that the pilgrim who finds himself in a barren place finds that the very barrenness itself teaches, blesses and refreshes him in a way no mere professor could appreciate.

A friend of mine told me of an incident whilst journeying through the deserts in Asia when he and his companions came to a well, but found it dry. He said no language could depict their disappointment and grief. Their troubles, when after long hours of traveling they came at night to encamp by the well and found that the sun had dried it up, were indeed most acute.

In the same manner therefore, that none but pilgrims through the dry and parched valley could adequately feel the sweetness of the natural well; so only true spiritual pilgrims, afflicted, exercised, and harassed, can appreciate the sweetness of the "pure water of life" with which the Lord at times refreshes the soul.

24th

"They go from strength to strength, every one of them in Zion appeareth before God."
Psalm 84:7

"They go from strength to strength," is the interpretation put on the original Hebrew by the translators, and an alternate rendering of

June

the original has been given as "from company to company." I rather think, that the meaning implied is, "they go from resting place to resting place."

There were certain fixed spots where the whole company of pilgrims rested at night, as we read of in the gospel. The infant Jesus tarried at Jerusalem, but his parents knew it not because they supposed that he was "in the company," that is, he had gone on with the traveling pilgrims, but when night came they looked for him and he was not there.

These resting places were spots where the caravan of travellers rested at night, and by these successive restings their strength was renewed, and they were enabled to bear the long journey, rising each morning refreshed with their night's rest. The Psalmist viewing it spiritually may well have rendered it, "They go from strengthening place to strengthening place," and so they were enabled to pursue their journey.

Is not this true in grace? Are there not resting places in the divine life, spots of refreshment, where the true pilgrims renew their strength? For instance, every manifestation of the Lord is a communication of divine strength, a recruiting place, where the soul recruits its strength to travel onward. Every promise that comes with sweet power is another resting place where the traveller may break his journey. Every discovery of saving interest in Christ, every glimpse of the grace and glory of Jesus, every word from the Lord's lips and every smile from the Lord's face uplifts us. Every token for good, everything that encourages, supports, blesses, and comforts the soul, enabling it to go onwards towards its heavenly home, is a resting place, where the pilgrim pauses, and where he recruits his weary limbs.

Now, where can we rest, except where God rests? Does not God "rest in his love?" (Zep. 3:17). Can we therefore rest anywhere short of God's love shed abroad in our heart? Does he not also rest in his dear Son? Did not his voice proclaim from glory, "This is my beloved Son, in whom I am well pleased?" (Matt. 3:17).

All the satisfaction of God centres in Jesus; all the delight of the Father rests in the Son of his love. "Behold my servant, whom I uphold; mine elect, in whom my soul delighteth," (Isa. 42:1). We cannot then rest anywhere but where God rests.

It is spiritually with us as it was with the Israelites of old, when the cloud tarried, they tarried; when the cloud went, they went; when the cloud moved onward, they followed it; and when the cloud stopped, they halted, and rested beneath its shadow.

June

25th

"They go from strength to strength, every one of them in Zion appeareth before God."
Psalm 84:7

    As the Lord is true, no spiritual pilgrim will ever fall and die in the valley of Baca. Some may fear that through temptation their strong passions or boiling lusts will one day break out and destroy them. It cannot happen if they are true pilgrims. "Every one of them in Zion appeareth before God." Others may think they never shall have a testimony; they never shall read their name clearly in the Book of Life; the Lord will never appear in their heart or bless their soul; they never shall be able to say, "Abba, Father," (Rom. 8:15). I can assure you, dear reader, if Jesus be theirs then they shall.
    Are they spiritual pilgrims? Do they find it a valley of tears? Are their faces Zionward? Have they come out of the world? Do they sometimes make the valley of Baca a well, and does the rain fill the pools? Have they ever felt their strength made perfect in weakness? Then every one of them will appear before God in Zion. Blessed end! Sweet accomplishment of the pilgrim's hopes, desires, and expectations! The crowning blessing of all that God has to bestow! Every one of them will appear before God washed in the Saviour's blood, clothed in the Redeemer's righteousness, adorned with all the graces of the Spirit, and made fit for the inheritance of the saints in light.
    No weeping then! The valley of Baca is passed, and tears wiped from off all faces. No thorns to lacerate the weary feet there; no prowling wild beasts to seize the unwary traveller there; no roving bandits to surprise stragglers there; no doubts and fears and cutting sorrows to grieve, perplex, and burden them there. Safe in Zion, safe in the Redeemer's bosom, safe in their Husband's arms, safe before the throne, every one of them appears before God in glory!

26th

"Blessed are the poor in spirit: for theirs is the kingdom of heaven."
Matthew 5:3

    Spiritual poverty is a miserable feeling of soul-emptiness before God. It is an inward sinking sensation that there is nothing in our hearts spiritually good, nothing which can deliver us from the justly merited wrath of God, or save us from the lowest hell.

Intimately blended with these poignant feelings of guilt and condemnation is a spiritual consciousness that there is such a thing enjoyed by the elect as the Spirit of adoption. There are such sweet realities as divine manifestations, and the blood of Jesus Christ being sprinkled by the Holy Spirit upon the consciences of the redeemed to cleanse them from all guilt and filth.

Thus by comparing its own needs with the known blessings, and having an inward light wherein the truth of God's word is seen, together with an inward life whereby it is felt, a soul wading in the depths of spiritual poverty is brought to feel that only the manifestation of the light of God's countenance can deliver. Only the testimony of God spoken by his own lips to the heart can save such a soul. The lack of that testimony is the lack of everything that can manifest that soul to be a vessel of mercy here, and fit it for eternal glory and bliss, as well as carry it thither.

To be poor, then, is to have this wretched emptiness of spirit, and feel this nakedness and destitution of soul before God. Nor is it, perhaps, ever more deeply felt than in the lonely watches of the night, when no eye can see, nor ear hear, but the eye and ear of Jehovah. In these solemn moments of deep recollection, when the stillness and darkness around us are but the counterpart of the stillness and darkness of the soul, he that is spiritually poor often feels how empty he is of everything heavenly and divine, a sinking wretch without a grain of godliness in him.

Without drawing too rigid a line of exclusion, we may unhesitatingly say that he who has never thus known what it is to groan before the Lord with breakings-forth of heart as a needy, naked wretch has yet to understand our subject. He that has never felt his miserable destitution and emptiness before the eyes of a heart-searching God, has not yet experienced what it is to be poor in spirit.

27th

"Remembering without ceasing your work of faith, and labour of love, and patience of hope in our Lord Jesus Christ."
1Thessalonians 1:3

What is meant by the expression 'patience of hope'? It means endurance, as though hope had to endure, faith had to work, and love had to labour. It is the 'patience of hope' that proves its reality and genuineness. Hope does not go forward fighting and cutting its way. Hope is like a quiet sufferer, unwearyingly bearing what comes upon it. Hope is manifested in enduring, as faith is manifested in acting. For instance, when the Lord hides his face and testimonies sink out of sight, and when signs are not seen and Satan tempts us sore, the work of grace upon the soul seems to be all obscured. In consequence, feelings of despondency begin to set in, and then it is that the 'patience of hope' is needed to endure all things, and to stand firm and to maintain its hold.

It acts in the same way, according to the beautiful figure of Paul, as the anchor which holds the ship. What is the main value, the chief requisite in the cable holding the anchor? Is it not endurance? The cable doesn't lay hold of the seabed, it does not act as the brake; it simply holds on and endures. It does not make a great ado in the water, and its primary quality, the only quality the captain needs in it, is strength to endure and not break. When the waves rise and the billows beat, when the storm blows and the tide runs strong, then the work of the cable is not to part from the anchor, but firmly to maintain the hold it has once taken. Thus it is with the anchor too. It is not active and need do nothing more than lay where it is dropped. Holding fast to the foundation of the sea is all its work and all its excellence.

Hope in a sinner's breast is the same. Has the Lord ever shown himself gracious unto such a one? Has the Lord ever made himself precious to his soul? Has he ever dropped a testimony into his conscience, or ever spoken with power to his heart? Has his soul ever felt the Spirit inwardly testifying that he is one of God's people? Then his hope is manifested by enduring patiently everything that is brought against it to crush it, and if God did not keep it, to utterly to destroy it.

28th

"And he is the propitiation for our sins."
1John 2:2

What is propitiation? By propitiation we are to understand an atoning sacrifice acceptable to Jehovah, by which God in all his attributes is satisfied, whereby He can be favourable and his mercy, grace, and pardon can freely flow forth.

Now sin, and the law condemning sin, barred out and held back the favour of God. They were the opposing obstacle to the love of

God, for God, as God, cannot love sin and sinners. Therefore, the sin of man, and the holy law of God, which is the transcript of his infinite and eternal purity barred back, so to speak, the favour of God.

It was needful, then, that this barrier should be removed, that a channel might be provided, through which the grace, favour, and mercy of God might flow. Sin needed to be blotted out, and the law accomplished and fulfilled in all its strict requirements and in such a manner that God "might be just," retaining every righteous attribute and not sacrificing even one of his holy perfections whilst also being "the justifier of him which believeth in Jesus," (Rom. 3:26.)

How was this to be effected? No seraph, no bright angel could ever have devised a way, for it lay locked up in the bosom of the Three-In-One God from everlasting. The only-begotten Son of God, who rested in the bosom of the Father from all eternity, "the brightness of his glory, and the express image of his Person," (Heb. 1:3), must needs become a bleeding Lamb, "the Lamb slain from [before] the foundation of the world," (Rev. 13:8). He had to take into union with his own divine Person a human nature, the flesh and blood of the children, remaining pure, spotless, and holy, and offer up that nature, that body which God prepared for him, a holy sacrifice. When he came into the world, the sacrifice began; and every holy thought, every holy word, and every holy action, in suffering and performing, that passed through the heart, dropped from the lips, or was performed by the hands of the only-begotten Son of God, when he was on earth, was part of that sacrifice. The grand consummation of it, (the offering up of that body especially), was when it was nailed to the accursed tree and blood was shed to put away sin.

This therefore is the propitiation, the atoning sacrifice and the redemption; it is the way, the only way, whereby sin is expiated, and whereby sin is pardoned.

Howbeit, in order that this blessed and atoning sacrifice may pass over to us; that its value, validity, efficacy, and blessedness may be felt in our consciences, there must be that wrought in our souls whereby it is embraced. The only salvation for our souls is the atoning sacrifice made by Jesus upon Calvary's tree. There is no other sacrifice for sin but that. Yet how is that salvation to pass into our hearts? How is the efficacy of this atoning sacrifice to be made personally ours? It is by faith. Does not the Holy Spirit declare this by the mouth of the Apostle? He says, "Whom God hath set forth to be a propitiation through faith in his blood," (Rom. 3:25).

Now, this is the turning point in the soul's salvation. This is the grand point which must be decided in a man's conscience before God, when, by living faith, he is enabled to see the atoning sacrifice through the blood of the Lamb. When he feels his very heart and soul going out after, leaning upon, and taking a measure of solid rest and peace in the blood of the sacrifice offered upon Calvary. Then he begins to receive into his conscience a measure of the favour and grace of the Lord God Almighty.

29th

**"Jesus Christ himself being the chief corner stone."
Ephesians 2:20**

The meaning of this expression, which frequently occurs in the New Testament, is, we think, often misunderstood. It is taken in the first instance from the declaration concerning our Lord in the Psalms, which he in the gospels, (Mark 12:10; Luke 20:17), specially claimed and appropriated to himself. "The stone which the builders refused has become the head-stone of the corner," (Psa. 118:22).

The head of the corner, or the chief corner stone, the meaning of both expressions being one and the same, signifies not the stone which stands at the top of the building, uniting the corners of the two walls just under the roof, but the broad foundation stone, which is firmly fixed at the very bottom. It is called the corner stone because that is where it sits, a huge and broad stone for a foundation of the whole building, each wall meeting upon it at the corners, with it equally supporting and upholding them all. The two walls which thus meet together represent Jew and Gentile; but each of these walls equally rests upon the broad foundation stone which is common to both, and not only supports them separately, but unites them together at the corner, where each meets and rests upon it.

It is the word 'head' which has oft caused the misapprehension of the expression 'corner stone' to which we have alluded. Yet the word 'head' in Hebrew properly signifies the first or chief; and thus as the foundation is not only the chief stone as supporting the whole, but the first which is laid, so our gracious Lord is not only chief in dignity, but was laid first in place, for the Church was chosen in him. In all things he must have the pre-eminence.

Thus he is first in dignity, as the Son of the Father in truth and love; first in choice, God choosing the elect in him; and first in suffering, for what sorrows were like his sorrows? He is first in resurrection, for he is "the first-fruits of those who slept," (1Cor. 15:20); first in power, for all power is given unto him in heaven and in earth, (Matt. 28:18), and first in glory, for he is gone before to prepare a place for his people. We may well add that he is first in their hearts and affections, for he that loveth father or mother, son or daughter, more than him is not worthy of him.

30th

"Perplexed, but not in despair."
2Corinthians 4:8

Oh! what a mercy, amid every degree of inward or outward perplexity, to be out of the reach of Giant Despair; not to be shut up in the iron cage; not to be abandoned, as Judas or Ahithophel, to utter desperation and suicide, and, after a long life of profession, concerning faith to make dreadful shipwreck! Now the child of God, with all his doubts, fears, sinkings, misgivings, and trying perplexities is never really and truly in despair. He may tread so near the borders of that black country that it may be debatable whether he is walking in that land or still only upon the borders of it.

I believe many children of God have at times come to the solemn conclusion that there is no hope for them, for they cannot see how they can be saved or have their aggravated sins pardoned. This may not be black despair, nor such utter, irremediable desperation as seized Saul and Judas, for there is still a "Who can tell," (John 3:9). Yet it certainly is walking very near the borders of that dark and terrible land.

I cannot tell, nor do I believe any can, how low a child of God may sink, or how long he may continue under the terrors of the Almighty. However, we have the warrant of God's word to believe that he is never given up to utter despair, for the Lord holds up his feet from falling into that terrible pit, and being cast into that sea to which there is neither bottom nor shore.

July

July

1st

"As the hart panteth after the water brooks, so panteth my soul after thee, O God."
Psalm 42:1

David has used a very striking figure in these words. Conceive a wounded stag, with an arrow in his flank, pursued by a crowd of hunters and hounds, all eager to pull him down. Conceive him to have run for some long time under a burning sun over crags and dry plains; and conceive that at a distance this poor hunted animal sees water gently flowing along. Oh, how it pants! How its heaving sides gasp, and how it longs for the cooling stream, not only that it may drink large draughts of the fresh waters and lave its panting flanks and weary, parched limbs - but, by swimming across, may haply escape the dogs and hunters at its heels.

How strong and how striking is the figure, and yet how earnestly does David employ it to set forth the panting of his own soul after God. Of ourselves we cannot, perhaps, rise up into the fullness of this figure, and we dare not stretch out our feelings side by side with his, or claim the same burning, vehement, ardent craving for God. Even so we may at least see from them what the saints of God have experienced in times of temptation and trial in days of old. We may in some measure compare the feelings of our soul with theirs, sometimes to fill us with shame and confusion at our shortcomings and sometimes to stimulate and encourage us so far as we experience a degree of similar teachings, for these things are written "for our admonition, upon whom the ends of the world are come," (1Cor. 10:11).

Thus in various ways and to various ends we may, with God's help and blessing, look into such expressions as we find in the words of David, and in the fear of God search our hearts to see if we can find anything there corresponding to the work of grace that the Holy Spirit describes in his soul. Neither need we be utterly cast down nor wholly discouraged if you cannot find a full or close similarity. Can you find *any?* If so, take encouragement, for the Lord despises not the day of small things. It is his own work upon the heart and his own work alone to which he has regard, as David felt when he said, "The LORD will perfect that which concerneth me: thy mercy, O LORD, endureth for ever: forsake not the works of thine own hands," (Psa. 138:8).

That work will ever be a copy in full or in miniature, a complete or reduced photograph, of the work of grace described in the Scripture as carried out by the Spirit in the hearts of God's saints of old.

July 2nd

"For the Jews require a sign, and the Greeks seek after wisdom - but we preach Christ crucified, unto the Jews a stumbling block, and unto the Greeks foolishness."
1Corinthians 1:22-23

The mystery of the cross can be received only by faith. To the Jews it was a stumbling block, and to the Greeks foolishness, but to those who are called, both Jews and Greeks, it is the power of God and the wisdom of God. When, then, we can believe that the Son of God took our flesh and blood out of love and compassion for our souls, the stumbling block is removed. In seeing that there is no other way which even heaven itself could devise, no other means that the wisdom of God could contrive whereby sinners could be saved other than the death of the cross, then the mystery shines forth with unspeakable lustre and glory. The shame and ignominy, what the Apostle calls the "weakness" and "foolishness" of the cross disappear, swallowed up in a flood of surpassing grace, and faith views it as a glorious scheme of God's own devising, and of the Son of God's approving and accomplishing.

Viewed in this light how glorious it appears, that by suffering in our nature all the penalties of our sin, Jesus should redeem us from the lowest hell and raise us up to the highest heaven. How full of unspeakable wisdom was that plan whereby he united God and man by himself becoming God-man, empowering poor worms of earth to soar above the skies and live forever in the presence of him who is a consuming fire. How glorious is that scheme whereby reconciling aliens and enemies unto his heavenly Father, he summons them, when death cuts their mortal thread, to mount up into an eternity of bliss, there to view face to face the great and glorious I AM; to be forever enwrapped in the blaze of Deity, and ever folded in the arms of a Triune God.

It is this blessed end, this reward of the Redeemer's sufferings, blood shedding and death, which lifts our view beyond the depths of the fall and the misery of sin that we see and feel in this miserable world. It is this view by faith of the glory which shall be revealed that enables us to see the depth of wisdom and mercy that were in the heart of God when he permitted Adam to fall. It is as if we could see the glory of God breaking forth through it in all the splendour of atoning blood and dying love, securing to guilty man the joys of salvation, and bringing to God an eternal revenue of praise.

July 3rd

"But God forbid that I should glory, save in the cross of our Lord Jesus Christ, by whom the world is crucified unto me, and I unto the world."
Galatians 6:14

An experimental knowledge of crucifixion with his crucified Lord made Paul preach the cross, not only in its power to save, but also in its power to sanctify. As then, so now, this preaching of the cross not only as the meritorious cause of all salvation, but as the instrumental cause of all sanctification, is "to them that perish foolishness," (1Cor. 1:18). As men have devised some other way of salvation than by the blood of the cross, so have they devised some other way of holiness than by the power of the cross. More accurately, they have altogether set aside obedience, fruitfulness, self-denial, mortification of the deeds of the body, and crucifixion of the flesh and the world.

Extremes are said to agree at times, and certainly men of most opposite sentiments will unite in despising the cross and counting it foolishness. The Arminian despises it for justification, and the Antinomian for sanctification. 'Believe and be holy' is as strange a sound to the latter as 'Believe and be saved' to the former. Yet, 'without holiness no man shall see the Lord', (Heb. 12:14), is as much written on the portal of life as, "By grace are ye saved through faith," (Eph. 2:8). Through the cross, that is, through union and communion with him who suffered upon it, not only is there a fountain opened for all sin, but for all uncleanness. Blood and water gushed from the side of Jesus when pierced by the Roman spear.

"This fountain so dear, he'll freely impart;
Unlocked by the spear, it gushed from the heart,
With blood and with water; the first to atone,
To cleanse us the latter; the fountain's but one."

"All my springs are in thee," said the man after God's own heart, (Psa. 87:7); and well may we re-echo his words. All our springs, not only of pardon, peace, acceptance and justification, but also of happiness and holiness, of wisdom and strength, of victory over the world, of mortification of a body of sin and death rise in his crucifixion. He is the source of every fresh revival, every renewal of hope and confidence, of all prayer and praise, and, as with Aaron's rod, of every new budding forth of the soul in blossom and fruit. Every gracious feeling, spiritual desire, warm supplication, honest confession, melting contrition, and godly sorrow for sin flows from

July

that fountain of life which is hidden with Christ in God, and is found in a crucified Lord.

Thus Christ crucified is, "unto us which are saved... the power of God," (1Cor. 1:18), and by God "is made unto us wisdom, and righteousness, and sanctification, and redemption," (1Cor. 1:30). At the cross alone can we be made wise unto salvation. Only there can we become righteous by a free justification, receive of his Spirit to make us holy, and be redeemed, washed and delivered by blood and power from sin, Satan, death, and hell.

4th

"For the scripture saith, Whosoever believeth on him shall not be ashamed."
Romans 10:11

A child of God may be often deeply exercised whether he has any faith at all; for when he reads what faith has done and can do, and sees and feels how little it has done for him, he is seized with doubts and fears whether he has ever been blessed with the faith of God's elect. This makes him often say, 'Woe is me; do I indeed possess one grain of saving faith?'

But possess it he does; it is his very faith which makes him so anxiously ask himself the question. It is his very faith that makes him see and feel the nature and amount of his unbelief. It is the very light of God shining into his soul that shows him his sins, their true nature and number, and convinces him of their guilt and enormity. This light lays the burden of them upon his conscience and discovers to him the workings of an unbelieving heart. Yet besides all this, if he had no faith at all he could not hear the voice of God speaking in the gospel, nor could he receive it as a message of mercy or of condemnation. He assuredly has faith, though he feels little of its witnessing evidence or abounding comfort.

This faith will save his soul; for "the gifts and calling of God are without repentance," (Rom. 11:29); that is, God never repents of any gift that he bestows or of any calling which he has granted. If, then, he has ever blessed you with faith, however small that faith may be in itself or in your own view of it, he will never take it away out of your heart, but rather will he fan the smoking flax until it bursts forth into a flame. He will never forsake the work of his own hands, for he which "he which hath begun a good work in you will perform it until the day of Jesus Christ," (Phil. 1:6).

July

If ever, nay, if but once in your life, you have felt the gospel to be the power of God unto salvation; if you have ever had just one view of Christ by living faith, that work has been begun. If but once only, under the influence of his blessed Spirit on your heart, you have laid hold of him and felt even for a few minutes that he was yours, your soul is as safe as though it were continually bathing in the river which makes glad the city of God. It is as though you are continually drinking of the milk and honey of the gospel, and walking all day long in the full light of his most gracious countenance.

Now, a man should not be satisfied with living at a poor, cold, dying rate, he should seek for the work once begun to be completed. Notwithstanding, it is a part of God's truth that as regards salvation, it is not the amount, but the reality of faith that saves the soul.

5th

"It shall bring forth new fruit according to his months, because their waters they issued out of the sanctuary." Ezekiel 47:12

There is always something new in the things of God. Here is a passage perhaps in the word of God that we have read and read again and again without seeing or feeling anything in it; but all of a sudden there may come a blessed flash of light upon it; we now see something in it that we have never seen before, something exceedingly sweet and precious. It is now all new; it is received as new, felt as new, fed upon as new, relished as new. It seems as though we never saw anything in the passage before.

As with reading the word, so it is with hearing. You may perhaps have had your soul shut up in distress and bondage and misery for months; you could scarcely trace anything of the life of God in you. But under the preached word, it may have pleased God to drop something which has come into your heart with warmth, and life, and feeling. Oh, how new it is! It is as new as though it were never heard before; it seems as though the eyes were now first opened to see new things, and the ears were opened to hear new things, and the heart opened to receive new things.

The Lord thus fulfils that blessed promise given through the apostle John, "And he that sat upon the throne said, Behold, I make all things new," (Rev. 21:5), and fulfils that spoken of by Paul, "Therefore if any man be in Christ, he is a new creature: old things are passed away; behold, all things are become new," (2Cor. 5:17).

July 6th

"And those that walk in pride he is able to abase."
Daniel 4:37

Among all the evils which lie naked and open before the eyes of Him with whom we have to do, pride seems especially to incur his holy abhorrence; and the outward manifestations of it have perhaps drawn down as much as, or more than, any other sin, his marked thunderbolts. Pride cost Sennacherib his army and Herod his life; pride opened the earth to Korah, Dathan, and Abiram, and hung up Absalom in the boughs of an oak; pride filled the breast of Saul with murderous hatred against David, and tore ten tribes at one stroke from the hand of Rehoboam. Pride drove Nebuchadnezzar from the society of his fellow-men, and made him eat grass as oxen, and his body to be wet with the dew of heaven, until his hairs were grown as eagles' feathers, and his nails like birds' claws.

As it has cut off the wicked from the earth, and left them neither son nor nephew, root nor branch, so has it made sad havoc even among the family of God. Pride shut Aaron out of the promised land and made Miriam a leper, and whilst working in the heart of David it brought about a pestilence which cut off seventy thousand men. Pride carried captive to Babylon Hezekiah's treasure and descendants, and cast Jonah into the whale's belly, which to him was like unto the very belly of hell.

It is the only source of contention; the certain forerunner of a fall; the instigator of persecution; a snare for the feet; a chain to compass the whole body; the main element of deceitfulness, and the grave of all uprightness. The very opposite to charity, pride is not patient, and is never kind; she always envies, and ever boasts of herself; is continually puffed up, always behaves herself unseemly, ever seeks her own, is easily provoked, perpetually thinks evil, rejoices in iniquity, but rejoices not in the truth. She bears nothing, believes nothing, (good in a brother), hopes nothing, and endures nothing. She is ever restless and ever miserable, tormenting herself and tormenting others, the bane of churches, the fomenter of strife, and the extinguisher of love. May it be our wisdom to see, our grace to abhor, and our victory to overcome her, and may the experience of that verse in Deer's hymn be ours–

"Your garden is the place
Where pride can not intrude;
For should it dare to enter there,
Would soon be drowned in blood."

July 7th

"And I give unto them eternal life; and they shall never perish, neither shall any man pluck them out of my hand." John 10:28

The Lord says, "I give unto them, (that is, my sheep), eternal life;" he doesn't say "I *will* give unto them eternal life." It is not something to be given at a future date, but it has been given unto them now. We therefore read, "He that believeth on the Son hath everlasting life," (John 3:36). The believer has it now, as a present, felt, and enjoyed possession. This life is given manifestly when Christ reveals himself to the soul; for eternal life is then received out of his fullness as an enjoyed possession. All, then, who have truly fled for refuge to lay hold of the hope set before them, embrace in so doing eternal life. They live, as being manifestly in Christ, for he is "our life;" and as they embrace it in him they feel its sweet movements in their breast, in the joy it communicates, in the peace it imparts, in the prospects it opens, in the doubts it removes, and in the fears it disperses.

Thus, in real religion, there is something, if I may so speak, tangible, something to be laid hold of; and this distinguishes a good hope through grace from every other hope which is delusive, enthusiastic, or visionary. Depend upon it, there is a reality in vital godliness, a possession for eternity, which, therefore, kills and deadens the living child of God to a perishing world, and the fading things of time and sense. Whenever we get a view of Christ, there is a view of eternal life in him; for he is the eternal Son of God, and when he makes himself known to the soul as such, he shows us that all our life is in him.

The work that he accomplished is for eternity; he lives himself forever and ever; and those whom he has redeemed by his blood, justified by his righteousness, and sanctified by his grace, will live forever and ever in his glorious presence. It is the eternity of his love which stamps it with its main value and blessedness; for this life being eternal, secures not only perpetuity, but immutability, prevents it from any change in time as well as from any change in eternity, and secures it firm and stable to all the heirs of promise. As, then, they lay hold of eternal life in laying hold of him who is the life, and as the sweet movements of hope spring up in their breast, it opens before their eyes a vista of immortal joy.

July 8th

"Because he hath set his love upon me, therefore will I deliver him: I will set him on high, because he hath known my name."
Psalm 91:14

A man must know the Lord's name before ever he can feel any real love to him. Now this is needful, this is what the Lord does for his people; he causes them to know his name. "They shall all know me, from the least of them unto the greatest," (Jer. 31:34). "They shall..." The Lord has declared it. They shall know me.

Now what is the name of the Lord? When God revealed himself unto Moses, did he not say, "I AM THAT I AM?" This was the way God taught Moses his name, and we may gather from it that whatever God is, that is his name. God is holy, God is just, God is merciful, and God is a God of love. Now the penitent sinner must know this. He must know that God is a pure and holy God, and at first when he is beginning to learn this lesson, he is completely astonished and appalled by it. It causes him to shrink away and hide himself from God. 'How can I appear before God, who is of purer eyes than to behold iniquity?' he cries, and it brings distress into his conscience.

It is the first work of the Spirit to convince men of sin, and a sense of God's holiness is that which brings upon us this conviction – our sin and God's purity. How can the sinner appear before and approach to God? Whilst he is under the terrors of the law, he is full of distress, and at times, perhaps, wishes he had never been born, and at other times he is tempted with hard thoughts of God, reaping where he had not sown, and gathering where he had not strowed. This is how God is seen in his perverted mind. The devil is at him, and tries all he can to harden his heart against the Almighty, but the terrors of the Almighty have taken hold of him. He tries many ways to get these arrows extracted, but all his tugging and pulling only make the wound worse.

So he goes on struggling until he is brought to see that God is a God of mercy – and this is revealed to him in and through the Lord Jesus. This is what clears up the mystery - when he sees Christ bleeding on the cross. Here he sees God is both a just God and a Saviour. God is pure and holy, and exacts to the utmost farthing all the enormous debt he owes, and yet to the bleeding, broken heart, he, through Christ, can and does manifest his mercy.

July 9th

"But none of these things move me, neither count I my life dear unto myself, so that I might finish my course with joy, and the ministry, which I have received of the Lord Jesus, to testify the gospel of the grace of God."
Acts 20:24

What does the word 'gospel' signify? Its literal meaning is either God's word or message, or rather, good news, or good tidings, which is more agreeable to the original. If it be 'good news', it must be good news of something for someone. There must be some good tidings brought, and there must be some person by whom, as good tidings, it is received. In order, then, that the gospel should be good news, and glad tidings, there must be a message from God to man, God being the Speaker, and man the hearer; he the gracious Giver, and man the happy receiver. But if the gospel means good news from heaven to earth, it can only be worthy of that title if it proclaims grace, mercy, pardon, deliverance, and salvation, and all as free gifts of God's unmerited favour. Otherwise, it would not be a gospel adapted to our needs; it would not be good news, or glad tidings to us poor sinners, to us law-breakers, to us guilty criminals, to us vile transgressors, to us arraigned at the bar of infinite justice, to us condemned to die by the unswerving demands of God's holiness. And as it must be a gospel adapted to us to receive, so must it be a gospel worthy of God to give.

This gospel then, pure, clear, and free, is good news or glad tidings, as proclaiming pardon through the blood of Jesus and justification by his righteousness. It reveals an obedience whereby the law was magnified and made honourable, and an atoning sacrifice for sin by which it was forever blotted out and put away; and thus it brings glory to God and salvation to the soul. It is a pure revelation of sovereign mercy, love and grace, whereby each Person in the divine Trinity is exalted and magnified. In it, mercy and truth meet together, and righteousness and peace kiss. As revealed in it, truth springeth out of earth in the hearts of contrite sinners, and righteousness, eternally satisfied by Christ's obedience, looks down from heaven, (Psa. 85:11).

If you love a pure, a clear, a free gospel, "the gospel of the grace of God," you love it not only because it is so fully suitable to your needs, so thoroughly adapted to your fallen state, but because you have felt its sweetness and power. You love it because it not only speaks of pardon, but brings pardon; it not only proclaims mercy, but brings mercy; it not only points out a way of salvation, but brings salvation, with all its rich attendant blessings, into your heart. It thus becomes "the power of God unto salvation to every one that believeth," (Rom. 1:16).

10th

"I am the vine, ye are the branches: He that abideth in me, and I in him, the same bringeth forth much fruit: for without me ye can do nothing."
John 15:5

Without a union with Christ, we have no spiritual existence. We may boldly say that we no more have a spiritual being in the mind of God independent of Christ, than the branch of a tree has an independent existence out of the stem in which it grows.

Yet you will also observe in this figure of the vine and the branches, how all the fruitfulness of the branch depends upon its union with the vine. Whatever life there is in the branch, it flows out of the stem; whatever strength there is in the branch, it comes from its union with the stem; whatever foliage, whatever fruit, all comes out of its union with the stem. This is the case whether the branch be great or small, from the stoutest limb of a tree to the smallest twig, all are in union with the stem and all derive life and nourishment from it.

So it is in grace. Not only does our very being, as sons and daughters of the Lord Almighty, result from our union with Christ, but our well-being also. All our knowledge, therefore, of heavenly mysteries, all our faith, all our hope, and all our love springs from him. All our grace, whether much or little, whether that of a babe, a child, a young man, or a father – flows out of a personal, spiritual, and experimental union with the Lord Jesus, for we are nothing but what we are in him, and we have nothing but what we possess by virtue of our union with him.

11th

"And our hope of you is stedfast, knowing, that as ye are partakers of the sufferings, so shall ye be also of the consolation."
2Corinthians 1:7

The Lord has appointed the path of sorrow for the redeemed to walk in. Why? One purpose is to wean them from the world; another purpose is to show them the weakness of the creature; a third purpose is to make them feel the liberty and vitality of genuine godliness made manifest in their soul's experience.

What am I, and what are you when we have no trials? Light, frothy, worldly-minded, carnal, and frivolous. We may talk of the things of God, but they are at a distance; there are no solemn feelings, no melting sensations, no real brokenness, no genuine contrition, no weeping at the divine feet, no embracing of Christ in the arms of affection.

But when affliction, be it in providence or be it in grace, brings a man down; when it empties him of all his high thoughts, lays him low in his own eyes, brings trouble into his heart, I assure you he needs something more than mere external religion. He needs power; he needs to experience in his soul the operations of the blessed Spirit; he wants to have a precious Jesus manifesting himself to his soul in love and blood. When trouble strikes he needs to see his lovely countenance beaming upon him in ravishing smiles; he needs to hear the sweet whispers of dying love speaking inward peace; he needs to have the blessed Lord come into his soul, manifesting himself to him as he does not manifest himself to the world.

What brings a man here? A few dry notions floating to and fro in his brain, like a few drops of oil in a pail of water? That will never bring the life and power of vital godliness into a man's heart. It must be by being experimentally acquainted with trouble. When he is led into the path of tribulation, he then begins to long after, and, in God's own time and way, he begins to drink into, the sweetness of vital godliness, made manifest in his heart by the power of God.

12th

"Then they that were in the ship came and worshipped him, saying, Of a truth thou art the Son of God."
Matthew 14:33

What a beauty and blessedness there is in the deity of the Lord Jesus Christ, when viewed by the spiritual eye! Our reasoning minds, it is true, may be deeply stumbled at the doctrine of an incarnate God. My own mind, I know, has sometimes been driven almost to its wits' end by this great mystery of deity and humanity combined in the Person of Christ, for it so surpasses all human comprehension, and is so removed beyond the grasp of all our reasoning faculties. It is not contrary to reason, for there is nothing in it impossible or self-contradictory; but it is beyond and above the reach of human thought and tangible apprehension.

Consider what would be the most certain and most fearful consequences if the Lord Jesus Christ were not what he declares himself to be, God as well as man. Such contemplation compels us, from the very necessity of the case, to cast ourselves with all the weight of our sins and sorrows upon an incarnate God, as the shipwrecked sailor gladly casts himself upon the rock in the ocean as the only refuge from the devouring sea.

When we feel what sinners we are and have been, and looking down into the depths of the fall see in some feeble and faint measure what sin is in the sight of a holy and pure God, what can save us from despair unless we see the deity of the Lord Jesus Christ? What can rescue us apart from his work upon the cross and his obedience with a merit that shall suffice to justify our guilty souls, wash away our aggravated iniquities, blot out our fearful crimes, and make us fit to appear in the presence of a righteous God? Thus we are sometimes absolutely compelled to throw ourselves upon the deity of Christ, as ready to perish, because in such a divine Saviour, in such precious blood we see a refuge, and we see elsewhere no other.

We then feel that if the deity of Christ be taken away, the Church of God is lost. Where can you find pardon? Where will be justification? From whence comes reconciliation to God? Where is the atoning blood, if there is no Saviour who merited as God and suffered as man? We might as well leap into hell at once with all our sins upon our head, as a sailor might spring over the prow of a burning ship into the boiling waves, to meet death instead of waiting for it, unless we believe by a living faith in the deity of the Son of God.

Yet sometimes we are sweetly led into this glorious truth, not merely driven by sheer necessity, but blessedly drawn into this great mystery of godliness when Christ is revealed to our souls by the power of God. Then, seeing light in God's light, we view the deity of Christ investing every thought, word, and act of his suffering humanity with unspeakable merit. Then we see how this glorious fact of deity and humanity in the Person of Immanuel satisfies every need, puts away every sin, heals every wound, wipes away every tear, and sweetly brings the soul to repose on the bosom of God.

Sometimes from necessity, driven by storms of guilt and waves of temptation, and sometimes sweetly drawn by the leadings and teachings of the Holy Spirit, we lay hold of the hope set before us in the essential deity and suffering humanity of the Son of God, knowing that there is a refuge in him from sin, death, hell, and despair.

July 13th

"We have such an high priest, who is set on the right hand of the throne of the Majesty in the heavens; a minister of the sanctuary, and of the true tabernacle, which the Lord pitched, and not man."
Hebrews 8:1-2

Our blessed Lord was to be "an High Priest after the order of Melchizedec," (Heb. 5:10). It will be remembered that Melchizedec met Abraham returning from the slaughter of the kings, and blessed him, (Gen. 14:19). In the same way our great High Priest blesses the seed of Abraham; for "they which be of faith are blessed with faithful Abraham," (Gal. 3:9), and as believers in the Lord Jesus Christ, they walk in his steps who "believed God, and it was counted unto him for righteousness," (Rom. 4:3).

Howbeit that Melchizedec the type could only *ask* God to bless Abraham; he could not himself confer the blessing. Jesus, the antitype, our great Melchizedec, whose priesthood is "after the power of an endless life," (Heb. 7:16), blesses his people, not by merely asking God to bless them, but by himself showering down blessings upon them, and by communicating to them out of his own fullness every grace which can sanctify as well as save.

Even before his incarnation, when he appeared in human form, anticipating in appearance that flesh and blood which he should afterwards assume in reality, he had power to bless. We read that when Jacob wrestled with the angel, which angel was no created angel, but the Angel of the covenant, even the Son of God himself in human form, he said, "I will not let thee go, except thou bless me," (Gen. 32:26). In answer to his wrestling cry we read that "he blessed him there," (v29). Jacob knew that no created angel could bless him, and after he received the blessing said, "I have seen God face to face, and my life is preserved," (v30).

To this blessing Jacob afterwards referred when, in blessing Ephraim and Manasseh, he said, "The angel which redeemed me from all evil bless the lads," (Gen. 48:16). Thus, also, our gracious Lord, immediately before his ascension to heaven, in anticipation of the gifts and graces which he was to send down upon his disciples when exalted to the right hand of the Father, "lifted up his hands and blessed them," (Luke 24:50). Yet, as if to show that he would ever continue to bless them, "it came to pass, while he blessed them, he was parted from them, and carried up into heaven," as if he were blessing them all the way up to heaven, even before he took possession of his mediatorial throne, (Luke 24:51).

July

14th

"But ye, beloved, building up yourselves on your most holy faith, praying in the Holy Ghost."
Jude 20

By the words "most holy faith," we may understand chiefly the grand truths of the everlasting gospel which are revealed unto and embraced by faith. They are called our "most holy faith" because they are imbued with all the holiness of God, and as they are received into believing hearts they communicate sanctification, because they have a liberating, sanctifying efficacy.

The words "building up" assume that there is a foundation to build upon, and so it is. Christ is that foundation which God has laid in Zion, a chief cornerstone, elect and precious; and where Christ is revealed to the soul by divine power, a foundation is laid in the heart on which every subsequent truth is to be built up.

The grand thing to be clear of in our own experience is, whether Christ has been laid as a foundation in our souls or not, and if he has, we have been driven from every other as finding no rest or peace but in him. If he has been revealed to our souls by the mighty power of God, then we will have seen and felt in him that foundation on which we can stand, and that for eternity.

As the Son of the Father in truth and love; as having come to finish the work which the Father gave him to do; and as having put away sin by the sacrifice of himself, and brought in an everlasting righteousness in which we stand justified, there is a foundation on which a poor, guilty soul may rest.

When this foundation is brought near, and we, by the power of God's grace, are lifted up to rest upon it, we can say; "How firm a foundation, ye saints of the Lord, Is laid for your faith in his excellent word."

"For other foundation can no man lay than that is laid, which is Jesus Christ," (1Cor. 3:11).

15th

"Keep yourselves in the love of God."
Jude 21

When Christ is made known to our soul by the power of God, we have views of truth in him, of happiness in him, and of deliverance in him. "As ye have therefore received Christ Jesus the Lord, so walk ye in him," (Col. 2:6). We receive him as the Son of the Father in truth and love; we receive him as suitable to our needs and woes; we receive him as putting away sin by the sacrifice of himself, and endearing himself to our heart in the sweet manifestation of his Person, goodness, and love. Now as long as Christ and the soul are together, there is no place for error, and no place for evil. He makes the soul tender, the heart upright, the spirit broken and contrite, truth precious, error hateful, and sin loathsome and detestable. Whilst he and the soul are engaged together, error cannot approach nor evil find an entrance so as to get any standing-ground in the heart.

However, error is very subtle. It addresses itself to our reasoning powers, and when we lose sight of Christ, then error very easily creeps in. If not an error of doctrine, some special lust, or something ungodly, seems by degrees to obtain power and influence, and we gradually decline from the strength of faith, the confidence of hope, and the sweet affections of love. We drop almost unnoticed into a cold, carnal, careless, lifeless state, where, no longer together with Christ, we lie open to the full invasion of error and the temptations of Satan as an angel of light or an angel of darkness.

Jude now comes and says, 'Keep yourselves in the love of God, and I will tell you, if you will listen to me, how you shall do it. You must build up yourselves on your most holy faith'.

God has laid a foundation for your faith in his holy word; he has laid Christ as a foundation in your own soul. That is a very strong foundation; it is of God's own laying. It is very solid, and will bear any weight that is laid upon it. And therefore you must build up yourselves upon that most holy faith if you would have a religion which stands. If your religion, or any part of your religion, be built upon another foundation, it will not stand, but if you build up yourselves on your most holy faith, then everything you build upon it will stand, because it rests upon the foundation, and is in harmony with it.

16th

"Search me, O God, and know my heart - try me, and know my thoughts and see if there be any wicked way in me, and lead me in the way everlasting."
Psalm 139:23-24

The people of God cannot take their religion upon credit; they cannot be satisfied with the endorsement of this or that good man.

July

They must have it wrought by God himself. They are often exercised as to whence their religion came. Do you not find it so, and that it costs you many exercises? If, for instance, you are cast down, you are exercised whether it springs from godly sorrow for sin. If you are comforted, you cannot take the comfort for granted; you must have it weighed up in the gospel balance. If you meet with providential deliverances, you cannot take them as so many certain evidences that all is right with your soul. So that every step you take you have to examine, and weigh it whether it be of God.

The dead professors, the hypocrites in Zion never have their religion tried and weighed up in this way. They know nothing of these inward exercises. They take things for granted; they nestle under some good man's wing, or get their religion endorsed by some minister, and are satisfied.

But the people of God must have testimonies from the Lord himself; and they will often be sharply exercised whether they have that work in their souls which will stand in the trying hour. If in answer to their cries the Lord is pleased to shine into their souls, and raise up clear tokens that it is from heaven, it fills their hearts with gratitude, sinks the things of time and sense, and lifts up their affections to that blessed fountain whence these testimonies came down. Those very things which seem against them are for them, and they derive their sweetest consolations out of their heaviest afflictions. They would not change their trying path, with all its bitter things, for the smooth flowery path in which they see thousands walk, knowing that a religion without trials and temptations will only lead the soul down into a never-ending hell.

Thus at times they can feel good spring out of their exercises, and would rather be all their days a tempted, tried people, and bear those things which God inflicts, than walk in a path which seems right in the eyes of a man, and at the end find eternal destruction. They would rather have those chastisements which prove they are children and not bastards, than walk in a flesh-pleasing way of which the end is eternal damnation.

17th

"Then what prayer or what supplication soever shall be made of any man, or of all thy people Israel, when every one shall know his own sore and his own grief, and shall spread forth his hands in this house:"
2Chronicles 6:29

July

Solomon comes to experience; he puts his hand upon the right spot. It is in a man knowing his "own sore" and his "own grief."

You may know another man's sores and griefs, but that will not profit you. You may read of experience in books, love to hear experimental ministers and will hear no others; and yet know not your own sore and your own grief. Like a physician who may know the symptoms of every malady, and yet not have one malady of his own; so you may hear described every symptom of every disease, and yet be untouched by one.

Yet the man for whom Solomon's prayer is made is he that knows and feels, painfully feels, his own sore and his own grief, whose heart is indeed a grief unto him, whose sins do indeed trouble him. How painful this sore often is! How it runs night and day! How full of ulcerous matter it seems, and how it shrinks from the probe!

Most of the Lord's family have a "sore." Each some tender spot, something perhaps known to himself and to God alone, and the cause of his greatest grief. It may be some secret slip he has made, some sin he has committed, some word he has spoken, or some evil thing he has done. He has been entangled, entrapped, and cast down; and this is his grief and his sore which he feels, and that at times deeply before God.

For such Solomon prays. He casts his net upon the right side of the ship as he pleads their cause, "Then hear thou from heaven thy dwelling place, and forgive, and render unto every man according unto all his ways, whose heart thou knowest; for thou only knowest the hearts of the children of men," (2Chro. 6:30).

Yes; God alone knows the heart and he knows it completely, and he sees to its very bottom.

18th

"Likewise the Spirit also helpeth our infirmities: for we know not what we should pray for as we ought: but the Spirit itself maketh intercession for us with groanings which cannot be uttered."
Romans 8:26

"We know not what we should pray for as we ought." How often do we find and feel this to be our case. Darkness covers our mind; ignorance pervades our soul; unbelief vexes our spirit; guilt troubles our conscience; and a crowd of evil imaginations, or foolish or worse than foolish wanderings distract our thoughts. Satan himself hurls in thick and fast his fiery darts and a dense cloud is spread over the mercy-seat; infidelity whispers its vile suggestions, until, amid all this rabble throng, such confusion and bondage prevail that words seem idle breath, and prayer to the God of heaven but empty mockery.

In this scene of confusion and distraction, when all seems going to the wreck, how kind, how gracious is it in the blessed Spirit to come, as it were, to the rescue of the poor bewildered saint, and to teach him how to pray and what to pray for. He is therefore said to help our infirmities, for these evils of which we have been speaking are not wilful, deliberate sins, but wretched infirmities of the flesh.

He helps our infirmities by subduing the power and prevalence of unbelief; by commanding in the mind a solemn calm, and by rebuking and chasing away Satan and his fiery darts. He awes the soul with a reverential sense of the power and presence of God and presents Jesus before our eyes as the Mediator at the right hand of the Father. He raises up and draws forth faith upon his Person and work, and upon his blood and righteousness; and, above all, himself intercedes for us and in us "with groanings which cannot be uttered."

When the soul is favoured thus to pray, its petitions are a spiritual sacrifice, and its cries enter the ears of the Lord Almighty, for "And he that searcheth the hearts knoweth what is the mind of the Spirit, because he maketh intercession for the saints according to the will of God," (Rom. 8:27).

19th

"Because they have no changes, therefore they fear not God."
Psalm 55:19

True religion is certainly the most weighty, and yet the most mysterious matter that we ever have had or ever can have to deal with in this world; and I will tell you this, that it will either comfort you, or it will distress you. It will either exercise your mind, trouble your soul, cast down your spirit, and make you truly miserable, or else it will be the source of your choicest comfort and your greatest happiness. From true religion come our deepest sorrows and highest joys, the greatest uneasiness and the sweetest peace.

There is this peculiar feature about true religion that in the greatest prosperity it may be the cause to us of the chief trouble, or in the greatest adversity it may be to us the cause of the purest joy. What are wealth or health, rank or titles, and every comfort the world can afford to a wounded spirit? What are poverty, sickness, persecution, contempt, a garret or a prison to a soul basking in the smiles of eternal love?

Religion will surely make itself felt wherever it exists, and will testify by its power to its presence. If, then, you are a partaker of true religion, be you who, where, or what you may, you cannot be at ease in Zion, for there will be ever something working up out of your own heart or arising from some other quarter to make you uneasy.

Job was once at ease, but he was not allowed to die in his soft nest. He therefore says, "I was at ease, but he hath broken me asunder: he hath also taken me by my neck, and shaken me to pieces, and set me up for his mark," (Job16:12). And yet with all this unexpected and apparently cruel treatment, he could still say, "Behold, my witness is in heaven, and my record is on high," (Job 16:19).

He was so exercised and distressed that he had to cry out, "My bone cleaveth to my skin and to my flesh, and I am escaped with the skin of my teeth. Have pity upon me, have pity upon me, O ye my friends; for the hand of God hath touched me," (Job 19:20-21). Yet he could add, in all the confidence of faith, as desirous that his words might stand forever upon record:

"Oh that my words were now written! Oh that they were printed in a book! That they were graven with an iron pen and lead in the rock for ever! For I know that my redeemer liveth, and that he shall stand at the latter day upon the earth: and though after my skin worms destroy this body, yet in my flesh shall I see God; whom I shall see for myself, and mine eyes shall behold, and not another; though my reins be consumed within me," Job 19:23-27.

20th

"Deal bountifully with thy servant, that I may live, and keep thy word."
Psalm 119:17

Can the Lord deal any way but bountifully with his servants? Why indeed has he made you his servants? Why did he strike the chains of former servitude off your hands? Why did he bring you out of the service of sin, the world, Satan, and self? Why did he ever make himself precious to your heart, win your affections, and enable you to give yourselves wholly unto him?

Was it that he might cast you off? That he might mock your calamity? That he might trample you one day into hell? That he might leave you to yourself, that he might allow Satan to overcome you, permit your lusts to destroy you; or allow your sins to be tied one day like a mill-stone round your neck to sink you into hell?

Oh, can our hearts ever indulge thoughts so derogatory to sovereign grace? Was it not because the Lord had bounty in his heart towards you, that he first turned your heart towards himself? Was it not because the Lord had purposes of love towards you, that he first led your feet into his paths? Was it not because God first loved you, that he gave his Son to die for you?

Now if he has taught you, led you, upheld you, kept you, all this time, is it to cast you off now – to let you sink at last? He cannot do so, and will not do so. Those whom he loves, he loves to the end; the good work which he has begun, he will accomplish, and bring to final perfection; and therefore all the Lord's acts are acts of bounty.

21st

"So then it is not of him that willeth, nor of him that runneth, but of God that sheweth mercy."
Romans 9:16

He that is not interested in the eternal election of God the Father, in the atoning blood and justifying righteousness of God the Son, or in the work and witness of God the Holy Spirit, whatever be his name, sect, denomination or profession, he will surely die in his sin. Whatever be his outward conduct, the doctrines he professes, or the creed to which he signs his name, he will die as Esau died, as Balaam died, as Saul died, as Judas and Ahithophel died. He will never see the King in his beauty; never see the land afar off; never see the new Jerusalem, nor "the blood of sprinkling, that speaketh better things than that of Abel," (Heb. 12:24).

Howbeit every living soul that has been feelingly taught his lost condition, that has known something of a resting-place in Christ, that has turned his back upon the world and the professing church, and gone weeping Zionward will have a different end. He in whose heart God the Holy Spirit has implanted solemn desires and solemn determinations under divine teaching, not of free will but of grace, strengthened by the Spirit of God, "to join himself to the Lord in a perpetual covenant never to be forgotten" will be borne safely through this waste-howling wilderness.

The one who is determined to live in Jesus and die in Jesus, to live out of Jesus and unto Jesus, that he may feel his power, taste his love, know his blood, rejoice in his grace shall, like Israel of old be

July

carried through this valley of tears. He will be taken to enjoy eternal bliss and glory in the presence of Him whom to see as he is, constitutes the blessedness of the redeemed.

Every such poor, exercised, tempted soul shall be brought into a personal enjoyment of Christ below and of Christ above, so as to enjoy a foretaste of heaven here, and hereafter to bathe in the ocean of endless bliss.

22nd

"Now no chastening for the present seemeth to be joyous, but grievous: nevertheless afterward it yieldeth the peaceable fruit of righteousness unto them which are exercised thereby."
Hebrews 12:11

Although the Apostle speaks here of chastening generally, this includes spiritual exercises which 'for the present seem not to be joyous, but grievous; but afterward will yield the peaceable fruit of righteousness unto those who are exercised thereby'.

Why the Lord allows so many of his people to be so long and so deeply tried about their saving interest in Christ, *why* he does not more speedily and fully manifest his pardoning love to their souls, is a mystery which we cannot fathom. I have however observed that, where the first work was not attended with deep and powerful convictions of sin, it is usually the case, as if what was lacking in depth has to be made up in length, and a slow, continuous work compensates, as it were, for a shorter and more intense one.

Whatever the length or depth, I consider it a great mercy where there are these exercises, for I am well convinced that exercise is as much needed for the health of the soul as it is for the health of the body. Without movement, air becomes pestilential and water putrescent. Motion is the life of the natural creation, and equally so of the supernatural creation; and what are exercises, doubts, and fears, accompanied as they always are by desires and prayers, but means by which the soul is stirred up, and kept alive and healthy? As Hezekiah said, "O Lord, by these things men live, and in all these things is the life of my spirit," (Isa. 38:16).

If you cannot see what good such exercises have done, can you see from what evil they have kept you? They have kept you from being entangled in a worldly system; they have preserved you from resting in the form of Godliness without the power, and they have kept you from a notional dead-letter faith which has ruined so many thousands. Without such exercises you would be without a revealed Christ, without manifested pardon of sin, without the love of God being shed abroad in your heart by the Holy Spirit.

And here most are, who are not exercised - resting in 'a name to live', and in the doctrine without the experience. Being sick, you need a physician; being guilty, you need mercy; and being a sinner, you need salvation; and you need all this not in word and name, but in reality, and divine revelation and application.

Your exercises give you errands to the throne of mercy, and make you see in Christ and his precious gospel what otherwise would neither be seen nor cared for.

At the same time, it would be wrong to rest in exercises as marks and evidences of grace. Thirst is good as preparatory for water; hunger is good as antecedent to food; but who can rest in thirst or hunger? Without them, water and food are not desired; so, without exercises, Christ, the Water and Bread of life, is not desired nor longed for.

These exercises are given to quicken longing desires after Christ, and ultimately make him very precious.

23rd

"Turn thou us unto thee, O LORD, and we shall be turned; renew our days as of old."
Lamentations 5:21

If we do not wish to deceive ourselves, if God has made us honest, if he has planted his fear in our hearts, if he has begun and is carrying on a good work in us, there will be evidences of the existence of the life of God within. Life is the commencement of salvation as an inward reality; for whatever the eternal purposes of God are, or whatever standing the vessel of mercy has in Christ previous to effectual calling, there is no more movement in the soul Godwards until life is imparted, than there is life and motion in a breathless corpse that lies in a churchyard.

Howbeit, wherever divine life is implanted there will be certain fruits and feelings that spring out of this life. One fruit will be 'complaint'. This will arise sometimes from a feeling of the burden of sin, and at others from a sense of merited chastisement from God on account of it. Yet wherever this complaining is spiritual, there will be accompanying it an 'accepting the punishment of our iniquity', (Lev. 26:41), and 'a putting of our mouth in the dust' (Lam. 3:29). Thus where there is spiritual life there will be complaint, confession, and submission; the effect being meekness, brokenness, and humility.

This breaks to pieces self-conceit and self-justification, and the result is a searching and trying our ways whether they are of God. The fruit of this search will be, for the most part, a solemn and painful conviction that the greater part of our ways have been in the flesh; or, at least, there will be many anxious suspicions of that which cannot be relieved except by an express testimony from the Lord himself.

This produces a going out of soul unto him, the cry now being, 'Let us turn again to the Lord' (Lam. 3:40); and towards him the heart turns as to the only Source and Author of every good and perfect gift. As the quickened soul knows that he is a heart-searching God, this appeal will purge away much hypocrisy and insincerity, and deepen uprightness, sincerity, and godly integrity. And the blessed fruit and end of all this sifting work will be a coming down of gracious answers, divine testimonies, smiles of the Saviour's loving countenance, soft whispers of God's eternal favour, and the blessed witness of the Spirit within.

24th

"But God, who is rich in mercy, for his great love wherewith he loved us, even when we were dead in sins, hath quickened us together with Christ, (by grace ye are saved;) and hath raised us up together, and made us sit together in heavenly places in Christ Jesus."
Ephesians 2:4-6

Eighteen hundred years have rolled away since the body of Christ was quickened in the sepulchre; but the virtual effect of that quickening reached all the election of grace, and will stretch down to the remotest period of time. Now, by virtue of this quickening, when the Holy Spirit comes forward for the execution of his purpose, life enters into the soul. "You hath he quickened, who were dead in trespasses and sins," (Eph. 2:1). With quickening comes living sensations, such as conviction of sin, guilt of conscience, the fear of God, the heart broken, the spirit of prayer, repentance unto life; in short, all the first work of grace in the soul.

As in the body of Christ, when quickened by the Holy Spirit, there were vital movements before that body left the sepulchre, so there are vital movements in the soul of a child of God under the quickening operations of God the Holy Spirit, before raised up and brought forth. He is quickened into life, and under that quickening sees, feels, trembles, cries, groans, begs, and sues for mercy; every faculty of his renewed mind is alive and open to the things of God. Never do we pray for, read of, hear, or feel so much the power of eternal things as when the Lord by his Spirit and grace is first pleased to quicken us into this spiritual life; but there is no resurrection yet; only the quickening precedes.

In the same way that the breath of the Holy Spirit quickened the body of Christ as it lay in the tomb, and it was but a preparation for the raising of that dead body to life, so the quickening operations of God the Holy Spirit in the heart of a child of God are but preparatory to his being raised up to life with Christ.

Christ's body did not remain in the tomb, though it was alive in the tomb; so those whom God has quickened, and who are still lying in the tomb of sin, misery, and wretchedness, but are sighing, suing, and begging for mercy at his hands will certainly be brought out. Christ's body was not left where it was quickened, neither will any of you who are quickened be left in your sin and misery, and in your condemnation and guilt. The same divine operation that quickened you into spiritual life will bring you out of this state of concern and anxiety into the resurrection life of Christ, as was done for his body when he rose out of the tomb.

Now, when the power of God is put forth in the soul; when mercy reaches the heart; when Christ is revealed and his word applied, it comes forth out of the dark tomb in which it has lain, like Lazarus, bound with grave-clothes, and yet alive. When the door of hope thus is set open, and the soul is raised up to believe, hope and love, then it is 'raised up together with Christ'.

Thus we see that the resurrection of Christ was not merely the grand testimony that God put upon him as his own dear Son, for he was declared to be "the Son of God with power, by the resurrection from the dead," (Rom. 1:4). He was also "raised again for our justification," (Rom. 4:25), and we likewise rose in him, if we believe in his name.

All the elect of God rose with him, for they are "members of his body, of his flesh, and of his bones," (Eph. 5:30). When he died, they died. When he rose again, they rose again. They rose virtually in the Person of the Son of God when he rose triumphant from the tomb. Therefore, when the Holy Spirit applies to the heart and conscience the benefits and blessings of his death and resurrection, he raises them up and brings them out of the dark sepulchre into the open light of a glorious gospel day.

This is the true meaning of being 'raised up together' with Christ.

July 25th

"And hath raised us up together, and made us sit together in heavenly places in Christ Jesus."
Ephesians 2:6

Jesus did not tarry upon the earth after his resurrection; he ascended up where he was before, and took his seat at the right hand of the Majesty on high; but when he ascended up on high, all the election of grace ascended with him. He did not leave his members behind upon earth, but he took them all 'virtually' into heaven. This is his pledge that they will one day be with him in the realms of eternal bliss because they have already ascended with him as members of his mystical body. This, in experimental manifestation, is the lifting up of the affections, the raising up of the soul to sit together with Christ in heavenly places.

Having sin, death, hell, and Satan, together with all the misery and wretchedness we have brought upon ourselves firmly under our feet, in like manner as Christ reigns having put all enemies under his feet, is to sit with Christ in heavenly places. One of the last acts that God usually does for the soul, is the lifting of it up thus to sit with Christ in the anticipation of eternal glory. Seeing death dethroned, hell destroyed, sin abolished is sitting together with Christ. Viewing the glorious immortality reserved for the saints of God, and enjoying this in the sweet anticipation and blessed foretastes, so as to be in heaven before we get there is to sit down with Christ in heavenly places. We sit with him by virtue of his sitting down "on the right hand of the Majesty on high," (Heb. 1:3).

Now, see what benefits and blessings spring out of a union with the Son of God. Why did God quicken your soul? Because you were a member of Christ. Why were you raised up to "a good hope through grace?" Why did mercy, peace, and pardon flow into your soul? Why were you brought out of misery and death into the light of God's countenance, and had a precious Christ revealed to your heart? Because in the day, when the Son of God rose triumphant from the tomb, you, as a member of his mystical body, rose there and then with him. Why are you sometimes privileged to have your affections on things above, attain any victory over sin, death, hell, and the grave, find your enemies put under your feet, and look forward at times with a sweet anticipation of eternal joys? Because, as a member of Christ's mystical body, you have already ascended, and are already sitting at the right hand of God with Christ, who is sitting as the Head of his body there.

July 26th

"Only let your conversation be as it becometh the gospel of Christ."
Philippians 1:27

What is this conversation? The word means the whole of your life before God and before man. It is a very comprehensive term in the original, meaning, literally, 'Conduct yourselves as citizens'. It therefore includes the whole of our spiritual fellowship and daily communion with God and man. It thus views us as citizens of no base city; as citizens, I may indeed say, of a heavenly city, the new Jerusalem; and it bids us walk and speak, live and act, as becomes citizens of a heavenly country. This, then, is the meaning of the word "conversation" in our text, and by it we are called to walk with God as becomes the gospel. He has reconciled us to himself by the blood of his dear Son; and when we receive the atonement, or reconciliation, as the word means, then we can walk with God in peace, equity, and amity, for sin, which made the breach, is removed out of the way.

So Levi, as ministering at the altar, and those near to God, walked of old. "My covenant was with him of life and peace; and I gave them to him for the fear wherewith he feared me, and was afraid before my name. The law of truth was in his mouth, and iniquity was not found in his lips: he walked with me in peace and equity, and did turn many away from iniquity," (Mal. 2:5-6). This is walking in the light as He is in the light, and so far as we can do this, our fellowship is with the Father, (1John 1:3-7).

And our conversation with God, our walk with God, must be as becomes the gospel of Christ. If we walk at freedom with God, in sweet liberty, with holy access, pouring out our heart before him, enjoying his presence, and having some discoveries of his goodness and mercy, then our conversation with God becomes the gospel. The gospel is a message of mercy. When, then, we embrace that mercy, and feel the power of it; when that mercy reaches our heart, melts our inmost soul, dissolves our doubts and fears, and removes legality and bondage, then we walk worthy of the gospel, as walking before God in the light of his countenance through the power of the gospel. God does not send the gospel to condemn us, for, "There is therefore now no condemnation to them which are in Christ Jesus, who walk not after the flesh, but after the Spirit," (Rom. 8:1), and they walk after the Spirit when they have access by him through Christ unto the Father.

July

27th

"And so were the churches established in the faith, and increased in number daily."
Acts 16:5

Oh what an inestimable mercy it is for a man to know the truth for himself by divine teaching and divine testimony! What a privilege to have it applied to his heart by a gracious influence and a heavenly power; to know for himself what salvation is, whence it comes, and above all to enjoy the sweet persuasion that this salvation has reached his heart! He will then know where to go in the hour of trouble, and whom to resort to when sorrow and affliction come into his house, or illness or infirmity shake his tabernacle. He will not be a stranger to the throne of grace, nor to the sweetness of the covenant ordered in all things and sure.

There will be given him from above, out of the fullness of Christ, such grace and strength as will support him in the trying hour. It is by these gracious dealings upon his soul, that a believer becomes "established in the faith."

The very storms through which he passes will only strengthen him to take a firmer hold of Christ, and thus become more established in the faith of him. It is in these storms that he learns more of his own weakness and more of Christ's strength; more of his own misery and more of Christ's mercy; and more of his own sinfulness compared to the super-abounding grace of God. As he sees his own poverty he finds Christ's riches, and as he realises his own desert of hell, he is shown his title to heaven.

Thus he becomes "established in faith," for the same blessed Spirit who began the work carries it on, goes on to fill up the original outline, and to engrave the image of Christ in deeper characters upon his heart, and to teach him more and more experimentally the truth as it is in Jesus.

28th

"But mine eyes are unto thee, O GOD the Lord: in thee is my trust; leave not my soul destitute."
Psalm 141:8

The very cry is a pledge that the Lord will not leave the soul destitute. Strange though it be to us; it is the light that shows darkness; it is life that makes us feel deadness; no, more, it is fertility and fruitfulness that make us feel barrenness; it is riches that make us feel poverty; it is God's teaching and presence that make us feel destitution. This very mourning over our barrenness; this very feeling of our inability to do good, is a proof of the life of God in the soul, an evidence of the work of grace in the heart.

"Leave not my soul destitute." This is something genuine; this is heart-work; these are the footsteps of the flock; these are the leadings and teachings of God the Spirit in the hearts of the redeemed. These things are saving; these things will lead the soul to eternal glory. The man that knows any of these things by personal experience will one day see the glory of the Lord face to face.

What then do we know of these things? Can we lay our experience side by side with this experience of the Psalmist, and say, "mine eyes are unto thee, O God the Lord; in thee is my trust; leave not my soul destitute?"

Wherever that prayer is, it will bring an answer; and wherever that answer is, there will be matter for everlasting praise. Blessed are the souls that know these things from genuine heartfelt experience. They will shine forth as stars forever and ever; and when the Lord of life and glory comes a second time without sin unto salvation, then shall they also appear with him in glory.

29th

"Beloved, let us love one another: for love is of God; and every one that loveth is born of God, and knoweth God." 1John 4:7

"Love is of God." I can have no satisfaction, real satisfaction, that I am a partaker of the Spirit and grace of Christ except I feel some measure of the love of God shed abroad in my heart. I may have hopes, or expectations, or even evidences, fainter or brighter; but I have no sure, clear certainty in my own soul that I have the Spirit and grace of Christ there except I am blessed with the love of God. For until love comes there is fear, which has torment, and whilst we have such fear, there is no being made perfect in love.

A man has no clear assurance in his breast that God has loved him with an everlasting love; nor has he any bright testimony that the Spirit of God has made his body his temple until this love comes into his soul. Howbeit when the crowning blessing comes of the love of God, experimentally felt and enjoyed by his own shedding of it abroad in the heart, with the communication of the Spirit of adoption to cry "Abba, Father," *that* is the sealing testimony of his possession of the true spirit.

It is a spirit of "power, and of love, and of a sound mind," (2Tim. 1:7), and where there is this, there is also a spirit of love and affection to all the family of God.

30th

"For the oppression of the poor, for the sighing of the needy, now will I arise, saith the LORD."
Psalm 12:5

The distinguishing mark and character of a needy soul is to be full of needs. Day after day he needs divine realities to be revealed to his soul, to hear the sweet voice of mercy speaking into his heart, as from the lips of God himself, that he is an accepted child, that he may bathe, as it were, in sweet manifestations of the love and mercy of God. In the supply of need he believes the marrow of all true religion and vital godliness to consist. So that he cannot take up with his present state of need for religion. If he is in doubts and fears, or is passing through heavy temptations, and is writing bitter things against himself, he cannot say 'this is religion'. He wants something different from what he feels, even the blessed testimonies and manifestations that he is one of the Lord's own dear family. I am very well assured from soul experience, that nothing but the application of heavenly blessings to the soul can ever satisfy the man who has had life implanted in his heart by the hand of God himself.

We therefore read of this needy person that he 'sighs'. "For the oppression of the poor, for the *sighing* of the needy." He is sighing after God; groaning in the depths of his soul after the lifting up of the light of God's countenance. He is sighing under the weight of unbelief, the burden of infidelity, the power of temptation, the wretchedness of his heart, the carnality of his mind, the barrenness of his frame, his stupidity, his brutality, filth and corruption. He is sighing to the Lord under the burden of these things lying as a load on his conscience, and begging the Lord that he would only lift up the light of his countenance, that he would only drop one sweet testimony, that he would speak but one word to his soul, to bring with it sweet deliverance, and lift him out into all the light, and life, and liberty, and peace of the glorious gospel of the blessed God.

July 31st

"Then they cried unto the LORD in their trouble, and he delivered them out of their distresses."
Psalm 107:6

    Oh what a mercy it is that there is a God to go to, and a God who hears and answers prayer! What a blessing it is to be able to unbosom before him the burdened spirit!
    Observe the words, "Then they cried unto the Lord in their *trouble."* If you have trouble, it is a sufficient warrant for you to go to God with it. Do not trouble yourself with the question, whether you are elect or non-elect. God does not put it in that shape, and neither need you. The answer will best show on which side of the line you stand. Does he not say, "call upon me in the day of trouble: I will deliver thee, and thou shalt glorify me," (Psa. 50:15)? If you have a day of trouble, you have here a sufficient warrant to call upon God.
    Write not, then, bitter things against yourself. If you are enabled to sigh and cry unto the Lord there is life in your soul. God has quickened you by his blessed Spirit if he has put a sigh and cry into your bosom. Remember the men in Ezekiel on whom the Lord put the approving seal. It was those who sighed and cried for the abominations which they saw and felt in themselves and others, (Ezek. 9:4). If, then, the Lord has put a sigh and cry into your bosom on account of your felt inward abominations, you are one of those on whom he has set his seal.
    Sanctified troubles are some of our greatest blessings; and one of their blessed fruits is that they keep us from settling on our lees and being at ease in Zion. Careless, worldly-minded, proud, covetous professors, sunk in carnality and death, where is there ever a cry in their soul? They may have a formal prayer – a morning prayer, an evening prayer, a family prayer, and all as round as a ball and as cold as ice. Stiff and frozen in carnality they are ice themselves, and they bring their ice with them wherever they come. But God does not allow his people to go on in this cold, lifeless, frozen, icy way, with mere formal devotion, lip service, and prayers worn out like an old shoe with long and continual treading. He sends afflictions, trials, and troubles upon them, takes them into the wilderness, exercises them well in the path of tribulation, and supporting them under it, raises up a cry which he is sure to hear.

August

August 1st

"Let thy work appear unto thy servants, and thy glory unto their children."
Psalm 90:16

"Let thy work appear unto thy servants." Creature works we here read nothing of. They had been long ago cut to the very ground. And what had been their deathblow? What had driven the dagger into their very heart? 'Days of affliction, and years of evil'. These had been their destruction; creature righteousness they had stabbed to the very heart, and let out the life-blood of human merit. There is no petition, then, "Let *our* works appear!" No. These were buried in the grave of corruption; these were swallowed up and lost in 'days of affliction, and years of evil'.

Rather it is, "Let *thy* work," the finished work of the Son of God; the obedience of Jesus to the law; the atoning blood which he shed upon Calvary's tree; the work which he undertook, went through, and completed. "Oh," breathes forth the man of God in earnest cry, (and our hearts if they have been taught by the same Spirit will unite in the same strain), "let *thy* work appear unto thy servants!"

'What?' says one. 'Can we not see that work in the word of God and is not that sufficient? Can we not hear that work set forth by good men and is not that sufficient? Can we not read it as opened up by the pen of ready writers and is not that sufficient?' Yes, for those who have never seen 'days of affliction, and years of evil', it is amply sufficient.

It will never do for God's exercised children, though; they have other thoughts and other feelings upon these matters. They know what darkness of mind is, the power of unbelief, and creature helplessness. They know that nothing short of the light of God's countenance, the manifestation of His mercy, and the teaching and witness of the Spirit, can make the work of Jesus appear in all its beauty, suitability, and glory.

Therefore they can say, 'Let thy work appear unto thy servants. Give me, O Lord, a sight by living faith of the atonement of Jesus Christ'. Their soul would cry in the language of Moses, 'Show me thy glory; reveal in my heart the finished work of Christ; sprinkle my conscience with his atoning blood; discover him to me, and thus give me a sweet manifestation of his Person, love, blood, and complete salvation. Let it, Lord, appear before my eyes, and in my heart, and seal it with divine power upon my conscience'.

August

2nd

"Underneath are the everlasting arms."
Deuteronomy 33:27

How Moses brought before the people the eternity of God! He will have nothing to do with time. What is time? A fragment, merely like the foam upon the sea compared with the mighty ocean. Eternity is as vast as the ocean; time is but the foam upon a single wave.

"Underneath are the everlasting arms." And depend upon it, if the everlasting arms are underneath the saints of God, for it is unto them that the words are spoken, they are put there for some purpose. God puts affliction upon affliction to bring the soul down, that it may fall into and upon the everlasting arms, and there find how firm and strong they are.

Have you not often found it so? Do not lie against your right. How many trials in providence you have been brought through. How conspicuously the Lord has appeared in this and that instance, so that your unbelief and infidelity were, for the time at least, thoroughly silenced, and faith saw the hand of God so clearly that you felt as if you could never doubt again. Have you not had many sweet supports on your bed of languishing, many precious seasons when you could bless God for laying upon you his afflicting hand? And have you not found that strength was always given to you according to your day, that with every trial power was given you to bear it, and that out of your deepest afflictions came your greatest blessings?

Why are you not in hell? Do you not deserve to be there? Why still upon praying ground, with a good hope through grace, and your soul waiting for the Lord to appear, more than those that watch for the morning? If these arms have once supported you, will they not support you again? Would they be everlasting if they could part asunder and let you fall through? Rest upon them and you will find how strong they are.

3rd

"When Christ, who is our life, shall appear, then shall ye also appear with him in glory."
Colossians 3:4

Is Christ your life here upon earth? Do you have a living faith in his divine Majesty? Have any drops of his love ever bedewed your soul? Has any sweet smile ever comforted your heart? If you can say yes, then the Apostle would say unto you, "When Christ, who is *your* life, shall appear, then shall ye also appear with him in glory."

No longer pestered by sin and Satan, no longer carrying about a weak, infirm tabernacle, the seat of innumerable evils and maladies, but endued with a soul pure as he is pure, and a spiritual body capable of enjoying the bliss and blessedness of eternity, "then shall ye appear," you suffering saints, who have set your affections on him whom you have not seen, and yet in whom you believe, "then shall ye also appear with him in glory."

Is not this worth struggling for? Is not this a blessed goal at the end of the race? Is not this a worthy prize to run for? Is not this an ample reward of all your temptations, troubles, griefs and sorrows, to believe, and not in vain, that when he shall appear, you shall appear with him in glory?

May the Lord, if it be his will, lead our souls into these divine and blessed realities! They are the substance of vital godliness; and so far as we feel them, and live under the sweet influences and bedewing operations of the Spirit of grace, these things will prove all our salvation, as they must be, if we be rightly taught, all our desire.

4th

"But the God of all grace, who hath called us unto his eternal glory by Christ Jesus, after that ye have suffered a while, make you perfect, stablish, strengthen, settle you."
1Peter 5:10

There is no Christian perfection, no divine establishment, no spiritual strength, no solid settlement, except by suffering. Yet after the soul has suffered, and after it has felt God's chastising hand, the effect is to perfect, to establish, to strengthen, and to settle it. By suffering, a man becomes settled into a solemn conviction of the character of Jehovah as revealed in the Scripture, and in a measure made experimentally manifest in his conscience.

He is settled in the belief of an "everlasting covenant, ordered in all things, and sure," (2Sam. 23:5). He is fully persuaded that "all things work together for good to them that love God, to them who are the called according to his purpose," (Rom. 8:28). He has a firm conviction that all things he suffers come to pass according to God's eternal purpose, and are all tending to the good of the Church, and to God's eternal glory.

August

His soul, also, is settled down into a deep persuasion of the misery, wretchedness, and emptiness of the creature; into the conviction that the world is but a shadow, and that the things of time and sense are but bubbles that burst the moment they are grasped. He knows that of all things sin is most to be dreaded, and above all things the favour of God is most to be coveted. He accepts without reservation that nothing is really worth knowing except Jesus Christ and him crucified; that all things are passing away; and that he himself is rapidly hurrying down the stream of life and into the boundless ocean of eternity.

Thus he becomes settled in a knowledge of the truth, and his soul remains at anchor, looking to the Lord to preserve him here, and bring him in peace and safety to his eternal home.

5th

"And this is life eternal, that they might know thee the only true God, and Jesus Christ, whom thou hast sent."
John 17:3

How many appear anxious to know the way of salvation, how eternal life is to be obtained, and how to "flee from the wrath to come." Yet here the Lord Jesus has shown in one short sentence in what eternal life consists, that it is in the knowledge of the "only true God, and of Jesus Christ, whom [he] has sent." He therefore that knows the Father and the Son has eternal life in his soul.

The Lord Jesus, in the sixth chapter of John, quoted this among other passages of the Old Testament, and says, "It is written in the prophets, And they shall be all taught of God. Every man therefore that hath heard, and hath learned of the Father, cometh unto me," (John 6:45). He lays this down, then, as one especial fruit of divine teaching, that it produces a coming unto him.

The Spirit, who teaches to profit, holds up before the eyes of the soul, the Person, work, blood, love, grace, and righteousness of the Lord Jesus Christ. He shows the soul that he is just such a Saviour as it needs. He opens up the dignity of his Person, and shows that he is God-man. He makes known in the conscience that he has offered up himself a sacrifice for sin, and that he has shed his atoning blood so that the sin of the Church is forever put away from the sight of a just God.

He opens up before the eyes of the mind his glorious righteousness, as that in which the Father is well pleased, and in which if the soul has but a saving interest, it is secure from the

August

wrath to come. He unfolds to the heart the willingness of Christ to receive every coming sinner, and reveals the treasures of mercy and grace which are locked up in him.

He brings down in the heart the comforting words that he spoke in the days of his flesh. "Come unto me, all ye that labour and are heavy laden, and I will give you rest," (Matt. 11:28), or "him that cometh to me I will in no wise cast out," (John 6:37), and "if any man thirst, let him come unto me, and drink," (John 7:37).

6th

"He that is slow to anger is better than the mighty; and he that ruleth his spirit than he that taketh a city."
Proverbs 16:32

What a foe to one's peace is one's own spirit! And what shall I call it? It is often an infernal spirit. Why? Because it bears upon it the mark of Satan. The pride of our spirit, the presumption of our spirit, the hypocrisy of our spirit, and the intense selfishness of our spirit are often hidden from us. This wily devil, SELF, can wear such masks and assume such forms; this serpent, self, can so creep and crawl, can so twist and turn, and can disguise itself under such false appearances, that it is so often hidden from ourselves.

Who is the greatest enemy we have to fear? We all have our enemies, but who is our greatest enemy? He that you carry in your own bosom; the one you believe to be your friend; your daily, hourly, and moment by moment companion, that entwines himself in nearly every thought of your heart; that suggests well near every motive; that sometimes puffs up with pride, sometimes inflames with lust, sometimes inflates with presumption, and sometimes works under feigned humility and fleshly holiness.

Now this self must be overcome; for if self overcomes us eventually, we shall perish in the condemnation of self. God is determined to stain the pride of human glory. He will never let self, (which is but another word for the creature), wear the crown of victory. It must be crucified, denied, and mortified; it must be put off, so that Jesus may be put on; that in the denying of self, Jesus may be believed in; and that in the crucifixion of self, there may be a solemn spiritual union with Him who was crucified on Calvary.

Now, are we overcoming self? Are we buffeted? What says self? "Buffet back." Are we despised? What says self? "Despise back; retort angry look for angry look, and hasty word, for hasty word; an eye for an eye, and a tooth for a tooth." But what says the Spirit of

God in a tender conscience? "Be not overcome of evil, but overcome evil with good," (Rom. 12:21).

The way to overcome self is by looking out of self to Him who was crucified upon Calvary's tree. It is to receive his image into our heart and to be clothed with his likeness. It is to drink into his spirit, and thereby "of his fullness have all we received, and grace for grace," (John 1:16).

7th

"And wisdom and knowledge shall be the stability of thy times, and strength of salvation: the fear of the LORD is his treasure."
Isaiah 33:6

"The fear of the Lord is his treasure," and, oh, what a treasure it is!

Treasure in ancient times was generally hidden; it was concealed from the eye of man, hoarded up, and not brought ostentatiously out to view. Wealthy men of old hid the knowledge of their treasures, lest they should be robbed of them by the hand of violence. So spiritually, the fear of the Lord is hidden in the heart, and lies deep in the soul; it is not spread out ostentatiously to view, but is buried out of sight in a man's conscience.

Although hidden from others, and even from ourselves at times, this "fear of the Lord" will reliably act as circumstances draw it forth. There may be times and seasons when we seem almost hardened and conscience-seared; sin appears to have such power over us, and evil thoughts and desires so carry us away, that we cannot trace one atom of godly fear within; and the soul cries, "What will become of me! Where am I going now! What will come next on such a wretch as I feel myself to be!"

But place him in such circumstances, say, as befell Joseph, then he will find that the "fear of the Lord" is in him a fountain of life, a holy principle springing up in his soul. Thus, this fear, which is a part of the heavenly treasure, acts when most needed. The more the life of God is felt in the soul, the more the fear of God flows forth as a fountain of life to depart from the snares of death. The more lively the grace of God is in the soul, the more lively will godly fear be in the heart; and the more the Spirit of God works with power in the conscience, the deeper will be the fear of God in the soul.

August

8th

"Jesus saith unto him, I am the way, the truth, and the life: no man cometh unto the Father, but by me."
John 14:6

How is Jesus the way? In everything that he is to God's people he is the way.

His blood is the way to heaven, for as Deer speaks "the whole path is lined with his blood." By his precious blood shed upon Calvary's tree he has put away sin by the sacrifice of himself, and opened a way of access to God. His righteousness, is part of the way, for only so far as we stand clothed in his glorious righteousness have we any access unto, and any acceptance with God the Father. His love is the way, for if we walk in love, we walk in him, for he is love. Every part of the way was devised and is executed by the love of his tender heart.

Howbeit the way is also the way of tribulation. Was not Jesus himself the great Sufferer? If he be the way, and the only way, I must be conformed to his likeness in suffering. Not to know affliction and tribulation, is not to know Christ. He was "a man of sorrows and acquainted with grief," (Isa. 53:3), and if so, for us to have no sorrow, to have no acquaintance with grief, and to know not tribulation, is to proclaim to all with a loud clear voice that we have no union and communion with the Lord Jesus Christ.

Yet we are continually turning aside 'to the right hand' or 'to the left'. There is that cowardice in the heart which cannot bear the cross; there is that slipping into carnal ease and fleshly security, so as to get away from under the painful cross of affliction and suffering. When we thus turn aside 'to the right hand' or 'to the left', the voice the Lord calls after us. "This is the way, walk ye in it, when ye turn to the right hand, and when ye turn to the left," (Isa. 30:21). The way of affliction, the way of tribulation, the way of trial, the way of exercise; there is no other.

This is the way in which the King walked of old, and this is the way in which all his people have walked before him and after him, for this is the only path in which the footsteps of the flock can be found.

9th

"Unto the upright there ariseth light in the darkness: he is gracious, and full of compassion, and righteous."
Psalm 112:4

We often get into such dark paths that we seem altogether out of the ways of God, and feel as if there were no more grace in our souls, than in one altogether dead in trespasses and sins. No matter whether we look back at the past, view the present, or turn our eyes to the future, one dark cloud seems to rest upon the whole. Nor can we, with all our searching, find to our satisfaction that we have one spark of true religion, or one atom of grace, or one grain of vital godliness, or any trace that the Spirit of God has touched our consciences with his finger.

Now, when we are in this dark, benighted state, we need light, we need the blessed Sun of righteousness to arise. We need the south wind to blow a heavenly gale and drive away the mists. We need the clouds to part and the light of God's countenance to shine into our souls so as to show us where we are and what we are. We need his light to make it clear that base and vile as we are, yet we have a saving interest in the love of the Father, the blood of the Son, and the teachings of the Holy Spirit.

When his word begins to distil like the rain and to drop like the dew, when the Lord himself is pleased to speak home one sweet testimony, one little word, one kind intimation – what a change it makes! The clouds break away, the fog clears off, the mists dissolve, and the soul becomes sweetly persuaded of its saving interest in the blood and love of the Lamb.

10th

"And the angel answered and said unto the women, Fear not ye: for I know that ye seek Jesus, which was crucified." Matthew 28:5

Whatever be our state and case, if it can truly be said of us that the angel said to the women at the sepulchre, "I know that ye seek Jesus, who was crucified," we have a divine warrant to believe that 'he is gone before us into Galilee, and there shall we see him'.

He is risen; he has ascended up on high, and has "received gifts for men; yea, for the rebellious also, that the LORD God might dwell among them," (Psa. 68:18). He is now upon the mercy-seat, and he invites and draws poor needy sinners to himself. He says, "Come unto me, all ye that labour and are heavy laden, and I will give you rest," (Matt. 11:28). He allows us, nay he invites us, to pour out our heart before him, to show before him our trouble, to spread our needs at his feet, as Hezekiah spread the letter in the temple. If we seek communion with him, we may and shall tell him how deeply we need him, that without him it is not life to live, and with him it is not death to die.

We shall beg of him to heal our backslidings, to manifest his love and blood to our conscience, to show us the evil of sin, to bless us with godly sorrow for our slips and falls, and keep us from evil that it may not grieve us. We shall ask him to lead us into his sacred truth, to preserve us from all error, to plant his fear deep in our hearts, to apply some precious promise to our souls, and to be with us in all our ways. We will implore him to watch over us in all our goings out and comings in, to preserve us from pride, self-deception, and self-righteousness, to give us renewed tokens of our saving interest in his finished work, to subdue our iniquities, to make and keep our conscience tender and work in us everything which is pleasing in his sight.

What is communion but mutual giving and receiving, the flowing together of two hearts, the melting into one of two wills, the exchange of two loves – each party maintaining its distinct identity, yet being to the other an object of affection and delight? Have we nothing, then, to give to Christ? Yes, our sins, our sorrows, our burdens, our trials, and above all the salvation and sanctification of our souls. And what has he to give us? Do you even need to ask? He gives us everything worth having, everything worth a moment's anxious thought, everything for time and eternity.

11th

"They shall come with weeping, and with supplications will I lead them: I will cause them to walk by the rivers of waters in a straight way, wherein they shall not stumble: for I am a father to Israel, and Ephraim is my firstborn."
Jeremiah 31:9

Oh how much is needed to bring the soul to its only rest and centre! What trials and afflictions, what furnaces, floods, rods, and strokes, as well as smiles, promises, and gracious drawings! What pride and self to be brought out of, and what love and blood to be brought into! What lessons to learn of the dreadful evil of sin! What lessons to learn of the freeness and fullness of salvation! What sinkings in self! What risings in Christ! What guilt and condemnation on account of sin, what self-loathing and self-abasement, what distrust of self, what fears of falling and what prayers and desires to be kept. What clinging to Christ and what

August

looking up and unto his divine Majesty as faith views him at the right hand of the Father. What desires never more to sin against him, but to live, move, and act in the holy fear of God. Do we not find, more or less daily, all these in a living soul!

From whence springs all this inward experience? Is it not from the fellowship and communion which there is between Christ and the soul? It is, as the apostle says, because "we are members of his body, of his flesh, and of his bones," (Eph. 5:30).

As such there is a mutual participation in sorrow and joy, for "He hath borne our griefs, and carried our sorrows," (Isa. 53:4), and "was in all points tempted like as we are, yet without sin," (Heb. 4:15). He can, therefore, "be touched with the feeling of our infirmities," can pity and sympathise with our plight, and thus, as we may cast upon him our sins and sorrows, when faith enables, so can he supply, out of his own fullness, that grace and strength which can bring us off eventually more than conquerors.

12th

"For if the blood of bulls and of goats, and the ashes of an heifer sprinkling the unclean, sanctifieth to the purifying of the flesh, how much more shall the blood of Christ, who through the eternal Spirit offered himself without spot to God, purge your conscience from dead works to serve the living God?"
Hebrews 9:13-14

What a mercy it is to have a conscience in any measure purged from dead works to serve the living God. What a relief to feel any free access to his gracious Majesty, any happy liberty in walking before him, any deliverance from doubt and fear, any removal of those exercises which try the mind and often bring heavy burdens upon the soul!

Still, after all our wanderings, we must ever come to the same spot. After all our departings and backslidings, still, again and again we must be brought to the same place to get the guilt removed, the mercy proclaimed, and the peace revealed. For is not this the blessedness - that the blood of Christ cleanses from all sin?

Having obtained eternal redemption for us, his blood will never lose its efficacy, but will ever purge the conscience as long as the conscience of any burdened member of his mystical body remains to be purged, until he presents all his ransomed saints faultless before the presence of his glory with exceeding joy.

August 13th

"A new heart also will I give you, and a new spirit will I put within you: and I will take away the stony heart out of your flesh, and I will give you an heart of flesh."
Ezekiel 36:26

This "new spirit" is a broken spirit, a soft, tender spirit, and is therefore called a 'heart of flesh', as opposed to the 'heart of stone', the rocky, obdurate, unfeeling, impenitent heart of one dead in sin, or dead in a profession.

How is this soft, penitent heart communicated? He will put 'new spirit, his spirit, within us'. The same divine truth is set forth in the gracious promise which God gave to Zechariah. "I will pour upon the house of David, and upon the inhabitants of Jerusalem, the spirit of grace and of supplications: and they shall look upon me whom they have pierced, and they shall mourn for him, as one mourneth for his only son, and shall be in bitterness for him, as one that is in bitterness for his firstborn," (Zech. 12:10).

What is the immediate effect of the pouring out of the spirit of grace and of supplications? It is a looking to him whom they have pierced, a mourning for him as one mourns for an only son, and a being in bitterness for him as one that is in bitterness for his firstborn. This is evangelical repentance, as distinguished from legal repentance. It is godly sorrow working repentance unto salvation not to be repented of, as distinct from the sorrow of the world which worketh only death.

These two kinds of repentance are to be carefully distinguished from each other, though they are often sadly confounded. Cain, Esau, Saul, Ahab, Judas, all repented; but their repentance was the remorse of natural conscience, not the godly sorrow of a broken heart and a contrite spirit. They trembled before God as an angry judge, but they were not melted into contrition before him as a forgiving Father. They neither hated their sins nor forsook them, and they neither loved holiness nor sought it. Cain went out from the presence of the Lord; Esau plotted Jacob's death; Saul consulted the witch of Endor; Ahab put honest Micaiah into prison; and Judas hanged himself.

How different from this forced and false repentance of a reprobate is the repentance of a child of God – that true repentance for sin, that godly sorrow, that holy mourning which flows from the Spirit's gracious operations. This does not spring from a sense of the wrath of God in a broken law, but of his mercy in a blessed gospel. It comes from a view by faith of the sufferings of Christ in the garden and on the cross and from a manifestation of pardoning love. It is

August

always attended with self-loathing and self-abhorrence, with deep and unreserved confession of sin and forsaking it, with most hearty, sincere, and earnest petitions to be kept from all evil, and a holy longing to live to the praise and glory of God.

14th

"I will worship toward thy holy temple, and praise thy name for thy lovingkindness and for thy truth: for thou hast magnified thy word above all thy name."
Psalm 138:2

This verse contains one of those expressions in Scripture that seem so comprehensive, and yet so amazing. To my mind one of the most remarkable expressions in the whole book of God is, "Thou hast magnified thy word above all thy name."

The name of God includes all the perfections of God. Everything that he is and everything that he is shown to possess. His justice, majesty, holiness, greatness and glory, and whatever he is in himself; that is God's name. Yet he has magnified something above all his name; his word!

'Word' has two distinct meanings in scripture – the Incarnate Word, the Son of God, who is called the Word, and the scripture itself. Either and both meanings are in view in this text.

In both his epistle and his gospel, the apostle John refers to the Son of God as the word. "For there are three that bear record in heaven, the Father, the Word, and the Holy Ghost: and these three are one," (1John 5:7). "In the beginning was the Word, and the Word was with God, and the Word was God," (John 1:1). Then in the book of Deuteronomy, Moses records God describing the commandments he gave to the people on Horeb, which would become our Scripture, as being his words. "Gather me the people together, and I will make them hear my words, that they may learn to fear me," (Deut. 4:10).

You may therefore take the words of our text as meaning that God has magnified his Word – his eternal Son – above all his great name, setting Christ on high above all the other perfections of his majesty. You may also take it as meaning that he has magnified his written word, that is, the sacred Scriptures, all his promises therein, and the fulfilment of them, above his great name, his faithfulness being so dear unto him, that he has exalted keeping his word above all his other attributes. He has so magnified his faithfulness that his love, his mercy, his grace and all his other perfections would all sooner fail than his faithfulness, than the word of his mouth and what he has revealed in the Scriptures.

What a firm salvation, then, is ours, which rests upon his word, when God has magnified that word above all his name! What a comprehensive declaration is this! What volumes of blessedness and truth are contained therein! So that, if God has revealed his truth to your soul, and given you faith to anchor in the word of promise, sooner than that should fail, he would suffer the loss of all - for he has magnified his word above all his name.

15th

"The life which I now live in the flesh I live by the faith of the Son of God, who loved me, and gave himself for me." Galatians 2:20

There is no way except by being spiritually baptised into Christ's death and life, that we can ever get a victory over our besetting sins. If, on the one hand, we have a view of a suffering Christ, and thus become baptised into his sufferings and death, the feeling, while it lasts, will subdue the power of sin. Or, on the other hand, if we get a believing view of a risen Christ, and receive supplies of grace out of his fullness, that will lift us above sin's dominion. If sin is powerfully working in us, we need one of these two things to subdue it; either we must have something come down to us to give us a victory over our sin in our strugglings against it, or we must have something to lift us up out of sin into a purer and better element.

When there is a view of the sufferings and sorrows, agonies and death of the Son of God, power comes down to the soul in its struggles against sin, and gives it a measure of holy resistance and subduing strength against it. So, when there is a coming in of the grace and love of Christ, it lifts up the soul from the love and power of sin into a purer and holier atmosphere. Sin cannot be subdued in any other way. You must either be baptised into Christ's sufferings and death, or you must be baptised, (and these follow each other), into Christ's resurrection and life.

A sight of him as a suffering God, or a view of him as a risen Jesus, must be connected with every successful attempt to get the victory over sin, death, hell, and the grave. You may strive, vow, and repent; and what does it all amount to? You sink deeper and deeper into sin than before. Pride, lust, and covetousness come in like a flood, and you are swamped and carried away almost before you are aware. But if you get a view of a suffering Christ, or of a risen Christ; if you get a taste of his dying love, a drop of his atoning blood, or any manifestation of his beauty and blessedness, there comes from this spiritual baptism into his death or his life a subduing power. It is this that gives a victory over temptation and sin, which nothing else can or will give.

Yet I believe we are often many years learning this divine secret, striving to repent and reform, and finding that we cannot. At last, by divine teaching, we come to learn a little of what the Apostle meant when he said, "The life I now live in the flesh, I live by the faith of the Son of God." When we can get into this life, this hidden life of Christ's faith not our own faith, then our affections change and are set on things above. There is no use setting people to work by legal strivings for they only plunge themselves deeper in the ditch. You must get Christ into your soul by the power of God, and then he will subdue, by his smiles, blood, love, and presence, every internal foe.

16th

"And ye shall know the truth, and the truth shall make you free."
John 8:32

The truths of the gospel, though to an enlightened eye they shine as with a ray of light all through the word, yet are they, for the most part, laid up as precious veins deep in the rock. "Surely there is a vein for the silver, and a place for gold where they fine it," (Job 28:1). "As for the earth, out of it cometh bread: and under it is turned up as it were fire. The stones of it are the place of sapphires: and it hath dust of gold," (Job 28:5-6).

Where is this 'place of sapphires' and where is this 'dust of gold' to be found? In the "path which no fowl, (unclean professor), knoweth, and which the vulture's eye, keen though it be after this world's carrion, hath not seen," (Job 28:7-8).

To a spiritual mind, sweet and self-rewarding is the task, if task it can be called, of searching the word as for hidden treasure. No sweeter, no better employment can engage heart and hands than, in the spirit of prayer and meditation, and of separation from the world, to go mining for this treasure. No greater reward awaits those who, in a spirit of holy fear, and with a desire to know and do the will of God, with humility, simplicity, and godly sincerity, seek to enter into those heavenly mysteries which are stored up in the Scriptures. This, not to furnish the head with notions, but to feed the soul with the bread of life.

August

Truth, received in the love and power of it, informs and establishes the judgment, softens and melts the heart, warms and draws upward the affections. It makes and keeps the conscience alive and tender, is the food of faith, the strength of hope, and the mainspring of love.

To know the truth is to be "a disciple indeed," and to be made blessedly free; free from error, and the vile heresies which abound everywhere; free from presumption and self-righteousness; free from the curse and bondage of the law and the condemnation of a guilty conscience. To know this truth is to be free from a slavish fear of the opinion of men and the contempt and scorn of the world and worldly professors. It is to be free from following a multitude to do evil, and free from companionship with those who have a name to live but are dead.

It makes us free to love the Lord and his dear people; free to speak well of his name; and free to glorify him with body and soul, which are anyway his. We become free to approach the throne of grace and see a blood-besprinkled mercy-seat; free to hear and do every good word and work. We are set free to "whatsoever things are true, whatsoever things are honest, whatsoever things are just, whatsoever things are pure, whatsoever things are lovely, whatsoever things are of good report," (Phil. 4:8).

17th

"But now, O LORD, thou art our father; we are the clay, and thou our potter; and we all are the work of thy hand." Isaiah 64:8

Until free-will, self-righteousness, creature exertions, and human merit are dried up and withered away, until they all die, we can never come into that spot where we are the clay, and God is the Potter. Can the clay make itself into a vessel? Can it mould itself into shape and form? Can it start from its bed, and work itself up into a vessel for use or ornament? No more can we make ourselves fit for glory, or mould ourselves into vessels of honour. If the Lord does but give us the feeling in our souls, our sweetest privilege, our dearest enjoyment, is to be the clay.

Free-will, self-righteousness, human wisdom, and creature strength – we give them all to the Pharisees; let them make the most of them. When the Lord indulges our souls with some measure of access to himself, and brings us in all humility and brokenness to lie low before his throne, we feel that we are nothing but what he makes us, have nothing but what he gives us, experience nothing but what he works in us, and do nothing but what he does in and for us.

To be here, and to lie here, is to be the clay. It is to find the Lord working in us holy desires, fervent breathings, secret cries, and the actings of faith, hope, and love. To feel these things freely given, graciously communicated, and divinely wrought, and to know that the Lord is doing all this for us and in us, is to find him the Potter, and is to be brought to the sweetest, lowliest, and happiest spot that a soul can come into.

18th

"But let patience have her perfect work, that ye may be perfect and entire, wanting nothing."
James 1:4

Patience then has its work; and what is that? It is firstly to endure all trials, live through all temptations, bear all crosses, carry all loads, fight all battles, toil through all difficulties, and overcome all enemies. Then secondly it is to submit to the will of God, to own that he is Lord and King, to have no will or way of its own, no scheme or plan to please the flesh, avoid the cross, or escape the rod. It is to submit simply to God's righteous dealings, both in providence and grace, believing that he does all things well, that he is a Sovereign, and "worketh all things after the counsel of his own will," (Eph. 1:11).

Now until the soul is brought to this point, the work of patience is not perfect; it may be going on, but it is not consummated. You may be in the furnace of temptation now, passing through the fiery trial. Are you rebellious or submissive? If still rebellious, you must abide in the furnace until you are brought to submission; and not only so, but it must be thorough submission, or else patience has not done its perfect work. The dross and slag of rebellion must be scummed off, and the pure metal flow down. It is all of God's grace to feel this for a single moment.

Are there not, and have there not been, times and seasons, in your soul, when you could be still and know that he is God? Have there been times when you could submit to his will, believing that he is too wise to err and too good to be unkind? When this submission is felt, patience has its perfect work.

Look at Jesus, our great example – see him in the gloomy garden, with the cross in awful prospect before him on the coming morn.

August

How he could say, "Not my will, but thine be done," (Luke 22:42)? Only because there was the perfect work of patience in the perfect soul of the Redeemer. Now we must have a work in our soul corresponding to this, or else we are not conformed to the suffering image of our crucified Lord.

Patience in us must have its perfect work, and God will take care that it shall be so. In a beautiful piece of machinery, if the engineer sees a cog loose or a wheel out of gear, he must adjust the defective part, that it may work easily and properly, and in harmony with the whole. So it is if the God of all our salvation sees a particular grace not in operation or not properly performing its appointed work, he by his Spirit so influences the heart that it is again brought to work as he designed it should do.

Measure your faith and patience by this standard, but do not take in conjunction, or confound with them the workings of your carnal mind. Here we often err. We may be submissive as regards our spirit, meek and patient, and quiet and resigned in the inward man, and yet feel many uprisings and rebellings of the flesh; thus patience may not seem to have her perfect work.

Yet looking for perfect submission in the flesh is to look for perfection in the flesh, which was never promised and is never given. Look to what the Spirit is working in you, not to the carnal mind which is not subject to the law of God, neither indeed can be, and therefore knows neither subjection nor submission. Look at that inward principality of which the Prince of Peace is Lord and Ruler, and see whether in the still depths of your soul, and where he lives and reigns, there is submission to the will of God.

19th

"We are troubled on every side, yet not distressed; we are perplexed, but not in despair."
2Corinthians 4:8

The saint of God is "troubled on every side" because he has on every side that with which he may be troubled. He has a spiritual side as well as a temporal side, a side in his soul as well as a side in his body, a side in his supernatural life as well as in his natural life, and a side in his new man of grace as well as a side in his old man of sin. Therefore, as it is necessary for him to be conformed to the suffering image of Christ, trouble comes upon him from every side and from every quarter, to make him like unto his blessed Lord. Now, his troubles are multiplied in proportion to his grace, for the more the afflictions abound the more abundant are the consolations, and an abundance of consolation is but an abundance of grace. Thus, the more grace he has the greater will be his sufferings, and the more he walks in a path agreeable to the Lord, and in conformity to his will and word, the more will he be baptised with the baptism of sorrow and tribulation with which his great Head was baptised before him.

Howbeit there is more to our verse, for the apostle says he is "Yet not distressed." The words "not distressed" literally signify that we are not shut up in a narrow spot from which there is no outlet whatever. It corresponds to an expression of the Apostle's in another place where he says that God will, "with the temptation also make a way to escape, that ye may be able to bear it," (1Cor. 10:13). This tallies well with the words of David, "thou hast known my soul in adversities," (Psa. 31:7), but though there be trouble on every side he adds in the next verse, "And hast not shut me up into the hand of the enemy: thou hast set my feet in a large room." Not being shut up into the hand of the enemy is not being abandoned of God to the foeman's death-stroke; and having the feet set in a large room is to have a place to move about in, one which affords an escape from death and destruction.

Thus, the dying Christian has a God to go to, a Saviour into whose arms he may cast his weary soul, and a blessed Spirit who from time to time relieves his doubts and fears. Thus God applies a sweet promise to his burdened spirit, gives him resignation and submission to his afflicting hand, and illuminates the dark valley of the shadow of death, which he has to tread, with a blessed ray of gospel light.

20th

"Wherefore the rather, brethren, give diligence to make your calling and election sure: for if ye do these things, ye shall never fall: for so an entrance shall be ministered unto you abundantly into the everlasting kingdom of our Lord and Saviour Jesus Christ."
2Peter 1:10-11

I believe many of God's people, if not most, have much ado to 'make their calling and election sure'. They are not a people to take things for granted; they cannot sit at ease and say, 'I have no doubt that I am a child of God'; they need something powerful, something applied, something spoken by the mouth of God himself; and short of that, they must be exercised with doubts and fears as to their state before him.

Now, therefore, let conscience speak; let us turn over the leaves of conscience. What says that faithful witness? Has God spoken with power to your soul? Has he pardoned your sins? Has he given you a sweet testimony of your saving interest in the Son of his love? Say you, 'Why, I do not know that I can say all that, I do not know that God has pardoned my sins'.

Well, if you cannot say that, we will come a little lower and take easier ground. Can you say that you are sighing and groaning and crying at times, not always for sure, but as the Lord works in you, for the sweet manifestations of Jesus' love to your soul? Here is a door open for you, the door of hope in the valley of Achor. Can you come in here?

Well then and good, these are marks of being one of God's peculiar people. But you cannot be satisfied, short of God himself making it known to you; you need an immediate testimony from his blessed mouth, and nothing but that can satisfy you. When he sheds abroad his love in your soul, it will give you peace and comfort, and nothing short of his love can do that.

21st

"A bruised reed shall he not break, and smoking flax shall he not quench, till he send forth judgment unto victory." Matthew 12:20

The gracious Man of Sorrows will never ever 'break the bruised reed, nor quench the smoking flax'. It is true that he sends forth judgment, for he means to bring the soul down into the dust. Yet while this judgment is going on, he secretly supports; for he kills that he may make alive; he brings down to the grave that he may bring up, (Deut. 32:39). In sending forth this judgment, it is unto victory, and conquest is at the end. There may be a long conflict, a hard and fearful battle with the garments rolled in sweat and blood, but victory is sure at last for he will never rest until he fully gains the day. Oh, how Satan would triumph if any saint ever fell out of the embraces of the good Shepherd; if he could point his derisive finger up to heaven's gate and to its risen King, and say, 'Your blood was shed in vain for this wretch, he is mine, he is mine!' Such a boast would fill hell with a yell of triumph, but no, no! It never will be so; the blood that "cleanseth us from all sin," (1John 1:7), never was, and never can be shed in vain.

August

Though the reed is bruised, it will never be broken; though the flax only smokes, it will never be extinguished; for he that sends forth judgment sends it "unto victory." Long indeed may the battle ebb and flow; again and again may the enemy charge; again and again may the event seem doubtful. Victory may be delayed even unto a late hour, until evening is drawing on and the shades of night are about to fall; maybe even until you are lying prone and helpless on the field of battle, but *it is sure* at the last.

It is also the Lord who does the whole. We have no power in ourselves to win the battle. Is there one temptation that you can master? Is there any one sin that you can, without divine help, crucify, or one lust that, without special grace, you can subdue? We are total weakness in this matter, but the blessed Lord makes his strength perfect in this weakness. We may and indeed must be bruised, and under painful feelings may think no one was so hardly dealt with, and that our case is singular.

Yet without this bruising we would not judge ourselves, "For if we would judge ourselves, we should not be judged," (1Cor. 11:31). If you justify yourself, the Lord will condemn you; if you condemn yourself, the Lord will justify you. Likewise if you exalt yourself, and the Lord will humble you; humble yourself, and the Lord will exalt you.

22nd

"O send out thy light and thy truth: let them lead me; let them bring me unto thy holy hill, and to thy tabernacles." Psalm 43:3

"O send out thy light." The Psalmist desired that light might be sent out, that is, that there might be a communication of it. The soul walking in darkness, and enabled under that darkness to pant and cry after light, is not satisfied with the conviction, however deep, that with God is light. The thirsty man is not satisfied with knowing that there is water in the well; nor the man who has lost his way in a mine, with knowing that there is light in the sun. One faint ray gleaming through a chink were worth to him a thousand suns, blazing, unseen by him, in the sky.

Thus the benighted saint cannot rest in the bare knowledge "that God is light, and in him is no darkness at all," (1John 1:5), but his sigh and cry is that this light may be sent out of the fullness of the Godhead into his soul. He needs an inward light shed abroad in his heart, whereby he may see the truth of God; whereby he may see

God's glory in the face of Christ and see his name written in the book of life, discerning his saving interest in the "everlasting covenant, which is ordered in all things, and sure," (2Sam. 23:5).

He needs this light to see Christ, and in seeing Christ he sees his own eternal union with Christ, and in that union he enjoys sweet communion with him and feels his presence in his soul, and has his glory revealed, and manifested to his heart.

David also wanted something more than light. He says, "O send out thy light and thy truth," (Psa. 43:3). What was "the truth" which he sought to know, and realise its inward power by its being sent out of the fullness of the Godhead? Doubtless, it was the same truth that saints are crying out for today, which can be nothing less than 'the truth as it is in Jesus'. It is the truth of his blood as atoning for sin and the truth of his righteousness as justifying us from all things from which we could not be justified by the law of Moses. It is the truth of personal and everlasting deliverance from all curse and condemnation, that truth whereby the soul is made free, according to those words, "Ye shall know the truth, and the truth shall make you free," (John 8:32). It is the truth whereby the affections are separated from the things of time and sense, and fixed on the realities of eternity.

In short, it is to know Jesus himself by his own sweet revelation, for he is "the way, the truth, and the life," and to enjoy him in our souls as the sum and substance of truth.

23rd

"They shall ask the way to Zion with their faces thitherward, saying, Come, and let us join ourselves to the LORD in a perpetual covenant that shall not be forgotten." Jeremiah 50:5

"Come, let us join ourselves to the Lord." This seems to imply power in the creature to join himself to the Lord, but on close inspection, it implies this - that after the Lord has united us to himself, then we can't help but unite ourselves to him. It is only the Lord who can set the face of a believer towards Zion. When he therefore brings such an one into a manifested union with himself, there is a leaping forth of the soul, a going forth of the affections, a cleaving to him with purpose of heart, and a believing in him with all the powers of the mind. There is a solemn renunciation, a casting aside, a trampling under foot, and a rejection of everything but that which stands in the power of God, as made known to the soul by the Holy Spirit.

It is not spoken in a presumptuous way. It does not indicate any bold claim upon the Lord, as if by being on the road to Zion, and being possessed of certain evidences, they could somehow claim the inheritance, and rush in to lay hold of gospel blessings. Rather it expresses the hidden longings of the heart, and points out the actings of living faith in the soul, which go forth when raised up and drawn out by the blessed Spirit.

The vain confidence and rash forwardness of those who are at ease in Zion is a very different thing from the meek faith of those who are going on weeping, and asking the way to Zion with their faces set towards it. Those whose hearts are melted by the Spirit into contrition, who renounce everything but Christ and him crucified, and desire to feel and taste the sweet manifestation of the love of a dying Lord are not those who would force their way in.

These only, without presumption or bold familiarity, can say, 'Come, let us join ourselves to the Lord', as feeling in their souls the actings of that living faith, whereby they cleave to and lean upon him, as the only prop between them and hell.

24th

"And he is the head of the body, the church: who is the beginning, the firstborn from the dead; that in all things he might have the pre-eminence."
Colossians 1:18

That the Lord Jesus Christ should have a people in whom he should be eternally glorified was the original promise made by the Father to the Son. "Ask of me, and I shall give you the heathen for your inheritance, and the uttermost parts of the earth for your possession" (Psa. 2:8). This was 'the joy that was set before him' for which 'he endured the cross, despising the shame', (Heb. 12:2). This was 'the purchased possession', 'the travail of his soul', and the reward of his humiliation and sufferings, (Phil. 2:9-10).

This people form the members of his mystical body, all of which were written in his book, the book of life, when as yet, as regards their actual existence, there was none of them, (Psa. 139:16). All these were given to him in eternity, when he was constituted their covenant Head in the everlasting covenant, ordered in all things, and sure. They thus became, in prospect of his incarnation, "members of his body, of his flesh, and of his bones," (Eph. 5:30).

August

How touchingly did the blessed Redeemer remind his Father of those covenant transactions, when he said in his memorable prayer, "I pray for them: I pray not for the world, but for them which thou hast given me; for they are thine; and all mine are thine, and thine are mine; and I am glorified in them," (John 17:9-10). Being thus given to Christ, and constituted members of his mystical body, they can no more perish than Christ himself. He is their Head; and as he is possessed of all power, full of all love, filled with all wisdom, and replete with all mercy, grace, and truth, how can he, how will he, allow any of his members to fall out of his body, and be lost to him as well as to themselves? Will any man willingly allow his eye, or his hand, or his foot, or even the tip of his little finger, to be taken out or cut off? If any member of our earthly body perish, if we lose an arm or a leg, it is because we have not power to prevent it. Yet all power belongs to Christ, in heaven and in earth, and therefore no one member of his mystical body can perish for lack of power in him to save it.

However truly blessed this doctrine is, it is only when we are quickened and made alive unto God by a spiritual birth that we savingly and experimentally know and realise it; and we are, for the most part, led into it thus.

First, we are made to feel our need of Christ as a Saviour from the wrath to come, from the fear of death, the curse of the law, and the accusations of a guilty conscience.

Then, when enabled by the blessed Spirit's operations to receive him into our heart by faith as the Christ of God, and to realise in some measure a saving interest in him, we are taught to feel our need of continual supplies of grace and strength out of his fullness. We have to learn something of the depths of the fall, of the evils of our heart, of the temptations of Satan, of the strength of sin, and of our own weakness and worthlessness in order to appreciate the enormity of our salvation. Every fresh discovery of helplessness and wretchedness makes a way for looking to and hanging upon him; we become more and more dependent on him as of God made unto us wisdom, righteousness, sanctification, and redemption.

25th

"I am the resurrection, and the life."
John 11:25

How often we sink into places where we are in our feelings dead men. Has sin never slain you? Have convictions never, so to speak, knocked the life of God out of your soul? Has Satan never come with his fiery darts, with all the artillery of hell, and sought to scorch up every gracious feeling and every living desire? And have you not sunk at times in your soul into such miserable deadness of spirit, that it seemed that not only there and then you were devoid of all grace, but that it was an impossibility for grace ever again to renew and revive your soul?

Here you were dead. I have often been here, which enables me to describe it to you. Yet with all this, there is a longing look, a heartfelt groan, a heaving sigh, a resisting unto blood, not an utter giving way, nor sinking down into miserable despair. God the Spirit kept alive his work upon the soul, and Christ himself as the resurrection dropped into our bosom, raised up and drew forth towards himself some fresh movements of that life which is in him. Thus is fulfilled that gracious consequence of his resurrection, "he that believeth in me, though he were dead, yet shall he live," (John 11:25).

Oh, amid all our deadness, all our gloom and desolation, all our emptiness, barrenness, and helplessness, if there be in our souls a longing look, a heartfelt cry, an earnest groan, a sincere desire toward him who is the resurrection, our prayer will ascend into his pitying, sympathising ear. Because he is the resurrection, he will once more raise up into life and feeling our dead and drooping soul. We have no other source of life. If we were altogether and really dead, we would always continue dead unless he were the resurrection, but because he is the resurrection, he can re-animate, revive, renew, and re-quicken us by pouring into our hearts fresh life and feeling. It will be our mercy to be ever looking unto him, hanging upon him, believing in him, trusting to him, and giving him no rest until he appear again and again to the joy and rejoicing of our heart.

26th

"He that believeth in me, though he were dead, yet shall he live."
John 11:25

How can anyone who is dead believe? He can, or our Lord would not have said so. I will show you how. He is a living man as quickened into life by the power of the Spirit of God, and yet he is dead. This is the deep mystery, that though he is dead in law, dead in conscience, dead in helplessness, yet God the Holy Spirit has breathed into him and deposited in him a seed of living faith. By this faith he cries, by this faith he sighs, and by this faith he hungers and thirsts after righteousness; yes, more, by this faith he looks unto and believes in the Son of God. He scarcely knows that he has faith. His faith is so weak and so small in his own estimation, that he dare not say he has faith; and yet he has all the fruits of faith, all the marks of faith, and all the evidences of faith.

Take as a parallel case Jonah in the whale's belly. Had he faith or had he not faith? How low he sank when the waves were heaped over his head, when carried through the boundless deep in the belly of the whale. Yet even there he could say, "I will look again toward thy holy temple," (John 2:4). Had he no faith? Yes, he had; and by that faith he was saved, justified, accepted, brought out, and delivered, and able to say, "Salvation is of the Lord!" (John. 2:8).

Take also King Hezekiah upon his bed of sickness. Had he no faith? How then could he turn his face to the wall and pray unto the Lord? How could his eyes fail with looking upward, when he said, "O Lord, I am oppressed, undertake for me?" (Isa. 38:14).

Take too David in his mournful journey out of Jerusalem, as he went weeping and barefoot up the Mount Olivet with his head covered at the time of Absalom's rebellion. Had he no faith? How then came he to pray, "O LORD, I pray thee, turn the counsel of Ahithophel into foolishness?" Why did the Lord answer that prayer, if it were not the prayer of faith?

In all these men of God, sunken though they were almost to the last and lowest point, there was still the life of faith, and by that faith they called upon God. They looked unto him and were lightened, and their faces were not ashamed anymore.

Here, then, we find the connection between the resurrection of the Lord Jesus Christ from the dead and the experience of this seemingly dead soul. When Christ died on the cross, he bore the sins of this poor dead soul in his body there on the tree, and thus atoned for them and put them away. When Christ rose from the dead, this poor dead soul rose with him, as a member of his mystical body. When Christ went up on high, the now living soul ascended up with him, and when Christ sat down at the right hand of the Father, the once dead soul virtually and mystically sat down with him in heavenly bliss.

Therefore, because Jesus is the resurrection, and because as such the redeemed soul has a saving interest in him, "he that believeth in him, though he were dead, yet shall he live."

27th

"Being made so much better than the angels, as he hath by inheritance obtained a more excellent name than they." Hebrews 1:4

August

Christ was made so much better than the angels, not as the Son of God, because being their Maker and Creator he was already better than they were. Neither did he take up the position of God's Son by being "appointed heir of all things", (Heb. 1:2), and thereby obtaining that more excellent name. He was the natural heir. If I have an only son, and he inherits my property, his being my heir does not make him my son, but his being my son makes him my heir. In like manner is the blessed Jesus God's heir.

However, the beauty and blessedness, the grace and glory, the joy and consolation of his being the "heir of all things" lies in this; that he is heir in our nature! That the same blessed Immanuel who groaned and wept, suffered and bled here below, is now at the right hand of the Father as our High Priest, Mediator, Advocate, Representative, and Intercessor. All power is given unto him in heaven and earth as the God-man, (Matt. 28:18), and the Father hath "set him at his own right hand in the heavenly places, far above all principality, and power, and might, and dominion, and every name that is named, not only in this world, but also in that which is to come," (Eph. 1:20-21).

But he has all this pre-eminence and glory not to make him the Son of God, or because he always was the Son of God, but because, as a *man*, God lifted him up. "Who, being in the form of God, thought it not robbery to be equal with God, but made himself of no reputation and took upon him the form of a servant and was made in the likeness of men; and being found in fashion as a man, he humbled himself, and became obedient unto death, even the death of the cross. Wherefore God also hath highly exalted him, and given him a name which is above every name, that at the name of Jesus every knee should bow, of things in heaven, and things in earth, and things under the earth; and that every tongue should confess that Jesus Christ is Lord, to the glory of God the Father," (Phil. 2:6-11).

The joy of heaven above, the delight of the saints here below, their only hope and help, their strength and wisdom, spring from this, that the Son of God is exalted to the right hand of the Father in the very nature which he assumed in the womb of the virgin, as a man like unto us.

28th

"The full soul loatheth an honeycomb; but to the hungry soul every bitter thing is sweet."
Proverbs 27:7

August

Afflictions, trials, and sorrows are very bitter things, and they must needs be bitter, for God never meant that they should be otherwise. When he takes the rod, it is to make it felt; and when he brings trouble on his children, it is that they may smart under it. Our text therefore does not, I believe, mean that the "bitter thing" is sweet when it is taken, for then it would cease to be bitter; but it is sweet on account of the blessed nourishment that is brought to the soul out of it.

I remember reading, many years ago, the travels of Franklin to the North Pole, and a very interesting book it is naturally, but there is one incident mentioned in it which just strikes my mind. In wandering over the snows of the polar regions there was no food to be gotten for weeks, except a lichen or kind of moss that grew upon the rocks, and that was so exceedingly bitter, (something like 'Iceland moss'), that it could only be taken with the greatest disgust, yet upon that Franklin and his companions lived. They had no alternative; they must either eat that or die. Yet that bitter moss became sweet after it had passed their palates, for it had a nutriment in it which kept their bodies alive.

Likewise, many of God's people, who have endured the most dreadful trials, have afterwards found nutriment for their souls to spring out of them. What bitter things are God's reproofs and rebukes in the conscience! Yet what Christian would be without them?

I appeal to you who fear God, would you deliberately choose never to experience marks of divine disapprobation, and never feel the frowns of God's anger at any time when you go wrong? I believe in my conscience that you whose hearts are tender in God's fear would say, 'Lord, let me have your frowns; for if I have not your frowns and a conscience to feel them, what sins would I not recklessly plunge into? Where would not my wicked nature carry me, if I had not your solemn reproofs!' These very rebukes then become sweet, not in themselves, nor at the time, but because of the solid profit that comes out of them.

29th

"For we are his workmanship, created in Christ Jesus unto good works, which God hath before ordained that we should walk in them."
Ephesians 2:10

Good works, properly so-called, spring out of the inward operation of God's grace. By making the tree good he makes the fruit good,

(Matt. 12:33). He works in us first the will to do that which is good, and then he gives us the power to do it. He thus works in us both to will and to do of his good pleasure, (Phil. 2:13). Under the operations of his grace we are transformed by the renewing of our mind to prove what is that good, and acceptable, and perfect will of God, (Rom. 12:2); and because this will is sought after to be known and done, good works follow as the necessary fruit.

All the acts of love and affection, of kindness, sympathy, and liberality towards the Lord's people, and all those instances of self-denial and willingness to suffer rather than to do wrong spring out of the goodness of God within us. All the myriad proofs of unselfish desire to do all the good we can according to our means, position, and circumstances of life, all that striving after and maintaining integrity and uprightness of conduct in all matters of business and trust and all that strict and scrupulous adherence to our word, even to our own injury reflect Him. All this, and the Christian fulfilment of our relative duties, the social relationships of husband and father or wife and mother which the Scripture has enjoined, and all else which by unanimous consent is called 'good' by men, is only really and truly good as wrought in the heart, life, and lip by the power of God within us.

30th

"And they overcame him by the blood of the Lamb, and by the word of their testimony; and they loved not their lives unto the death."
Revelation 12:11

It is not "the blood of the Lamb" as revealed in the word of God, but as applied to and sprinkled on the conscience, which answers the accusations of Satan? Yes indeed, but we may observe that there is our coming unto 'the blood of sprinkling', and there is 'the blood of sprinkling' coming unto us.

The apostle writes, "Ye are come... to the blood of sprinkling, that speaketh better things than that of Abel," (Heb. 12:24). This coming to the blood is the first step in gaining the victory, but in Christian warfare defeat generally, if not always, precedes conquest. It is not, therefore, so easy to overcome sin, death, and hell, which are all continually striving against us; and usually we never look to the right quarter for help until well-near all hope is gone. The first gleam generally comes from a view of 'the blood of the Lamb', as it were, in the distance.

August

The lighthouse casts its glimmering rays far over the wide waste of waters, to guide into harbour or guard from the rocks the storm-tossed mariner. So it is when there is a view in the soul of 'the blood of the Lamb', even at a distance, it is a beacon light, which draws towards it the eyes and heart of those who are doing business 'in deep waters'. The light may not at first seem very bright or clear, but still it is a day-star, heralding the rising of the sun. The Spirit shines on the word, and raises up faith in the soul to believe that the Lamb has been slain, that blood has been shed, that a sacrifice has been offered, and that 'a new and living way' has been opened and consecrated 'through the veil', that is the torn "flesh" of our Lord Jesus.

This affords the accused soul some foothold on which it can stand and answer Satan's accusations. 'True', he says, 'I am a guilty wretch, a sinner, and even the chief of sinners, for I have sinned against light, against convictions, against conscience, and the fear of God. My heart is altogether evil, my mind wholly corrupt, and my nature utterly depraved. I have never done any good thing of myself, and I am a wretch, the worst of wretches, and I can never say anything too bad of myself, nor others of me; but, with all that, the Lamb of God has shed his precious blood, and that blood cleanses from all sin'.

"When the enemy shall come in like a flood, the Spirit of the LORD shall lift up a standard against him," (Isa. 59:19). That standard is the blood-stained flag of the crucified Redeemer; and to come for refuge under this banner dipped in blood is to make headway against Satan. Yet the victory is still not fully gained. It is only when there is a coming of the blood into the heart, a sprinkling of it on the conscience, a manifestation and application of it to the soul, that Satan is effectually put to flight.

31st

"He giveth power to the faint; and to them that have no might he increaseth strength."
Isaiah 40:29

The Lord often gives his people power to take a longing, languishing look at the blood and righteousness of Jesus, and to come to the Lord, as 'mighty to save', with the same feelings with which Esther went into the presence of the king. "I will go in, and if I perish, I perish," (Est. 4:16). It is with them sometimes as with the four lepers who sat at the entering in of the gate of Samaria and said one to another, "Why sit we here until we die? If we say, We will enter into the city, then the famine is in the city, and we shall die there: and if we sit still here, we die also. Now therefore come, and let us fall unto the host of the Syrians: if they save us alive, we shall live; and if they kill us, we shall but die," (2Kings 7:3-4). So are the Lord's people sometimes brought to this state – 'If I perish, I will perish at his footstool'. If he gives no answer of mercy, they will still cling to his feet, and beseech him to look upon them and save them.

Now this is the power spoken of in our text, real power. Despair would instead have laid hold upon their soul if this secret power had not been given to them. Sometimes we learn this by painful experience. Our trials sometimes stun us, and then there is no power to seek or pray. At other times power is given, and there is a pleading with the Lord, a going out of the heart's desires after him, and a fulfilment in the soul of the experience described by the prophet, "I will wait upon the LORD, that hideth his face from the house of Jacob, and I will look for him," (Isa. 8:17).

God gives power also to believe; for it is the work of the blessed Spirit to raise up living faith in the heart. He gives power to hope; for it is only so far as he communicates power, that we can cast forth this anchor of the soul. He gives power to love; for it is only as he gives power, that we feel any measure of affection either to the Lord or to his people. In short, every spiritual desire, every breath of fervent prayer, every movement of the soul heavenward, every trusting in God's name, relying on his word, and hanging upon his promises, springs out of power communicated by the Lord to the faint and feeble.

September

September

1st

"But now we see not yet all things put under him."
Hebrews 2:8

It is God's special prerogative to bring good out of evil, and order out of chaos. If you were to watch carefully from an astronomical observatory the movements of the planets, you would see them all in the greatest apparent disorder. Sometimes they would seem to move forward, sometimes backward, and sometimes not move at all. This confused and contradictory motion sadly puzzled astronomers until Sir Isaac Newton explained the whole. Then all was seen to be the most beautiful harmony and order, where before there was the most puzzling confusion.

Take too a scriptural instance, the highest and greatest that we can give, to show that where, to outward appearance, all is disorder, and there the greatest wisdom and most determinate will reigns supreme. Look at the crucifixion of our blessed Lord. Can you not almost see the scene as painted in the word of truth? See those scheming priests, that wild mob, those rough soldiers, that faltering Roman governor, the pale and terrified disciples, and the weeping women. See too, at the very centre of it all, the innocent Sufferer with the crown of thorns, enduring that last scene of surpassing woe which made the earth quake and the sun withdraw his light. What confusion! What disorder! What triumphant guilt! What oppressed and vanquished innocence! Yet was it really so? Was there no wisdom and power of God here? Was he not accomplishing even by the instrumentality of human wickedness his own eternal purposes? Has not he testified to this point? "Him, being delivered by the determinate counsel and foreknowledge of God, ye have taken, and by wicked hands have crucified and slain," (Acts 2:23).

The determinate counsel and foreknowledge of God, in the great and glorious work of redemption, was accomplished by the wicked hands of man; and if so, in this the worst and wickedest of all possible cases, is not the same eternal will also now executed in instances of a similar nature, though to us at present it is less visible?

2nd

"But unto you that fear my name shall the Sun of righteousness arise with healing in his wings;"
Malachi 4:2

Oh, what a mercy it is for the Church of Christ, that the God and Father of the Lord Jesus Christ has not left her, as he might justly have done so, to perish in her sins. What a mercy it is that he has provided for her a Saviour, and a great one, and does from time to time encourage every poor, self-condemned sinner to hope in his mercy!

The very things, poor exercised soul, that most try your mind, are the very things that make such a Saviour suitable to you. You are dark; this makes the Sun of righteousness exactly suitable to enlighten you. You are cold; this makes you need the Sun to warm you. You are cheerless and cast down; this makes you need the Sun to gladden you. You are barren and unfruitful, and lament that you cannot bring forth fruit to God's glory; you need the Sun to fertilise you. You are, at times, very dead in your feelings, and can scarcely find any inclination to pray, meditate, or read the Scriptures; you need the Sun to enliven and revive you.

Are these not, then, the very trials and temptations necessary to make you feel that the Lord Jesus is the Sun you need, the Sun that made David sing unto him? (Psa. 84:11).

What value do those put upon the Lord Jesus who make a fire for themselves, and walk in the sparks of their own kindling? (Isa. 50:11). What is Jesus to those who know no trouble of soul? What real and earnest prayer do such offer, or what fervent desire do they have they after him? What ardent longing do they feel for his appearing, and what breathings do they experience to see and feel his blood and righteousness? Oh, it is sharp exercises, manifold trials, and powerful temptations that make the soul really value the Lord Jesus.

3rd

"God is faithful, by whom ye were called unto the fellowship of his Son Jesus Christ our Lord."
1Corinthians 1:9

Nothing distinguishes the divine religion of the saint of God, not only from the dead profanity of the openly ungodly, but from the formal lip-service of the lifeless professor, so much as communion with God.

How clearly do we see this exemplified in the saints of old. Abel sought after fellowship with God when "he brought of the firstlings of his flock, and of the fat thereof," (Gen. 4:4), for he looked to the

September

atoning blood of the Lamb of God. God accepted the offering, by manifesting his respect unto it. Here was fellowship between Abel and God.

Enoch "walked with God... three hundred years," (Gen. 5), but how can two walk together except they be agreed, and for so long time? There is no doubt that Enoch and God were agreed, and therefore were in fellowship and communion.

Abraham was "the friend of God," (Jas. 2:23). "The Lord spoke to Moses face to face," (Ex. 33:11), and David was "the man after God's own heart," (1Sam. 13:14). All the testimonies of the Holy Spirit concerning these three implied that they were reconciled, brought near, and walked in holy communion with the Lord God Almighty.

So we see that all the saints of old, whose sufferings and exploits are recorded in Hebrews 11, lived a life of faith and prayer, a life of fellowship and communion with their Father and their Friend. Even though they were stoned, sawn asunder, tempted and slain with the sword, and wandered about in sheep-skins and goat-skins, being destitute, afflicted, tormented, (Heb. 11:37), they had communion with the Lord. Though they wandered in deserts and in mountains, and in dens and caves of the earth, (Heb. 11:38), yet were they all sustained in their sufferings and sorrows by the Spirit and grace, by the presence and power of the living God, with whom they held sweet communion. Though they were tortured, they would accept no deliverance by denying their Lord, "that they might obtain a better resurrection," (Heb. 11:35), and see him as he is in glory, by whose grace they were brought into fellowship with him on earth.

This same communion with himself is that which God now calls his saints unto, as we read, "God is faithful, by whom ye were called unto the fellowship of his Son Jesus Christ our Lord," (1Cor. 1:9), for to have fellowship with his Son is to have fellowship with him.

As then he called Abraham out of the land of the Chaldees, so he calls elect souls out of the world today, out of darkness, sin, and death, out of formality and self-righteousness, out of a deceptive profession, to have fellowship with himself, to be blessed with manifestations of his love and mercy.

It is to this point that all his dealings with their souls tend. It is to bring them near to himself that all their afflictions, trials, and sorrows are sent. In giving them tastes of holy fellowship here, he grants them foretastes of that eternity of bliss which will be theirs when time shall be no more, when they shall be forever swallowed up with his presence and love.

September 4th

"And we have known and believed the love that God hath to us. God is love; and he that dwelleth in love dwelleth in God, and God in him."
1John 4:16

Love is communicative. This is a part of its very nature and essence. Its delight is to give, and especially to give itself; and all it wants or asks is a return. To love and to be beloved. To enjoy and to express that ardent and mutual affection by words and deeds – this is love's delight, love's heaven. To love, and not be loved – this is love's misery, love's hell. God is love. This is his very nature, an essential attribute of his glorious being; and as he, the infinite and eternal Jehovah, exists in a Trinity of distinct Persons, though undivided Unity of Essence, there is a mutual, ineffable love between Father, Son, and Holy Spirit.

To this mutual, ineffable love of the three Persons in the sacred Godhead, the Scripture abundantly testifies. "The Father loveth the Son," (John 3:35); and "thou... hast loved them, as thou hast loved me," (John 17:23); and "This is my beloved Son in whom I am well pleased," (Matt. 17:5). As the Father loves the Son, so does the Son love the Father; "But that the world may know that I love the Father," (John 14:31), are his own blessed words. That the Holy Spirit loves the Father and the Son is evident not only from his divine personality in the Godhead, but because he is essentially the very 'Spirit of love' (Rom. 15:30), and as such sheds abroad the love of God in the hearts of the election of grace, (Rom. 5:5).

Thus man was not needed by the holy and ever-blessed Trinity as an object of divine love. Sufficient, eternally and amply sufficient, to all the bliss and blessedness, perfection and glory of Jehovah was and ever would have been the mutual love and intercommunion of the three Persons in the sacred Godhead. Yet love – the equal and undivided love of Father, Son, and Holy Spirit – flowed out beyond its original and essential being to man; and not merely to man as man, that is to human nature as the body prepared for the Son of God to assume, but to thousands and millions of individuals that make up the human race.

We are all loved personally and individually with the whole sum of God's infinite love as much as if that love were fixed on only one, and that one were loved as God loves his dear Son. "I have loved you with an everlasting love," (Jer. 31:3), is spoken to each individual of the elect as much as to the whole Church, viewed as the mystical Bride and Spouse of the Lamb.

September

Thus the love of a Triune God is not only to the physical nature which in due time the Son of God should assume, the flesh and blood of the children, the seed of Abraham, which he should take on him, (Heb. 2:14-16), and for this reason viewed by the Triune Jehovah with eyes of intense delight. The love of the Triune God is equally towards that innumerable multitude of human beings who were to form the mystical body of Christ.

Were Scripture less express, we might still believe that it was the physical nature alone, which one of the sacred Trinity was later to assume, that would be delighted in and loved by the holy Three-in-One. Howbeit we have the testimony of the Holy Spirit on this point, which puts it beyond all doubt or question.

At the creation of that nature, when all else was complete, the Holy Trinity said, "Let us make man in our image, after our likeness," (Gen. 1:26). In pursuance of that divine council, "the LORD God formed man of the dust of the ground, and breathed into his nostrils the breath of life," so that man "became a living soul," (Gen. 2:7). God thereby united an immortal soul to an earthly body, and this human nature was created in the moral image of God, not just after the pattern of that body which was prepared for the Son of God by the Father. Therefore we have God's own testimony that it is not just our physical nature that is loved, but our spiritual nature too.

5th

"In whom are hid all the treasures of wisdom and knowledge."
Colossians 2:3

What poor, blind fools are we by nature! How insufficient is all our earthly wisdom and all our natural knowledge, to guide us into the truth! When the soul really is under divine teaching, how ignorant it feels as to every single thing it desires to know! What clouds of darkness perpetually hang over the mind! What a veil of ignorance seems continually spread over the heart! The simplest truths of God's word seem hidden in the deepest obscurity, and the soul can neither see the truth, nor see or feel its personal interest in it.

Now, when a man is here, he does not go to the Lord with lying lips and a mocking tongue, and ask him to give him wisdom, merely because he has heard that other persons have asked it of God, or because he reads in the Bible that Christ is made of God "wisdom" to his people. He goes as a poor, blind fool, as one completely

September

ignorant, as one totally unable to understand a single spiritual truth of himself, as one thoroughly helpless to get into the marrow of vital godliness, into the mysteries of true religion, or into the very heart of Christ.

For it is not a few doctrines received into the head, nor a sound creed in the mind that can satisfy a soul convinced of its ignorance. Nothing else can satisfy him, but having that divine illumination whereby he sees light in God's light, and has spiritual wisdom communicated whereby he feels himself "made wise unto salvation," (2Tim. 3:15). He craves that unctuous light to be shed abroad in his heart, which is the only key to gospel truth, and is its own blessed evidence that he knows the truth by a divine application of it to his soul.

6th

"O God, thou art my God; early will I seek thee: my soul thirsteth for thee, my flesh longeth for thee in a dry and thirsty land, where no water is; to see thy power and thy glory, so as I have seen thee in the sanctuary."
Psalm 63:2

Every place is "a sanctuary" where God manifests himself in power and glory to the soul. Moses, doubtless, had often passed by the bush which grew in Horeb. It was but a common thorny bush and in no way distinguished from the other bushes of the grove until on one solemn occasion it was all "in a flame of fire," (Gen. 3:2). "The angel of the Lord" had appeared unto him in the midst of it, and though it burnt with fire, it was not consumed for it was not natural fire. God being in the bush, the ground round about was holy, and Moses was bidden to take his shoes from off his feet. Was not this a sanctuary to Moses? It was, for a holy God was there.

Thus wherever God manifests himself, *that* becomes a sanctuary to a believing soul. Sanctuaries are not places made holy by the ceremonies of man, but places made holy by the presence of our God. Then a stable, a hovel, a hedge, any homely corner may be, and often becomes a sanctuary, when God fills your heart with his sacred presence, and causes every holy feeling and gracious affection to spring up in your soul.

If ever you have seen this in times past, you have seen God in the sanctuary, for at such time your heart becomes the sanctuary of God. According to his own words, "Ye are the temple of the living God; as God hath said, I will dwell in them, and walk in them; and I will be their God, and they shall be my people," (2Cor. 6:16). Are not our very bodies also called the temples of the Holy Spirit, (1Cor. 6:19)? Does not Christ dwell in the heart by faith, (Eph. 3:17), and is he not formed there, the hope of glory, (Col. 1:27)?

It is, therefore, not only in seeing Christ without, but in seeing Christ within that we experience the power and glory of God. It is in this way that we become consecrated to the service and glory of God, set our affections upon heavenly things, and obtain a foretaste of eternal joy.

7th

"I will give thee the treasures of darkness."
Isaiah 45:3

Is not this a strange expression? "Treasures of darkness!" How can there be darkness in the City of Salvation of which the Lord the Lamb is the eternal light? The expression does not mean that the treasures themselves are darkness, but that they were hidden in darkness until they were brought to light. The treasures of Belshazzar, like bank bullion, were buried in darkness until they were broken up and given to Cyrus.

It is so in a spiritual sense. Are there not treasures in the Lord Jesus? Oh, what treasures of grace there are in his glorious Person! What treasures of pardon in his precious blood! What treasures of righteousness in his perfect obedience! What treasures of salvation in all that he is and has as the great High Priest over the house of God!

Yet, all these treasures are "treasures of darkness," so far as they are hidden from our eyes and hearts, until we are brought by his special power into the City of Salvation. Then these treasures are not only brought to light, revealed, and made known, but the soul is at once put into possession of them. They are not only seen, as a bank clerk sees notes and sovereigns, but are by a special deed of gift from the Court of Heaven made over to him who by faith in the Lord Jesus receives him into his heart. No one has the least conception of the treasures of grace that are in the Lord Jesus until he is brought out of darkness into God's marvellous light, and knows him and the power of his resurrection by the sweet manifestations of his presence and love.

But the word "treasures" signifies not only something laid up and hidden from general view, but, being plural, expresses a vast, incalculable amount! An amount which can never be expended and used up, but suffices, and suffices, and suffices again for all needs and for all believing comers.

When we get a view by faith of the Person and work of the Lord Jesus and see the ever-flowing and overflowing fullness of his grace, and how it superabounds over all the aboundings of sin, it may well fill our minds with holy wonder and admiration. When we get a glimpse of the virtue and efficacy of his atoning blood, that precious blood which "cleanses from all sin," and that divine righteousness which is "unto all and upon all those who believe," what treasures of mercy, pardon, and peace are seen laid up in him!

To see this by the eye of faith, and enter into its beauty and blessedness, is indeed to comprehend with all saints the length, and breadth, and depth, and height, and to know something of the love of Christ which passes knowledge. The sun will cease to give his light, and the earth to yield her increase; but these treasures will still be unexhausted, for they are in themselves infinite and inexhaustible.

8th

"Every valley shall be exalted, and every mountain and hill shall be made low: and the crooked shall be made straight, and the rough places plain."
Isaiah 40:4

If in your road heavenward, no valley ever sank before you and no mountain rose up in front of you; if you walked no crooked paths through dense and tangled woods, nor stumbled through rough places with many a rolling stone; and if you were not scratched and bleeding from the dragging thorny briar, it would not seem that you were treading the well-worn path of the saints of God at all. Nor would it appear as if you needed special help from the sanctuary, or any peculiar power to be put forth for your help and deliverance.

Howbeit you are in this path by God's own appointment, finding before your eyes valleys of depression which you cannot raise up, and mountains of difficulty that you cannot lay low. You are hemmed in by crooked things which you cannot make straight, and rough places that you cannot make smooth. You are compelled, from a felt necessity, to look for help from above.

These perplexing difficulties, then, are the very things that make yours a case for the gospel, and make yours a state of mind to which salvation by grace is thoroughly adapted. Yours is the very condition of soul to which the revelation of the glory of God in the face of Jesus Christ is altogether suitable. If you could but view these trials with spiritual eyes, and know that they are all appointed by unerring wisdom and eternal love, and are designed for the good of your soul, you would rather bless God that your pathway was so cast in providence and grace that you had a valley or a mountain, or a crook and a thorn.

And even as regards the present experience of your soul, you would feel that these very difficulties in the road were all productive of so many errands to the throne - that they all called upon you, as with so many speaking voices, to beg of the Lord that he would manifest himself in love to your heart.

We all desire ease; we love a smooth path. We would like to be carried to heaven in a palanquin; to enjoy every comfort that earth can give or heart desire, and then, dying without a pang of body or mind, find ourselves safe in heaven. Yet that is not God's way. The word of truth, the sufferings of Christ, and the universal experience of the saints through the ages all testify against the path of ease and testify for the path of trial.

They all proclaim, as with one united voice, "wide is the gate, and broad is the way, that leadeth to destruction, and many there be which go in there at," (Matt. 7:13). This is the way of ease and of that prosperity which destroys fools, (Prov. 1:32); but "strait is the gate, and narrow is the way, which leadeth unto life, and few there be that find it," and this is frequently the path of suffering and sorrow.

9th

"But this man, after he had offered one sacrifice for sins for ever, sat down on the right hand of God."
Hebrews 10:12

It is a fundamental article of our most holy faith, that the man Christ Jesus is now at God's right hand, and very man, not a shadowy, ethereal ghost. "For there is one God, and one mediator between God and men, the man Christ Jesus," (1Tim. 2:5). God looks at him as such with eyes of intense delight, with ever-new approbation and love; and views him as the representative of all that are savingly interested in him; he being the Head, and the Church being the members. He is the Bridegroom, and the Church is the bride. He is the great High Priest, and the Church is the house of God.

He lives for her at the right hand of the Father, ever presenting on her behalf the validity of his intercession. The fact, the reality that he is there, is the Church's joy, as it is all her hope and all her boast. "Because I live, ye shall live also," (John 14:19).

To him, then, do we direct our prayers, and on his glorious Person do we fix our believing eyes. Upon his blood do we hang all our hope and under his righteousness do we ever desire to shelter. To feel his presence, taste his grace, experience his love, and know his power is what our soul, under divine teaching, is ever longing for.

See, then, the grounds of holy boldness for a poor sinner to enter into the holiest. Blood has been shed, which blood has the validity of Godhead stamped upon it. A new and living way has been consecrated, in which a living soul may walk. A great High Priest is set over the house of God, who is ever presenting the merits of his intercession. Thus, those who feel their need of him, who cannot live, and dare not die without him, whose eyes are upon him and hearts are towards him, are encouraged to enter with all holy boldness into the holiest, that they may have communion with Father, Son, and Holy Spirit.

10th

"Nay, in all these things we are more than conquerors through him that loved us."
Romans 8:37

Those who know nothing of their own heart, of their own infirmities, of their own frailties, of their own inward or outward slips and backslidings, know nothing of the secret of super-abounding grace, nothing of the secret of atoning blood, nothing of the secret of the Spirit's inward testimony. They cannot. Only in proportion as we are emptied of self in all its various forms, are we filled out of the fullness of Him who fills all in all.

Now you, perhaps, (I address myself personally to some poor, tempted child of God, that in touching one, I may touch others), are a poor, tempted creature; and your daily sorrow, your continual trouble is, that you are so soon overcome; that your temper, your lusts, your pride, your worldliness, your carnal, corrupt heart are perpetually getting the mastery. From this you sometimes draw bitter conclusions. You say, in the depth of your heart, "Can I be a child of God, and be thus? What mark and testimony have I of being in favour with God when I am so easily and so continually overcome?"

September

Now I want you to look to the end. What is the issue of these defeats? Remember, it is a solemn truth, and one that we learn very slowly – that we must *be* overcome in order *to* overcome. There is no setting out with a stock of strength, daily adding to it, weekly increasing it, and then gaining the victory by our own resolutions, our own innate strength. Such sham holiness may come under a gospel garb, may wear a fair appearance; but it only more hides the rottenness of the flesh.

Then also remember this - that in order to gain the victory, we must know our weakness, and we can only know our weakness by its being experimentally opened up in our consciences. We cannot learn it from others, we must learn it in our own souls and that often in a very painful manner. These painful sensations in a tender conscience lead a man more humbly, more feelingly, more believingly to the Lord of life and glory, to receive out of his fullness. Thus every defeat only leads to and ensures victory at the last.

Our text says, "In all these things we are more than conquerors." Is this through resolutions and human wisdom? No. It is "through Him that loved us." There is no other way to overcome, but by His strength made perfect in our weakness, (2Cor. 12:19).

11th

"And my speech and my preaching was not with enticing words of man's wisdom, but in demonstration of the Spirit and of power."
1Corinthians 2:4

It is not the work of the Spirit to produce doubts and fears, but to overcome them; yet still we are continually subject to them. Infidel thoughts fly across the mind; doubts and questionings suggest themselves, and Satan is ever busy plying his arguments. A guilty conscience such as ours falls too readily at his accusations, and painful recollections of past slips, falls, and backslidings strengthen the power of unbelief. Coming to a spot wherein there is not the least shadow of a doubt about divine realities, and, what is far more important, of our own saving interest in them, is a rare circumstance. It is only attainable at those favoured moments when the Lord is pleased to shine into the soul and settle the matter between himself and our conscience.

Yet these very doubts, these very questionings, these cutting, killing fears, these anxious surmisings all work together for our good, and are mercifully overruled for our spiritual benefit. What else has brought us to the point where nothing short of demonstration can satisfy the soul that is truly born and taught of God? It must feel it and experience it – nothing else will do. We cannot live and die upon uncertainties. It won't do always to be in a state that we don't know whether we are going to heaven or to hell, being tossed up and down on a sea of uncertainty, scarcely knowing who commands the ship, what is our destination, what our present course, or what will be the end of the voyage.

Now, human wisdom leaves us upon this sea of doubt. Such wisdom is useful in nature, but useless in grace. It is, however, foolish and absurd, as some teach, to despise human learning, for without it we would be a horde of wild, wandering savages. Yet it is worse than foolish to make human wisdom our guide to eternity, and make man's reason the foundation of our faith or hope. What you would thus believe today, you would disbelieve tomorrow. All the arguments that may convince your reasoning mind, all the appeals to your natural passions will come up short. That which may seem for a time to soften your heart, and all the thoughts swaying to and fro which sometimes lead you to hope you are right and sometimes make you fear you are wrong - all these will be found insufficient when the soul comes into any time of real trial and perplexity.

We want, therefore, demonstration to remove and dispel all these anxious questionings, and settle the whole matter firmly in our heart and conscience. Only the Spirit can give us this by revealing Christ, by taking of the things of Christ and showing them unto us, by applying the word with power to our hearts, and bringing the sweetness, reality, and blessedness of divine things into our soul. It is only in this way that he overcomes all unbelief and infidelity, doubt and fear, and sweetly assures us that all is well between God and the soul.

12th

"But in demonstration of the Spirit and of power."
1Corinthians 2:4

In human reasoning, demonstration cannot usually be obtained except in mathematics, but not so in divine reasoning. There grace outshines and exceeds nature, for the teaching and testimony of the blessed Spirit is always demonstrative, that is, convincing beyond the possibility of doubt. It is not demonstration simply we require., not demonstration of the word, as if there were some innate proof and power in the word itself to demonstrate its own truth, though

September

doubtless it is so when the Spirit shines upon it as we read. It is the "demonstration of the Spirit." This is very necessary to observe, for you will often hear the word of God spoken of as if the Bible possessed not only demonstrative proof of its own inspiration, but was able to give that demonstration to the souls of men. The thing needed to convert sinners and satisfy saints is the demonstration not of the word itself, but of the Spirit in, through, and *by*, the word. This is proof indeed, not cold and hard like a mathematical demonstration, but warm, living, softening, and sanctifying; being the very light, life, and power of God himself in the soul.

Now Paul's preaching was this demonstration of the Spirit. The Spirit of God speaking in him and by him, so demonstrated the truth of what he preached that it came, as he elsewhere speaks, not "in word only, but also in power, and in the Holy Ghost, and in much assurance," (1Thes. 1:5). There are no Pauls now, and yet, unless we have a measure of the same demonstration of the Spirit, all which is said by us in the pulpit drops to the ground. It has no real effect, and there is no true or abiding fruit unto eternal life.

If there be in it some enticing words of man's wisdom, it may please the mind of those who are gratified by such arts. It may stimulate and occupy the attention for the time, but there it ceases, and all that has been heard fades quickly away like a dream of the night. As regards the family of God, we may apply to all such preaching the words of the prophet. "It shall even be as when an hungry man dreameth, and, behold, he eateth; but he awaketh, and his soul is empty: or as when a thirsty man dreameth, and, behold, he drinketh; but he awaketh, and, behold, he is faint, and his soul hath appetite," (Isa. 29:8).

Howbeit anything which is communicated by the Holy Spirit, that which is demonstrated by him to your soul, and that which is brought into your heart with light, life, and power, and there sealed and witnessed by that sacred Teacher and divine Comforter – *that* abides. You take it home with you and it comforts you, not only at the time, but when you look back on it in days to come. It is a bright spot in your soul's experience, when you can believe that then and there God was pleased to bless his word to your soul, and seal it home with a sweet influence upon your conscience. This is "demonstration of the Spirit."

And where there is this demonstration, there is also power, for the Spirit adds the words, "and of power" to the verse. The grand distinguishing mark of the kingdom of God is that it "is not in word, but in power," (1Cor. 4:20). Thus power is given to believe in the Son of God, and we cannot believe truly and savingly in him until power is put forth. It is the power to receive our Lord in all his covenant characters and gracious relationships in the gospel of his grace. It is the power to believe that what God has done he does forever, and it is the power to come out of every doubt and fear into the blessed light and liberty of the truth which makes free.

13th

"And Enoch walked with God."
Genesis 5:24

The chief way whereby we walk with God is by faith, and not by sight, (2Cor. 5:7). Abraham walked in this way, (Heb. 11:8-10). Unbelief severs the soul from God. There is no communion between God and an infidel. An unbelieving heart has no fellowship with the Lord Jesus Christ; but a believing heart has communion with him.

It is by faith that we have fellowship with God and his dear Son; and you will find that just in proportion to the strength or weakness of your faith is your walking with God. If you have faith in blessed exercise, as you look to the atoning blood, you find that you can walk with God; you can pour out your heart before him, tell him all your concerns, spread before him the inmost movements of your mind, and look to him for peace and consolation.

Yet when your faith is weak, when it gives way under trial, and cannot take hold of the promises, then communion is interrupted; there is no longer a walking with God. But in proportion as faith is strong, so there is a walking with God in sweet agreement; for faith keeps eyeing the atonement; faith looks not so much to sin, as to salvation from sin; at the way whereby sin is pardoned, overcome, and subdued. So it is by faith, and in proportion to our faith, that we walk together with God.

14th

"Blessed be the God and Father of our Lord Jesus Christ, who hath blessed us with all spiritual blessings in heavenly places in Christ."
Ephesians 1:3

If you are blessed with all spiritual blessings, it is only "in Christ" you are so blessed. If you were chosen before the foundation of the world, it was only "in Christ" that you were chosen. He is our covenant Head. What we are we are only in him. There is nothing in

September

SELF; no fixedness there. All is fluctuating here below; all is uncertain as regards man. Certainty is with God; and the fixedness of God's purposes is our grand, our only support. Thus the doctrine of election received into the heart diffuses a sacred blessedness over the whole truth of God, for it gives stability to it. It is not a dry doctrine which men may toss about from hand to hand like a tennis ball; it is not an article of a creed written down in church articles, or a theory to be argued by divines. Nor is it a mere loose, floating idea gathered from a few dim and doubtful passages of God's word. It is no meteor light dancing over morasses and swamps. It is a steady light set by the hand of God in the Scriptures, as he set of old lights in the skies of the heavens to give light upon the earth. It therefore diffuses its rays over the whole of God's truth.

For it is "in Christ" his people were chosen, and therefore election being in Christ, it is reflected with all the beams of the Sun of righteousness upon every gospel truth. There is not a single gospel truth, or a single spiritual blessing, which does not derive its blessedness from its connection with the Person and work of the Son of God; and what is true of all, is true of this, that the blessedness of election is because it is "in Christ."

Some may say, 'These things are hard to believe', and I would agree; they are very hard to believe, for our unbelieving heart finds it very hard to believe anything that is for our good. We can believe Satan's lies with great readiness, and we give an open, willing ear to anything which our evil heart suggests. But to believe God's truths so as to enter into their beauty and blessedness, to feel their quickening power, and live under their cheering, invigorating influence, this is another matter.

Yet where is the life of our religion when these things are taken away from it? Take, if you could take – and God be praised it is beyond the reach of human hand! – but take away that solemn fact, that God has blessed the Church with all spiritual blessings in heavenly places in Christ Jesus, and where would there be room for any blessing to rest upon our soul? Why, any sweet promise that comes rolling into your breast, any lifting up of the light of God's countenance in seasons of darkness and adversity, any liberty in prayer, any looking up and receiving out of Christ's fullness couldn't exist. They all hang upon this grand point, that the blessings with which God has already blessed us are in Christ Jesus.

All we have to do – and it is a great thing to do which God alone can enable within us – is to receive what God has been pleased so mercifully to give. As he has blessed us with all spiritual blessings in heavenly places in Christ Jesus, we need but to feel their power, to enjoy their sweetness, and to know for ourselves by the sealing of the Spirit that he has blessed us, even us, and that with life for evermore.

September 15th

"For the earth bringeth forth fruit of herself; first the blade, then the ear, after that the full corn in the ear."
Mark 4:28

    Faith, I believe, has in it always a measure of assurance, and what is assurance? It is merely the larger growth and fuller development of faith.
    The nature of assurance is much misunderstood. It is often considered something distinct from faith, but this is not at all the case at all. It is rather faith in a fuller, larger development. The word "assurance" in the original has a simple and yet beautiful meaning. It means, literally, "a full bearing;" and the word is applied sometimes to a large crop of corn or fruit, and sometimes to the tide coming in with a fuller wave. Now it is the same corn which grows in the fields, whether the crop be much or little, and it is the same tide which comes up the river, whether in a scanty or full flow. So it is with assurance and faith; it is the same faith, only increased, enlarged, bearing more abundant fruit, or flowing in a more abundant tide.
    Assurance in Scripture is not confined to faith. Firstly there is "the full assurance of understanding," (Col. 2:2), that is, a fuller measure and amount, a greater enlargement of understanding to know the truth of God. The understanding is the same, but there is a larger measure of it. Then there is "the full assurance of hope," (Heb. 6:11), that is, a hope strengthened and enlarged, bearing more fruit and flowing in a fuller tide. It is still the same hope, the same in kind, though larger in degree, and it is still an anchor, but a stronger anchor, (Heb. 6:19). Then there is the "full assurance of faith," (Heb. 10:22), that is, a larger, fuller measure of faith, a richer crop and a more abundant tide.
    Thus you have a certain measure of the assurance of faith if you have but any faith at all. If you had no assurance of the truth of these things, you would not follow after them. Why do you hang upon them, why do you hope in them, and why do you seek the power and experience of them in your soul? Is it not because you have arrived at this point already?
    "For we have not followed cunningly devised fables, when we made known unto you the power and coming of our Lord Jesus Christ, but were eyewitnesses of his majesty," (2Pet. 1:16). These things that we are following after are realities; these objects set before us are certainties which are borne witness to by the disciples and prophets.

I grant that you may be much exercised about your saving interest in them. Still, unless you know that they are certainties, why do you believe them? Why are you anxious to know your saving interest in them? Why do you sink in doubt and fear for lack of clearer evidences of a saving interest in them? And why do you spring up in peace and joy the moment that a little light from them beams upon your soul, and a little sweetness out of them drops into your heart? Because you know that these things are realities.

So far then you have an assurance that they are certainties, and in due time, as God is pleased, you will have the assurance in your own breast, not only that they are certainties, but that you have them in your own sure and certain possession.

16th

"Joseph is a fruitful bough, even a fruitful bough by a well; whose branches run over the wall. The archers have sorely grieved him, and shot at him, and hated him, but his bow abode in strength, and the arms of his hands were made strong by the hands of the mighty God of Jacob; (from thence is the shepherd, the stone of Israel:)"
Genesis 49:22-24

One would have thought that Joseph being a fruitful bough could have looked with complacency, almost with holy scorn, upon these archers who shot at him, but it was not so, for "they sorely grieved him." To be sold by his own brethren into Egypt; the dreams and visions God had given him to be derided; to be cast into prison as an ungodly man through the very person who was tempting him to ungodliness, and there to be neglected and forsaken; how these archers had shot their arrows against his bosom, and sorely grieved him!

Why was he grieved so? It was because he had the fear of God; it was because his feelings were tender, that the arrows found a place. If his bosom was of steel and his heart of stone, the arrows would have fallen off blunted and pointless; but it was because he had tender feelings, a living conscience, warm affections, godly fear, and a work of grace upon his soul, that he presented a tender spot for these arrows to strike. Therefore the archers not only shot at him and grieved him, but they hated him too.

But did they prove his destruction? Did anyone drain his life-blood? Did he sink and die like a wounded deer? Did he fall upon the plain and gasp out his forlorn life? Not at all! "His bow abode in strength, and the arms of his hands were made strong by the hands of the mighty God of Jacob."

He also had a bow, then, and knew how to shoot, but what was his bow, and whence his arrows? And where did he direct them, for do we read anywhere of him resisting his oppressors? He picked up the arrows that flew about him, or rather he plucked them out of his own wounded bosom; but instead of aiming the shafts back at those who had so sorely grieved him, he shot them upward. He redirected those arrows towards the throne of grace, to the Majesty on high, and there he turned the bitter shafts into prayers, supplications, and petitions.

Thus he used the very arrows that were shot at him to approach the throne of God, and thereby is our example. Never return evil for evil, nor railing for railing; never trade blow for blow. When we are shot at by the archers, and we surely will be, do not shoot back. Lay those arrows before the throne. Present your wounds, your groans and your sighs as they are. Bring them alongside your warm petitions, and spread them before our God, who hears and answers prayer; and you will find the benefit and blessing of it.

The world will beat you at shooting if you shoot at them. They can use language that you cannot. A man of birth and education, drawn into collision with a street ruffian, cannot bandy words with him; he must pass on; he would soon be beaten in the strife of words. So must you never trade arrow for arrow with the archers who sorely grieve you.

Like Joseph, you have a tender conscience; you have the fear of God; you weigh your words for you know what will grieve your mind when it comes back upon you, and are therefore sparing of your speech. Cease from that war; return not a single arrow, let them shoot away, then take their arrows, direct your bow upward, turn them all into prayers and supplications, and in due time sweet answers of mercy and peace will come into your bosom.

Thus Joseph's bow "abode in strength," and all their arrows neither struck it out of his hand, nor broke it asunder. He could shoot as well as they, but he shot in a different manner, and at a different target. We see, then, Joseph's fruitfulness; we see the source of it; we see the persecutions that grieved his soul; and we see the victory that he gained. May his God, the God of might and infinite mercy, lead our souls on that same blessed path, applying his truth to our hearts, and giving power to our bow that it may abide in strength, and may the arms of our hands may be made strong by the hands of the mighty God of Jacob.

September 17th

"I beseech you therefore, brethren, by the mercies of God, that ye present your bodies a living sacrifice, holy, acceptable unto God, which is your reasonable service."
Romans 12:1

If the Son of God has redeemed us by his blood, all that we are and all that we have belongs to him; our body, soul, and spirit are his. Nothing is our own, for we are bought, and that with a great price, (1Cor. 6:20). In laying down his precious life for us, he has redeemed us unto himself, that we should be his peculiar people, and not only render to him the calves of our lips, (Hos. 14:2), but give him body, soul, spirit, substance, and life itself; all that we are and have being his by sovereign right. He lays claim to them all, not only as our Creator, but as our Redeemer, having bought them back by his precious blood.

When we feel his mercy warm in our soul, can we keep anything back? Look at Abraham's example. When God called to him, and said, "Abraham!" what was his answer? 'Here am I. Here is my body, here is my soul, here is my substance, here is my future, here is my wife, here is my son; all are at your disposal. What would you have me to do, Lord? Take them; they are all yours. You have a right to them, and you must do with them, and you must do with me, what seems good in your sight'.

Under these feelings, then, we should 'present our bodies', not, indeed, leaving our souls behind. For what is the casket without the jewel? What is the body without the soul? Will God accept the body if the soul be left behind? That is popery; to give the body, and keep back the soul. Not so with the dear family of God; they present their bodies, but with their bodies they present the soul that lodges in their body - the house with its tenant, the jewel-case with the jewels in it.

But what is it to present our bodies? They must be presented as "a living sacrifice." God accepts no dead sacrifices. You will recollect, under the Jewish law the sacrifice was to be a living animal, and that without spot or blemish, and it died there upon the altar. A dead lamb could never be presented. Only a living animal, perfect in its kind, could be the victim. So if we are to present our bodies, there must be "a living sacrifice."

It may well be asked, 'What have we sacrificed for the Lord's sake?' Have we been called upon to sacrifice our property, prospects, idols, or affections? Maybe it was our name or reputation, or our worldly interests? Have we obeyed the call?

September

Abraham did not offer Isaac until the voice of the Lord called him to make the sacrifice; but when the Lord called him to do so, Abraham at once rendered obedience to the voice. God does not expect us to give up everything with which he has blessed us the moment it is given, or realised, but as with Abraham so it must be with those that follow in his footsteps. If they are called upon, as all are, sooner or later, to make those sacrifices, those sacrifices they must make.

Now, in thus presenting our bodies "a living sacrifice," it becomes also a "holy" offering, because what is done in faith is accepted by God as being sanctified by his blessed Spirit. If we make such a sacrifice without the blessed Spirit's operation upon our heart, it is a dead sacrifice. Men go into monasteries and deluded women enter convents becoming brothers, or sisters of mercy, supposedly offering their bodies as a sacrifice to God, but it is not a living sacrifice because there is no spiritual life in either offeror or offering. Cain also brought his offering to God alongside Abel, but it wasn't what God asked and it was done with a wrong heart, so it was not accepted. Yet when we sacrifice our warmest affections, our prospects in life, and everything that our flesh loves because the gospel claims it at our hands, and we do it through the constraining love of Christ, *that* is a living sacrifice, and is "holy" because it sprang out of the sanctifying influences and operations of the Holy Spirit.

We indeed, looking at ourselves, see nothing holy in such a sacrifice, for sin is mingled in with all we do, but God's eye discerns the precious from the vile. He sees the purity of his own work. He can separate what we cannot, the acting of the spirit and the working of the flesh. God looks at that which his own Spirit inspires, and his own grace produces, and he that is acceptable to him – it is holy.

18th

"And be not conformed to this world."
Romans 12:2

In proportion as we are conformed to the spirit of this world, our understanding becomes dull in the things of God, our affections become cold and torpid, and our consciences become less tender and sensitive. There is an eternal opposition between God and the world, which lies in wickedness. In order, then, that our spiritual experience of the truth of God should maintain its ground, it must not be dulled and deadened by conformity to the world. It is like the sabre that the soldier carries into battle; it must not trail unsheathed upon the ground lest point and edge be dulled; both must be kept keen and sharp that execution may be done upon the foe. So it is with our enlightened understanding, with our tender conscience, and our heavenly affections. If we let them fall uncared for upon the world, it is like a soldier trailing his sabre upon the pavement; he might still be advancing, but every step he takes dulls both the edge and point of his weapon.

When we allow ourselves to become conformed to this world, we lose the sweet understanding that we once had of the precious truth of God; we lose that tender sensitiveness of conscience, whereby sin, any sin, becomes a grief and a burden to the soul. A Christian should be what was said of an ancient knight: "Without fear and without reproach." So the Christian's shield should be without a stain, his reputation without a blot. His character should not only be free from blemish, but free even from suspicion, as untarnished as the modesty of a chaste woman, or the honour and bravery of a valiant man.

Now, we often get into this worldly conformity, and run the risk of dulling the sword and sullying the shield by degrees by giving way in this and in that thing. True it is that we are hedged in by the precepts of the gospel, the alarms of a tender conscience, and many powerful restraints; we have so many banks and dykes to keep out the sea of the world. In Holland, if one breach be made in the dyke, the north sea at once rushes in, and so it is with the conscience. If one gap be opened up, then the sea of worldliness rushes through the breach, and but for God's grace would soon deluge the soul. Even without a peculiar temptation to make such a wide breach, our social ties, our daily occupation, the friends and relations whom we love in the flesh, all, through their power over our natural affections, draw us aside from time to time into this worldly conformity.

Here, then, is the point where we have to make our stand; for if we are conformed to the maxims, the principles, the customs, and the spirit of the world, we so far lose that spiritual position which is a believer's highest blessing and privilege. We descend from the mount of communion with the Lord, and fall into a cold, miserable spot, where the life of God, though not extinct, is reduced to its lowest ebb.

19th

**"Be ye transformed by the renewing of your mind."
Romans 12:2**

September

As worldly conformity is subdued and departed from, there is the transforming process of which the Apostle here speaks, whereby we become renewed in the spirit of our mind. In other words, the Holy Spirit, by his work upon the soul, renews the life of God, revives faith, hope, love, prayer, praise, and spirituality of mind with every tender feeling and every godly sensation that stirs and moves in a living heart.

As, then, the Spirit of God renews his work upon the heart, he brings us out of this worldly conformity. He discovers to us the evil of it, and he makes and keeps the conscience tender and sensitive. He shows us that if we are conformed to the world we lose our evidences; that they become dulled and obscured; that we are soon deprived of communion with God, of comfortable access to our best, our heavenly Friend; that our taste and appetite for spiritual things get palled; and that our very profession itself becomes a burden. As the conscience then gets more and more awakened to see and feel these things, we become convinced that we do but reap what we have sown. The Spirit of God by pressing the charge more closely home, shows us, and sometimes by painful experience, such as long days of darkness, and heavy, dragging nights of desertion, the evil of worldly conformity.

Now, as he thus brings us out of worldly conformity, by showing us the evil of it, and that by this miserable cleaving to earth we rob ourselves of our happiest hours, our sweetest hopes, and our dearest enjoyments, he draws the soul nearer to Christ. As he keeps renewing us in the spirit of our mind, by dropping one precious truth after another into the heart, he revives faith, renews hope, communicates love, draws forth prayer, and bestows spirituality of mind and affection. By these means a transforming process takes place, whereby the soul is brought out of worldly conformity, and is transformed into the likeness of the suffering Christ.

How we need, then, the blessed Spirit of God to be renewing us daily in the spirit of our minds, and thus transforming us into the suffering image of the sorrowing Son of God. There is no medium between spirituality and carnality, or between the image of Christ and conformity to the world. As there is no middle path between the strait road and the broad road, so there is no middle way between fruitfulness and barrenness, nor a halfway house between prayerfulness and prayerlessness, watchfulness and carelessness, repentance and hardness, and faith and unbelief. Neither therefore can we live both the life of a Christian and the life of a worldling.

September 20th

> "That ye may prove what is that good, and acceptable, and perfect, will of God."
> Romans 12:2

The will of God is good, perfect, and acceptable, but how are we to prove personally and experimentally that this is the case? That good and perfect will runs counter, over and over again, to our natural inclinations, and sets itself firmly against our fleshly desires. God's will calls for self-denial, but I want self-gratification; it requires obedience, but my carnal mind is the essence of disobedience; it demands many sacrifices, but my coward flesh revolts from them; it bids me walk in the path of suffering, sorrow, and tribulation, but my fleshly mind shrinks back, and says, "No, I cannot tread in that path!"

Therefore, as long as I am conformed to the world, I cannot see the path, for this worldly conformity has thrown a veil over my eyes. If, perchance, I do dimly make it out, I am not willing or able to walk in it, because my carnal mind rebels against all trouble or self-denial, or anything connected with the cross of Christ. If, on the other hand, by any gracious operations of the Spirit on my heart, I am drawn out of this worldly conformity, am renewed in the spirit of my mind, and transformed into the likeness of the suffering Son of God, then "that good, and acceptable, and perfect, will of God," becomes commended to my conscience.

God's will so described is far, far out of the sight of the carnal eye, out of the sound of the worldly ear, out of the touch of the worldly hand; but is made manifest to the spiritual eye, listened to by the spiritual ear, and laid hold of by the spiritual hand. To realise this for ourselves, we shall find it good sometimes to look back and see how that divine will has previously proved itself acceptable to our renewed mind. We can see how supremely that will has reigned, and further, how that reign has in all points been for our good. It has ordered or overruled in all circumstances and in all events, amid a complication of difficulties in providence and grace. No injury has taken us, but all things, according to the promise, have worked together for our good.

Yet there is one thing that we must deeply bear in mind. As we cannot deliver ourselves from worldly conformity, so we cannot renew ourselves in the spirit of our mind. The blessed Spirit must do both for us, and "to will and to do of his good pleasure," (Phil. 2:13). As we are led to feel the misery of the one state, and the blessedness of the other, we shall seek after these gracious operations and divine influences. As the blessed Spirit from time to time brings the soul out of this worldly conformity and transforms it into the suffering image of Christ, it sees more and more the beauty and blessedness of walking in this path. Our soul will cleave to Christ and his cross with the tenderest of affections, proving for itself the goodness, acceptability, and perfection of the will of God.

21st

"But the anointing which ye have received of him abideth in you."
1John 2:27

All the powers of earth and hell are combined against the holy anointing here spoken of, and with which the children of God are so highly favoured. Yet if God has locked up in the bosom of a saint but one drop of this divine unction, that one drop is armour against all the assaults of sin, all the attacks of Satan, all the enmity of self, and all the charms, pleasures, and amusements of the world. Waves and billows of affliction may roll over the soul; but they cannot wash away this holy drop of anointing oil. Satan may shoot a thousand fiery darts to inflame all the combustible material of our carnal mind; but all his fiery darts cannot burn up that one drop of anointing oil which God has laid up in the depths of a broken spirit. The world, with all its charms and pleasures, and its deadly opposition to the truth of God, may stir up waves of ungodliness against this holy anointing; but all the powers of earth combined can never extinguish that one drop which God has himself lodged in the depths of a believer's heart.

Jonah had it locked up in the depths of his soul when he was in the whale's belly, but not all the waves and billows that went over his head, nor even the very depths of hell itself, in whose belly he felt he was, could wash away the drop of anointing oil that God had lodged in his soul. David sank deep into sin and remorse, but all his sin and misery never drank up the drop of anointing oil that God the Spirit had dropped into his heart. The prodigal son went into a far country, but he never lost that drop of anointing oil, though he wasted all his substance in riotous living. Heman complained out of the depths of his affliction, but all his troubles never consumed the holy anointing oil that God had put into his soul. Hezekiah on his apparent death-bed, when he turned his face to the wall, was severely tried, and almost in despair; yet all his affliction and despondency never drained the holy drop of anointing oil.

So it has been with thousands and tens of thousands of the dear saints of God. Not all their sorrows, I may say more, not all their sins, backslidings, slips, falls, miseries, and wretchedness, have ever, all combined, drunk up the anointing that God has bestowed upon them. If sin could have done it, we would have sinned ourselves into hell long ago. If the world or Satan could have destroyed it or us, they would have long ago destroyed both. If our carnal mind could have done it, it would have swept us away into the floods of destruction. Howbeit the anointing abides sure, and cannot be destroyed; and where it has been once lodged in the soul, it is secure against all the assaults of earth, sin, hell and the devil.

The saints of God *feel* that it abides, for it springs up at times in prayer and desires after the living God, and breaks forth into faith, hope, and love. Thus it not only abides as a divine reality, but as a living principle, springing up into eternal life. Were it not so, there would be no revivals, no fresh communications, no renewed testimonies, no breakings forth, no tender meltings, no breathings out of desire for the Lord's presence, no mourning over his absence. However, the anointing abides, and this preserves the soul from death, and keeps it alive in famine.

22nd

"Father, I will that they also, whom thou hast given me, be with me where I am; that they may behold my glory, which thou hast given me: for thou lovedst me before the foundation of the world."
John 17:24

How great, how elevated above all utterance or all conception of men or angels, must the glory of Christ be when viewed as the Son of the Father in truth and in love! Not only is the Lord Jesus Christ glorious in his essential Deity as the Son of God, but glorious also in his holy, spotless humanity which he assumed in the womb of the Virgin Mary. For although he was the flesh and blood of the children, he was also that holy One who was born of the Holy Spirit, (Luke 1:35), and was taken into union with his eternal Deity, that he might be Immanuel, God with us, (Matt. 1:23).

The purity, holiness and innocence, the spotless beauty and perfection of this human nature, make it in itself exceedingly glorious; but its greater glory is the union that it possesses and enjoys with the divine nature of the Son of God. The pure humanity of Jesus veils his Deity, and yet the Deity shines through it, filling it with unutterable brightness, and irradiating it with inconceivable glory. There is no blending of the two natures, for humanity cannot become Deity, nor can Deity become humanity; each nature remains distinct, and each nature has its own peculiar glory. Yet there is a unique glory also in the union of both natures in the person of the God-man. That such wisdom should have been displayed, such grace manifested, such love revealed, and that the union of the two natures should even have originated is a wondrous mystery in itself. That this unique God-man should still unceasingly uphold and eternally maintain salvation with all its present fruits of grace, and all its future fruits of glory, makes the union of the two natures unspeakably glorious.

When we consider further that through this union of humanity with Deity, the Church is brought into the most intimate nearness and closest relationship with the Father and the Holy Spirit, what a glory is seen to illuminate the Person of the God-man. As God he is one with God, and as man he is one with man, and thus unites the two natures bringing about the fulfilment of those wonderful words, "That they all may be one; as thou, Father, art in me, and I in thee, that they also may be one in us," (John 17:21). And again, "I in them, and thou in me, that they may be made perfect in one," (John 17:23).

Thus there is the glory of Christ as God, the glory of Christ as man, and the glory of Christ as God-man. And this threefold glory of Christ corresponds in a measure with what he was before he came into the world, with what he was whilst in the world, and with what he is now as having gone to the Father, according to his own words, (John 16:28). Before he came into the world his chief glory was that which belonged to him as the Son of God; while in the world his chief glory was in being the perfect Son of man; and now that he is gone back to heaven his chief glory is that of his being God and man untied in one glorious Person.

This latter glory of Christ, which is, in an especial sense, his mediatorial glory, is seen by faith here, and will be seen in the open vision of bliss hereafter. The three disciples on the Mount of transfiguration, Stephen at the time of his martyrdom, Paul when caught up into the third heaven, and John on the Isle of Patmos, all had special and supernatural manifestations of this united glory of Christ, surpassing the view generally given to all believers.

The way in which we now see his glory is through the Holy Spirit receiving of that which is his and showing it to the soul. This divine Teacher testifies of him, takes away the veil of ignorance and unbelief which hides him from us, and shines with a holy and sacred light on the Scriptures that speak of him. Raising up faith to believe in his name, he sets him before the eyes of the enlightened understanding, so that he is looked unto and upon, and although not seen with the bodily eye, he is loved, believed, and rejoiced in with joy unspeakable and full of glory.

Thus seen by the eye of faith, all that he is and has, and all that he says and does is made precious and glorious. His miracles of mercy whilst here below; his words so full of grace, wisdom, and truth; his going about doing good; his sweet example of patience, meekness, and submission; his sufferings and sorrows in the garden and on the cross; his spotless holiness and purity and his tender compassion to poor lost sinners; his atoning blood and justifying obedience; his dying love, so strong and firm, yet so tried by earth, heaven, and hell; his lowly, yet honourable burial; his glorious resurrection, as the first-begotten of the dead, by which he was declared to be the Son of God with power; his ascension to the right hand of the Father, where he reigns and rules, all power being given unto him in heaven and earth. Yet despite all his lowliness and humility, he still intercedes for his people as the great High Priest over the house of God. What beauty and glory shine forth in all these divine realities when faith can view them in union with the work and Person of Immanuel!

23rd

"And he humbled thee, and suffered thee to hunger, and fed thee with manna, which thou knewest not, neither did thy fathers know; that he might make thee know that man doth not live by bread only, but by every word that proceedeth out of the mouth of the LORD doth man live."
Deuteronomy 8:3

This is the grand lesson which we have to learn in our wilderness journey, "that man doth not live by bread only," that is, by those providential supplies which relieve our natural necessities. Thanks be to God for any bread that he gives us in his kind and bountiful providence – an honest living is a great mercy. To be enabled by the labour of our hands or by the labour of our brain to maintain our families and bring them up in a degree of comfort, if not abundance, is a great blessing, but God has determined that his people shall not live by bread alone. They shall be separated from the mass of men who live only in this carnal way, who have no care beyond earthly possessions, and the sum of whose thoughts and desires is what they shall eat, what they shall drink, and with what they shall be clothed. His people are to look beyond the purse, the business, the daily occupation, the safe return and the profitable investment, and even how to provide for themselves and their families.

God has planted in the breast of his people a higher life, a nobler principle, a more blessed appetite than to live upon this world's bread alone. We bless him for his providence, but we love him for his grace. We thank him for our daily food and clothing, but these mercies are but for time, perishing in their very use, and he has provided us with that which is for eternity, that which moth and rust doth not corrupt, and which thieves cannot break in and steal, (Matt. 6:19).

What then does he mean the soul to live upon if not bread only? It is to live upon "every word that proceedeth out of the mouth of the Lord." But where can we find these fruitful words that proceed out of the mouth of God? In the Scriptures, for that is the food of the Church, and especially in Scripture as applied to the heart, those words that God is pleased to drop into the soul by a divine power, which we receive from his gracious mouth, and lay hold upon with a believing hand. That is the food and nutriment of our soul; the truth of God applied to our heart and made life and spirit to our souls by his own teaching and testimony. Look and see how large and ample is the supply! Review through the whole compass of God's revealed word, and see in it what a store there is of provision laid up for the Church of God. How this should both stimulate and encourage us to search the Scriptures as for hid treasure, to read them constantly, to meditate upon them, to seek to enter into the mind of God as revealed in them, and thus to find them to be the food of our soul. If we were fully persuaded that every word of the Scripture came out of God's mouth, and was meant to feed our soul, how much more we would prize it, read it, and study it.

24th

"His going forth is prepared as the morning."
Hosea 6:3

It is to the living soul walking in darkness, and unable to find God, that this text speaks, "His going forth is prepared as the morning." There is an appointed time for the Lord to go forth and this is sweetly compared to the rising of the sun. Does not 'the dayspring know his place?' (Job 38:12). Does not the sun rise every day according to the appointed minute? Is he ever before his time, or ever after his time? Did the free will of the creature ever hurry or retard his rising for a single second? Thus it is with the going forth of the Lord for the salvation of his people, the going forth of the Lord in the revelation of his presence and his power, the going forth of the Lord from the place where he has for a while hidden himself, to come down with light and life into the soul. All his glorious goings forth are as much prepared, and the moment is as much appointed, as the time is fixed every morning for the sun to rise.

Yet what is the state of our world before the sun rises? Does not night precede day, does not darkness come before dawn? And when it is midnight naturally, can we bid the sun arise and disperse the darkness? Is there not, as the Psalmist says, a waiting for the morning, in nature? "My soul waiteth for the Lord more than they that watch for the morning," (Psa. 130:6). Do not the sick turn on their restless couch, waiting for morning? Is not the shipwrecked mariner who has been driven on to rocks waiting anxiously for the morning to know what is his prospect, and whether a friendly sail may be in sight? Is not the man benighted on the hills waiting for the morning, that the sun may arise, and he might find his way homeward? Yet with all their waiting, they cannot bid the sun arise; they must wait until the appointed time.

So the going forth of the Sun of righteousness, the appearance of Christ in the heart, the sweet revelation of the Son of God, the lifting up of the light of his blessed countenance, is "prepared as the morning." It is as fixed, as appointed in the mind of God as the morning to come in its season, but no more to be hurried than the sun is to be hurried up into the sky. Aye, and it is as much an impossibility for us to bring the Lord into our souls before the appointed time, or keep him there when he has come, as for us to play the part of Joshua, and say, "Sun, stand thou still upon Gibeon; and thou, Moon, in the valley of Ajalon," (Jos. 10:12).

Yet "his going forth is prepared as the morning," and when he goes forth, he goes forth "conquering and to conquer," (Rev. 6:2), mounted on the white horse spoken of in Revelation. He goes forth to conquer our enemies, to overcome our temptations, to lay our souls at his footstool, to arise like the sun in his strength, and to come into the heart with healing in his wings.

25th

"Likewise reckon ye also yourselves to be dead indeed unto sin, but alive unto God through Jesus Christ our Lord."
Romans 6:11

September

How many poor souls are struggling against the power of sin, and yet never get any victory over it! How many are daily led captive by the lusts of the flesh, the love of the world, and the pride of life, and never get any victory over them! How many fight and grapple with tears, vows, and strong resolutions against the besetting sins of temper, levity, or covetousness, who are still entangled and overcome by them again and again! Now, why is this? Because they know not the secret of spiritual strength against them, and spiritual victory over them.

It is only by virtue of a living union with the Lord Jesus Christ, drinking into his sufferings and death, and receiving out of his fullness, that we can gain any victory over the world, sin, death, or hell. Let me bring this down a little to your own experience. Say your soul has been, on one particular occasion, very sweetly favoured; a melting sense of the Saviour's precious love and blood has come into your heart, and you could then believe, with a faith of God's own giving, that he was eternally yours. Through this faith, as an open channel of divine communication, his merits and mediation, blood, righteousness, and dying love came sweetly streaming into your soul.

What was the effect? Did it lead you to sin, to presumption, to licentiousness? I'll warrant not, but rather the contrary. I am sure it led to a holy obedience in heart, lip, and life. Sin is never really or effectually subdued in any other way. Saul, being struck down at the gates of Damascus, turned from persecution to praying, and is for us a scriptural instance of the death of sin by the power of Christ. It is not, then, by legal strivings and earnest resolutions, vows, and tears, which are but monkery at best, a milder form of the hair shirt, the bleeding scourge, and the damp cloister. It is not the vain struggle of religious flesh to subdue sinful flesh that can overcome sin. It is by a believing acquaintance with, and a spiritual entrance into the sufferings and sorrows of the Son of God, having a living faith in him, and receiving out of his fullness supplies of grace and strength - strength made perfect in our weakness.

In this sense the Apostle says to the Colossians, "For ye are dead," (Col. 3:3), and not merely by the law having condemned and slain you, as to all legal hopes, but by virtue of a participation in the death of the Lord Jesus Christ, by virtue of a living union with the suffering Son of God.

"For sin shall not have dominion over you: for ye are not under the law," where sin reigns with increased dominion, "but under grace," which subdues sin by pardoning it, (Rom. 6:14). If you read the whole of the sixth chapter of Paul's letter to the Romans with an enlightened eye, you will see how the Apostle traces out the death of the believer unto the power and prevalence of sin, by virtue of a spiritual baptism into the death and resurrection of the Lord Jesus.

September 26th

"For the LORD God is a sun and shield: the LORD will give grace and glory: no good thing will he withhold from them that walk uprightly."
Psalm 84:11

There are those who walk uprightly, very uprightly, in the fear of God, and yet have little comfortable or abiding evidence that they are at present partakers of God's grace, or will be hereafter sharers of Christ's glory. Yet this one evidence they certainly do possess, though they can take no present comfort from it, that they walk uprightly before God and man. Let no one, however deeply experienced or highly favoured, despise this evidence of grace in others; and you who walk uprightly from a living principle of godly fear have here a marked testimony from the Lord himself that he has a special regard for you.

So, what is it to "walk uprightly?" Here is the grand difficulty in religion. We may talk; we may preach; we may hear; we may seem to believe; but it is when we come to *act,* to walk, and carry out into daily and hourly practice that which we profess, that the main difficulty is felt and found. "The soul of religion," says Bunyan, "is the practical part;" and it is when we come to this practical part that the daily, hourly cross commences. The walk, the talk, the dress, the daily, hourly conduct is often our hardest challenge, and it is primary amongst the all-important fruits of a Christian profession. To walk daily and consistently under all varied circumstances and temptations that beset us, uprightly, tenderly, and sincerely in the fear of God is far from easy. To feel continually that heart, lip, and life are all open before his all-penetrating eye, and to do that which he approves whilst fleeing from that which he abhors – oh, this in religion is the daily hill of difficulty that is such a struggle to climb!

We can talk fast enough, yes, but oh, to walk in the straight and narrow way; to be a Christian outwardly as well as inwardly, before man as well as God, before the world as well as the Church seems to be beyond the natural man. To follow in the footsteps of our Lord, and in all points to speak and act with undeviating consistency in our profession – this is what nature never has done, and what nature never can do. In thus acting, as much as in believing, do we need God's power and grace to work in, and be made manifest in us.

September 27th

> "Being justified freely by his grace through the redemption that is in Christ Jesus - whom God has set forth to be an atoning sacrifice through faith in his blood."
> Romans 3:24-25

Before we can have faith in Christ's atoning blood, we must see the glory of the Person of the Lord of life. "We beheld his glory," said John, speaking of himself and the other favoured disciples, "we beheld his glory, the glory as of the only begotten of the Father," (John 1:14). May I ask you a question, you who profess to know these things? Were your eyes ever anointed to behold the glory of Jesus? Did faith ever contemplate, did hope ever anchor in, did love ever flow forth unto the glorious Person of Immanuel? Was he ever precious to your soul? Was he ever "altogether lovely" in your eyes? Have you been able to say, "Whom have I in heaven but thee? and there is none upon earth that I desire beside thee," (Psa. 23:5)?

If you have seen his Person by the eye of faith, you have had faith flowing out of your soul to his atoning blood; for his atoning blood derives all its value, all its validity, and all its efficacy from its being the blood of that glorious Person. Upon that atoning blood we view infinite dignity stamped. We see it as the blood of Him who was God-man; and we see the dignity, immensity, and glory of the Godhead of Jesus, stamped upon the sufferings and blood that flowed from his pure humanity. When we see that by the eye of faith, what a rich stream does it become! What a fountain opened up for sin and uncleanness! What value is stamped upon it to purge and cleanse a guilty conscience!

When this is known and felt, the soul is justified. Justification passes over from the mind of God into the bosom of the sinner. He never really was, in the mind of God, in an unjustified state, for God is out of time and saw the end from the beginning. He was in his own conscience, however, and he was as touching the law, and as regards his standing as a sinner before the eyes of a holy Jehovah. The moment he is enabled, by living faith, to touch and wash in the atoning blood of the Lamb of God, justification passes over into his soul, and he becomes freely justified, pardoned and accepted through the blood of sprinkling upon his conscience. He stands before God whiter and brighter than snow, for "the blood of Jesus Christ his Son cleanseth us from all sin," (1John 1:7).

September 28th

"Say to them that are of a fearful heart, Be strong, fear not."
Isaiah 35:4

"Fear not," says the Lord. 'Ah but Lord,' replies the soul, 'I do fear! I fear myself more than anybody. I fear my base, wicked heart, my strong lusts and passions, and my numerous inward enemies, the snares of Satan, and the smooth temptations of the world. You ask me to, "Fear not," but I do fear. I cannot help but fear'. Still the Lord repeats his call, "Fear not." Let us see if we cannot find something to explain this a little more clearly.

There is a crowd yonder, and a timid wife in company with a strong husband. He says to his partner, them all trembling and fearing to pass the crush, 'Fear not; take hold of my arm, cling close to me'. The timid one takes a firm hold and fears not. So it is with the timid soul and its enemies. It says, 'How can I press through this crowd of difficulties? How can I make my way through these opposing doubts and fears? How can I withstand these manifold temptations which so drag at me?' The strong husband, the Lord, comes and says to that soul, "Fear not; take hold of my strength; cleave close to me!" The soul hears, obeys, and clings to the Lord. Its enemies buffet and stretch forth their hands and fain would steal away that soul, but the Lord has a far stronger grip. At length the enemies give off trying to unstick the soul from its Lord and give way. The doubts and fears part asunder, and that soul is safely delivered through.

You could take another familiar comparison. Here is a child trembling before a large mastiff, but the father says, 'Fear not, he will not hurt you, only keep close to me'. We hear David cry in similar vein, "Deliver my soul from the sword; my darling from the power of the dog," (Psa. 22:20). Who is that dog? Satan is the huge mastiff, whose jaws are reeking with blood. If the Lord says, "Fear not," why need we fear? He is a chained enemy.

Oh how the timid soul needs these divine "Fear nots," for without him, it is all weakness but with him, all strength. Without him, all is trembling, but with him, all is boldness. "Where the word of a king is, there is power," (Eccl. 8:4), and this makes the Lord's "Fear nots" so efficacious. As Augustine once prayed, "Give what you command, and command what you will." The burden still remains, but strength is given to bear it; the trials are not lessened, but power to endure them is increased; the evils of the heart are not removed, but grace is communicated to subdue them.

September 29th

"Say to them that are of a fearful heart, Be strong, fear not: behold, your God will come with vengeance, even God with a recompense; he will come and save you."
Isaiah 35:4

"Behold, your God will come." The Lord then has not yet come; but he says he will come, and the promise of his coming takes away the fear. He says, 'Behold'. Even that little word contains something in it noteworthy. The Lord is in the distance; he knows thy need and is ready, for he "maketh the clouds his chariot: who walketh upon the wings of the wind," (Psa. 104:3). As the Lord said to his disciples, "lift up your heads; for your redemption draweth nigh," (Luke 21:28), so by the word, 'Behold', the Lord would take the eyes of his people from being ever bent on the ground or ever looking at their own miserable hearts and the difficulties and dangers of the way. "Look up!" he says. "Look up; thy God is coming to save thee!"

I like to dwell on every crumb as it were of our text. The jots and tittles of God's word, like diamond dust, are to be gathered up and treasured. In Scripture there is much in a little; not like our sermons, where there is often little in much. The word of God is full to overflowing with the very essence of concentrated truth. Look at the next crumb. Is it not the very quintessence of blessedness? "Your God." Well, is he your God? That is the very dropping of everlasting love. In that one word is concentrated the essence of every blessing of the new covenant. For, if God is truly your God, your doubts, fears, and misgivings do not break that sacred covenant tie.

Imagine you are a spouse, and your partner is afflicted with some mental disease the nature of which is such that she hardly recognises your face, altogether doubts your affection, and does not believe you are her husband at all. Such cases we know to be frequent, but do her doubts or denial dissolve your love? Do they cancel the marriage tie? The state of her mind, however painful, does not alter the marriage relationship. So if the Lord's espoused ones, through Satan's temptations, doubt their union with him, do their fears break the wedding ring or cancel the marriage writings? If covenant love matched them in eternity, and covenant grace joined their hands in time, they are still his Hephzibahs and Beulahs, for the Lord "hateth putting away," (Mal. 2:16).

September 30th

"Blessed are they which do hunger and thirst after righteousness: for they shall be filled."
Matthew 5:6

Hunger is a painful sensation. It is not merely an appetite for food; but an appetite for food attended with pain as the body physically suffers from lack of nutrients. So it is spiritually.

It is not merely a desire after Christ, or even a hankering for a morsel from the preacher that constitutes spiritual hunger. As Solomon wisely says, "The soul of the sluggard desireth, and hath nothing," (Prov. 13:4). Spiritual hunger is a desire attended with pain; not merely a wish for spiritual food, but also with such painful sensations, that unless this appetite is satisfied, the soul must perish and die. Nothing short of this constitutes spiritual hunger. There are many who say, 'I have a desire', and if it be a spiritual desire, it will be granted. Howbeit, true spiritual desire is always attended with painful sensations of which many who claim such desire are completely ignorant. "The desire of the slothful killeth him," (Prov. 21:25). Why is this? Because he rests satisfied with a desire, "his hands refuse to labour," and he never takes the kingdom of heaven by violence. Only "the soul of the diligent shall be made fat," (Prov. 13:4).

The expression "thirst" conveys a still larger meaning. Hunger is more supportable than thirst. People die sooner when left without water than without food. Intense thirst is perhaps the most gnawing of all bodily sensations that a human being can experience. The Spirit has therefore made use of this figure in order to convey the intense desire of a living soul. Such an one must have Christ, or perish. He must feel His blood sprinkled upon the conscience or die in his sin. He must "know him, and the power of his resurrection," (Phil. 3:10), or he must pass into the gloomy chambers of eternal woe. He must have the presence of Jesus sensibly realised within him, and the love of God shed round about him, or else of all men he will be the most miserable.

October

October

1st

"The lofty looks of man shall be humbled, and the haughtiness of men shall be bowed down, and the LORD alone shall be exalted in that day."
Isaiah 2:11

How does the Lord humble? By discovering unto man what he is; by opening up the depth of his fall, by making him feel what a vile and guilty wretch he is before the footstool of mercy, by breaking him to pieces, by slaughtering and laying him low and by making him abhor himself in dust and ashes. Was not that the way the Lord took with the saints of old? How did he humble Isaiah? Was it not by some discovery of his divine Majesty, to make him cry, "I am a man of unclean lips!" How did he humble Daniel? Was it not by manifesting himself in his almighty purity, and turning Daniel's loveliness into corruption? How did he humble Hezekiah? By laying him upon a sick-bed, and laying his sins and iniquities with weight and power upon his conscience. None of these men produced humility in themselves. How did the Lord humble Job? By sifting him in Satan's sieve, and discovering as that riddle moved to and fro in Satan's hands the pride, peevishness, and self-righteousness of his carnal mind.

There are many who cannot bear to hear the malady touched upon. They cannot bear to hear the corruptions of the heart even hinted at. But what real humility can a man have except through a knowledge of himself? How can I be humbled except I feel that in myself which covers me with shame and confusion of face, and makes me loathe and abhor myself before the eyes of a heart-searching God?

Therefore the more the glorious majesty of heaven is pleased to unfold itself in all its divine purity in my conscience, and the deeper discovery I have of what I am as a fallen wretch and a guilty sinner, the more will my heart be humbled, the more shall I become lowly and abased, the more shall I loathe myself in dust and ashes as the saints and prophets of old.

2nd

"Grace and peace be multiplied unto you through the knowledge of God, and of Jesus our Lord."
2Peter 1:2

If we do not know Jesus for ourselves, by some spiritual discovery of his Person and work, what testimony have we of a saving interest in his grace? Because there is no grace except that which flows through him, for "grace and truth came by Jesus Christ," (John 1:17). This is what we should ever labour after.

Our daily, hourly desire and prayer should be to have spiritual discoveries of Christ; to see him by the eye of faith; to enter into his glorious Person and finished work; to realise his presence, taste his love, and know him and the power of his resurrection. This is what Paul so earnestly laboured after, (Phil. 3:7-11), and for the excellency of this knowledge he suffered the loss of all things, and counted them but dung that he might win Christ. To know him as our Surety and Sin-bearer, our Advocate and Intercessor, our Friend, Husband, and Brother, and to understand our saving interest in him, and our union with him, why this is bliss itself. To feel our place in his heart and see our name on his breast, to touch our memorial in the palms of his hands – what can surpass the blessedness of such a certain knowledge as this?

Through this spiritual, experimental knowledge of him, grace flows. As a watercourse opening from a river bank it brings down its irrigating stream into the parched meadow, so a knowledge of Christ opens up a channel through which the grace that is in him flows into the barren, parched soul. Thus, as through grace alone we know him, so every fresh communication of grace not only makes him better known, but flows in through and deepens that very channel of knowledge.

The grace that comes through this knowledge of him brings also peace, for "he is our peace," (Eph. 2:4). He "hath broken down the middle wall of partition between us; having abolished in his flesh the enmity, even the law of commandments contained in ordinances; for to make in himself of twain one new man, so making peace," (Eph. 2 14-15). He therefore "came and preached peace to you which were afar off, and to them that were nigh," (Eph. 2:14).

Our saviour's blood speaks peace to a guilty conscience; his voice says peace to the winds and waves of the surging heart; his legacy, bestowed at the last supper, was "Peace I leave with you, my peace I give unto you," (John 14:27). His promise to us all during that final discourse was, "that in me ye might have peace," (John 16:33), and as the Prince of peace at God's right hand he is able to fill us "with all joy and peace in believing," (Rom. 15:13), for his kingdom is "righteousness, and peace, and joy in the Holy Ghost," (Rom. 14:17). Thus, through the knowledge of God, and of Jesus as our Lord, "grace and peace" are both "multiplied unto [us]," (2Pet. 1:2).

October 3rd

"Thy life will I give unto thee for a prey in all places whither thou goest."
Jeremiah 45:5

There is a life given to the elect when the blessed Spirit quickens their souls – a life eternal, communicated to them out of the fullness of the Son of God. This life is a personal, individual life; and thus there seems to be a sweetness contained in the expression, "*thy* life will I give unto thee for a prey." This life which is treasured up in the fullness of Christ is breathed into the soul in the appointed time by the Holy Spirit, is kept alive there by his almighty power, and will burn brighter and brighter in the realms of endless day.

We should observe from the expression made use of in the text that this life which is given to the child of God is given to him in a peculiar way, "thy life will I give unto thee *for a prey*." The word "prey" indicates that this life is the object of attack. We hear of beasts of prey, and of birds of prey, and the expression often describes the prize of a carnivorous hunter. We would be safe to infer that there are ravenous beasts at large continually seeking to devour this life, voracious enemies on watch eager to prey upon the life which the Holy Spirit has kindled in thy soul.

How accurately and how experimentally do these words describe the inward kingdom of God! Eternal life is given by God, and it is kept by him when given, and preserved by his power from ever being extinguished. It is preserved by a perpetual miracle, like a burning lamp set afloat upon the waves of the sea; or, to use a figure that I have somewhere seen, like a lighted candle carried over a hill in the midst of a gale of wind.

Thus, our life is given us for a prey, and the power, faithfulness, and wisdom of God are manifested in keeping this life unhurt amid all its enemies. As Daniel was preserved in the den of lions, and as the three men were preserved in the burning fiery furnace, so the life of God is preserved in the soul. For as David says, "My soul is among lions," (Psa. 57:4), or as the prophet Isaiah enjoins, "glorify ye the LORD in the fires," (Isa. 24:15).

And so we find that the life of the child of God is one continual conflict between faith and unbelief, between enmity and love, between the grace of God and the rebellion of the carnal mind, and between the sinkings of the drooping spirit and the liftings-up of the light of God's countenance.

October

4th

"Whither the forerunner is for us entered, even Jesus."
Hebrews 6:20

How blessedly did the Lord comfort his sorrowing disciples when he said to them, "In my Father's house are many mansions: if it were not so, I would have told you. I go to prepare a place for you," (John 14:2). He has gone to take possession beforehand of his and their everlasting home, for he is ascended to his Father and their Father, to his God and their God. He has, as it were, filled heaven with new beauty, new happiness, and new glory. In him dwells all the fullness of the Godhead bodily. His glorious Person as Immanuel has become the object of heaven's praise and adoration. The elect angels adore him as God-man, and the spirits of just men made perfect worship him in company with the angelic host.

What a view had holy John of heaven's glorious worship when he saw the four living creatures and the twenty-four elders fall down before the Lamb. How clear it was to him when he heard their new song and the voice of many angels round about the throne, and all saying with a loud voice, "Worthy is the Lamb that was slain to receive power, and riches, and wisdom, and strength, and honour, and glory, and blessing," (Rev. 5:12).

The whole of heaven is waiting for the completion of the great mystery of godliness, when the finished Church shall be assembled around the throne; when the marriage supper of the Lamb shall come, and when the headstone shall be brought forth by the hands of the spiritual Zerubbabel, with shoutings of Grace, grace unto it, (Zech. 4:7). Earth itself is groaning under the weight of sin and sorrow; and the souls of those under the altar who were slain for the word of God, and for the testimony which they held, are crying with a loud voice, "How long, O Lord, holy and true, dost thou not judge and avenge our blood on them that dwell on the earth?" (Rev. 6:10).

The very signs of the times themselves are all proclaiming as with one voice that it cannot be long before the Lord will come a second time without sin unto salvation.

5th

"Wherefore doth a living man complain, a man for the punishment of his sins?"
Lamentations 3:39

We must not understand in the word "punishment" as used here anything of a vindictive nature, For God never punishes the sins of his elect penally; that is, not as he punishes the sins of the reprobate. The eternal covenant forbids this. "Fury is not in me," says the Lord, (Isa. 27:4). The elect are accepted in Jesus, are pardoned in him, and are complete in him. This is their eternal and unalterable covenant standing, the fruit and effect of their everlasting union with the Son of God.

Yet though this covenant forbids our punishment in its strictly penal sense, it by no means excludes *chastisement.* Thus we are not to understand by our text the infliction of God's righteous wrath, a foretaste of eternal damnation with which, even in this life, he sometimes visits the ungodly. It signifies that chastisement which is the privilege of the heir, and distinguishes him from the bastard. It is under this chastisement, then, that the living man is brought to complain, and he will often see in the afflictions that befall him the rod of the Lord as the chastisement of sin. When he thus sees light in God's light, he may justly say, 'Why should any living man complain when punished for his sins? Are they not chastisements rather than punishments? Are they not the rod of a father's correction rather than the vindictive stroke of offended justice?'

Perhaps his property is lost through unlooked-for circumstances, or the roguery of others and he is brought down from comparative affluence to be a poor man. When he can see that this is a chastisement for his pride and carnality in former days, he is able to put his mouth in the dust. Maybe the Lord afflicts him in his body so that he shall scarcely enjoy a day's health, but when he recalls how he abused his health and strength when he possessed it, and sees how many hurtful snares his bodily affliction now preserves him from, he is able most times to bear it meekly and patiently as unto the Lord.

He may have serious afflictions within his family, or find, like David, "his house not so with God" as he could wish, but when he sees that a sickly wife or disobedient children are but so many strokes of chastisement, and far lighter than his sins demand, he forbears to protest. When he sees that they come from the hand of love and not from eternal wrath, that they are the stripes of a Father, not the vindictive strokes of an angry judge, he feels then that love is mingled with chastisement. His spirit is meekened, and his heart softened, and he is brought down to say, 'Why should any living man complain when punished for his sins?'

Now, until a man gets to this point he can do nothing other than complain. Until he is brought spiritually to see that his afflictions, griefs, and sorrows are chastisements and not punishments, and is able to receive them as the stripes of love, he must and he will complain. Generally speaking, before the Lord lifts up the light of his countenance upon him, before he gives him a sense of peace in his conscience, he will bring him to accept of the punishment of his iniquity, (Lev. 26:41). He will then receive these strokes of chastisement with a subdued spirit, and will confess that they are justly deserved. With his obstinacy and rebelliousness being in a measure broken, he will lie as a poor and needy supplicant at the foot of the cross.

6th

"Persecuted, but not forsaken."
2Corinthians 4:9

Whatever injury persecutors may do or attempt to do to a Christian, they cannot rob him of his God. They may mangle and destroy his body, they may torture and twist his mind, but they cannot harm his soul. They may wound his reputation, they will try and test his conscience, and they may strip him of all his earthly goods, but they cannot lay their unhallowed hands upon the treasure which God has lodged in his breast. Yes, all may forsake him as they forsook his divine Master, but God has said, "I will never leave thee, nor forsake thee," (Heb. 13:5). Why, then, need we dread persecution for righteousness sake? If the Lord be on our side, whom need we fear? Who can harm us if we be followers of that which is good?

We do well to remember that the persecution must be suffered for righteousness' sake. Do not call it persecution if you are buffeted for your faults. Do not think yourselves persecuted if by your inconsistencies you have brought upon yourself the reproach of men, or the just censure of those who fear God. If your persecutions are brought upon you from doing the will of God, and that from the heart, you will find the approbation of God in your conscience. You will find that your very persecutions draw down into your soul a blessed sense of the sympathy of your great High Priest, so that as your afflictions abound, so will your consolation.

Sad indeed it would be for the Church of God, if, amid her persecutions, the Lord added to the weight of her trouble by withdrawing from her the light of his countenance and the consolations of his sensible presence. Yet in truth, she never more sensibly reclines on his bosom than when he gives her to drink of his own cup, and thus conforms her to his suffering image.

October 7th

"At that time Jesus answered and said, I thank thee, O Father, Lord of heaven and earth, because thou hast hid these things from the wise and prudent, and hast revealed them unto babes."
Matthew 11:25

Whatever religious knowledge, whatever carnal wisdom, or whatever worldly prudence a man may possess, if he is devoid of the life of God in his soul, he is destitute of the workings of godly fear. He has no solemn awe or reverence for Jehovah, he has never seen his sins in the light of God's countenance, he has never trembled at "the wrath to come," he has never prostrated himself with a reverential spirit before the eyes of a heart-searching Jehovah who sees into the secret recesses of his bosom.

All his knowledge, all his wisdom, and all his prudence do him no good, and leave him just where they found him — carnal, sensual, worldly, unconverted, dead in trespasses and sins. His wisdom will never reach beyond the surface; it will never break up the crust of unbelief, so as to enter through that seared shell into the conscience, and produce living effects in it, as made tender by the touch of God's finger. His knowledge, his wisdom, his prudence are merely floating in his judgment, and never descend into the depths of his heart.

God hides the workings of spiritual fear from those who are "wise and prudent," (Luke 10:21). He does not condescend to manifest himself to them. He does not show them light in his light and he does not reveal himself to their consciences. He does not come with power into their hearts, nor take the veil of unbelief and blindness from their carnal minds and show them himself. He takes them not where he took Moses, into the cleft of the rock whilst his glory passed by, (Ex. 33:22). He deals not with them as he dealt with Isaiah when he manifested his glory in the temple, nor does he discover himself to them as he did to Job who at the presence of God abhorred himself in dust and ashes, (Job 42:6).

All their knowledge of God, therefore, is external and intellectual, a mere exercise of the faculties of the mind without any spiritual teaching or any special revelation of the presence, power, glory, and majesty of God to their consciences. Yet the babe in Christ, the living babe in Zion, without any wisdom or prudence from this world, has "the fear of the Lord," in his soul which is "the beginning of wisdom," (Prov. 9:10).

Therefore, having this fountain of life within him, he has it springing up in spiritual exercises. As the Apostle says, he "serves God acceptably with reverence and godly fear," (Heb. 12:28). He dare not rush with presumption into his holy presence. When he comes into his sanctuary a solemn dread from time to time falls upon his spirit.

He has the feelings of Isaiah when he cried, "Woe is me! for I am undone; because I am a man of unclean lips, and I dwell in the midst of a people of unclean lips: for mine eyes have seen the King, the LORD of hosts," (Isa. 6:5). He shares the feelings of Jacob when he was afraid, and said, "How dreadful is this place! this is none other but the house of God, and this is the gate of heaven!" (Ge. 28:17). He knows the experience of Moses when he stood by the burning bush and put his shoes from off his feet, for the spot whereon he stood was holy ground, (Ex. 3:5). He shares the awe of the high priest in the temple on that day of atonement, when he entered alone, "not without blood," into the sanctuary, the holy of holies, and beheld the Shekinah glory, the Divine presence as a cloud resting on the mercy-seat, (Heb. 9:7).

The new born Christian has these exercises of godly fear implanted within, exercises of which the carnal, unhumbled, worldly-wise professors know nothing. Though at times he seems to have no religion which he can really call spiritual or which satisfies himself, yet he has that tenderness, awe, and reverence with which the carnal professor is utterly unacquainted, however high his doctrine or soaring his vain confidence.

8th

"Ye were sealed with that holy Spirit of promise, which is the earnest of our inheritance until the redemption of the purchased possession."
Ephesians 1:14

The Church has been redeemed by a price, but is not as yet fully redeemed by power. With his precious blood Christ has bought both the souls and bodies of his people, but he has not yet redeemed them openly. This redemption is still future, and will not be accomplished until the glorious resurrection morn, when the bodies of the dead saints will be raised, and the bodies of the living saints will be changed in a moment, in the twinkling of an eye, at the last trumpet, (1Cor. 15:52). This then is "the redemption of the purchased possession," and being in the future, we have to wait for it, as the Apostle speaks, "But if we hope for that we see not, then do we with patience wait for it," (Rom. 8:25).

Our body is not yet redeemed from its native corruption, but in the resurrection morn, when the dead will be raised incorruptible, then the redemption of the body will be complete. We will enter fully into our inheritance which is, as risen and glorified saints, nothing less than Christ himself, and he will in turn receive us. His purchased possession will be forever delivered from every foe and every fear, from every sin and every sorrow, from every corruption of body or soul, and be crowned with an exceeding and eternal weight of glory.

Unto this day of redemption the Holy Spirit has sealed all the living family of God, (Eph. 4:30), not only by assuring them of their saving interest in the inheritance, and himself being the earnest of it, but as thereby securing to them the most certain possession of it.

9th

"The heart is deceitful above all things, and desperately wicked: who can know it?"
Jeremiah 17:9

The sin of our fallen nature is a very mysterious thing. We read of the mystery of iniquity as well as of the mystery of godliness; and the former has lengths, depths, and breadths as well as the latter; depths which no human plumb-line ever fathomed, and lengths which no mortal measuring line ever spanned. Thus the way in which sin sometimes seems to sleep, and at other times to wake up with renewed strength, its active, irritable, impatient, restless nature, the many shapes and colours it wears, the filthy holes and puddles in which it grovels, the corners into which it creeps, its deceitfulness, hypocrisy, craftiness, persuasiveness, intense selfishness, utter recklessness, desperate madness, and insatiable greediness are secrets, painful secrets, only learned by bitter experience.

In the spiritual knowledge of these two mysteries, the mystery of sin and the mystery of salvation, all true religion consists. In the school of experience we are kept, day after day, learning and forgetting these two lessons, being never able to understand them, and yet not satisfied unless we know them, pursuing after an acquaintance with them, and finding that they still, like a rainbow, recede from us as fast as we pursue them.

Thus we find realised in our own life and walk those heavenly contradictions, those divine paradoxes, that the wiser we get, the more foolish we become, (1Cor. 3:18), and the stronger we grow, the weaker we are, (2Cor. 12:9-10). The more we possess, the less we have, (2Cor. 6:10), and the more completely bankrupt we are, the more frankly we are forgiven, (Luke 7:42). The more utterly lost we find ourselves, the more perfectly we are saved, (Luke 19:10), and when most like a little child, then are we the greatest in the kingdom of heaven, (Matt. 18:4).

10th

"And hope maketh not ashamed; because the love of God is shed abroad in our hearts by the Holy Ghost which is given unto us."
Romans 5:5

The Scriptures speak of a "good hope through grace," (2Thes. 2:16), and call such hope "an anchor of the soul, both sure and steadfast, and which entereth into that within the veil," (Heb. 6:19). What a blessed grace must this hope be which is not only sure and steadfast, but enters into the very presence of Christ, and the throne room of God! Still further, the word of God speaks of it as the twin to both faith and love, (1Cor. 13:13); and declares in our text that it "maketh not ashamed" because it springs out of the love of God shed abroad in the heart by the Holy Spirit.

Now, we learn what a "good hope through grace" is, by being tossed up and down on the waves of despondency, and almost at times sinking into despair over our sin. Evidences so darkened, the heart so shut up, the mind so bewildered, sin so present, the Lord so absent, a nature so carnal, sensual, idolatrous, and adulterous – no wonder that amid so many evils felt or feared, the soul should at times sink into despondency!

Yet at such seasons the blessedness of a "good hope through grace" is found! When this anchor of hope is cast to steady us, and it duly enters within the veil, taking hold of the blood and righteousness of the great High Priest, how strongly and securely it holds the ship. No more can we be utterly overwhelmed in the billows of despair, or dashed by a surging tide of sin upon the rocks of this world's distraction.

October 11th

"The Lord has laid on him the iniquity of us all."
Isaiah 53:6

What heart can conceive, what tongue express what the holy soul of Christ endured when "the Lord laid on him the iniquity of us all?" In the garden of Gethsemane, what a load of guilt, what a weight of sin, what an intolerable burden of God's wrath did that sacred humanity endure, until the pressure of sorrow and woe forced the drops of blood to fall as sweat from his brow. The human nature in its weakness recoiled, as it were, from the cup of anguish put into his hand. His body could scarcely bear the load that pressed him down; his soul, under the waves and billows of God's wrath, sank in deep mire where there was no standing, and came into deep waters where the floods overflowed him, (Psa. 69:1-2).

How could it be otherwise when that sacred humanity was enduring all the wrath of God, suffering the very pangs of hell laid up for unrepentant sinners, and wading in all the depths of guilt and terror? When the blessed Lord was made sin and a sin-offering for us, he endured in his holy soul all the pangs of distress, horror, alarm, misery, and guilt that the elect would have felt in hell forever. Yet more than that, he felt this not as an individual, but as the collective whole would have experienced under the outpouring of the everlasting wrath of God. The anguish, the distress, the darkness, the condemnation, the shame, the guilt, the unutterable horror that any and all of his quickened family have ever experienced under a sense of God's wrath, the curse of the law, and the terrors of hell, are only faint, feeble reflections of what the Lord felt in the garden and on the cross. In his case the attendant circumstances were such as were not and cannot be in ours and theirs, and which made the distress and agony of his holy soul, both in nature and degree, such as none but he could feel or know.

As the eternal Son of God, he had lain in his bosom before all worlds, and had known all the united blessedness and happiness of the love and favour of the Father, his own Father, shining upon him, for he was "by him, as one brought up with him: and was daily his delight, rejoicing always before him," (Prov. 8:30).

Yet now, instead of his father's love he felt his hate, instead of beams of favour he experienced frowns and terrors of wrath, instead of the light of his countenance he tasted the darkness and gloom of desertion. What heart can conceive, what tongue express the bitter anguish which must have wrung the soul of our suffering Surety under this agonising experience?

October 12th

"With long life will I satisfy him, and shew him my salvation."
Psalm 91:16

Other scripture teaches that it is not the number of our years that prepares us for death, nor is it length of life that give a man satisfaction. Scripture can never contradict itself, so such cannot be true. Then what can the promise in our Psalm mean? Why, simply that God will satisfy his people with and within whatever length of life he blesses them, whether it be short or long. God takes his children home at all ages, and yet he always satisfies them. He always brings them to see and feel that this life is empty and vain, and that it is better, far better, to live eternally in his presence. You may be harassed by the thoughts of death and be in bondage through the fears of the grave; your mind may be mulling, 'How will it be with me then?' I will tell you.

If you are a child of God, I firmly believe you will not be removed unwillingly and reluctantly, but you will be willing in the day of the Lord's power. You will be willing to breathe out your soul into his dear hands, to whom you will commend your spirit; you will be willing to be with Christ, which is far better. You may not now be willing. If you pluck at an unripe apple, it resists the touch, but let it be fully ripe, how little, how slight a touch will cause it to drop from the tree. You shall be gathered as a shock of corn in its season. Why, a farmer will not gather in his grain until it is fully ripe; and do you think the Lord will gather his grain into his heavenly garner and it be in an unfit and unripe state, (Matt. 3:12)? We cannot think it. Be that thought far from us, as it is far from the Lord.

"...I satisfy him, and shew him my salvation." Ah! the soul will never see it unless the Lord shows it to him, but the Lord will show it him because he says he will. What can a man want more than to see God's salvation? All that he may want, all that he may need in his journey through this wilderness is summed up in that revelation. Is there not a sufficiency? Is there not that which he feels is enough? If these promises be mine and be yours, and if they be fulfilled to you and to me, what more can we possibly want?

October 13th

"But the Comforter, which is the Holy Ghost, whom the Father will send in my name, he shall teach you all things, and bring all things to your remembrance, whatsoever I have said unto you."
John 14:26

If the Lord has given to any of you eyes to see and hearts to receive this divine Comforter, praise, bless, and adore your God and Father, and most merciful Benefactor, for his distinguishing grace in giving you to know him as your Comforter. Further, if he has ever dropped into your soul any of his sweet teachings, bless him that you have received him also as the Spirit of truth into your conscience.

What but sovereign grace, rich, free and super-abounding, has made the difference between you and the world who cannot receive him? Without his divine operations upon your soul, you would still be of the world, hardening your heart against everything good and godlike, walking on in the pride and ignorance of unbelief and self-righteousness, until you sank down into the chambers of death.

Oh, it is a mercy if but one drop of heavenly consolation has ever been distilled into your soul, or if ever you have felt or found any relief in your sorrows and distresses from the work and witness of the Holy Spirit. It is of his doing if you have ever gleaned solid comfort from a promise applied with power, from a text dropped into your heart with a sealing testimony, from a manifestation of the love and blood of Christ. Liberty, joy, and peace are produced only by the operation and influence of the Spirit of God.

Such comfort may have been but little, and lasted but a short while, yet it was sufficient for your need and it gave you a taste of its blessedness. It made you long for another sip, another crumb, another visit to the fountain.

Yet look to it well and examine carefully whether it be real, and whether, when weighed in the balance of the sanctuary, what you received with such comfort to your soul was distilled into your heart by the Comforter. Check diligently that the truth which you have felt and believed, and also professed, was opened up to your conscience by the Spirit of truth.

October 14th

"In him, not having mine own righteousness, which is of the law, but that which is through the faith of Christ, the righteousness which is of God by faith."
Philippians 3:9

Here are the two righteousness's clearly laid down, and in one or the other we must all stand before God. The righteousness which is of the law, and the righteousness which is of Christ and thereby of God through faith.

Now bear in mind that for righteousness to be acceptable before God it must be perfect righteousness. Such perfect righteousness no man ever did or ever can produce by his own obedience to the law. No man ever yet loved God with all his heart, soul strength and mind, or his neighbour as himself, (Luke 10:27). A man who does not thus love God and his neighbour is accursed and condemned already by that righteous law he seeks to keep, "for it is written, Cursed is every one that continueth not in all things which are written in the book of the law to do them," (Gal. 3:10).

The apostle felt that as this righteousness could not be yielded by himself as a fallen sinner, he must necessarily fall under the condemnation and curse attached to that holy law. Trembling therefore in his conscience and feeling that the wrath of God was revealed against him and all unjustified sinners in a broken law, he knew that he must sink forever under the terrible indignation of the Almighty if he had no covering for his needy, naked soul but his own righteousness. He therefore fled from the impossibly righteous demands of the law to find justification, acceptance, mercy, and peace in the righteousness of Christ. Thenceforth he was "determined not to know anything among you, save Jesus Christ, and him crucified," (1Cor. 2:2), and Jesus became to him his all in all.

Once he had been favoured with a view of the righteousness of the Son of God, he wanted no other for time or eternity. He saw by faith the words and works of the God-man, and he beheld Deity stamped upon every thought, word, and action of that pure humanity with which it was in union, investing them with a merit beyond all conception or expression of men or angels. He saw him by faith bearing his sins in his own body on the tree, and by his active and passive obedience working out a righteousness acceptable to God, such as he and all the redeemed could stand in before the great white throne without spot or blemish.

October

As a traveller overtaken by a violent thunderstorm gladly flies to a house by the wayside to shelter from the lightning-stroke and the sweeping rain, or as a ship threatened with a hurricane bends every sail to reach the harbour, so does the soul terrified by the thunders and lightnings of God's righteous law, seek for shelter in the wounded side of Christ, and hide itself beneath his justifying obedience.

This righteousness is here called "the righteousness of God," for God the Father contrived it, God the Son performed it, and God the Holy Spirit applies it. It is said to be "by faith" and "through the faith of Christ" because faith views it, believes in it, receives it, and gives the soul a manifested saving interest in it.

15th

"My doctrine shall drop as the rain, my speech shall distil as the dew, as the small rain upon the tender herb, and as the showers upon the grass."
Deuteronomy 32:2

We have in our text four degrees of precipitation - the rain, the dew, the small rain, and the showers, and this graduated scale of heavenly moisture shows that there are degrees of spiritual blessing. We must not expect all to be blessed to the same extent, nor all to receive the same measure. Yet these blessings are all of the same nature.

Examine the dew; it is water. The small rain is water also, as is the rain, and the showers. They are all water. You cannot find any difference between the water of the dew, the water of the small rain, of the heavy rain, or of the showers – it is all alike pure water, distilled from the sky.

So it is with the blessing of God upon the soul. It may fall upon one almost unnoticed as the dew, or upon another as the small rain, upon a third as the showers, or on a fourth as an outpouring of heavy rain; yet all are equally and alike spiritual and divine. It is given by the same God; comes through the same Jesus; and is communicated by the same Spirit. In every soul it produces more or less the same effects – to soften, to moisten, to fertilise, and to revive. It all descends from the heaven of Christ's gospel and falls from the same skies of grace and mercy, truth and love, and redeeming blood and salvation.

Therefore, only the teaching that testifies of Christ and only the speech that proclaims him to be a Rock and declares his work to be perfect, 'drops as the rain and distils as the dew'. There is a power in truth when God is pleased to apply it to the heart; and whether it come in large or in small measure, whether it be in dew or shower, it is equally a proof of his mercy and love, and equally a proof that his power attends his own divine truth to our soul.

16th

**"Your life is hid with Christ in God."
Colossians 3:3**

There is nothing so deep, nothing so hidden, as the life of God in the soul. It seems to be enshrined in the lowest depths of a man's heart. It does not float upon the surface, like a cork upon the water, but sinks deep, very deep, right to the very bottom of the soul. Therefore is it hidden from the eyes of a profane world; hidden from the professing world; and what is more, sometimes even hidden from the subject of it himself. A child of God often cannot see his own faith, nor can he discern the life that is bubbling and streaming up in his own bosom. It is not a lake, spread abroad in the meridian sunshine to attract every eye, nor is it a brook rushing noisily over pebbles and rocks. It is described as a well, "but the water that I shall give him shall be in him a well of water springing up into everlasting life," (John 4:14). As with water in a well, therefore it is deep, hidden from view.

The best part of our religion is that which is least seen. The secret cries, groans, tears, confessions, supplications, and breathings after God do not for the most part come abroad. The despondency, heart sickness, trials, perplexities, and powerful temptations with which many a dear saint of God is exercised do not come to view, nor do his fears, sinkings, guilt, misery, and self-condemnation. Yes, the best part of his religion is hidden from view, for the weightiest ever sinks the deepest.

As it is with the dealings of his soul with God, so it is with the dealings of God with his soul, making and keeping his conscience tender, reviving the fear of Him, drawing the heart upward into prayer and meditation, watering his spirit and bedewing it with the secret dew and rain of his grace. Thus the best part, because it is the spiritual part of a man's religion, is hidden from the eyes of all, except as the fruits thereof are manifest.

Take your stand upon yon hill, and see that thread of verdure spreading itself through the barren plain. Whence comes that green strip which you see? Coming down to examine it, you find a little brooklet threading its way through the barren plain. It is this brooklet that, watering the roots of the grass, gives it that verdure, yet the brooklet itself is hidden until the eye is brought close as it is sought out. So it is with the hidden life of God in the soul. We see the effects, the verdure produced by the brook of blessing, but the brook itself, the life and grace of God in the innermost soul is hidden, "hid with Christ in God."

Yet it is not merely hidden, but hidden with Christ in God, what a sacred, what a holy, what a truly divine life it must be! If this be spiritual religion, that it dwells with Christ himself in the bosom of God, what a divine thing, what a heavenly possession! How full of eternal blessedness must the religion of a child of God be! It is locked up in two distinct places, yet united with each other by virtue of the humanity of Christ, and the faith that embraces it. If I may use the expression, one end is in the bosom of God, and the other in the believer's breast! Compare man's paltry, beggarly religion with this supernatural life of God in the soul, Christ himself formed in the heart the hope of glory. Words would fail to express the eternal distinction between them!

Yet the word "hidden" carries also another idea, being out of reach, treasured up, safe. What would long ago have become of the life of God in the soul if it could have been robbed, trodden out, or lost? But this can never be, for it is locked up in the Person of the Son of God. Can you imagine anyone stealing anything that has been left in the care of our all-seeing and all-knowing God? It is, therefore, out of the reach of Satan, sin, death, and hell; safe in Christ's keeping, locked up in his eternal bosom. Were it otherwise, where should you and I long ago have been? Where would our religion have gone to, unless we had reason to believe that it had been kindled by the power of God, and was maintained by the same power which first gave it birth? This is the grand consolation of a child of God – to believe that he has the life of God in his soul, and to feel, day by day, that he who gave that life maintains it in firm and living exercise.

17th

"Grace unto you, and peace, be multiplied."
1Peter 1:2

When we see and feel how we need grace every moment of our lives, we at once perceive a beauty in the blessing thus asked for in an abundant, overflowing measure. We cannot walk the length of

October

the street without sin. Our carnal minds, our vain imaginations, are perpetually on the lookout for evil. Sin presents itself at every avenue, and lurks like a robber in the wilderness or a prowling night thief taking every opportunity of open or secret plunder. In fact, in ourselves, in our fallen nature, except as restrained and influenced by grace, we sin with well-near every breath that we draw. We need, therefore, grace upon grace, or, in the words of the text, grace to be "multiplied" in proportion to our sins. Shall I say in proportion? No, if sin abounds, as to our shame and sorrow we know it does, we need grace to much more abound, (Rom. 5:20). When the deep tide of sin flows in with the mud and mire, we need the spring tide of grace to flow higher still, to carry out the slime and filth into the depths of the ocean, so that when our sins are sought for they may no more be found.

Thus we need grace, free grace; grace today, grace tomorrow, grace this moment, grace the next, grace all the day long; healing, reviving, restoring, saving, sanctifying; and we need it multiplied to cover all our needs and woes, sins, slips and falls, unceasing and aggravated backslidings. We need grace to believe, grace to hope, grace to love, grace to fight, and grace to conquer; grace to stand, grace to live, and grace to die. Every moment of our lives we need this keeping, supporting, holding, and withholding grace; for, as a good man has said, 'If the Lord were to leave us for a moment, he would leave us for a moment too long.'

In our text the Apostle adds peace unto grace. Sin breaks our peace, and sets our souls at a distance from God. Trials, also, and temptations, sins and sorrows occur every day to mar our rest and so we need peace to be multiplied as well as grace; peace like a river, of which the stream is ever flowing; peace like the sea, of which the tides, if they do ebb, yet rise higher than they fall. We also need peace to establish our hearts in the truth, and in the love of it, so as to prevent our being carried about with every wind of doctrine. We are often entangled in the wily snares of Satan, and we need peace to be restored to our soul. When it is thus sadly broken, and sin has filled us with guilt and terror, we need peace to come and heal all those wounds, and establish our souls firmly in the gospel of peace.

And when we shall be called upon to enter the dark valley of the shadow of death, how then we shall need peace to be multiplied, that we may fear no evil, but find the comforting staff and supporting rod. Thus we never can have too much grace or too much peace. The more we know of sin the more shall we need grace, and the more we know of sorrow the more we shall need peace.

October 18th

"Jesus answered and said unto them, This is the work of God, that ye believe on him whom he hath sent."
John 6:29

Oh, how many a living saint is there who wants to believe in Jesus, who longs to trust in his holy name, and yet he cannot, so plagued and pestered is he by the risings of inward unbelief. He knows that he does not yet so believe in him as to obtain deliverance; for he has an inward testimony in his conscience, that if he believed in the Lord Jesus by the power of the Holy Spirit, it would bring the love of God into his heart, extract the sting of death, and fill him with joy and peace. But as long as he feels condemned by the law and his own guilty conscience, he has an inward testimony that he has not as yet that living faith in Christ which, he is persuaded, would save and deliver him from all his guilty fears and dismal apprehensions. Therefore he labours after this special, this peculiar faith in the Lord Jesus, that he may attain unto it, or rather that God would, of his infinite mercy, bestow it upon him.

Here, then, is the main labour of faith, to believe in Jesus Christ so as to obtain pardon, peace, and deliverance. Many a poor soul is labouring hard at this work, yet with a deep and increasing conviction that it is a work which he cannot perform except by the immediate power of God. So powerful an antagonist is unbelief, that, with all his attempts, he feels that he cannot subdue it, nor raise up one grain of that true faith whereby Christ is experimentally brought into the heart.

Yet this very struggle plainly shows that there is life within and a work of God on his soul, for all this conflict proceeds from the movements of his grace, and the opposition of his carnal mind to them. In due time, the blessed Spirit brings Christ near to his eyes and heart and reveals him within. He takes of his atoning blood and sprinkles it on his conscience. His righteousness is brought forth and put upon him, and he sheds abroad the love of God and raises up that special faith in the Lord Jesus whereby the soul hangs. That faith then hooks itself upon his Person as God-man, upon his blood as cleansing from all sin, upon his righteousness as perfectly justifying, upon his grace as super-abounding over all the aboundings of evil, and upon his dying love as a balmy cordial against all the woes and sorrows by which it is distressed. This is believing in the Son of God. This is believing in Jesus Christ, whom God sent, to the salvation of the soul.

October 19th

"Hast thou not procured this unto thyself, in that thou hast forsaken the LORD thy God, when he led thee by the way?"
Jeremiah 2:17

No man knows better, I believe, than myself, that we cannot do anything of a spiritual nature to bring ourselves near to God, but I am equally sure that we can do many things that set us very far from him. Let all the shame and guilt be ours, for all the grace and glory are God's. Every drop of felt mercy, every ray of gracious hope, every sweet application of truth to the heart, every sense of saving interest, every blessed testimony, every sweet indulgence, every heavenly smile, every tender desire, and every spiritual feeling, all, all are of God. If ever my heart is softened, my spirit blessed, my soul watered, if Christ is ever felt to be precious, it is all of his grace. It is all given freely, sovereignly, without money and without price.

But can it be denied – I for one cannot deny it – that by our carnality, inconsistency, worldly-mindedness, negligence, ingratitude, and forsaking and forgetting the God of our mercies, we are continually bringing leanness and barrenness, deadness and darkness into our own souls? Thus we are forced to plead 'Guilty, guilty!' to put our mouth in the dust, (Lam. 3:29), acknowledge ourselves to be vile, and confess ourselves indeed 'of sinners chief, and of saints less than the least.'

Yet thus does God, in his mysterious dealings, open up a way for his sovereign grace and mercy to visit the soul. The more we feel ourselves condemned, cut off, gashed, and wounded by a sense of sin and folly, backslidings and wanderings from God, the lower we shall lie, the more we shall put our mouth in the dust, the more freely we shall confess our baseness before him. And if the Lord should be pleased, in these solemn moments, to open our poor blind eyes to see something of the precious blood of the Lamb, to apply some sweet promise to the soul, or to bring to the heart a sense of his goodness and mercy, how sweet and suitable is that grace, as coming over all the mountains and hills of our sin and shame. Thus is the goodness of God, as it were, reflected on and by our baseness and vileness, as we see the sun sometimes shining on and reflected by a black cloud. The black cloud of our vileness but serves to heighten the glory of the rays of free grace and the bright beams of the Sun of righteousness.

October 20th

"Thou therefore endure hardness, as a good soldier of Jesus Christ."
2Timothy 2:3

How is the Christian soldier made? Is it by going to chapel, by reading the Bible, by singing hymns, and by talking with his fellows about religion? No more is the veteran warrior made by merely living in the barracks. He must go into the battle and fight hand to hand with Satan and the flesh. He must endure cruel wounds given by both outward and inward foes. He must lie upon the cold ground of desolation and desertion. He must rush up the breach when called to storm the castles of sin and evil, and never 'yield or abandon the field', but press on, determined to win the day or die.

Through these battles of the Lord, in due time he learns how to handle his weapons, how to call upon God in supplication and prayer, and how to trust in Jesus Christ with all his heart. He is shown how to beat back Satan, how to crucify self, and how to live a life of faith in the Son of God amidst a world of evil.

Religion is not a matter of theory or of doctrine – although any skilled soldier knows, understands and prepares for the fight. It is to be in the thick of the battle, fighting with the enemy hand to hand, foot to foot, shoulder to shoulder. This actual, not sham, warfare makes the Christian soldier hardy, strengthens the muscles of his arm, gives him skill to wield his weapons, and power sometimes to put his enemies to flight. Thus it works endurance and makes him a veteran. He is no longer a raw recruit, but one able to fight the Lord's battles and to "endure hardness, as a good soldier of Jesus Christ."

What then have been your best friends in life? Your spiritual trials. Where have you learned your best lessons? In the school of temptation. What has made you look to Jesus? A sense of your sin and misery. Why have you hung upon the word of promise? Because you had nothing else to hang upon.

Thus, could you look at the results, you would see that trials and temptations produced upon your spirit two effects. They tried your faith, and that sometimes to the uttermost so that in the trial it seemed as if all your faith were gone, and they have wrought patience, they have made you able to endure.

Why have you not long ago given up all religion? Have your trials made you disposed to give it up? They have made you hold all the faster to it. Have your temptations induced you to let it go as a matter of little consequence? Why, you never had more real religion than when you were tried whether you had any, and never held faith with a tighter grasp than when Satan was pulling it all away. The strongest believers are not the men of doctrine, but the men of experience; not the boasters, but the fighters; not the parade officers in all the millinery of spotless regimentals, but the tattered, soiled, wounded, half-dead soldiers that give and take no quarter from sin or Satan.

21st

"Behold, I will bring evil upon all flesh, saith the LORD." Jeremiah 45:5

The Lord may be said spiritually to "bring evil upon all flesh" when he lays trouble and calamity upon the flesh itself, and upon all that the flesh holds dear. The blow falls upon the fruits of the flesh, when it cuts down fleshly religion, and roots up false hopes, vain confidence, and self-dependence. The effect of these strokes is to lay the soul poor and needy at the footstool of mercy; and as the Holy Spirit enlightens the eyes to see, quickens the soul to feel, and raises up power to ask, there is now a seeking after real things - substance as opposed to shadows. Thus pardon, mercy, the testimony of God in the soul, the lifting up of the light of his countenance, the sprinkling of the blood of Jesus upon the conscience with all the other spiritual blessings revealed in the word, are sought after, valued, and prized.

It is no longer enough that they are heard from a minister, assented to in the judgment, or received on the testimony of others. They are only now so far enjoyed as they are tasted, felt, and handled in the depths of the heart. I can say for myself that until evil came upon me in this way through a long illness, (though if I now have life, I had it before), until trouble came, and I was brought low in body and soul, I never sought before as I have done ever since, the visitations and manifestations of the Lord's favour. Deceived by Satan and my own heart, I was seeking rather to make myself wise in the letter than to feel the power of vital godliness in my soul. Since that time, amid many discouragements and with many alternations and changes, I have felt led, as I never knew before, or at least not from the same pressing sense of need, to seek after the visitations and manifestations of the Lord's favour. To crave the dew of his Spirit, the application of his atoning blood, and the inward testimonies of his love and grace. Nor can I rest for salvation upon anything else.

I am not, therefore, speaking at a peradventure, for I know the ground and have travelled it, and have lined it with laborious footsteps. Therefore, having tracked it out, I speak in my measure that which I know, and testify that which I feel.

When the Lord, then, thus brings evil upon our flesh, it is not to sweep away any real religion that we may possess, but to sweep away our false religion. This winnowing fan is to fan away the chaff and leave the pure grain. The keen knife of the heavenly Surgeon is used only to cut away the diseased and unhealthy tumours and leave the sound parts uninjured. When the Lord brings distress into the soul, it is not to destroy any one grace that has been communicated by the blessed Spirit, but to fulfil that word, "Every plant, which my heavenly Father hath not planted, shall be rooted up," (Matt. 15:13). He puts his "vessels of gold and silver," (2Tim. 2:20), into the furnace to take away their dross, that they may be sanctified, and fit for the Master's use. For he has chosen his Zion in the furnace of affliction, and he shall sit "as a refiner and purifier of silver: and he shall purify the sons of Levi, and purge them as gold and silver, that they may offer unto the LORD an offering in righteousness," (Mal. 3:3).

22nd

"And the Word was made flesh, and dwelt among us, (and we beheld his glory, the glory as of the only begotten of the Father,) full of grace and truth."
John 1:14

The glory of Christ in his suffering humanity was veiled from the eyes of all but those who were taught by the blessed Spirit and enlightened to see it, and oh, what glory is still to be seen by believing eyes in an incarnate God! The grandeur of Deity, tempered by the weakness of humanity, and yet shining through it, as the noonday sun shines through the clouds, which so far veil his rays that though they permit him to be seen they do not dazzle nor blind the eye! The Son of God, the babe of Bethlehem, the "only begotten of the Father," sweating great drops of blood in the Garden and hanging upon the cross at Calvary. Yet in his lowest state, when covered to man's eye with ignominy and shame, we see glory streaming from every pore of his sacred body, majesty and beauty shining forth from every lineament of his marred visage, and love and mercy characterising every word issuing from his languid lips!

October

None will ever see the glory of a risen, ascended, and glorified Christ in the open bliss of heaven who do not first see him on earth in his humiliation as a suffering Christ. Indeed, it is his very suffering glory which is now so blessed and so suitable to a guilty sinner. To see this suffering glory of the Son of God revealed to his soul by a divine power, made over to him as his salvation, and containing in it the essence of all his present and future happiness; this is the glory that a redeemed and regenerated saint longs to see and feel.

What glory can the world give compared with the glory of the marred countenance of the suffering Son of God? By the side of his cross all earthly glory pales, withers, and dies, for death puts an end to everything naturally bright and glorious. Well has God spoken of the end of all human glory; "Therefore hell hath enlarged herself, and opened her mouth without measure: and their glory, and their multitude, and their pomp, and he that rejoiceth, shall descend into it," (Isa. 5:14).

Yet that glory which begins with the cross ends with a crown, for if we suffer with him, we shall also be glorified together with him, (Rom. 8:17. To see this glory of the suffering Christ by the eye of faith; to feel the heart deeply penetrated and inwardly possessed by it; to have it for our daily bread and our daily drink; to come as led by the Spirit to this ever-spread table of the flesh of Christ, this ever-flowing fountain of his atoning blood, and hear the Lord himself saying, "Eat, O friends; drink, yea, drink abundantly, O beloved," (Song 5:1), here is food to feed your immortal soul. Here are streams of pardon and peace; here are the rivers of eternal life, "Let him that is athirst come; and whosoever will, let him take the water of life freely," (Rev. 22:17). Why, to see, to enjoy, to feel, and experience all this in his own dry, thirsty and weary bosom, this is to see the glory of God, as revealed in the Person, work, blood, obedience, and love of his dear Son.

23rd

"Surely, shall one say, in the LORD have I righteousness and strength: Even to him shall men come."
Isaiah 45:24

Our God has given an absolute promise that "In the LORD shall all the seed of Israel be justified, and shall glory," (Isa. 45:25). No less absolute is the addition and divine corollary to that promise that, "to him shall men come." Who is it that gives them will and power to come? Why, the Father himself, according to the Lord's own words. "No man can come to me, except the Father which hath sent me draw him," (John 6:44). Yet will the Father draw all the chosen vessels of mercy to Jesus? Surely he will; for the Lord adds, "It is written in the prophets, And they shall be all taught of God. Every man therefore that hath heard, and hath learned of the Father, cometh unto me," (John 6:45).

Every act of faith whereby you look to Jesus is a 'coming'. Every beam and ray of hope in his blood and righteousness is a 'coming'. Every sigh, groan, or tear; every contrite feeling, every breathing desire of a broken heart, all are a 'coming'. You may not be able to realise as fully as you could wish a saving interest in the former part of the promise. "Surely, shall one say, in the Lord have I righteousness and strength," yet there is wrought in your soul by a divine power that secret coming whereby you have a manifested saving interest in the second part of it, "even to him shall men come."

We cannot come until we are drawn. "Draw me," says the bride, "we will run after you," (Song 1:4). "The LORD hath appeared of old unto me, saying, Yea, I have loved thee with an everlasting love: therefore with lovingkindness have I drawn thee," (Jer. 31:3). When we are drawn, then we come, and we cannot but come. It is good to come. Even those who have received must be ever coming. We get nothing but by coming. Our daily life, as one of faith and hope, is a life of coming. Our continual prayer is a continual coming. For the language of the Church still is, "And the Spirit and the bride say, Come. And let him that heareth say, Come. And let him that is athirst come. And whosoever will, let him take the water of life freely," (Rev. 22:17). Thus must we be ever coming that we may be ever receiving; and so everything that makes us come has in it a real or an implied blessing. Nor will you come in vain, be you who or what you may, for "him that cometh to me I will in no wise cast out," says our Lord himself in the gospel, (John 6:37).

24th

"For I say unto you, That except your righteousness shall exceed the righteousness of the scribes and Pharisees, ye shall in no case enter into the kingdom of heaven."
Matthew 5:20

There are three kinds of righteousness, or at least three kinds of righteousness which truly bear that name. First, there is inherent righteousness, of which we have none. Then there is imputed righteousness, which is all our justification. Lastly there is imparted righteousness, when God the Spirit makes us new creatures, and raises up in the heart that "new man, which after [the image of] God is created in righteousness and true holiness," (Eph. 4:24).

Therefore, when the Lord said, "except your righteousness shall exceed the righteousness of the scribes and Pharisees, ye shall in no case enter into the kingdom of heaven," he was not speaking of an external righteousness wrought out by obedience to the law, but an internal righteousness wrought out by the Holy Spirit.

This is why we read of the inward as well as the outward apparel of the Church. "The King's daughter is all glorious within; her clothing is of wrought gold," (Psa. 45:13). There are two kinds of righteousness which belong to the children of God. First our imputed righteousness which is our outward robe, "the clothing of wrought gold," and second our imparted righteousness which is our inward adorning, which makes us "all-glorious within." This inward glory is the new man in the heart, with all his gifts and graces, what Peter calls "the divine nature," (2Pet. 1:4), and what Paul calls "Christ in you, the hope of glory," (Col. 1:27).

25th

"And we know that the Son of God is come, and hath given us an understanding, that we may know him that is true, and we are in him that is true, even in his Son Jesus Christ. This is the true God, and eternal life."
1John 5:20

When the Lord Jesus is pleased in some solemn hour to reveal himself to our soul, when he graciously condescends to take the veil from off our heart that we may behold his glory, the glory as of the only begotten of the Father, full of grace and truth, when he kindly favours us with some manifestation and discovery of himself as the Son of God, the brightness of the Father's glory and the express image of his Person, then we know that the Son of God has come.

How do you know that the sun rose this morning? Why, by the light which is now cast about you. We may also say spiritually, "How do you know that the Son of God has come?" The answer is similar, by the Sun of righteousness arising upon you with healing in his wings and the light of understanding and belief which he shines in your heart. So the Lord speaks to Zion, "Arise, shine; for thy light is come, and the glory of the LORD is risen upon thee," (Isa. 60:1).

That is also the way in which the darkness is dispersed; for he adds, "behold, the darkness shall cover the earth, and gross darkness the people: but the LORD shall arise upon thee, and his glory shall be seen upon thee," (Isa. 60:2). Did not our blessed Lord say, "I am come a light into the world, that whosoever believeth on me should not abide in darkness," (John 12:46)? Has he not promised, "he that followeth me shall not walk in darkness, but shall have the light of life," (John 8:12)? Now as God is light, when he is pleased to shine into the soul, we walk in the light as he is in the light, and then we have fellowship with one another and the blood of Jesus Christ cleanses us from all sin. This is the best, this is the surest, this is the safest way to know that the Son of God is come.

We know also that the Son of God is come by his presence, by his power put forth on our behalf, and by the answers which he gives to prayer. We can feel his presence by the way he appears in dark and gloomy hours, making crooked things straight and rough places plain, by his discovering himself to us as the Way, the Truth, and the Life, showing unto us that in him there is rest and peace, solid, abiding happiness, and in no other.

He thus draws and fixes our eyes upon himself, where he sits at the right hand of the Father in the fullness of his grace, glory, and majesty. Thus we know that the Son of God has come. Every prayer, every petition, every sigh and cry, every longing look that you cast up to him, and every word of his grace, every sweet promise, every glimpse or glance of the King in his beauty which you receive out of his fullness are all so many testimonies that the Son of God has come and that you know that he has come.

26th

"These wait all upon thee; that thou mayest give them their meat in due season."
Psalm 104:27

The meat which God's children long after, is to have the truth as it is in Jesus, in all its various branches, revealed with power to their heart. Not merely to see a certain truth in God's word – that is like a hungry beggar looking at savoury provision through a window from which he is barred out. Such a sight simply whets his appetite rather than satisfies it. The food that God's people are longing after, and the only thing which can assuage their spiritual hunger, is the truth as it is found in Christ. It must be manifested, revealed, discovered, and applied with power to their souls as dew, with unction, savour, sweetness, life, light, and liberty accompanying the word, so that truth falls as heavenly manna into their hearts. It is not sufficient that the Holy Spirit should create the appetite, but he must overshadow the soul with his divine influences, breathe abroad a heavenly savour, and fill it with some sensations of his presence, with some meltings of heart at the feet of Christ, and with some drawing forth of affection to God. Thus he communicates an inward reception of the truth, and an enjoyment of its sweetness and savour.

Notice that our verse says "give them." This meat is not to be taken out of the Bible because it may be read. It is not to be caught up as the minister throws it forth because it may be heard. It is not to be got out of books because they have been written, but it is to be bestowed by the holy hand of Jehovah himself. It is to be received in the posture of a penitent, in the attitude of a suppliant, as a sinner prostrate at the foot of the cross, without anything in self but wounds, condemnation, and guilt.

There is also an appointed time, "thou mayest give them their meat in due season." There are many living souls, who are hungering after divine blessings, but the "due season" has not come. "It is not for you to know the times or the seasons, which the Father hath put in his own power," (Acts 1:7). You are not yet fit for it. The Lord has to bring you lower. You have yet to travel darker paths and pass through sorer exercises. There is a "due season" for the manifestation of gospel blessings. There is a fitting time which the Searcher of hearts knows, and that Searcher of hearts knows that many of the true Church of God are at this present time in that state, and that he will not manifest to them his greatest and richest blessings.

There is a "due season," in which they are to be revealed and manifested to the soul, and that season will be as suitable to all its wants as it will be most glorious to God. That "due season" will most probably be when the soul least expects to receive it. The promise has been so long delayed, it seems as though it will never come. The blessing has been so long withheld, it appears as though the Lord would never bestow it. Having denied his countenance so long, it seems as though he has drawn a black cloud over the throne, and through that cloud the rays of the Sun will never shine.

Yet in its "due season" it will surely come. "For the vision is yet for an appointed time, but at the end it shall speak, and not lie: though it tarry, wait for it; because it will surely come, it will not tarry," (Hab. 2:3). There is a time set to favour Zion, (Psa. 32:3), and when that set time arrives, the Lord will build up Zion and appear in his glory, for "he will regard the prayer of the destitute, and not despise their prayer," (Psa. 102:17).

October 27th

> "Whether Paul, or Apollos, or Cephas, or the world, or life, or death, or things present, or things to come; all are yours;"
> 1Corinthians 3:22

"All are yours", says the Apostle, including "life", but how can this be? In two ways is the answer – our life present, and our life to come. Both are the Christian's, according to the words of Paul to Timothy, "Godliness is profitable unto all things, having promise of the life that now is, and of that which is to come," (1Tim. 4:8), yet life present is natural as well as spiritual. Therefore in three senses is life the portion of Christ's people – life natural, life spiritual, and life eternal.

Life natural is theirs, for they alone can truly enjoy it. What is natural life if it hangs by a thread over a dreadful eternity? How soon spent and gone, and how soon death and judgment close the scene. For a Christian, though, his natural life is the season for faith and prayer, the seedtime of an immortal harvest. The unregenerate are life's slaves, but he is life's master. To most, the natural life is but an opportunity of evil, but to him an opportunity of good.

However, spiritual life is peculiarly theirs for they alone possesses it. Natural man shares natural life, but only the Christian enjoys spiritual life. This life is his because Christ is his, and Christ is his life. Because Christ lives, he lives also.

Finally, there is life eternal, which commencing now in life spiritual is transplanted above to bloom in immortality.

Then, more wondrous still, "death", that last enemy, that king of terrors, who makes the strongest tremble, and the stoutest heart quake. That also is yours if you are Christ's. Death is not your enemy if you are Christ's, but your friend. He may in the dim and distant prospect seem to come in the guise of an enemy and you may dread the thought of his approach. You may even sink down with fear how it may be with you in that solemn hour, but if you are Christ's, death is yours as well as life, for he has abolished death and has brought life and immortality to light, (2Tim. 1:10).

Death then cannot harm you, because Christ died for you. Death will merely cause your failing body to drop into the ground whilst opening to your soul the everlasting doors through which the King of glory, the Lord mighty in battle, entered as your forerunner when he went above to prepare a place for you.

October 28th

"And ye are Christ's; and Christ is God's."
1Corinthians 3:23

"Christ is God's." These are remarkable words, and need to be carefully and reverently opened up. The fullness of the mystery is beyond our grasp. Still, we may attempt to look at it in faith and godly fear. How, then, is Christ God's?

First, he is God's son. Not by covenant or by office, not adopted as we are, but a true and proper Son – a Son by nature, by his eternal mode of subsistence as a Person in the Godhead. "This is my beloved Son" was proclaimed twice by God the Father with an audible voice from heaven, (Matt. 3:17-Matt. 17:5).

Second, but he is also God's servant. "Behold my servant whom I uphold," (Isa. 42:1). "It is a light thing that you should be my servant to raise up the tribes of Jacob," (Isa. 49:6), and this he was as Messiah. Howbeit, because he is by office God's servant, he is not any less by nature God's Son.

Here, however, he is spoken of as the God-man mediator, the Son of the Father in truth and love, and the great High Priest over the house of God. More especially is he viewed in union with the Church, the Bridegroom with the bride, the Vine with the branches, the Shepherd with the sheep, the living foundation with the living stones built into and upon it.

Christ, therefore, in our text is said to be God's not only as the only-begotten Son of God, but as "the head of the body, the Church," (Col. 1:18). For, as says the Apostle, "We are members of his body, of his flesh, and of his bones," (Eph. 5:30). Christ is therefore God's with all those that belong to him – he as much as they, they as much as he.

Look at the glorious truths in our text in sequence. "Ye are Christ's," because by donation, purchase, and possession you are members of his body. "Christ is God's," as Son, as Servant, as Mediator, as Head of the Church, and therefore you too are God's, because you are Christ's; for the members are one with their covenant Head.

29th

"They that be whole need not a physician, but they that are sick."
Matthew 9:12

A physician is not needed without a case to attend, but the harder the case, the wiser and better physician we need. Thus a guilty conscience is a case for atoning blood, a wounded spirit for healing balm, a filthy garment for a justifying robe, a drowning wretch for an Almighty hand, a criminal on the gallows for a full pardon, an incurable disease for a heavenly physician, and a sinner sinking into hell for a Saviour stooping down from heaven. A man with a real case must have a real salvation. He is no longer to be cheated, deluded, and tricked with pretences, as a nervous patient is sometimes cured with fake pills; but he must have a real remedy because he has a real disease.

Christ hidden in the Bible, Christ sitting as an unknown Saviour in the heavens, Christ afar off, unmanifested and unrevealed, is no Christ to him. 'Near, near, let him come near! To feel him in my heart, in my soul, revealed in me, manifested unto me, formed within me - this, this is the Christ I need! O for just one drop of his atoning blood, just one smile of his blessed countenance, just one testimony of his love, and one single gleam of his justifying righteousness!"

Thus when this divine Redeemer appears in his garments stained with blood, the sinking soul hails his approach, the fowls of the mountains take flight, the beasts of the earth slink off to their dens, the dreary stump pushes forth its shoots, and the voice sounds forth from the inmost depths of the soul.

"This is our God; we have waited for him, and he will save us: this is the LORD; we have waited for him, we will be glad and rejoice in his salvation," (Isa. 25:9).

30th

"My people are bent to backsliding from me."
Hosea 11:7

What a dreadful error it is to deny backsliding! What ignorance it manifests of a man's own heart! How it stamps a man as a perverter of truth, and one that trifles with sin and the displeasure of the Most High! Who that knows himself and the idolatry of his fallen nature, dares deny that he backslides perpetually in heart, lip, or life? Can any of us deny that we have backslidden from our first love? Backslidden from simplicity and godly sincerity, backslidden from reverence and godly fear, backslidden from spirituality and heavenly-mindedness, backslidden from the breathings of affection and pouring forth of the heart into the bosom of the Lord?

October

If we have been so blessed as not being allowed to backslide into open sin, if the Lord has kept us, and not let us be cast down into the mire, yet have we not committed that twofold evil with which the Lord through his prophet charges his people? "For my people have committed two evils; they have forsaken me the fountain of living waters, and hewed them out cisterns, broken cisterns, that can hold no water," (Jer. 2:13)?

And what do we reap from backsliding? Do we reap pleasure, comfort, or peace? Do we reap the smiles of God, or the solemn testimony of the Spirit in the conscience? No. If conscience speaks in your bosom, what does it say? That every departure from the Lord has brought grief and trouble; that so far from justifying yourself in your sin, you have been ready almost to weep tears of blood that you have so wickedly departed from the Lord. It has been our mercy that the Lord has not given us up to hardness of heart and searedness of conscience, that we have not been allowed to say with Israel of old, "I am innocent, I have not sinned," (Jer. 2:35); but that he has led us with weeping and with supplications, (Jer. 31:9).

Have not some of us, (I am sure I have for one), been obliged "to go and weep," and tell the Lord a piteous tale of backsliding, how we have departed from his fear, and sinned basely against him, and how unwilling we have been to take his yoke upon us and walk in his precepts? Have we not been forced to tell him that we have been disobedient, stubborn, filthy and vile? Has he not, in some faint measure, led us 'to turn our faces Zionward', (Jer. 50:5), and to turn our back upon all false ministers, upon all idol shepherds, upon all the strength and wisdom and righteousness and will of the creature? Has he not given to us some simplicity, uprightness, and integrity of heart and conscience whereby we have turned our face Zionward, looking for a blessing to come out of Zion, looking for grace, looking for glory?

"I will make you sick in smiting you," says the Lord, (Mic. 6:13), alluding to the feeling of sickness produced by a wound, ("I am made sick," 1Kings 22:34, *margin*). Have not these wounds in our conscience made us, in our measure, sick of the world, sick of the professing church, sick of hypocrites, sick of whitewashed Pharisees, sick of carnal professors, sick of our backslidings, sick of all but the word of God revealed with power. Are we not sick of all but the blood and love of the Redeemer, of all teachings but the teachings of the Holy Spirit, and of all company but the company of the children of God, and even God only?

Can you say thus much? that you have turned your back upon everything but Christ, and him crucified? that you have turned away from all doctrines but those which centre in the blood of the Lamb?

that you have turned away from universal charity and general philanthropy, as substituted for the power of vital godliness, (though you would desire to love and serve your fellow men as men), and that your spiritual affections are toward God and his people? And has there been in your soul any such feeling as Ruth had when she said, "thy people shall be my people, and thy God my God," (Ruth 1:16), Any sweet response in your bosom to the voice of the Lord, "My son, give me your heart?" "Take it, Lord, with all that I have and am!" Any casting yourself at the foot of the cross, and there entreating the Lord of life and glory to speak peace to your soul?

31st

"By grace ye are saved."
Ephesians 2:5

Oh! the volumes of blessed truth that are couched in these few words; thrown in out of the Apostle's full heart as if to give a moment's vent to his love of salvation by grace! Mercy, love, and grace are all in the bosom of God toward his saints; and yet they differ from each other, but how?

Mercy regards the criminal; love regards the object; grace, perhaps, is a blending of the two – the union of mercy and love. There is an object of love in which there is no mixture of mercy, for God loves his holy unfallen angels – having never sinned they have no need of mercy. God also shows no mercy to the fallen angels, and there we see his justice and wrath without mercy. In the case of the saints of God, the election of grace, we have not only mercy and love, but we have the joint attribute. That uniting mercy and love in one stream flows onward to the Church as the river of the water of life, the pure crystal river of grace.

Grace means the pure, unmerited favour of God, and, as such, is sovereign, distinguishing, free, and super-abounding. Every attribute of Jehovah is distinct, and yet so blended that the whole shines forth in a single glorious effulgence. The rays of the sun united form one complete body of pure, bright light; but the prism or the rainbow separates out these rays into distinct colours. So the attributes of God are not confused though blended, and all shine forth in one pure bright glory. This is the peculiar character of *grace,* that any intermixture of worth or worthiness in the object would destroy it, for if the gospel require merit, we are damned by it as inevitably as by the law. This Luther felt when, racked and torn by the words "the righteousness of God without the law is manifested," he cried out in the agony of his soul, "What! Am I damned not only by the law, but damned by the gospel also!"

This pure, free, unadulterated grace is the joy of every soul that is able to receive it, for it comes as a blessed cordial when sinking and swooning under a sight and sense of the deserved wrath of God. When, then, the pure gospel of the grace of God comes as a cordial from the Most High, it lifts up his drooping head, revives his sinking soul, and pours oil and wine into his bleeding wounds. By this grace we are justified, pardoned, accepted, sanctified, and saved with an everlasting salvation. Oh! These are glad tidings to perishing sinners! What blessed news to those who are sinking under a sense of guilt and misery, in whom the law of God is discharging its dreadful curse!

When we get a view by faith, and a sweet taste of the pure grace of God, what a balm, what a cordial, what a sweet reviving draught it is. It is this which makes us prize so highly and exalt so gladly the free grace of God; because it is so pure, so free, and so superabounding over all the aboundings of sin, guilt, filth, and folly. It never can be laid down too clearly, it never can be too much insisted on that "by grace," and grace alone, "ye are saved," (Eph. 2:8). If free grace has reached your soul, it has saved your soul. If free grace has come into your heart, it has blessed you with an everlasting salvation, and you will live to prove it when your happy soul joins the throng of the blessed.

If anything can lift up a drooping sinner, restore a backslider, break a hard heart or soften a stony heart it is grace. If anything can draw forth songs of praise and tears of contrition, produce repentance and godly sorrow for sin, humble a mind and make tender a conscience, it is the sweet experience of the superabounding grace of God.

Can we then exalt it too much? Can we prize it too highly? Can we cleave to it too closely? No. In proportion as we feel our ruin and misery, we shall cleave to it with every desire of our soul, for it is all our salvation, as it is all our desire.

November

November 1st

"The entrance of thy words giveth light."
Psalm 119:130

The blessed Spirit is pleased sometimes to give some testimony concerning Jesus, to open up some passage of Scripture which speaks of Him, to cast a divine light before the astonished eyes, and to throw some of the blessed beams of gospel truth into our souls, whereby we see our Lord. At such times we are brought in soul feeling to the desires of those Greeks who came up to worship at the feast and went to Philip saying, "Sir, we would see Jesus," (John 12:21). From some apprehension of his beauty and loveliness, we pour out our soul before God, and say, "We would see Jesus." We want to feel his love, to have our eyes anointed to behold his glory. We want to look upon him as crucified for us and bearing our sins in his own body on the tree, that we may have a sweet and blessed fellowship with him as our suffering Surety, and thus, by faith, enter into the "breadth, and length, and depth, and height; and to know the love of Christ, which passeth knowledge," (Eph. 3:18).

Wherever there is a work of grace upon the soul, there will be this pining after Christ for the soul that is really taught of God can never rest satisfied short of Jesus. "There remaineth therefore a rest to the people of God," (Heb. 4:9), and they can never be satisfied short of that rest, which consists in an experimental knowledge of the Son of God as revealed by the Holy Spirit to their souls.

Howbeit, before the enjoyment of this spiritual rest, there is often long delay. Clouds of darkness may for months and years envelope the mercy seat. The cross of Christ cannot be seen, and the Holy Spirit holds back in taking of the things of Christ and showing them to the soul. In the absence of these heavenly manifestations, we cannot realise our saving interest in the things of salvation, nor can we feel our hearts sweetly composed and settled down in the blessed assurance, that when this life shall come to a close, we shall inhabit mansions prepared for us before the foundation of the world. When "with clouds he covereth the light; and commandeth it not to shine by the cloud that cometh betwixt," (Job 36:32), there are many doubts, fears, suspicions, surmises, and jealousies whether we are not deceived and deluded altogether. At such seasons, everything seems to be against us, and to stamp us as being nothing but nominal professors.

It is in such dark and gloomy seasons as these that the entrance of God's words giveth light, and some such promise as this is made sweet to the soul. "Come unto me, all ye that labour and are heavy laden, and I will give you rest," (Matt. 11:28). As that promise is brought home with power to the heart, and is shed abroad with sweetness in the soul, it draws forth and strengthens faith, and the toiling pilgrim comes to the Lord feeling "weary and heavy laden," but as he comes, he is indulged sometimes with a few sweet moments of rest. He is enabled to look out of fallen self, with all its miseries, and to look upon Jesus in his grace and beauty. He is favoured to cast himself simply, as he is, upon Jesus, and some sense of his atoning blood, his dying love, and his complete atoning sacrifice for sin is opened up to his heart. Faith springs up to lay hold of it and embrace it, and once again he begins to taste the savour and sweetness and healing efficacy of a Saviour's blood and love.

Thus "the entrance of [God's] words giveth light," and he feels by the divine coming in of what God has externally revealed, that inward light is shed abroad in the recesses of his soul, and he can, in some measure, realise the power of the cross of Jesus in his heart.

2nd

"And such were some of you: but ye are washed, but ye are sanctified, but ye are justified in the name of the Lord Jesus, and by the Spirit of our God."
1Corinthians 6:11

Justification and sanctification are two distinct blessings. The first springs out of and is connected with the finished work of the Son of God. The second springs out of and is connected with the work of the Holy Spirit on the soul. Sin has defiled our persons externally as well as polluted our souls internally. As a result, we cannot stand before God unless washed in the blood of the Lamb and clothed in his spotless righteousness. This righteousness forms our title to heaven in like manner as holiness constitutes our fitness for heaven. The former is our wedding robe, the latter our spiritual qualification. The hymn well draws this distinction.

> "Tis he adorned my naked soul,
> And made salvation mine;
> Upon a poor, polluted worm
> He makes his graces shine.
>
> And, lest the shadow of a spot
> Should on my soul be found,

November

He took the robe the Saviour wrought,
And cast it all around.

The Spirit wrought my faith, and love,
And hope, and every grace;
But Jesus spent his life to work
The robe of righteousness."

Without these two qualifications, what entrance could there be into heaven, or what happiness could we find there if entrance could be gained? For consider not only the infinite purity and holiness of God, but the blazing splendour of his immediate presence, the piercing ray of his deep-searching eye. Who or what can live in his presence but that which is absolutely perfect without and within?

Yet this the Church cannot ever be, unless she is washed in the blood and clothed in the righteousness of God's dear Son, and perfectly sanctified by the ceaseless operations and indwelling of his Spirit.

Paul therefore describes that sanctifying work by way of an example. "Husbands, love your wives, even as Christ also loved the church, and gave himself for it, that he might sanctify and cleanse it with the washing of water by the word, that he might present it to himself a glorious church, not having spot, or wrinkle, or any such thing; but that it should be holy and without blemish," (Eph. 5:25-27).

3rd

"It is good that a man should both hope and quietly wait for the salvation of the LORD."
Lamentations 3:26

The Lord does not bring his poor and needy children to a throne of grace just to send them away as soon as they have come. His purpose is to show them deeply what they are, to make them understand and value his favours, and to sink them lower and lower in self that they may rise higher and higher in Christ. It is to "teach them to profit," (Isa. 48:17), to write his laws upon their hearts in lines of the Spirit's drawing, in lines, "graven with an iron pen and lead in the rock for ever!" (Job 19:24). God's lessons are not traced out in characters on the sand, to be washed away by the rising tide or effaced by the wind, but are scribed in characters as permanent as the soul itself.

November

The work of the Spirit in the hearts of the redeemed is radical work, work that goes to the very bottom; nothing flimsy, nothing superficial, nothing which can be effaced and obliterated springs from him, but that which shall have an abiding effect - that which shall last for eternity. The Lord is fitting his people for eternity and therefore his work in them is thorough work; it goes right through them leaving nothing covered up and masked, but turns all up from the very bottom, "discovering the foundation unto the neck," (Hab. 3:13). He does to man spiritually what he threatened to do in Jerusalem literally, "I will wipe Jerusalem as a man wipeth a dish, wiping it, and turning it upside down," (2Kings 21:13).

Therefore, he does not answer the prayers of his children immediately when they come to his throne of mercy and grace, but rather he deepens those convictions that he implanted to cause the prayer in the first place. He makes the burdens heavier that he has put upon their back and hides himself instead of discovering himself. He thus draws back further instead of coming nearer in order to emphasise the need.

This is to make them wait with greater earnestness, with more unreserved simplicity and honesty, and with absolute dependence upon him and him alone to communicate the blessing. He is drawing out a greater separation of the heart from the strength of the creature, and a firmer resolution in the soul to cast away all its own righteousness and hang solely and wholly upon the Spirit's teachings and upon Jesus' sweet revelation of himself.

4th

"Love is of God."
1John 4:7

Love is a gift which the risen Mediator has received that he may freely communicate it out of his fullness to his people, and we must be brought to feel that it is a gift. Could we produce it or keep it alive in our own hearts, we would burn incense to our own skill or our own care. Some perhaps will scarcely believe that a child of God can feel enmity against Christ; but his carnal mind is unmitigated enmity against him. And oh, what a cutting feeling it is for a follower of the Lamb to discover a principle within him which hates Christ; which hates, bitterly hates, his Person, his holiness, and his purity, and which could join in the cry, "Crucify him, crucify him," and push and strike him with the Roman soldiers and the Jewish rabble. Unless painful experience convinced us that there was such a dreadful principle within, we could not believe that there was this devilish enmity in our heart against him whom our souls desire to love and adore.

Yet what can we know about love if we have not all this enmity, carnality, and coldness to try it? When we have been exercised with all these wretched feelings and the Lord begins to drop a little mercy and grace into our hearts and draw forth our affections unto him, then we begin to feel what a sweet thing love is.

Love is the sweetest balm a man can taste in this life. It is so naturally. There is a very real sweetness in love. When we love our wives, our children, and our friends, there is a sweetness and tenderness in the very feeling which, as moralists say of virtue, is its own reward. Coldness, dislike, envy, prejudice, jealousy, suspicion, peevishness, and quarrelling are sparks of hell which burn and torture every spot on which they fall.

So it follows that if ever there is hell in a man's bosom it is when he is full of hatred against God and his people, but if ever we feel a foretaste of heaven, it is when the Lord kindles some meltings of love and some drawings of affection toward Jesus and to those who are his. Then enmity and prejudice flee away; and we feel as if we could take all the people of God into our bosom, and say with the widowed daughter-in-law, "thy people shall be my people, and thy God my God," (Ruth 1:16).

5th

"There is... a time to weep."
Ecclesiastes 3:4

Does a man weep only once in his life? Does not the time of weeping run more or less through a Christian's whole life? Does not mourning run parallel with his existence in this tabernacle of clay, for "man is born unto trouble, as the sparks fly upward," (Job 5:7). Then as the preacher says, "a time to kill, and a time to heal; a time to break down, and a time to build up" must run parallel with a Christian's life, just as much as "a time to weep, and a time to laugh; a time to mourn, and a time to dance."

Living souls will know many times to weep. They will often have to sigh and cry over their base hearts and to mourn with tears of godly sorrow their backslidings from God. It is to them a regular thing to weep over their broken idols, faded hopes, and marred prospects, and to weep at having so grieved the Spirit of God by their disobedience, carnality, and worldliness. They know what it is to be melted into contrition at the feet of a dying Lord, so as in some measure to be led into the path in which Jesus walked as "a man of sorrows, and acquainted with grief," (Isa. 53:3). They will have to bewail the falling off of those friends whom once they looked upon as bidding fairer for the kingdom of God than themselves and to weep at the cruel arrows of calumny which are shot against them by professors of the faith. They will ever be mourning over the low state of Zion, how few there are who really serve the Lord acceptably with reverence and godly fear, and who adorn the doctrine in all things.

Yet, above all things, will they have to weep over the inward idolatries of their filthy nature, and to weep that they ever should have treated with such insult that God whom they now desire to love and adore. Bitter tears will be shed that they should so neglect and turn their backs upon that Saviour who crowns them with loving-kindness and tender mercies, and that they bear so little in mind the instruction that has been communicated to them by the Holy Spirit.

There is many a weeping time for God's children, and if there be one frame of mind in soul experience more to be coveted than another, it is to be weeping at Jesus' feet. We have two sweet instances of the Lord's manifesting himself to those who were weeping. The first was to the woman who was an immoral sinner, and who knelt behind him washing his feet with her tears, (Luke 7:38), and the second was to Mary Magdalene, who stood outside the sepulchre weeping, (John 20:15).

Oh, how different is the weeping, chastened spirit of a living soul from the hardened, seared presumption of a proud professor! How different are the feelings of a broken-hearted child of God from the lightness, the frivolity, the emptiness, and the worldliness of hundreds who stand in a profession of religion! How different is a mourning saint, weeping in his solitary corner over his base backslidings, from a reckless professor who justifies himself in every action, who thinks sin a light thing, and who, however inconsistently he acts, never feels conscience wounded thereby! "Blessed are they that mourn, for they shall be comforted," (Matt. 5:4).

6th

"The spirit indeed is willing, but the flesh is weak."
Matthew 26:41

Why is flesh so weak? Because it is fallen, because it is sinful, because it has an alliance with the temptation which is presented to it. It is weak against temptation for the same reason that a man

November

who loves strong drink is weak against the offered wine. If we had no inward lusting after evil, no pride, no rebelliousness, no fallen nature, no carnal mind, no vile affections, nothing in us earthly, sensual, or devilish; would we fear temptation? No, for then we would be armoured against it, tempting such a saint would be like dipping a match in water.

Here then our weakness lies. If by ourselves we could always resist we would conquer, but we cannot resist, except by the special power of God. This is a lesson we all need to learn. The weakness of the flesh manifests itself continually in compliance, in non-resistance, in giving way, in yielding, often almost without a struggle, no, sometimes even going beyond even the temptation and acting a worse and more wicked part still. How striking are the words of Deer – "That mariner's mad part I played, who sees, yet strikes the rock."

Is there any one that knows and fears God who can say he has never played that mad part? One who has never seen the rock ahead, and yet deliberately run upon it? One who has never mourned, sighed, cried, groaned and repented, and yet been again overcome, willingly, of the same sin? One who has never seen the evil of the snare, never felt the rope round his neck, and yet been willingly entangled – I might almost say strangled? It is through these things that we learn the weakness of the flesh; weak to believe, weak to hope, weak to love, weak to fight, weak to resist, weak to overcome, weak to watch, weak to pray, weak to stand, weak to everything good; strong to everything evil. The flesh indeed is weak. What use are all resolutions, all promises, all desires, all endeavours, all strugglings, all strivings, except the soul is held up by the mighty power of God?

Yet 'the spirit is willing'. Here the child of God is distinguished from those who are given up as a prey to temptation. He has a willing spirit which they have not. How is the spirit willing? It is made willing in the day of God's power, (Psa. 100:3). It is a new spirit, a free spirit, a holy spirit, a gracious spirit, and therefore a willing spirit.

What therefore is it willing to do? It is willing to obey, to watch, to pray, to be conformed to the will of God, to crucify the lusts and affections of the flesh, to put off the old man and to put on the new.

How does it show this willingness? By the very struggles it maintains against the flesh; flesh and spirit pulling contrary ways; the spirit all willingness, the flesh all weakness; flesh twining around spirit, spirit struggling under the firm and strong embrace of flesh.

Hence the conflict; the spirit willing to read God's word, to pray and seek God's face, and pour out the heart before him; the flesh weak, and finding prayer a burden. The spirit willing to make sacrifices, endure persecutions, bear afflictions, carry the cross, suffer with Jesus, resist even unto blood striving against sin; the flesh weak, dragging the spirit down with it, unable to stand a single moment, complying with every suggestion to evil, listening to every insinuation of Satan breathed into the ear, hearkening to the tempter, and almost as bad as he.

This then, the willingness of the spirit and the weakness of the flesh, is the reason why there should be, no, why there must be watchfulness and prayer. If there were no willing spirit, there would be no need of watchfulness; it would be useless; nor of prayer, for it would not ascend with acceptance into the ears of the Lord of Sabbath. If there were nothing but flesh, the believer would be all weakness; but possessing spirit, there is in him some willingness, and this God looks at.

7th

"My people hath been lost sheep."
Jeremiah 50:6

When God the Holy Spirit takes a soul in hand, just as the fingers of a man's hand wrote a sentence of condemnation upon the palace wall in Babylon, so does the blessed Spirit write the word "lost" upon the conscience of every vessel of mercy. When he has written this word with power on their consciences, they carry it about with them branded as it were in letters of fire, in such a manner that the impression is never to be erased until it is blotted out by the atoning blood of the Mediator.

Thus as the Holy Spirit teaches the consciences of God's family, "lost, lost, lost" is written on their heart, "lost, lost, lost" is the cry of their lips, and "lost, lost, lost" is the deep feeling of their soul. None in his family was ever found who had not the feeling 'lost' written deeply upon his heart. None was ever gathered into the arms of the heavenly Shepherd, sought out upon the mountains and the hills, laid upon his shoulders, and brought home with rejoicing that hadn't first been lost. None was ever brought into a spiritual acquaintance with Jesus, so as to enjoy communion with him, who had not sighed and groaned and cried under a sense of his lost state, as a guilty sinner before God.

Now when the soul has been taught by the Holy Spirit to feel, see and know itself to be without strength to deliver itself from the wrath to come, and is sunk down into despondency and dismay as a result, then is the time when the Holy Spirit usually gives it some discovery of the mercy of God in the face of Jesus Christ. We find this sweetly set forth in that remarkable chapter, Ezekiel 16. The vessel of mercy is there delineated under the figure of a new-born babe, abandoned by its mother, and "cast out in the open field, to the lothing of thy person, in the day that thou wast born," (Ezek. 16:5).

As unpitied, as abandoned, as polluted, as helpless, as perishing, as wretched and as an outcast is the quickened soul, but it is not left to perish. As the preacher wrote, "Now when I passed by thee, and looked upon thee, behold, thy time was the time of love; and I spread my skirt over thee," (which was the sign of espousal as we see in Ruth 3:9), "and covered thy nakedness: yea, I sware unto thee, and entered into a covenant with thee, saith the Lord GOD, and thou becamest mine," (Ezek. 16:8).

8th

"But we have this treasure in earthen vessels."
2Corinthians 4:7

Gold and silver, those precious metals, take no injury and receive no spot of corruption from any vessel in which they are contained, and let them be buried in the damp earth, no tarnish or rust forms upon them.

So it is spiritually. The grace of God in the heart, surrounded as it is with corruption, is not tarnished by it, nor is the heavenly treasure contaminated although it is lodged in an earthen vessel. Christ in the heart is not defiled by the inward workings of depravity, and by the base thoughts that strive perpetually against his grace, any more than the gold of the Bank of England is defiled by the dark and damp cellars in which it is stowed.

What a mercy it is that our corruptions cannot tarnish the grace of God, and that our unbelief cannot mix with and adulterate the faith of God's elect. What sweet relief that our despondency cannot spoil and ruin our gospel hope, and that our deadness, darkness, coldness, and rebellion cannot mingle with and defile the love of God in the soul! This heavenly treasure remains still as unpolluted and pure as when God first put it there, and being a part of "the divine nature," it remains uncontaminated by the filth and corruption that surround it.

Is not this a blessing for God's tried people, that spiritual knowledge, living faith, gospel hope, heavenly love, and the fruits and graces of God's Spirit in the soul can never be defiled, but, like the streams of a deep fountain, are ever gushing forth in pure water? What favour is bestowed that the pure grace of God in a man's heart cannot be contaminated by the filthy streams that are dashing from his vile nature against it like the torrents of water from a fire-engine against a burning house, but remains as pure as when God the Spirit first breathed it into the soul.

9th

"And he said, I will not let thee go, except thou bless me."
Genesis 32:26

What a strange intermixture there is in a believing heart of everything to cast down and yet of everything to encourage! How there is everything on the one side to perplex, to confuse, and put the soul to its wits' end, and yet how on the other there is everything to hold up its head, strengthen its faith, support its hope, and encourage it to hold on to the last gasp! Now this is that very trial of faith which is more precious than of gold that perishes, for faith is not a dead, sluggish grace, and is never more active than when it is being tried as with fire. You cannot give up from what you have felt and experienced, for that is the grand evidence, the persuasion that you have the life of God in your soul, and compared with that how worthless and valueless all other things seem to be in your eyes, because to give that up is to give up all your hope.

Here then is the grand mystery, to hang and hold on, to hold out and not allow oneself to be cast away, but the more the Lord would seem to put us away, the more to cling to him. Was not this the faith of the Syrophenician woman who, so to speak, would not take no for an answer, (Matt. 15:27)? Or yet like the faith of Ruth who said, "Intreat me not to leave thee," (Ruth 1:16), and like the faith of Hannah, when "she was in bitterness of soul, and prayed unto the Lord and wept sore," (1Sam. 1:10)? Does not this faith resemble that of Heman's, when he cried out, "Wilt thou shew wonders to the dead? Shall the dead arise and praise thee?" (Psa. 88:10), and that of Asaph when his feet were almost gone and his steps had well-nigh slipped, (Psa. 73:2)?

Thus the more the Lord seems to put us away, the more we cling to him. The viler we are, the more we need his grace; and the very magnitude of our sins only makes us hang more upon his atoning blood and cling more closely to his word and promises as suitable to our case. Nor will anything induce us to give up our hope or relinquish our hold of his mercy.

November
10th

"In the light of the king's countenance is life; and his favour is as a cloud of the latter rain."
Proverbs 16:15

What is religion without a living faith in, and a living love to the Lord Jesus Christ? How dull and dragging, how dry and heavy, what a burden to the mind and a weariness to the flesh is a 'round of forms' where the heart is not engaged and the affections not drawn forth! Reading, hearing, praying, meditation, conversation with the saints of God, what cold, what heartless work where Jesus is not known! But let him appear, let his presence and grace be felt, and his blessed Spirit move upon the heart, then there is a holy sweetness, a sacred blessedness in the worship of God and in communion with the Lord Jesus that makes, while it lasts, a little heaven on earth.

It is this inward sense of the blessedness of his presence and the misery of his absence, the heaven of his smile and the hell of his frown that makes the sheep of Christ seek communion with their shepherd. He has won their heart to himself by discovering to them his beauty and his love, and they having once seen the glory of his Person, heard the sweetness of his voice, and tasted the grace of his lips, follow him wherever he goes, seeking to know him and the power of his resurrection, and counting all things dung and loss that they may win him and have some manifestation of his love.

What is to support the soul under those trials and temptations that at times press it so sore? What can relieve those cruel doubts which so disquiet, and take away those fears of death which so alarm? What will subdue that rebelliousness which so condemns, wean from the world which so allures, and make it look beyond life and time, the cares of the passing hour, and the events of the fleeting day, to a solemn and blessed eternity? Only those visitations of the blessed Lord to the soul, which give it communion with himself, will do all this.

Thus were the saints of God led and taught in days of old, as the Holy Spirit has recorded their experience in the word of truth. Remembering the past, Job says, "Thy visitation hath preserved my spirit," (Job 10:12). Longing for renewal, David cries, "O when wilt thou come unto me," (Psa. 101:2), and under the enjoyment of his presence the bride says, "He brought me to the banqueting house, and his banner over me was love," (Song 2:4).

November

11th

"But if ye be led of the Spirit, ye are not under the law."
Galatians 5:18

If we are led of the Spirit by walking in him; if he be our Guide and Teacher; if he be continually operating upon our heart, and bringing near the influences of his grace, then the law is no more a terror unto us. If he be in us and with us, guiding us into all truth, making and keeping us believing, loving, prayerful, tender, watchful, humble, contrite, and sincere, and if we are thus led by the Spirit, we are not then under the law.

Now while the conflict is going on in your bosom, you are often in your feelings under the law. The law's curse is ringing in your ears, the law's condemnation piercing your conscience. The flesh in some unguarded moment prevails and you are entangled in some evil; you slip and fall into something which brings guilt upon your conscience. Now the law thunders. Inward condemnation re-echoes its peals, and the soul falls into bondage, doubt, and fear.

Howbeit, if you are led by the Spirit, if that blessed Guide is pleased to lead you out of yourself into Christ's blood and righteousness; if you are experimentally favoured with his blessed teachings and sweet influences, bringing with them light, life, liberty, and love, the law has no more curse for you. It cannot condemn you to hell, nor send your soul to lie forever under the curse of God.

For, being led by the Spirit, you are delivered from the curse of the law into the blessing of the gospel, and from the bondage of the law into the liberty of its truth. You are delivered from law charges into gospel mercies, and from the accusations of a guilty conscience into the witness of a good conscience, because it has been purged and sprinkled. To sum it all up in one sentence, you are thus translated from the power of darkness into the kingdom of God's dear Son. Oh the blessedness of walking in the Spirit, and being led by the Spirit!

12th

"He will subdue our iniquities; and thou wilt cast all their sins into the depths of the sea."
Micah 7:19

November

Sin subdued is the next greatest blessing to sin pardoned, and wherever God pardons sin, he subdues sin, for the same grace which saves sanctifies. The same grace which casts sin behind God's back, puts its foot upon the corruptions of the believer, and prevents iniquity from having dominion over him.

The Scripture is very plain and express upon this point. "Sin shall not have dominion over you," (Rom. 6:14). Why? "For ye are not under the law," which gives sin its strength and power, "but under grace," which is able to subdue its dominion. Nor do I believe that any child of God can ever rest satisfied except by the subduing of his sins as well as the pardoning of them.

To have his unbelief, infidelity, worldly-mindedness, pride, and covetousness subdued by the grace of God is his desire. To have its power taken out of it, its dominion dethroned, its authority destroyed, and its strength weakened and diminished, that he may not be under the dominion of any lust, or carried away by the strength of any secret or open sin is his longing. To walk before God in the light of his countenance, as desirous to know his will and do it – this is the desire and breathing of every one that knows sin in its guilt, filth, and power.

How gracious, then, is the promise, how sweet the favour, that the Lord has promised to subdue our iniquities by the same grace as that whereby he pardons them. How suitable that, as we receive the blood of Christ to sprinkle the conscience, so we receive the grace of Christ to sanctify and renew the soul, and the strength of Christ to overcome all our inward and outward foes.

13th

"And deliver them who through fear of death were all their lifetime subject to bondage."
Hebrews 2:15

It is no evidence against you if you are subject to bondage; it is no mark against you if you cannot look death in the face without doubt or fear. Is it not the children who feel the bondage, and did not the Lord come to deliver them from it, (Ex. 2:23)?

Are you then not a child because you fear death? If you had no sense of sin, no tenderness of conscience, you would be as careless about death as most other people are. Thus your very bondage, your very fears, if they make you sigh and cry for deliverance, are marks of life. And the day will surely come when the Lord will remove these chilling fears and put an end to these killing doubts.

November

As you draw near to the brink of Jordan, the Lord will be with you to deliver you, who, through fear of death, are now subject to bondage. He will extract its sting, and rob the grave of its victory, enabling you to shout 'Salvation!' through his blood, even at the moment when nature sinks lowest and the last enemy appears nearest in view.

Oh, what a blessed Jesus we have. What a heavenly Friend and what a divine Mediator stands between a holy God and our guilty souls! What love he displayed in taking our flesh and blood, and what kind condescension, what wondrous depths of unspeakable grace he uncovered. He loved us so much that he laid down his life for us! Did he not for our sakes endure the agony of the cross, the hidings of God's face, the burden of sin, and the very pangs of hell itself? And if he has done all this for us on earth, will he leave his work undone in heaven? Has he not quickened you into life, made you feel your sin, taught you to seek for mercy, raised up a good hope in your heart, applied a promise to your soul, given you a testimony? He may have done all this, and yet at times your conscience may be held down in bondage and imprisonment. But it is only to make further way for his grace; to open up more and more of his willingness and ability to save to the uttermost all that come unto God by him. It is only to make himself in the end more precious to you; to show you more of his finished work, more of his dying love and atoning blood, and more of what he is able to do in delivering you from all your fears.

Thus, as the Adamic fall was ordained by the wisdom of God to make manifest the riches of his eternal love, mercy, and grace, so your very doubts, fears, and bondage are blessedly ordained to give you further discoveries of Christ. They are designed, to wean you more from the arm of flesh, and to make you know more experimentally what the Lord Jesus Christ is to those who seek his face and hang upon and trust him and him alone.

A man who believes that he may live and die and do so safely without an experimental knowledge of Christ, will never seek his face or call upon his name, or ever long for the manifestations of his love. Howbeit the man who feels that he can neither live nor die without him, who knows that he has a soul that only Christ can save, sins which only Christ's blood can pardon, and iniquities that only Christ's righteousness can cover, will be often crying to the Lord to visit his soul with his salvation. He will find no rest until Christ appears, but when Christ appears to the joy of his soul he will bless and praise him with joyful lips. Oh, what a glorious trophy will that man be of Christ's eternal victory over sin and Satan, when he will reign with him and with his assembled saints in one immortal day!

November

14th

"Having a good conscience."
1Peter 3:16

We cannot often see our faith, but we can sometimes see our conscience. We cannot always rejoice in the Lord, but we can see whether we fear his great name. We cannot always triumph over our enemies, but we can sometimes observe whether there is a sentinel upon the look out.

Thus, if you want to know whether you have faith, look at faith's companion, see what faith is attended by; and if you don't find a "a good conscience," write death upon your religion. Throw away your sword for it is useless; it is of human manufacture and will break in pieces when you have to encounter your enemy, the king of terrors. God's lightning will shatter it then.

Howbeit, if the Lord has given you "a good conscience," a tender conscience, a pure conscience, he will strengthen your arm to fight the good fight of faith. You will often think your sword is so short, and your arm so weak that you cannot fight the Lord's battles, but if he has given you "a good conscience," a conscience tender in his fear, he has put into your hands the sword of faith. He will one day manifest clearly that he has himself equipped you with it by giving you victory over all your foes.

Oh, may the Lord raise up in our hearts some sweet testimony that we have "a good conscience," and then we shall have this blessed consolation, that concerning faith we shall not make shipwreck.

15th

"My Father, which gave them me, is greater than all; and no man is able to pluck them out of my Father's hand."
John 10:29

In that most sublime and touching prayer which the Lord Jesus Christ, as the great High Priest over the house of God, offered up to his heavenly Father before he shed his precious blood on the cross, there is one petition, or rather an expression of his holy will, which is full of unspeakable blessedness.

"Father, I will that they also, whom thou hast given me, be with me where I am; that they may behold my glory, which thou hast given me: for thou lovedst me before the foundation of the world," (John 17:24).

The change from 'petitioning as a Priest' to 'willing as a King' is very remarkable, and casts a gracious light upon the nature of Christ's mediatorial intercession at the right hand of God. On the footing of his covenant engagements, atoning sacrifice, and finished work, as well as from the perfect equality of his divine nature with that of the Father and of the Holy Spirit, he utters the expression of that sovereign will which was and is identically the same with the eternal will and fixed decrees of his heavenly Father.

And oh, how full and comprehensive, how gracious and condescending is the will of Christ as thus expressed! How it embraces in its firm and sovereign grasp all the members of his mystical body, all the sheep of his pasture and the flock of his hand, all that the Father gave him to be eternally his own! Yes; all the countless millions who before the foundation of the world were given to him - as his joy and crown, as his eternal inheritance, as the delight of his heart, and the promised reward of his incarnation, sufferings, and death, were included in this expression of his holy and unchanging will. Whatever be their state and condition here below, whatever sins and sorrows they may have to sigh and groan under, whatever opposition they may encounter from earth or hell, this will of Christ holds them up so that they cannot fall out of his hand, or be deprived of their glorious inheritance.

16th

"Be careful for nothing; but in every thing by prayer and supplication with thanksgiving let your requests be made known unto God."
Philippians 4:6

What a word is this! "Every thing!" You are privileged, saint of God, to go to the throne of God with everything. What, with every little occurrence? Yes. What, with things that people call trifles? Yes. With your daily concerns? Yes. If you feel that there is a God who can hear you, it is your privilege to go to him in everything. All things are comprehended; nothing is excluded. In everything, and that by prayer and supplication. Sometimes we pray, sometimes we supplicate.

Prayer is something more gentle than supplication, less earnest, less fervent, less powerful, yet no less effectual. I have sometimes compared prayer and supplication to two things in nature. The one to a river, a stream, such as we see in our low country that flows with gentle but unstoppable course to the sea, and the other to the torrents found in the mountains, leaping from precipice to precipice. The one is the calm prayer of the assured soul, but the other is the fervent cry of the heart, the earnest supplication, the breathed agony of the spirit rushing along into the bosom of God with many a broken sigh and many an earnest groan.

Here the two seem contrasted. There is prayer, calm and gentle, the simple pouring out of the soul into the bosom of God, and then there is supplication, which is earnest and calls upon the Lord as though the soul must be heard. We see it in the blessed Jesus himself. We read on one occasion that he went into a mountain the whole night to pray. Now we have no reason to believe he prayed on that occasion in the same way that he prayed in the garden and upon the cross. In the one case he had sweet union and communion with his Father; in the other he cried with groans and tears, but in both he was heard. The one was prayer, the other supplication.

When your soul is calmed by the presence of God and you feel the breath of prayer to enter your bosom, then you can pray to the Lord with sweetness and with spirit. Howbeit there are times and seasons when the soul, under the attacks of Satan and a terrible sense of guilt and shame, is obliged to cry as one that must be heard, and that is supplication.

There is yet another thing which is to be mingled with our prayers, a thing much omitted, and that is thanksgiving. These are the three constituents of a spiritual service - prayer, supplication, and thanksgiving.

17th

"Simon Peter, a servant and an apostle of Jesus Christ, to them that have obtained like precious faith with us."
2Peter 1:1

What a thought it is, that if you and I possess one grain of living faith, the same precious grace is in our hearts that was in the hearts of all the saints of God. From Abel the first martyr through all the saints and prophets of the Old Testament, down through the apostles, servants and martyrs of the new testament, right up to the saints of today, and such as will exists in the bosom of every saint right on to the remotest period of time.

"There is one body, and one Spirit... One Lord, one faith, one baptism... One God and Father of all, who is above all, and through all, and in you all," (Eph. 4:4-6), and by the possession of this "like precious faith" all the family of God are knit together into one glorious body, of which the Lord Jesus Christ is the risen Head.

You, in yourself, may be very poor and needy, for faith makes us to feel our poverty and need. You may think and feel yourself unworthy of the least notice by God's favouring eye, but if the blessed Spirit has raised up one grain of living faith in your soul, you stand on the same holy platform with saints, apostles, prophets, and martyrs. You are as much "accepted in the Beloved," (Eph. 1:6), as much "beloved of God," (Rom. 1:7), and as much a member of the mystical "body of Christ", (1Cor. 12:27), as though you were either of the apostles Peter or Paul, the patriarchs Enoch or Abel, the prophets Isaiah or Elijah, or any of the righteous kings of Israel.

18th

"And it is yet far more evident: for that after the similitude of Melchisedec there ariseth another priest, Who is made, not after the law of a carnal commandment, but after the power of an endless life."
Hebrews 7:15-16

We may say of the life which the Lord Jesus lives in the courts of heavenly bliss that it is a threefold life. There is, first, his eternal life, by which I mean the eternal life of God in his divine nature. This he lives IN himself, "For as the Father hath life in himself; so hath he given to the Son to have life in himself," (John 5:26). He is thereby "Alpha and Omega, the beginning and the end, the first and the last," (Rev. 22:13), and this life is the foundation of all his acts of mediation, as being God over all, blessed forever.

There is however a life which he lives FOR himself, that is, a life of inconceivable glory in his human nature. This is the life which he laid down that he might take it again. This life is the cause of, and is attended with all that ineffable glory which he now enjoys in heaven. This life he lives for himself, his reward, and the glory and honour with which he is crowned. As the Psalmist says, "Thou settest a crown of pure gold on his head. He asked life of thee, and thou gavest it him, even length of days for ever and ever," (Psa. 21:3-4).

However, there is another life which he lives - a mediatorial life which he lives for US. Thus we read that he was made a priest "after the power of an endless life," and he says of himself, "I am he that liveth, and was dead; and, behold, I am alive for evermore, Amen; and have the keys of hell and of death," (Rev. 1:18). Now this life differs from the second life of which I have spoken in that when the work of mediation is accomplished, he will cease to live a mediatorial life. He will then "have delivered up the kingdom to God, even the Father; when he shall have put down all rule and all authority and power," (1Cor. 15:24).

19th

"But we had the sentence of death in ourselves, that we should not trust in ourselves, but in God which raiseth the dead."
2Corinthians 1:9

What is life naturally and what is death naturally? Is not that life in which there is breath, energy, movement, sensation, and activity? And what is death but the utter cessation of all this moving activity, vital energy? To die is to lose life, and by losing life to lose all the movements and sensation of life. Thus, when the Lord takes everything we once held dear, everything in which we once had life, everything in which we lived and moved and seemed to have our earthly, natural, and enjoyed being, and condemns it by his holy word to a continual sentence of death, the judgement ever echoing in our conscience, he delivers us over unto death.

You will observe that none but the living family of God are so delivered, for, as the apostle writes, "we which live are alway delivered unto death for Jesus' sake," (2Cor. 4:11). Observe also that the reason for this mysterious deliverance is to bring to light the hidden life of Jesus within, for he adds, "that the life also of Jesus might be made manifest in our mortal flesh." Observe too the connection which the apostle has made between this sentence of death and the death of Christ. "Always bearing about in the body the dying of the Lord Jesus," (2Cor. 4:10).

We must suffer with our Lord if we are to be glorified with him; we must die with him if we are to live with him. His death is the example; it is the model and the means of our own; and as he had the sentence of death in himself upon the cross, so must we be crucified with him that we may be conformed to his suffering, dying image.

Thus there is a death by, under, and unto the law, so as to kill the soul to all creature hope and help, to all vain confidence, and to all self-righteousness. Howbeit, the continual teachings and dealings of God upon the heart, and especially in times and by means of heavy affliction, painful trial, and powerful temptation, does the Lord by his

Spirit and grace execute a sentence of death only in those to whom he is giving to drink of Christ's cup and to be baptised with Christ's baptism.

20th

"For thy Maker is thine husband; the LORD of hosts is his name; and thy Redeemer the Holy One of Israel; The God of the whole earth shall he be called."
Isaiah 54:5

As in the marriage union man and wife become one flesh, and, God having joined them together, no man may put them asunder, so when the Lord Jesus Christ, in "the everlasting covenant, ordered in all things and sure," betrothed the Church unto himself, he and they became one before the face of heaven in indissoluble ties. As he undertook in "the fullness of time" to be "made of a woman," the church became one with him in body by virtue of a common nature. It then became one with him in spirit when, as each individual member comes forth into time, the blessed Spirit unites them to him by regenerating grace.

Such is the testimony of scripture. "For we are members of his body, of his flesh, and of his bones," (Eph. 5:30), and "he that is joined unto the Lord is one spirit," (1Cor. 6:17). The churches union with his flesh ensures that her body will be conformed to His glorious body in the resurrection morn; and her union with his spirit ensures to her soul an eternity of bliss in the perfection of knowledge, holiness, and love. Thus the union of the Church with Christ, which commenced in the councils of eternal wisdom and love, is made known upon earth by regenerating grace and is perfected in heaven in the fullness of glory.

The Church, it is true, fell in Adam from that state of innocence and purity in which she was originally created. Yet see how the Adamic fall, in all its miserable consequences, instead of cancelling the bond and disannulling the everlasting covenant, only served more fully and gloriously to reveal and make known the love of Christ to his chosen bride in all its breadth and length and depth and height! She fell, it is true, into unspeakable, unfathomable depths of sin and misery, guilt and crime, but she never fell out of his heart or out of his arms.

Without the fall, what would have been known of dying love or of the mystery of the cross! Where would have been found the song of the redeemed? "Unto him that loved us, and washed us from our sins in his own blood... be glory and dominion for ever and ever. Amen!" (Rev. 1:5-6). Where would be the victory over death and hell, or the triumphs of super-abounding grace over the aboundings of sin, guilt, and despair? How could he have "led captivity captive," (Eph. 4:8), and "spoiled principalities and powers, [making] a shew of them openly, triumphing over them in himself?" (Col. 2:15). What would have been known of that most precious of the attributes of God, mercy? How would we have learned of his forbearance and long-suffering, and what of his abounding pity and compassion to the poor, lost children of men?

As then the Church's head and husband could not and would not dissolve the union, break the covenant, or alter the thing that had gone out of his lips, and yet could not still take her openly unto himself in all her filth and guilt and shame, he had to redeem her with his own heart's blood. With agonies and sufferings such as earth or heaven never before witnessed, with those dolorous cries under the hidings of his Father's face, which made the earth to quake, the rocks to rend, and the sun to withdraw its light, he gave his life for her. But his love was stronger than death, and he endured the cross, despising the shame, (Heb. 12:2), bearing her sins in his own body on the tree, (1Pet. 2:24), and thus suffering the penalty due to her crimes, reconciled her unto God "In the body of his flesh through death, to present you holy and unblameable and unreproveable in his sight," (Col. 1:22).

Having thus reconciled her unto God, as she comes forth from the womb of time, he visits member after member of his mystical body with his regenerating grace, that "he might sanctify and cleanse it with the washing of water by the word," (Eph. 5:26). Thus eventually he will be able to "present it to himself a glorious church, not having spot, or wrinkle, or any such thing; but that it should be holy and without blemish," (Eph. 5:27).

21st

"Deliver me from all my transgressions: make me not the reproach of the foolish."
Psalm 39:8

Who are these foolish? I think the best answer to this question is given by our Lord himself, in the parable of the wise and foolish virgins. The foolish were those who had oil in their lamps, but none in their vessels. By 'the foolish', therefore, we may understand those who have the light of knowledge in their heads, and the lamp of profession in their hands, but no oil of grace in their hearts.

They are foolish, because they know neither God nor themselves, neither sin nor salvation, and neither the depth of the fall nor the height of the remedy. They are foolish as regards themselves in thinking that light and knowledge will save them without life and grace, and they are foolish as regards others for lack of an experimental acquaintance with the heart. They know nothing, therefore, of the temptations of a child of God, and how he is beset on every hand; how Satan is ever thrusting at and enticing him, how his own heart is continually prompting him to evil, and how snares are in every direction laid for his feet. The foolish know nothing of these trials. They are Pharisees who "make clean the outside of the cup and of the platter," (Matt. 23:25), and who whitewash and adorn the outside of the sepulchre, "but are within full of dead men's bones, and of all uncleanness," (Matt. 23:27).

David knew well, and every child of God knows well, that if he were allowed to slip, if he were allowed to say or do anything unbecoming, these would be the very first to make him an open reproach. The foolish can and will make no allowances for the least slip of tongue or foot, for they themselves are ignorant of the weakness of the flesh, the subtlety of Satan, the strength of sin, and the power of temptation. Were the saint to stumble and fall, the foolish would be sure to point the finger of scorn at him.

In breathing forth, then, this petition, we may well suppose the psalmist to say, "Lord, whatever temptations I may be called upon to endure, whatever snares of Satan or lusts of the flesh may beset my path, behind and before, keep me! O keep me, keep me that I may not be 'the reproach of the foolish, that they may have nothing to take hold of, nothing to make me a bye-word, and noting through me to reproach thy name, cause, and truth."

22nd

"But we trusted that it had been he which should have redeemed Israel."
Luke 24:21

What a trial to their faith must the death of Jesus have been to his disciples and believing followers! When their Lord and Master died, their hopes, for the time at least, seem almost to have died with him, and indeed to the eye of sense, truth, holiness, and innocence all fell crushed by the arm of violence as Jesus hung on the cross. To the

November

spectator there, all his miracles of love and mercy, his words of grace and truth, his holy, spotless life, his claims to be the Son of God, the promised Messiah, the Redeemer of Israel, with every promise and every prophecy concerning him were all extinguished when, amid the triumph of his foes, in pain, shame, and ignominy, he yielded up his breath.

We now see that by his blood-shedding and death, the blessed Lord wrought out redemption, finished the work which the Father gave him to do and put away sin by the sacrifice of himself. He reconciled the Church unto God, triumphed over death and hell, vanquished Satan, magnified the law and made it honourable, exalted justice, brought in mercy, harmonised every apparently jarring attribute, glorified his heavenly Father, and saved millions with an everlasting salvation.

Yet would we have seen this as we see it now had we stood at the cross with weeping Mary and broken-hearted John, heard the railing taunts of the scribes and Pharisees, the crude laughter of the Roman soldiery, and the mocking cries of the Jewish mob? If we had viewed the darkened sky above, and felt the solid earth beneath rocking under our feet, where would our faith have been then? What but a miracle of almighty grace and power could have sustained it amid such clouds of darkness, such strength of sense, such a crowd of conflicting passions, such opposition of unbelief?

So it ever has been, and so it ever will be in this world. Truth, uprightness, godliness and the cause of God as distinct from and opposed to error and evil, have always suffered crucifixion, not only in the Person, but also in the example of a crucified Jesus. It is an ungodly world. Satan, not Jesus, is its god and prince. Not truth but falsehood, not good but evil, not love but enmity, not sincerity and uprightness but craft and deceptiveness, not righteousness and holiness but sin and godlessness prevail and triumph as they did at the cross.

This tries the faith of saints, but its relief and remedy are to look up amid these clouds to the cross, and see on it the suffering Son of God. Then we see that the triumphing of the wicked is but for a moment; that though truth is now suffering, it is suffering with Christ; and that as he died and rose again, so it will have a glorious resurrection, and an eternal triumph.

23rd

"Who against hope believed in hope."
Romans 4:18

November

Hope is a fruit of the Spirit. The absence of hope, the thorough, complete absence of it, stamps death upon that nominal branch, in which the absence of all hope is found. But some will say, 'Are not the children of God often plunged into despair?' No; they are never plunged totally into despair. They are often very near it, they are on the borders of it; they go to the very brink of it; the gusts from that pestiferous land may so blow their blasts and tug upon them, that in their feelings they shall be in despair; yet no living soul ever set his foot beyond the brink. No child of God ever stepped beyond the border, so as to get into the regions of complete despair. If he got there, he would no longer be in "the land of the living," (Ezek. 32:27). If ever he set his foot over the border that separates the land of hope from the land of despair, he would be no longer calling upon the Lord to save his soul from the lowest hell, but he would be at once overwhelmed by those torrents, which would sweep him away into endless perdition.

Hell is the place of despair, and of the conscience of the reprobate before he is cast into those devouring flames. Unless you know what the very feelings of the damned in hell are, (which you can never be certain you do however much you may think you know them), or unless you have gone into the very feelings of despair in the conscience of the reprobate as hell opens its jaws to receive him forever, however near you have been to the borders of that dreadful land, you never can say your foot has crossed the threshold.

No. There is always a 'Who can tell?' a secret support of "the everlasting arms." There is a band, a tie, wreathed around the soul by the God of all grace. There is a golden chain let down by God himself from the everlasting throne of mercy and truth which keeps the soul from ever being drawn into that whirlpool, going down those tremendous cataracts, and being swallowed up in the boiling abyss below. There is an invisible arm that preserves the soul from being swept away by the water-floods, and this secret help is manifested by a lifting up of the heart oftentimes in prayer, and the relief sometimes experienced in pouring forth the soul in fervent cries. Such upholds all who feel it from being overwhelmed in the torrent of despair, when the sluices of God's wrath seem opened to hurry them into eternal misery.

Therefore there is no child of God that has been quickened by the Spirit who does not have some degree of hope left in him which keeps him from making shipwreck altogether. It is this that ensures we do not go too far in saying that the absence of hope altogether stamps death upon a man.

November
24th

"But we are not of them who draw back unto perdition; but of them that believe to the saving of the soul."
Hebrews 10:39

The Scriptures have brought certain marks not only to test, but also to comfort God's people. In order to keep them tremblingly alive to the fear of being deceived, and in order to set up an effectual beacon lest their vessel should run upon the rocks, the blessed Spirit has revealed such passages as we find in the sixth and tenth chapters of the Hebrews. They seem set up by the Spirit of God as a lighthouse at the entrance of a harbour. Is it not so naturally? The mariner often has to guard against some shoal or sandbank that lies near a port entrance, but how is he guarded? A lighthouse is erected on or near the spot, which warns him of the danger.

Now, I look on the sixth and tenth chapters of the Epistle to the Hebrews as two lighthouses standing in the approach to the harbour of eternal life, and their language is, 'Beware of this shoal! Take care of that sand-bank! There are gifts without grace; there is profession without possession; there is form without power; there is a name to live while the soul is dead.'

The shoal often lies at the very entrance of a harbour, almost as though the harbour attracted it there. It is the same with the sandbank which often lies right in the optimum path for the ship making for port; but when the harbour is neared, the friendly beacon not only warns her of the shoal, but also points out the safe passage into the haven. And so spiritually, from these two chapters many of God's people have seen what shoals lie in the way, and have, perhaps, before they were warned off, come near enough to see the shipwrecked vessels. The gallant barks that sailed from the same port with themselves they have seen wrecked on the rocks, the freight lost, and the dead bodies and broken fragments floating on the waves.

But these never looked for the lighthouse, nor saw the bank; they were intoxicated, or fast asleep; they were sure of going to heaven; and on they went, reckless and thoughtless, until the vessel struck on the danger, and all on board perished. These dreadful warnings and solemn admonitions seem to me so written that they may scrape, so to speak, as nearly as possible the quick of a man's flesh, and they appear couched in language of purposed ambiguity that they may be deliberately trying passages. The very beauty and efficacy of them, and the real good to be wrought by them, is in their ambiguity, so that the people of God may take a more solemn warning by them, and may cry unto the Lord more earnestly that they may not be deceived.

Then it is not the poor, desponding children of God who are tried by these passages, and that have reason to fear them. Their being thus tried shows that their conscience is tender in God's fear, and that they are "the earth which drinketh in the rain that cometh oft upon it, and bringeth forth herbs meet for them by whom it is dressed, [and] receiveth blessing from God," (Heb. 6:7). Their fear shows that they are not that "that which beareth thorns and briers [and] is rejected, and is nigh unto cursing; whose end is to be burned," (Heb. 6:8).

Thus, these very fears and suspicions by which many of God's people are exercised, causing strong cries unto the Lord that he would teach, guide, and lead them, are so many blessed marks that they are not graceless persons, but partakers of the grace of God. At the same time proving, "that he which hath begun a good work in [them] will perform it until the day of Jesus Christ," (Phil. 1:6), and bring them into the eternal enjoyment of God that they may see him for themselves and not another.

25th

"There is a path which no fowl knoweth, and which the vulture's eye hath not seen."
Job 28:7

Growth in grace is not progressive sanctification and fleshly holiness on the one hand, nor a false and delusive establishment on the other. The narrow path lies between these two extremes. On the one side is Pharisaic holiness, on the other Antinomian security; and between these two sharp rocks lies the "path which no fowl knoweth, and which the vulture's eye hath not seen."

From dashing on either of these rocks a living man is kept only by the mysterious dealings of God with his spirit, and the internal exercises through which he continually passes. A constant acquaintance with his own vileness preserves him from a self-righteous holiness in the flesh; a daily cross and a rankling thorn keep him from careless presumption. His path is indeed a mysterious one, full of harmonious contradictions and heavenly paradoxes. He is never easy when at ease, nor without a burden when he has none. He is never satisfied without doing something, and yet is never satisfied with anything that he does. He is never so strong as when he sits still, never so fruitful as when he does nothing, and never so active as when he makes the least haste.

All outstrip him in the race, yet he alone gains the goal, and wins the prize. All are sure of heaven but himself, yet he enters into the kingdom, while they are thrust out. He wins pardon through guilt, hope through despair, deliverance through temptation, comfort through affliction, and a robe of righteousness through filthy rags.

Though a worm and no man, he overcomes Omnipotence itself through violence; and though less than vanity and nothing, he takes heaven itself by force. Thus amid the strange contradictions which meet in a believing heart, he is never so prayerful as when he says nothing; never so wise as when he is the greatest fool; never so much alone as when most in company; and never so much under the power of an inward religion as when most separated from an outward one.

26th

"For other foundation can no man lay than that is laid, which is Jesus Christ."
1Corinthians 3:11

We are very eager to put our hands to work. Like Uzzah, we must needs prop up the ark when we see it tumbling; when faith totters, we must come to bear a helping hand. But this is prejudicial to the work of God upon the soul. If the whole is to be a spiritual building; if we are "living stones" built upon a living Head, every stone in that spiritual temple must be laid by God the Spirit. And if so, everything of nature, of creature, of self, must be effectually laid low that Christ may be all – that Christ, and Christ alone, may be formed in our heart, the hope of glory.

How many trials some of you have passed through! How many sharp and cutting exercises, how many harassing temptations, how many sinkings of heart, how many fiery darts from hell, and how many doubts and fears have blocked your path. How much hard bondage has wearied you, and how many galling chains have bound you before the iron has oft entered into your soul!

Why is this? It is that you may be prevented from adding one stone by your own hands to the spiritual building.

The apostle tells us in our text that, "other foundation can no man lay than that is laid, which is Jesus Christ." He goes on to speak of those who build "wood, hay, and stubble," on this foundation as well as of those who used "gold, silver, and precious stones." Howbeit the "wood, hay, and stubble" must be burned with fire. It is after the Lord has already laid the foundation in the sinner's conscience, brought him near to himself, made himself precious to the sinner's soul and raised up hope and love in his heart, that he becomes apt to take up materials that God never recognises. He piles up the wood, hay, straw, and stubble of his own ideas and efforts to rear a flimsy superstructure of his own upon the divine foundation. Yet this gives way in the trying hour - it cannot stand up to a single gust of temptation. One spark of the wrath to come, one discovery of God's dread majesty, will burn up this "wood, hay, and stubble" like straw in the oven.

The Lord's people, therefore, have to pass through troubles, trials, exercises, and temptations, doubts and fears, and all that harassing path that they usually walk in, that they may be prevented from erecting a superstructure of nature upon the foundation of grace. The "wood, hay, and stubble" of man cannot stand upon the glorious mystery of an incarnate God.

27th

"And if Christ be in you, the body is dead because of sin; but the Spirit is life because of righteousness."
Romans 8:10

We need two things in lively operation – a spiritual death and a spiritual life. We need death put upon the flesh, upon sin, upon everything which is ungodly, that it may not reign or rule; and we need also the communication and maintenance of a divine life which shall act towards God, exist and co-exist in the same breast, and be in activity at the same moment.

Here is sin striving for the mastery, but here also is a view of the cross of Christ, a testimony of bleeding, dying love. This puts a death upon sin, but as death is put upon sin and the lust is mortified, crucified, resisted, or subdued, there springs up a life of faith and prayer, of hope and love, of repentance and godly sorrow for sin, of humility and spirituality, of a desire to live to God's praise and walk in his fear.

The cross gives both. From the cross comes death unto sin, and from the cross comes life unto righteousness. From the cross springs the healing of every bleeding wound, and from the cross springs every motive to a godly life. Thus, in God's mysterious wisdom, there is a way whereby sin can be pardoned, the law magnified, justice exalted, the sinner saved, sin subdued, righteousness given, and the soul made to walk in the ways of peace and holiness.

November

Oh, what depths of wisdom, mercy, and grace are here! Look where you will, try every mode, if you are sincere about your soul's salvation, if the Lord the Spirit has planted the fear of God in your heart you will find no other way but this. There is no other way that leads to holiness here and heaven hereafter. There is no other way whereby sin can be pardoned and the soul sanctified. It is this view of salvation from sin not only in its guilt but also in its power, this deliverance from the curse of the law and well-spring of all holy, acceptable obedience, which has in all ages so endeared the cross to the souls of God's family. It is this wonderful sufficiency that has made all of them more or less to be of Paul's mind, when he declared that he was determined to know nothing except Jesus Christ and him crucified.

28th

"But thou, O LORD, art a shield for me; my glory, and the lifter up of mine head."
Psalm 3:3

If your soul has ever been favoured with a taste of mercy, with a sip of the brook by the way; if ever your conscience has felt the application of atoning blood, or the love of God has ever been shed abroad in your heart by the Holy Spirit, when the law comes to curse you, remember always that the Lord Jesus Christ stands as a shield between it and you. The law has therefore nothing to do with those who believe, for it has cursed Christ in your stead. As the Apostle declares, he was "made a curse for us," (Gal. 3:13), and also, he "bare our sins in his own body on the tree," (1Pet. 2:24). Therefore, the law has nothing to do with you who believe in Christ Jesus. He has intercepted the curse for you, and, by receiving it into his own body and soul, bore it harmless away from you.

It is a blessed act of faith when you can thus take Christ in your arms and hold him up as a shield between the law and your conscience. The Apostle seems to hint at this in a measure when he says, "Above all, taking the shield of faith, wherewith ye shall be able to quench all the fiery darts of the wicked," (Eph. 6:16), for many of these fiery darts are taken from the law. It is indeed a great and special act of faith thus to take Jesus Christ in the arms, and holding him up in the face of the law, to be able to say, 'Law, thou hast nothing to do with me; Jesus hath fulfilled all thy righteous demands, and endured all thy tremendous curses. He is my shield, to protect me from thy condemning sentence; and all thy curses are harmless; they all fall short of me because they all fell wholly upon him.'

I say this is a special act of faith because we cannot do it except as divinely enabled. Otherwise, it would be but an act of presumption. I may add that it is a very rare thing to be enabled so to take Christ and hold him up as a shield against the curses of the law; but when done under the influences and operations of the blessed Spirit, it is an act of faith which God approves of and honours. Nor is there any other shield to intercept the tremendous curse of the law.

29th

"This charge I commit unto thee, son Timothy, according to the prophecies which went before on thee, that thou by them mightest war a good warfare; holding faith, and a good conscience; which some having put away concerning faith have made shipwreck."
1Timothy 1:18-19

This "good warfare" is carried on against three principal enemies – the flesh, the world, and the devil. Howbeit, each of these enemies is so closely allied to ourselves, and each is so powerful and so hostile, that they must surely overcome us unless we are "strengthened with might by his Spirit in the inner man," (Eph. 3:16).

There is the flesh, with all its baits, charms, and subtle attractions. It is continually laying its snares and traps for our feet, perpetually entangling us in some evil word or some evil work, and we in ourselves our utterly defenceless against it. Said I defenceless? Of ourselves yes, for we are eager to run into it, like the silly bird that sees the seeds of grain spread in the trap, but thinks not when it flutters around it that the trap will fall and confine it a prisoner. So we, allured by a few tempting morsels of grain spread before our eyes, often see not the snare until we are fast entangled therein.

Faith then is that eye of the soul which sees the concealed hook; by faith we call upon the Lord to deliver us from snatching at the bait; and by faith, as a spiritual weapon, we cut at times the snare asunder. Oh, how defenceless are we when the temptations and allurements of the flesh plead for indulgence unless faith is in exercise, unless faith realises the hatred of God against sin, and brings into our consciences a sense of God's heart-searching eye, and his wrath against all transgression!

Yet where the Lord has put this weapon of faith into the hand of his soldier he will often strengthen his arm to wield it in these seasons of extremity, even though that weapon should cut and wound his own flesh. See how Joseph was enabled to resist the snares spread for his feet by calling to mind the presence of the Lord! How he was strengthened to break asunder that bond which was fast twining round his heart, when faith sprang up in his soul, and he said, "How then can I do this great wickedness, and sin against God?" (Gen. 39:9).

See how the three young men who were about to be cast into the burning, fiery furnace unless they would worship the golden image that Nebuchadnezzar had set up, overcame that dreadful temptation to renounce their God and prove apostates by this living faith! Oh, what a weapon faith is when the Lord does but give us power to wield it! How, as Deer says, it "cuts the way through hosts of devils, while they fall before the word."

Yet when sin, temptation, and unbelief shake this weapon out of our hands, when it lies seemingly shattered at our feet, and we cannot get another such sword from God's armoury, how we stand naked and defenceless before our enemies! Therefore what need we have not merely of this heavenly grace in our souls, but to hold it fast and not let it go, lest the enchantress should catch our feet in her wiles and snares.

So, when Satan comes in with his fierce temptations and fiery darts, what but faith can enable the soul to stand up against them, as the Apostle says, "Above all, taking the shield of faith, wherewith ye shall be able to quench all the fiery darts of the wicked," (Eph. 6:16). Nothing but faith in God's power and presence; nothing but faith in Jesus's blood and righteousness; nothing but faith in the holy Spirit's lifting up a standard in the heart by means of his divine operations; in short nothing but faith in our triune God can enable the soul to battle against Satan's assaults. Therefore see how indispensable faith is to fight a good fight, yes, so indispensable that a good fight is called emphatically "the fight of faith," (1Tim. 6:12), and we are called to fight the good fight of faith, implying that true faith will enable a man to come off more than conqueror through every battle and to survive every conflict.

30th

"I will overturn, overturn, overturn, it: and it shall be no more, until he come whose right it is; and I will give it him." Ezekiel 21:27

There is then one to come who has a "right"; a King, who has a right to the throne and to the allegiance of his subjects; a right to all that they are and to all that they have; but whence has he gained this right? Rights to kingship are inherent, therefore his first right is conferred by being the Son of God, but what of his rights on this earth? His first rights here are by original donation and gift, the Father who created this earth, having given to the Son all the elect. "Father, I will that they also, whom thou hast given me, be with me where I am," (John 17:24), says Jesus, and also, "all that the Father giveth me shall come to me," (John 6:27). Then, so far as we are his, Jesus has a right to our persons; and in having a right to our persons, he has, by the same original donation of God the Father, a right to our hearts and affections.

Howbeit he has another right, and that is by purchase and redemption, having redeemed his people with his own blood and laid down his life for them. Thus he has bought and purchased them, and has established a right to them by the full and complete price which he himself paid down upon the cross for them. This twofold right he exercises every time he lays a solemn claim to any one of the people whom he has purchased. This also is the claim he lays when the blessed Spirit comes into the soul to arrest and apprehend a vessel of mercy, and bring it to his feet that he may be enthroned as King and Lord in its affections.

For be it remembered, that the possession of the heart with all its affections is his right. "I am the LORD: that is my name: and my glory will I not give to another, neither my praise to graven images," (Isa. 42:8). He will not allow his property to pass into other hands. Neither is he satisfied with merely having a right to the persons of his dear people, he wishes to give them all his love, and for that he must have their hearts. In exercising his right to bestow his affection and claim their affection, he will reign and rule supreme, blocking out any inferior rival, and therefore admitting no co-operation with self either, so that for their eternal benefit he alone is established as King and Lord in their hearts.

Then where is the soul before he comes into it in power, in sweetness, in beauty, and in preciousness? What and where do we find it? A heap of ruins, that's what.

No man ever found out about the preciousness of Christ whose soul was not made a heap of ruins, and in whom self had not been thoroughly overturned and cast to the ground. No man ever ardently panted that the Lord of life and glory should visit his heart with his salvation, should come in the power of his resurrection, in the glory of his righteousness and in the preciousness of his presence until self was strewn in pieces on the field of life. No man ever spiritually desired, sighed, cried, groaned, sued, and begged for the manifestation of Christ to his soul, who was not a ruined wretch before God, and in whom self had not been so overturned as to be a desolate heap, so overthrown that all the power of man could not put any one stone back in its place, or rebuild the former edifice.

December

December
1st

"According as he hath chosen us in him before the foundation of the world, that we should be holy and without blame before him in love: having predestinated us unto the adoption of children by Jesus Christ to himself, according to the good pleasure of his will."
Ephesians 1:4-5

It is a very solemn but a very true assertion that no man can quicken his own soul. It is an equally solemn, we might almost say a tremendous truth, that the gospel only comes in power to those whom God has chosen unto eternal life. Indeed the one flows from the other, for if no man can quicken his own soul, it necessarily follows that sovereign grace must quicken it if it is to be quickened at all. Acknowledge the fall, and acknowledge that a man is by nature so thoroughly dead in trespasses and sins that he cannot raise himself up out of this state to newness of life, and the doctrine of election necessarily follows.

A living soul may reason thus:

"Am I quickened? Yes.

Did I quicken myself? No. I could not, for I was dead in sin.

Did God then quicken me? Yes. Who but he could have given life to my dead soul!

Why did he quicken me? Because he loved me, and chose me in Christ to be an heir of his eternal glory.

Whether you can speak thus or not, there is no doubt that the Lord has a people who are dear to him, and to whom he makes himself dear. These, though despised or unnoticed by men, are the elect of God. If you are a vessel of mercy whom he has thus chosen to eternal life, the gospel either has come already, or in his own time and way it will be made to come with power to your heart and conscience.

2nd

"To declare, I say, at this time his righteousness: that he might be just, and the justifier of him which believeth in Jesus."
Romans 3:26

December

Every created thing, every finite intelligence, must sooner be annihilated than Jehovah can sacrifice or allow the slightest tarnish to come over any one of his eternal attributes. Yet God is just, infinitely just, scrupulously just, unchangeably just - and yet, whilst preserving his attribute of justice unchanging and unchangeable, he is still the justifier of those who believe in Jesus. The way by which this is effected will take a countless eternity to understand, and a boundless eternity to admire and adore.

Yet what is meant by the expression, "the justifier?" It means that God can change a man's status to count him as righteous, he can freely pardon his sins, he can graciously accept his person, he can impute to him righteousness without works and can bring him to the eternal enjoyment of himself. All this he can accomplish whilst remaining scrupulously and unchangeably just.

Who are these whom he thus brings to himself by so justifying them? Why, them "which believe in Jesus." What simplicity and yet what sweetness and suitability do we find imbued in the gospel plan!

Imagine that the passage ran thus, "that he might be just, and the justifier of him that worketh and pleaseth God by his own performances, and that produceth his own righteousness satisfactory to the eyes of infinite purity." Who then could be saved? Would there be a single soul in heaven? No. Such a sentence as that would be a sentence of death, and would trample down the whole human race into hell.

Howbeit, for our eternal sakes, the passage runs after this manner. "This is the mind and purpose of God, that in his eternal counsel, which cannot pass away, he is "the justifier of him which believeth in Jesus," so that the poor, the needy, the exercised, the tempted, the distressed, and the perplexed, which all believe in Jesus, which look unto him, lean upon him, and rest in his Person, blood, righteousness, and love for all things, need not fear. These are justified, these are pardoned, these are accepted, these are graciously received, and saved with an everlasting salvation."

How sweet and how suitable then does the gospel that declares this become to the living, believing soul!

3rd

"If we confess our sins, he is faithful and just to forgive us our sins, and to cleanse us from all unrighteousness."
1John 1:9

December

"He is faithful and just." Oh, what a word is just! There is scarcely to my mind such a word in the Bible as that; so great, so glorious, so comforting - "He is faithful and just."

'Just?' say you. 'Why, I know that God's mercy and grace can pardon sinners, but how can a just God pardon transgressors? Does not God's justice demand the punishment of sin? Does not God's justice blaze forth in eternal lightnings against the soul that transgresses his holy law? How then can it be true that God can be just and forgive rather than punish a confessing sinner?'

Yet I say it is true, divinely True, blessedly, eternally true, and in it is locked up that grand mystery of redemption by the blood and obedience of God's co-equal Son. It is all locked up in this one word, "just," and in this way. The Lord of life and glory became both security and substitute for those whom his Father gave to him. He entered into their place and stead. He endured the punishment that was due to them. For them he fulfilled the whole law by his doings and by his sufferings. For them he bled, and for them he died. For them he rose again, and for them ascended up to the right hand of the Father. So now, instead of demanding death, justice demands the sinner's pardon, and puts in its plea of righteousness.

See the difference. Mercy begs but justice demands. Mercy says, 'I ask it as a boon,' and as part of God's character, looks down with pity and compassion on the mourning criminal. Then justice answers, 'It is his due. It is his right. Such mercy belongs to him and is his because the Redeemer has discharged his debt, because the Surety has stood in his place, because the Saviour has obeyed that law for him which he could not obey in his own person.'

So when we can receive this blessed and glorious truth, that to those who confess their sins, "God is faithful," and not merely faithful but also "just to forgive them their sins," how it draws out of the bosom of Jehovah a full, free, and irrevocable pardon of all transgressions. How his mercy and justice smile, and yet more especially on those transgressions that the sinner confesses at his footstool!

4th

"For I am poor and needy, and my heart is wounded within me."
Psalm 109:22

The needy is a character who is not merely poor, empty, and naked before God, but who is feelingly in need of spiritual blessings to be applied to his soul. Some people can rest on temptations, and take temptations as evidences. Others can build on doubts and fears, and rest on doubts and fears as evidences. Some can take powerful past convictions, or present convictions, and lean on them as evidences. Others can look to a profession of religion, and take that as an evidence, but these are not alive.

A living soul must have heavenly blessings communicated immediately to his heart and conscience directly from the mouth of God. He must have deliverance manifested to his soul as a reality, and have the blood of Jesus sprinkled on his conscience with divine power to purge it from filth and dead works. He must have his eyes anointed with eye-salve to see Jesus, and his soul pants to be led up into sweet communion with his Lord. He needs to be taken spiritually into fellowship with Christ that he may see him with the eyes of his soul, that he may look upon him whom he has pierced, mourn over him and for him and with him, and have some sweet, spiritual, and supernatural manifestation of his dying love to his soul.

A nominal Christ will never do for a needy sinner. It must be Christ made spiritually known by the power of the Holy Spirit, sweetly revealed and coming into his heart with all his blessed efficacy, and shining into his soul like the sun in his strength, beaming forth blessed rays of grace and mercy. Nothing but this will ever satisfy a soul that has life in it.

5th

"For whom the Lord loveth he chasteneth, and scourgeth every son whom he receiveth."
Hebrews 12:6

Does not James say, "Blessed is the man that endureth temptation," (Jas. 1:12), and again, "count it all joy when ye fall into divers temptations," (Jas. 1:2)? Why is this? Is there any joy in trial, or any pleasure in sorrow? No. Yet there is joy in deliverance by the Lord therefrom, and in the power of God put forth to bring the soul out of trial. Therefore we have to walk in a dark path to make the light dear to our eyes; we have to pass through trials to taste the sweetness of the promises when applied with power, and we have to endure temptations that we may enjoy the blessedness of deliverance. This is the way, be sure of it, that God deals with his people.

Is your conscience made honest? Does that monitor in your bosom speak the truth? Tell me now what it says. Does it not agree that few trials bring few consolations, and few sorrows bring few joys? Will few difficulties yield but few testimonies from God and few sufferings result in only a few discoveries of love and blood? As the apostle says, "For as the sufferings of Christ abound in us, so our consolation also aboundeth by Christ," (2Cor. 1:5), and also of the sufferings, so shall ye be also of the consolation," (2Cor. 1:7)?

Further, he brings back to our minds the words of the wisest man who ever lived, (Prov. 3:11), regarding what the Lord says of his people and that the lot of a child is to endure chastisement.

"My son, despise not thou the chastening of the Lord, nor faint when thou art rebuked of him: for whom the Lord loveth he chasteneth, and scourgeth every son whom he receiveth. If ye endure chastening, God dealeth with you as with sons; for what son is he whom the father chasteneth not? But if ye be without chastisement," (O solemn word, and how applicable to thousands today!), "whereof all are partakers, then are ye bastards, and not sons," (Heb. 12: 5-8).

Is it then joyful to be tempted and tried by sin and Satan? Not in the endurance of it, I grant; but in the fact of it, in the deliverance from it, and in the realisation of sonship that it brings there is indeed great joy, and great assurance of soul.

6th

"O LORD of hosts, blessed is the man that trusteth in thee."
Psalm 84:12

Trust in God implies total self-renunciation. The moment that I trust in myself, I cease to trust in God. The moment I take any portion of my confidence away from the Lord and put a grain of it in myself, that moment I take away *all* my trust in God. My trust in God must be all or nothing. It must be unreserved and complete, or else it is false and delusive. Is not the Lord worthy to be trusted? And if he is worthy to be trusted at all, is he not worthy to be trusted with all? What real confidence could a man have in the wife of his bosom if he could trust her with one key, but not with all*?* Is that full confidence? So, if we can trust God for one thing and not for all, it shows that we have no real trust in him.

A man has no real trust in his wife who cannot give her all the keys, and a man has no real trust in God who cannot give him all his heart, and put everything into his hand; family, property, body, and soul. The province and work of true faith is to put everything into the hands of God, keeping back no part of the price. God hates this secret, hidden reserve. There is hypocrisy written on the very face of it. Trust in God for nothing or trust in him for all. God will not take a divided heart. Give him all, or give him none.

Is he not worthy of it? Has he ever disappointed you whenever you have really put your trust in him? Did he not say, "Have I been a wilderness unto Israel? a land of darkness? wherefore say my people, We are lords; we will come no more unto thee?" (Jer. 2:31).

Howbeit David saw how few there were that with all their hearts did trust in God. This feeling seems to have made him say, "Blessed is the man," that peculiar man, that rare individual, "that trusteth in thee," (Psa. 84:12). The blessing of God rests upon that happy, that highly-favoured man. He is blessed for time and for eternity. He has the blessing of God even now in his soul.

Oh how rare it is for us to be in that sweet, blessed frame when we can put our trust wholly in God, when we can trust him for life and death, and for all things, past, present, and to come. Yet without a measure of this faith, there is no solid peace, no real and abiding rest, and to this you must sooner or later come; for you cannot carry your own burdens without their breaking your back. But when you can cast your burden on the Lord, then you will surely find sweet relief.

May we not, then, join heart and voice with David and say, "O Lord of hosts, blessed is the man that trusteth in thee"? Such an one will never be disappointed. The Lord will hear his prayer; the Lord will bless his soul; the Lord will be with him in life, support him in death, and take him to be with him for all eternity.

7th

"He that overcometh shall inherit all things;"
Revelation 21:7

He "shall inherit all things." When? In eternity? Yes. Only in eternity? Oh no! In time also. There is a twofold inheritance, though it is but one and the same. One part is given in time, the other part in eternity. One part is the firstfruits, the other the harvest. One part is the pledge, the other the full sum. There is an inheriting here below and an inheriting up above, and he that receives no inheritance here on earth will receive no inheritance in heaven.

Now, in like proportion as we overcome in this life, are we put in possession of this inheritance. What therefore are we to inherit?

Riches, glory, honour, power, praise? These are worldly things; let the world enjoy them. By inheriting "all things," we are to inherit the things of God; the favour of God, the love of God, the mercy of God, and the glory of God. All that a covenant God gives in giving himself is ours; peace here and glory hereafter; pardon below and salvation above; the beginning of rest on earth and the fullness of rest in heaven.

Howbeit, whilst we are overcome, there is no being put into possession of this eternal inheritance. Does sin overcome us? Do we inherit pardon in being overcome? No, we inherit shame and confusion, guilt, fear and wrath. But do you, do I, ever overcome sin by the fear of God in our soul, as Joseph did? Do I ever overcome sin by looking to the Lord of life and glory to sprinkle his blood upon my conscience? Do I ever overcome sin by the leadings and teachings of the Spirit in my heart? No sooner do I thus overcome by the blood of the Lamb, and the word of his testimony, than I enter into the inheritance. There is therefore a connection, a beautiful and experimental connection, between overcoming here below, and inheriting here below.

To enter into this inheritance here below, we must be perpetually reminded that we have no strength of our own. Thus our slips, our falls, our backslidings, our frailties, (though we would not and dare not justify them), are mercifully overruled among the "all things" that work together for our good. They teach us our weakness, and by teaching us our weakness they lead us up to Christ's strength; and by leading us up to Christ's strength they enable us to "inherit all things," for in inheriting him, we inherit all that he is to God's people here on earth.

8th

"And I will be his God, and he shall be my son."
Revelation 21:7

What a promise! The God of heaven and earth will be not only our God, but our Father, our Benefactor, and our eternal, almighty Friend! Further, in overcoming we shall receive the adoption of sons, shall be manifested as the "sons and daughters" of the Almighty, and will receive the inheritance reserved for the children of God!

Now, the promise runs in connection with the qualifier "he that overcometh." If we do not overcome, then the promise is not for us. The promise of sonship is connected with overcoming, in the same manner as the inheritance is connected with it. Do I need to receive into my heart the Spirit of adoption? Do I need to feel the love of God the Father shed abroad in my soul? Do I need to establish a blessed title to the inheritance that he gives to his children? How am I to get it? How is it to be obtained? By making myself religious, by becoming holy, by subduing my lusts in my own strength? Friend, this sets me farther from God than I was before! This makes me a god to myself! If I am saved by my own holiness, by my own strength, by my own righteousness, I am worshiping myself, and in worshiping myself, I become my own god. That is idolatry, damnable idolatry, and he who lives and dies in the worship of self, will live and die under the wrath of God as an idolater.

Then how am I to receive adoption? By overcoming, but not in my own strength, rather only in the strength of the Lord of life and glory. If I rely on my own strength then am I shut up in self, and I inherit self and nothing more. If I shut out the Lord, then I am constrained only to inherit sin and the world, and I will have no part in heaven. If I inherit sin, I inherit death, and nothing more, for death is the wages of sin.

Yet if I overcome, if weak, helpless, and defenceless, I yield myself up to the hands of the Lord, as clay in the hands of the Potter, seeking not my own will, it is clear I am not relying on my own strength. If looking to the Lord to make known his will in my conscience and to work in me that which is well-pleasing in his sight, then I have an evidence of sonship! If there is one evidence, there will be a further evidence of it in the Spirit of adoption, enabling the soul to call God "Father." And he that calls God "Father" here below, will call God "Father" above, where he will enter into the full enjoyment of it, and bathe in the consolations of Father, Son, and Spirit to all eternity.

9th

"Then shall the dust return to the earth as it was: and the spirit shall return unto God who gave it."
Ecclesiastes 12:7

Nature shrinks from death, even apart from that which following after death makes it to so much a king of terrors. Even where grace has set up its throne, and mercy rejoices over judgment, many unbelieving, infidel thoughts at times will cross the mind and perplex the judgment about the separation of body and soul, and the launching of the spirit into an unseen, unknown world. Faith, it is true, can subdue these perplexing thoughts, better hinted at than

December

described, but faith needs some solid ground on which to build and rest. If, then, the soul is blessed with any assured hope or sweet persuasion of saving interest in the blood and obedience of the Lord Jesus Christ so as to remove guilty fears, how strengthening to faith is a view of his death, not merely as the only sacrifice for sin, but as the exemplar of our own.

We shall all die, and therefore looking by faith at the death of Jesus may be a profitable subject of meditation as a relief against the perplexing thoughts to which we have. Into his Father's hands the dying Lord commended his spirit, (Luke 23:46), and the Father received it, for the Father always hears him, (John 11:42). Thus his spirit returned unto him who gave it, and by the act of dying, the soul and body of the blessed Redeemer were, for a time, fully and actually separated - as fully and actually as ours will also be at death.

Now follow by faith that soul of Jesus when he breathed it forth, and view it at once and immediately entering paradise, into the blissful presence of God. What food for faith is here! How strengthening, how encouraging to a believing heart which has often been perplexed by such thoughts as we have named, to view the soul of Jesus thus passing at once into paradise.

May we not also view by faith the soul also of the believing malefactor, when the time of release was come, winging its flight into the same paradise where the soul of Jesus had preceded it? If we know anything painfully and experimentally of the assaults of unbelief, the arrows of infidelity, and the fiery darts of the wicked one, and how they are all quenched by the shield of faith, we have found already that in order to stand firm, faith must have the word of truth. It must have a "Thus says the Lord," to rest upon. We can now see how this stands as connected with the death of the blessed Lord. Fortified by his holy example, if blessed with faith in his Person, blood, and righteousness, the dying believer may commend his spirit into the hands of Christ as did martyred Stephen, in the same confidence that the Lord Jesus commended his spirit into the hands of his heavenly Father.

10th

"My soul thirsteth for God, for the living God."
Psalm 42:2

Has your heart ever panted after the Lord Jesus as the deer pants after the water brooks? Do you ever find yourself lying in the dust mourning over your sins against the bleeding, dying love of Jesus?

Do you ever ask God to kindle in your soul an intense desire to have Jesus as your Christ, that he may be your delight here and your portion forever? Surely there is that in him which is not to be found in anything below the skies, and which if not found here will not be found hereafter. If you have no love or affection for him, why is it but because he has not endeared himself to your soul? Yet if he has manifested himself to you, you have seen and felt enough of his blessedness to convince you that there is no real peace or happiness out of him.

It is true that you may have many trials and temptations to encounter, and many perplexities and sorrows may be spread in your path. However, be not dismayed, for the love of Christ, if you have ever felt that love shed abroad in your heart, will bear you more than conqueror through them all. May the Lord make and keep us faithful to the truth as it has been made known to our consciences, and may the goodness and mercy of God shine into our hearts and shed abroad its rays of light and joy in our darkest moments and under our severest trials. O how precious to be found in him on the great day, to be found members of his body and partakers of his flesh and bones, to be found the Lord's "peculiar treasure" when he makes up his jewels!

Where then will be those be who are not found in the Lord Jesus? They will call upon the mountains and the rocks to fall on them and hide them "from the face of him that sitteth on the throne, and from the wrath of the Lamb," (Rev. 6:16).

11th

"But so did not I, because of the fear of God."
Nehemiah 5:15

We can never praise God sufficiently for his restraining grace; for what would we be without it? What an unspeakable mercy, then, it is, that you cannot be what you would be, nor act as you would act, nor speak what you would speak, nor do the things you would do, because there is in you who fear God. What relief that there is a spiritual principle which holds you up, and keeps you back from the ways of sin and death in which the flesh would walk.

How this spirit of grace and godly fear kept Joseph in the hour of temptation! How it preserved David when he had Saul in his power as he slept in the cave! How it kept Nehemiah in the fear of God from extortion and oppression, and how, in many tens of thousands of instances, it has preserved the feet of the saints. How it has kept them from doing things that would have ruined their reputation, blighted their character, brought reproach upon the cause of God, and the greatest grief and distress into their own conscience!

12th

"I lead in the way of righteousness, in the midst of the paths of judgment; that I may cause those that love me to inherit substance."
Proverbs 8:20-21

How does it come about that God causes his people "to inherit substance," by leading them "in the way of righteousness, in the midst of the paths of judgment?" By leading them first into the way of righteousness through the opening up his holy law, which drives away all shadows.

We had been heaping together, with great toil, chaff and hay and straw and stubble; we had been as the prophet spoke, "when an hungry man dreameth, and, behold, he eateth; but he awaketh, and his soul is empty," (Isa. 29:8). So we were dreaming our life away continually with shadows, with a name to live, with a formal religion, with a mere external show of godliness, content with a few ordinances and sermons, and thinking that these would shelter us in the day of wrath.

Yet these were only shadows. Of no more avail to deliver our souls from the wrath to come were they than the shadowy form of a mountain in the morning sun. Howbeit, when the Lord began to lead us "in the way of righteousness," these previously precious shadows vanished. Something was then needed to conciliate the favour of God. Something was needed whereby the soul could escape those piercing eyes that looked it through and through, and the soul began to look after "substance." It needed realities, it needed a voice within from the Lord himself, a testimony of his eternal favour, and a manifestation of his love. There was "substance" needed.

The soul began to "hunger and thirst after righteousness," (Matt. 5:6), to pant and long after the manifestation of Jesus love, and to be restless and discontented and weary of everything short of the work and witness of the Holy Spirit. When the mouth is stopped, and the soul has become guilty before God, (Rom. 3:19), it wants pardon, peace, mercy, blood, and love; nothing else can satisfy it, and after this it pants with unutterable longings.

When Jesus leads his people "in the way of righteousness" by showing to them his glorious righteousness, they begin to "inherit the substance" after which they were panting. There is no substance to be found under the law; that is but a preparing of the soul to receive substance. It is emptying the soul that it may be filled; it is stripping the soul that it may be clothed; it is wounding the soul that it may be healed; it is bringing down the soul that it may be lifted up.

But when he leads "in the way of righteousness," that wonderful way whereby the soul is justified by his imputed righteousness, he causes that soul to "inherit substance," to inherit it even now upon earth, to have a taste of it, the beginnings of it, the pledge of it, and the firstfruits of it.

Oh, what a dreamy, shadowy thing is a mere profession of religion! What a delusive cheat is all the pleasure to be gained by sin! How it leaves a soul naked and bare, wounded, stripped, and guilty before God! Have we not oft promised ourselves pleasure in sin, but what have we found? The wormwood and the gall! All the anticipated pleasure vanished away, and its flight left us full of guilt and shame.

Yet if ever God indulged our souls in sweet communion with him, if ever he brought our affections to centre in himself, if ever he melted our souls at his feet, if ever he blessed us with the communications of his eternal favour and distinguishing love, there was substance in that. There was weight, there was power, there was the foretaste and pledge of a never-ending eternity.

13th

"And he shewed me Joshua the high priest standing before the angel of the LORD, and Satan standing at his right hand to resist him."
Zechariah 3:1

It is the object of Satan to keep those secure who are safe in his hands, nor does God see fit to disturb their quiet. Howbeit, where Satan perceives a work of grace in the heart, where he sees the eyes sometimes filled with tears, where he hears the sobs heaving with contrition, where he observes the knees oft bent in secret prayer, and where his listening ear hears the poor penitent oft confessing his sins, weaknesses, and backslidings before God he will soon be alongside. It is by these observations that Satan gains his intelligence, and wherever he sees this secret work going on in the soul, mad with wrath and filled with malice, he vents his hellish spleen against the chosen objects of God's love. Sometimes he tries to ensnare them into sin, sometimes to harass them with temptation, sometimes to stir up their wicked heart into desperate rebellion, sometimes to work upon their natural infidelity, and sometimes to plague them with many groundless doubts and fears as to their reality and sincerity before a heart-searching God.

So that whilst those who have no work of grace upon their hearts at all are left secure and free from doubt and fear, those in whom God is at work are exercised and troubled in their minds and often cannot really believe that they are the people in whom God takes delight. The depths of human hypocrisy, the dreadful lengths to which profession may go, the deceit of the carnal heart, the snares spread for the unwary feet, the fearful danger of being deceived at the last - these traps and pitfalls are not objects of anxiety to those dead in sin. As long as they can pacify natural conscience, and do something to soothe any transient conviction, they are glad to be deceived.

However, he that has a conscience tender in God's fear knows what a dreadful thing it is to be a hypocrite before God. He knows what it is to have a lie in his right hand, (Isa. 44:20), and be deluded by the prince of darkness. Therefore, until God himself with his own blessed lips speaks with power to his conscience, and establishes him in a blessed assurance of his saving interest in Christ by "shedding abroad his love in his heart," he must be tried and exercised in his mind. He must have these various tossings to and fro for this simple reason — because he cannot rest satisfied except in the personal manifestations of the mercy of God.

14th

"He that believeth on the Son of God hath the witness in himself."
1John 5:10

The grand point to have decided in a man's bosom is whether he is Christ's or not; and this is a problem which none but the Lord himself can solve. Blessed is he who has the witness in himself, and this he can only have by believing on the Son of God, as John speaks, "He that believeth on the Son of God hath the witness in himself." Moreover, as the apostle declares, this is the internal witness of the Spirit, "The Spirit itself beareth witness with our spirit, that we are the children of God," (Rom. 8:16).

What witness have you ever had in your bosom that you are a child of God? Or if you cannot discern this special witness, what marks or evidences, what tokens for good has the Lord bestowed upon you? Can you not remember something that the Lord has done for you in times past, some promise applied, some manifestation of his presence, some look of love, some softening touch of his gracious hand, which melted you into the dust, and brought sweet peace and assurance with it? It might not last long, or be very deep, but it was a precious evidence when felt that you belonged to Christ.

You remember the time and the circumstances, the darkness, distress and bondage before, and the deliverance into sweet liberty then enjoyed; but still you are dissatisfied. You want the Lord once more to appear; you want another smile, another word, another look, another promise, another testimony, and without it your soul often sinks down into doubt and fear.

Now this is the path in which most of God's saints walk. I will not say all because some are favoured with an abiding testimony, though even they have great sinkings and heavy trials, but with most it is a very chequered path. Thus, sometimes they are indulged with a smile, and then such darkness of mind falls upon them that they can scarcely see a single evidence. Then the sun shines again, but darkness once more covers the scene and down they sink into doubt, guilt, and fear. Then the Lord appears again, and then they love, and hope, and rejoice again; and so they go on, the scene ever changing, like an April day. The cycle continues until they come at last to the closing scene of life, when the Lord usually appears, scatters all their doubts and fears and darkness, and gives them a blessed dismissal into his own bosom of eternal rest and peace.

15th

"For our light affliction, which is but for a moment, worketh for us a far more exceeding and eternal weight of glory."
2Corinthians 4:17

The Hebrew word "glory" literally signifies "weight;" and the Apostle seems to have some allusion to that circumstance by connecting, as he does, the two words together. There is indeed a natural connection between what is weighty and what is solid and substantial. He would thus represent future glory as something solid, lasting, and durable, and therefore utterly distinct from the light, vain trifles of time, and even the passing afflictions of the day or hour.

But he seems chiefly to be alluding to the exceeding greatness of that glory which is to be revealed as compared with our present faculties of body and mind and all our present conceptions. It is as though he should say, 'In our present imperfect state, with our limited faculties of mind, and our weak, frail tabernacle, we could not bear the weight of that immortal glory which is prepared for the saints in the realms of bliss'. "Eye hath not seen, nor ear heard, neither have entered into the heart of man, the things which God hath prepared for them that love him," (1Cor. 2:9).

Heaven, with its opening bliss, would crush our present body and soul at once into the dust. As God said to Moses, "there shall no man see me, and live," (Ex. 33:20). When John in Patmos had a view of the glory of his risen Lord, though he had lain in his bosom at the last supper, yet he fell at his feet as dead. Therefore, we must have our soul purified from all stain of sin and expanded to the utmost of its immortal powers, and our body glorified and conformed to the body of the Lord Jesus Christ, that soul and body may alike be able to bear the weight of eternal glory with which they are to be clothed. As the Apostle speaks, "not for that we would be unclothed, but clothed upon, that mortality might be swallowed up of life," (2Cor. 5:4).

There is something more in the word "glory" that I must not pass by. The Lord, in that touching chapter, John 17, thus prays, or rather thus expresses his heavenly will, "Father, I will that they also, whom thou hast given me, be with me where I am; that they may behold my glory, which thou hast given me," (John 17:24). This is the "weight of glory" that the Apostle speaks of, not merely freedom from sin and sorrow, not merely seeing Christ as he is, but beholding and enjoying that unutterable glory which the Father gave him, which is all the glory of Godhead as revealed in, and shining through his human nature. The fullness and perfection of this glory is reserved for the saints of God to enjoy when they shall see him as he is, and know even also as they are known. We see a gleam of it when Christ is revealed to the soul, when the heavens are opened to faith, and when his beauty and blessedness are manifested to our heart by the power of God. Howbeit, the "exceeding and eternal weight of glory" can never be fully comprehended in this present life with our present body and present mind.

16th

"Not unto us, O LORD, not unto us, but unto thy name give glory, for thy mercy, and for thy truth's sake."
Psalm 115:1

Many of God's dear children cannot get much beyond gentle intimations of his mercy, passing touches of his gracious hand, and softenings of heart under a sense of undeserved goodness and love; yet they feel sensibly relieved by what their faith thus lays hold of and brings in, and give glory to God. Sometimes they hear the preached word and get a blessing under it, or some precious promise comes home to their soul with divine power as they read the word. Maybe as they are favoured in secret prayer, light and life breaking in upon their mind, they see such a glory in what is thus made known to them that they glorify God for what they see and feel. Yet more especially when the way of salvation is opened up to them, when Christ is revealed to their soul by the power of God, and when they see that wondrous plan unfolded, how God can be just, and yet the justifier of him who believes in Jesus; then as they view in the greatness of the mystery of the Person of Christ the blessed solution to the problem which has so exercised their mind, they freely and fully give all the glory to God.

'Lord,' they cry, 'who am I that thou should have pity and compassion upon me? Who am I that thou should touch my heart by thy grace and plant thy fear in my breast? Why hast thou led me to pray and seek thy face, and listened to my feeble cries? Why am I thus given to hope in thy mercy and am blessed in my soul with a manifestation of thy dear Son? Oh, who and what am I to be thus favoured, when thousands are left to perish in their sins? Oh, how glorious thou art! What a good God! How thy mercy melts my heart and thy goodness softens my soul! To thy name be all the honour and praise, both now and forever and ever.'

Here is giving glory to God, seeing and feeling his great mercy and benevolence, and ascribing it unto Him. Thus, true faith will always give God the glory. It will never take an atom of praise to itself, but will attribute the whole glory to God as its sole author and finisher, until blessings here end in blessings hereafter, and streams of grace on earth issue into the boundless ocean of glory in heaven.

17th

"Set your affection on things above, not on things on the earth."
Colossians 3:2

How are we to set our affections on things above? Can we do this great work of ourselves? No. Only the Lord manifesting his beauty and blessedness to our soul, and letting down the golden cord of his

December

love into our breast can draw up our affections and fix them where he sits at God's right hand. To do this, he captivates the heart by some look of love, some word of his grace, some sweet promise, or some divine truth spiritually applied. When he thus captivates the soul, and draws it up, then the affections flow unto him as the source and fountain of all blessings. We are not flogged into loving him, but drawn by love into love. Love cannot be bought or sold. It is an inward affection that flows naturally and necessarily towards its object and all connected with it. Thus, as love flows out to Christ, the affections instinctively and necessarily set themselves "on things above, not on things on the earth."

What, therefore, are these "things above?" They are the things which are stored up in Christ, breathed of Christ, and come out of Christ. Pardon, peace, righteousness, love, and "joy unspeakable and full of glory," (1Pet. 1:8), strength against sin, victory over death and hell, and power against besetting lusts and temptations. In short, they are all the blessings with which God has blessed his people "in heavenly places in Christ," (Eph. 1:3).

These, then, are the things above upon which the soul must set its affections, yet we must have some view by faith of the Person of Christ, the eternal Son of the eternal Father. He must be revealed to our soul by the power of God before we can see his beauty and blessedness, and so fall in love with him as "the chiefest among ten thousand," and "altogether lovely," (Song 5:10-16). Everything that speaks of Christ, savours of Christ, and breathes of Christ, becomes inexpressibly sweet and precious.

This is "the golden oil," (Zech. 4:12), that flows unceasing into the heart. This is the sweet-smelling myrrh which drops upon the handles of the lock, (Song 5:5); this is the aloes and cassia out of the ivory palaces, (Psa. 45:8); this is the love which "many waters cannot quench, neither can the floods drown," (Song. 8:7). It is by such experiences as these that the affections become set on "things above," and in no other way can they be lifted up from earth to heaven.

We cannot control our affections. They will ever run of their own accord. Therefore, if our affections are earthly they will run towards the earth, and if they are carnal and sensual they will flow toward carnal and sensual objects. Howbeit, when the Lord Jesus Christ by some manifestation of his glory and blessedness is set before us, or the Holy Spirit by taking of the things of Christ and revealing them to the soul sets Him before our eyes as the only object worthy of and claiming every desire of our heart, then the affections flood unstoppably out! Such an outpouring is both natural and spiritual, and when we experience it, then are the affections most certainly set on "things above."

December 18th

"God is the LORD, which hath shewed us light."
Psalm 118:27

The Psalmist was clearly possessed of light, for he says, "God is the LORD, which hath shewed us light," and this light was in him as "the light of life." This light had shone brightly into his heart, the rays and beams of divine truth penetrating deep into his conscience. He carried about with him a light which had come from God, and in this light he saw light itself and discerned everything which the light manifested. Thus, by this internal light he knew what was good and what was evil, what was sweet and what was bitter, what was true and what was false, what was spiritual and what was natural.

He did not say, 'This light came from creature exertion, this light was the produce of my own wisdom, this light was nature transmuted by some action of my own will, and thus gradually rose into existence from long and assiduous cultivation'. No, he ascribes the whole of that light which he possessed unto God the Lord, as the sole author and the only giver of it.

Now, if God the Lord has ever showed you and me the same light which he showed his servant of old, we carry about with us more or less a solemn conviction that we have received this light from him. There will indeed be many clouds of darkness to cover it. There will often be doubts and fears hovering like mists and fogs over our souls, whether the light which we have received be from God or not, yet there are solemn moments when the Lord is pleased a little to revive his work. There are times and seasons when he condescends to draw forth the affections of our hearts unto himself, to bring us into his presence, to hide us in some measure in the hollow of his hand and to give us access unto himself.

At such moments and seasons we carry this light about with us, in spite of all our unbelief and in spite of all the suggestions of the enemy. No matter all the doubts, fears, and suspicions that rise from the depths of the carnal mind, no matter all the counter-workings and underminings we daily face, we carry about with us at these times a solemn conviction that we have light, and that this light we have received from God.

Why so? Because we can look back to a time when we walked not in the light, when we felt not it's comfort and guidance, when everything spiritual and heavenly was dark to us, and we were dark to them.

December 19th

"God is our refuge and strength, a very present help in trouble."
Psalm 46:1

 The Christian who has known what it is to worship God in spirit and in truth has a God to help him in his direst extremities. As long as the spirit of prayer abides in his bosom – and that spirit once given is never taken away – he can at times and seasons pour out his heart before God, and find help and strength in him. This, then, is one of his blessed resources, that he has a God to go to, the Lord Almighty, into whose ears his cries may enter. Yet besides this, all the promises are on his side which are yes and amen in Christ Jesus. He is not without sword or shield either, or the whole armour of God, and added unto them is faith and hope, and secret supplies of strength made perfect in weakness. He is blessed too with a knowledge of the truth, and is not destitute of the manifold evidences of a saving interest in it.
 Thus, let a Christian be involved in the greatest perplexity, and there is still the voice of prayer in his bosom. There are still the goings up and actings of a living faith upon the Son of God who has been manifested to his soul, and there are still the firm anchorings of hope within the veil. He is not like a sailor cast upon a wide ocean without rudder, chart, or compass. He has a guide; he knows what to do; he knows what course to steer; he knows the land to which his eyes are ever directed. Let him sink into the greatest perplexity, let the storms and chaos of life swirl around him, and he still knows there is at the right hand of the Father a Jesus upon whom help is laid as one that is mighty to save.
 Still, still, the solemn fact is recorded deep in his mind, an ineffaceable impression has been left upon his soul from former discoveries of the King in his beauty, that this Jesus is able to save to the uttermost all who come unto God by him. Thus he is not left without resource, help, or hope.

20th

"To know the love of Christ, which passeth knowledge."
Ephesians 3:19

That eminent saint, the Apostle Paul, who had been in the third heaven, and there saw glorious sights, and heard unspeakable words, though he exhausted human language to set forth the surpassing excellency of the love of Christ, comes at last to this point – 'It passeth knowledge'. Indeed, and so it must pass knowledge. Is it not infinite? What measure can be assigned to the love of Christ? If Christ be God, and as such is the equal of the Father, his love is as infinite as he is.

Our love is the love of the creature, but the love of God is as great as Deity. It is as infinite as the self-existent I Am. It must needs therefore pass knowledge. You may wonder sometimes – and it is a wonder that will fill heaven itself with anthems of eternal praise – how such a glorious Christ as this can ever look down from heaven upon such creeping worms of the earth, upon such sinners who have provoked him over and over again by their misdeeds. That this exalted, pure, spotless Christ, in the height of his glory, can look down from sinless heaven, his dwelling-place, on such poor, miserable, wretched creatures as we is the mystery which fills angels with astonishment.

Yet it is the glory of Christ thus to love. It is his special glory to take his saints to heaven and there be witnesses of his glory and partakers of it. Therefore, because we are such crawling reptiles, because we are such undeserving creatures, because we are so utterly unworthy of the least notice from him, are we to put away all this matchless love from us, and say, 'Can Christ love one like me? Can the glorious Son of God from heaven his dwelling-place cast an eye of pity and compassion, love and tenderness upon one like me, who can scarcely at times bear with myself; who see and feel myself one of the vilest of the vile, and the worst of the worst? Oh, what must I be in the sight of the glorious Son of God?'

Yet, he says, "I have loved thee with an everlasting love," (Jer. 31:3). This love has breadths and lengths unknown. It has depths unplumbed and heights unscaled. Its breadth exceeds all human span; its length outvies all creature line; its depth surpasses all finite measure; and its height excels even angelic understanding.

This is the very reason why such love is so adapted to us. We need a love like this; a love to spread itself over us, to come down to our lowest depths; a love that can land us safe in heaven. A love short of this would be no love at all. We would exhaust it by our sins if this love were not what it is here represented. Long ago we would have out-sinned this love, and drained it dry by our ingratitude, rebellion, and misdoing. Yet because it is what it is, love so wondrous, so deep, so long, so broad, and so high, because it is what it is, it is suitable to every want and every woe.

December 21st

"Yea, though I walk through the valley of the shadow of death, I will fear no evil: for thou art with me; thy rod and thy staff they comfort me."
Psalm 23:4

Death, the gaunt king of terrors; Death, who with his resistless scythe mows down all the millions of humanity; Death, who awaits his victims at every corner; Death, that must soon lay you and I low in the grave, casts a shadow wherever he comes. He visits the sick room and casts a shadow there. He hangs over the cradle where his shadow falls on the infant's face. He comes in the letter from afar, or with the black seal and mourning envelope put into our hand at home, and these tidings or these tokens cast a deep shadow over our hearts. Indeed, where is the place where death does not cast his shadow? Where is the house where this shade has never fallen? Wherever he comes, he shadow falls on all. He is "the last enemy," (1Cor. 15:26), and he is the final fulfilment of the original curse.

Even though death, to a saint of God, is stripped of its ultimate terrors, robbed of its sting, and disarmed of its victory; though, to the expiring believer it is but a portal of life into the mansions of eternal bliss, yet, say what we may, even as a portal it casts a shadow. Even David, though full of sweet confidence that 'the Lord was his shepherd', at the very time when 'his cup ran over' with the Lord's goodness and love, calls it 'the valley of the shadow of death'. God's 'rod and staff' comforted him, and he 'feared no evil', but it was still a valley, overhung by frowning mountains and dark, overarching woods, and "the shadow of death" was spread upon it from the entrance to the end.

And yet, dear reader, it was to him but a shadow.

To the graceless, to the Christless, to the impenitent and the unbelieving, it is a substance, for the wrath of God which burns to the lowest hell awaits them at the end of the valley, there to plunge them into the lake that burns with fire and brimstone. Yet to those who die in the Lord, in the sweet enjoyment of peace through his blood, it is but a passing shadow, albeit sometimes a thunderously dark one. For them the substance died when Jesus died. It was buried with him in the tomb, but it did not rise with him, for he destroyed it when he "abolished death," and "brought life and immortality to light through the gospel," (2Tim. 1:10).

December
22nd

"But let patience have her perfect work, that ye may be perfect and entire, wanting nothing."
James 1:4

    The word "perfect" in the Scripture does not mean, when applied to a saint of God, anything approaching to the usual idea of perfection as implying spotless, sinless holiness. It means one who is 'matured' and ripened in the life of God, no longer a child but a grown man. As a tree grown to its full stature is said to have attained perfection, so when the Holy Spirit has brought forth the work of patience in your soul, as far as that work is concerned you are perfect, for it is God's work in you. You are "entire." You are in possession of all which that grace gives, and wanting, or lacking, nothing which that grace can communicate.
    To submit wholly to the will of God, and be lost and swallowed up in conformity to it, is the height of Christian perfection here below. He who has that lacks nothing, for he has all things in Christ. What, then, is the greatest height of grace to which the soul can arrive? Where did grace shine forth so conspicuously as in the Lord Jesus Christ, and where did grace manifest itself more than in the gloomy garden and on the suffering cross? Was not the human nature of Jesus more manifestly filled with the Spirit, and did not every grace shine forth in him more conspicuously in Gethsemane and on Calvary than when enraptured upon the Mount of Transfiguration?
    So it is that there is more manifested grace in the heart of a saint of God who, under trial and temptation, can say, "Thy will be done," and submit himself to the chastening rod of his heavenly Father than when he is basking in the full beams of the Sun of righteousness. How often we are mistaken in this matter; longing for enjoyment, instead of seeing that true grace makes us submit to the will of God, whether in the valley or upon the mount!

23rd

"And let the beauty of the LORD our God be upon us: and establish thou the work of our hands upon us; yea, the work of our hands establish thou it."
Psalm 90:17

December

What is this beauty? It is here described as "The beauty of the Lord our God." It is, therefore, the beauty of the God-man; the loveliness, the holiness, the perfection, and glory that ever dwells in the Son of God. Now "days of affliction," (Job 30:16), and years of evil have marred all creature loveliness. There was a time, perhaps, when we could take some pleasure and delight in what we were, or what we vainly fancied we would be. Our own righteousness had a beauty and loveliness to us; and our religion was amiable and pleasing in our own sight, but what has become of it? Marred, marred, totally marred. By what? By days of affliction and years of evil. These have effectually ruined, defaced, and polluted all creature loveliness. In truth, we were once deeply in love with self, but self is now shown to us such a hideous monster, in so vile and despicable a light, that we have fallen out of love with him altogether. We have seen, at times, such beauty, glory, loveliness, and suitability in the Son of God, that as we have fallen out of love with self, we have fallen in love with the saviour.

Thus as all our own beauty and our own loveliness have been marred and defaced, and are cast aside, and the beauty and loveliness of the Lord has risen in due proportion. This has become the desire of our soul.

Let the beauty of the Lord our God be upon us. Let us stand accepted in it; let it be put upon us by the imputation of God himself; let us be clothed with it manifestly before the eyes of a heart-searching Jehovah. Let the beauty of Jesus' atoning blood, the beauty of his perfect righteousness, the beauty of his dying love, the beauty and holiness of his glorious Person be upon us, covering all our filth, guilt and shame, spreading itself over all our nakedness, sin and pollution. When God looks upon us, may he not see us as we are – marred, defaced, and full of wounds, bruises and putrefying sores. May he see us standing accepted in the Beloved, with 'the beauty of the Lord our God' upon us.

Oh, what a matchless robe is this! It outshines angels, for it is the righteousness of God's only-begotten Son! If we stand with "the beauty of the Lord our God" upon us we can bid defiance to all charges of the law, to all the accusations of a guilty conscience, and to all the darts from hell.

24th

"Not by works of righteousness which we have done, but according to his mercy he saved us."
Titus 3:5

To view mercy in its real character, we must go to Calvary. It is not sufficient to contrast the purity of God with the impurity of man. That indeed affords us some view of what mercy must be to reach down into the depths of the fall, but it is a side face of that precious attribute. To see its full face shining upon the redeemed we must go by faith, under the secret teachings and leadings of the Holy Spirit, to see "Immanuel, God with us," on his knees in Gethsemane's garden. We must view him naked upon the cross, groaning, bleeding, agonising, dying. We must view Godhead and manhood united together in the Person of a suffering Jesus, and witness the power of the Godhead bearing up the suffering manhood. We must view that wondrous spectacle of love and blood, and feel our eyes flowing down in streams of sorrow, humility, and contrition at the sight, in order to enter a little into the depths of the tender mercy of God. Nothing but this can really break the sinner's heart.

"Law and terrors do but harden,
All the while they work alone;
But a sense of blood-bought pardon
Soon dissolves a heart of stone."

Law terrors, death and judgment, infinite purity, and eternal vengeance will not soften or break a sinner's heart. Howbeit, if he is led to view a suffering Immanuel, and a sweet testimony is raised up in his conscience that those sufferings were for him, this and this only will break his stubborn heart all to pieces. Thus, only by bringing a sweet sense of love and blood into his heart does the blessed Spirit show a sinner some of the depths of the tender mercy of God.

25th

"Who, being in the form of God, thought it not robbery to be equal with God, but made himself of no reputation, and took upon him the form of a servant, and was made in the likeness of men."
Philippians 2:6-7

The humanity of our blessed Lord was actual flesh and blood from the moment of its conception, a perfect human body, to which was united a perfect human soul. Both were without sin or else he could not be the Lamb without blemish. Both were without sin or his pure humanity would not have been that "holy One" born of the Virgin, who should be called the Son of God. Thus he came forth as the

Lamb of God, without spot or blemish. Well indeed might the Apostle say, "Great is the mystery of godliness," (1Tim. 3:16).

Here we see as in a mirror the wonderful love of Jesus, that he who is the Son of God, co-equal and co-eternal with the Father and the Holy Spirit, a sharer of the Father's essence and glory, should stoop so low to lift us up so high. What condescension that he should unite his glorious Person to our nature, flesh and blood, and wear a human body like our own. To feel as we do, to speak as we do, to walk as we do, to eat, drink, hunger and thirst as we do, and to weep, sigh, and mourn as we do. O what union he showed! Yet all the while he remained the Son of God, having a divine nature in as close union with his human nature as our soul has with our bodily frame.

We cannot tell how our soul is in union with our body. We know it is so, but how we cannot tell. We know the fact, but we cannot explain the mode. In like manner, we cannot tell how Christ's divine nature is in union with his human nature; we know it is so by the testimony of God, and by the express revelation of his word. That revelation to a believer answers all inquiry.

When any man says to me, "Can you explain the mystery of the two natures in Christ?" I ask in my turn, "Can you explain the mystery of your own existence? Can you explain to me how you are able to lift up your own hand, see with your own eye, hear with your own ear, move with your own foot? No man has ever yet been able to fully explain these apparently simple things, feats every child can perform, but facts which no philosopher can fathom. Tell me, how does your mind cause you to act upon matter? How is it that you can wish to do a thing with your mind, and can do it instantaneously with your body?

"If you can explain your own existence and unravel the mystery of your soul acting in union with your body, then I will allow that man may unravel the mystery of the union of Deity and humanity in the Person of the Son of God as he lived upon earth, and as he now lives in heaven."

Beautiful upon this mystery are the words of Deer, "How it was done we can't discuss; but this we know, 'twas done for us," and happy those who can use these words without a wavering tongue!

26th

"Now faith is the substance of things hoped for, the evidence of things not seen."
Hebrews 11:1

December

What an eminent grace is the grace of faith! I sometimes call it the Queen of graces, for faith seems to lead, though hope and love follow almost side by side. Yet still, faith, as the Queen, seems to go in the foremost rank and to claim the most eminent place.

Now, what is faith? That is a question of questions, for on it hangs heaven or hell. God himself has given us a clear definition of it where he says, "faith is the substance of things hoped for." In other words, faith in the soul gives a realisation to the things in which we are brought to hope. It takes what to most men are airy shadows, mere words and names, and gives them a substantial existence, a firm abiding place in the heart and conscience. The Apostle adds that it is "the evidence of things not seen." In other words faith, by believing the testimony of God, is to us an internal eye whereby we see those things which to the natural eye are invisible.

Thus adopting the Apostle's definition, we may call faith 'the eye of the soul', for we read that by faith Moses "endured, as seeing him who is invisible," (Heb. 11:27). For it is only by faith that we see either God, or the precious things of God. It is only by faith that we feel their power. It is only by faith that we know they are real, and that we have a substantial, saving interest in them. This faith is the special gift of God. It is not the exercise of any intellectual faculty. It is not the result of reasoning or argument. Nor does it spring from any historical proof. It is a special gift of God, a grace of the Spirit raised up by the power of God in the soul, and acting upon the truth of God as the blessed Spirit draws it forth. Jesus is the Author; Jesus is the finisher of it; and we have no more, and I believe no less faith, than he himself, by his almighty power, is pleased to grant and to sustain.

Now, looking at faith and some of its properties, we may branch out a little in describing how faith acts. There is an expression of the Apostle's that casts a sweet light upon the work of faith, where he says, "unto us was the gospel preached, as well as unto them: but the word preached did not profit them, not being mixed with faith in them that heard it," (Heb. 4:2). Here he brings forward a special operation of faith in that it mixes with the word of truth, and it does it thus.

God the Holy Spirit applies God's word to the conscience and thus raises up the grace of faith; this grace of faith embraces God's testimony, and so intermingles itself with this testimony that it enters into it, appropriates it, and gives it a substantial realisation and personal indwelling.

See how this was done in the instance of Abram. God comes to him in the night visions, and says to him, "Fear not, Abram: I am thy shield, and thy exceeding great reward," (Gen. 15:1), but Abram, in a fit of unbelief, says, "what wilt thou give me, seeing I go childless, and the steward of my house is this Eliezer of Damascus?" The Lord then takes him abroad and shows him the stars of the sky and tells him, "So shall thy seed be." Now here was the testimony of God in a certain promise made to Abram's conscience, and upon this, faith immediately sprang up in his soul, for we read, "and he believed in the LORD; and he counted it to him for righteousness," (Gen. 15:6).

When God spoke to his soul, Abram believed it by the operation of God's Spirit on his heart, and so it is with every child of God. He believes what God speaks to him, and inwardly credits it, because he feels the Holy Spirit applying it powerfully to his soul at the same time as the same Holy Spirit is raising up faith in his heart by the application of God's word. Thus the two are mixed, and the word is given a substantial realisation, and a firm abiding place in his conscience.

27th

"They shall mount up with wings as eagles."
Isaiah 40:31

It is said of the eagle that he mounts up towards the sun, and that of all birds he is the only one which can gaze upon the sun with unshrinking eye. So it is with faith in the soul. The Lord's people alone can look by faith upon the "Sun of righteousness," can gaze upon a glorious Immanuel at the right hand of the Father, and see a precious Jesus ever interceding for them and drawing them near to his bosom. When this blessed Jesus communicates a measure of his love and blood to their consciences, raising up and drawing forth faith in his name, then the soul begins to mount up with these wings like an eagle. It soars higher and higher until it comes into the very presence of God, with a spiralling spiritual flight until it penetrates into the very throne room of Jehovah.

Now, has not your soul thus sometimes soared as upon eagle's wings? Have there not been those communications of divine life and light, those mountains of faith, those anchorings of hope, those goings forth of love, whereby your soul was enabled to mount up and find delight in Jesus, and felt his name, love, and blood precious? Have you not also mounted up in the exercise of living faith and hope, and of heavenly affection?

Sometimes we are so fastened down to this earth, this valley of tears, this waste-howling wilderness, and so chained to it that we are like a bird with a broken wing. We simply cannot mount up anywhere. We are swallowed by the world, forgetting God and godliness. Yet are there not times and seasons when the soul is delivered from these chains and fetters, when earthly cares drop off from the mind. Do we not have seasons when our wings are strong and fresh pinions have been given, when the world and its temptations, sins and snares are left behind? Is there not, on times, a sweet mounting up of the feelings in heavenly affection?

This then is to "mount up with wings as eagles," and the soaring soul never ceases to mount until it comes into the very presence of the Three in One God of the spiritual Israel.

28th

"And now, brethren, I commend you to God, and to the word of his grace, which is able to build you up, and to give you an inheritance among all them which are sanctified."
Acts 20:32

Not only did Paul commend the church at Ephesus to God, but he commended them also in an especial manner to the word of his grace. There is a difference between grace and the word of his grace. Nothing but grace can save the soul; nothing but superabounding grace can blot out and hide from the view of justice our aggravated iniquities. Howbeit, the word of his grace is that word which brings this grace into the heart, which communicates life and power to the soul, which the Spirit by his inward teaching and testimony seals on the conscience. By this word of grace, he reveals and sheds abroad that favour of which he testifies.

This is what the Lord's people need, for it is the word of grace which reaches their soul. It is not the reading of grace in God's word that brings peace into a man's heart; it is the word of his grace when God is pleased to speak that word with a divine power into a man's soul that brings salvation with it.

Now, the Lord's people are continually in those trying states and circumstances out of which nothing can deliver them but the word of God's grace. If the soul is passing through severe trials, hearing of grace that will not deliver it from them. If it be beset with powerful temptations it is not reading about grace that can break them to pieces. Howbeit, the word of his grace, when the Lord himself is pleased to speak it with his own blessed lips and apply some promise with his own divine power, supports under trial, delivers from temptation, breaks snares to pieces, makes crooked things straight and rough places plain, brings the prisoner out of the prison-house, and takes off the yoke by reason of the anointing.

December 29th

"For the preaching of the cross is to them that perish foolishness; but unto us which are saved it is the power of God."
1Corinthians 1:18

Has the gospel ever come to you in power? If it has, it has done something for you. Has it ever, then, dispelled your many doubts and fears? Has it ever made Jesus precious to your soul; ever brought with it light, life, liberty, and love; ever given you access to the bosom of God? Has it ever communicated that spirit of holy boldness and filial confidence, whereby, as a successful wrestler, you were enabled to prevail with God, and get a blessing out of his hands and heart?

However, it is no use talking of power when nothing is done. If a manufacturer requires an engine of an hundred horsepower, but the engineer builds an engine of only ninety horsepower, upon trial the engine will be found so far useless. Now, what would his employer say to him, but, 'What a mistake you have made! I ordered an engine of an hundred horsepower, and this is only ninety. It will not do the work I want. Take it away.'

So it is in grace. We need a power that can move the many different weights we find ourselves under. First we need moved the weight of sin from off a guilty conscience, killing the fears of death and hell. Then there is the burden of unbelief and the heavy load of carnality, for none escape the fierce pull of many grievous temptations which make the soul cry, "O LORD, I am oppressed; undertake for me," (Isa. 3:14).

What heavy weights there are to be lifted off, and what huge stones need to be rolled away from the sepulchre! The world is to be overcome; lusts and passions crucified; the old man of sin mortified, and Satan to be defeated and put to flight! Yet besides all these weights to be removed, and enemies to be overcome, there is the soul to be saved, heaven to be brought near, hell put out of sight, the law to be forever silenced, death to be robbed of its sting, and the grave of its victory. There is an eternal course of glory to be won. Oh, what a mighty work has to be done in us and for us – a work which no man ever has done or ever can do for himself!

December 30th

> "To whom coming, as unto a living stone, disallowed indeed of men, but chosen of God, and precious."
> 1Peter 2:4

Though disallowed of men, the Lord Jesus Christ is chosen by God, and God, I speak it with reverence, cannot make an unwise choice. To think that, would be to attribute folly to the Most High. Christ is chosen of God, because he alone was fitted for the work of salvation. It would have crushed an archangel to bear what Jesus bore. No bright angel, nor glorious seraph, no created being, however exalted, could have borne the load of sin; and therefore none but God's own Son, not by office, but by eternal generation, the Son of the Father in truth and love, could carry the weight of imputed sin and guilt. As Deer says, "Such loads of guilt were on Him put, He alone could sustain the weight."

He was chosen of God that he might be Zion's Representative, Zion's Sin-bearer, and Zion's glorious Head. He was chosen that there might be a foundation for the Church to rest upon with all her miseries, all her sins, all her sorrows, all her base backslidings and idolatries, and all her weight of woe and depths of guilt. It needs be a strong foundation to bear this Church, so loaded with degradation, ignominy, and shame! God's own Son, and none else in heaven or in earth, could bear all this. "Look unto me, and be ye saved, all the ends of the earth: for I am God, and there is none else," (Isa. 45:22).

He was chosen of God in eternity, in the divine councils, that he might be a Mediator. He was chosen to become man; chosen to become the Rock of Ages, Zion's anchorage, her harbour, resting-place, and home. Therefore, Jesus ever was and ever will be unspeakably precious to the Father's heart. Man despises him, but God honours him; man disallows him, but God values him, for he is his co-equal Son. Yet God not only values him as his fellow, having chosen him to be the Mediator, but finds him unspeakably precious in his Deity, in his humanity, in his blood, obedience and sufferings. He is precious in his death, precious in his resurrection, precious in his ascension to God's right hand. He is precious in the eyes of God as the Great High Priest over the house of God, and the only Mediator between God and man. Is he not worthy of all your trust, of all your confidence, all your hope, and of all your acceptance?

Look where we will, he is our only hope. Look at the world, what can you reap from that but a harvest of sorrow? Look at everything that man calls good and great and all that man highly values; some of it is good perhaps for time, but it is valueless for eternity. Few could put a higher value than I upon what man naturally regards as good and great, especially upon human learning, and attainments in knowledge and science. Yet I have seen them as compared with eternity, seen them to be but breath and smoke - vapours that pass away and are no more seen.

Yet the things of eternity, the peace of God in the heart, the work of the Spirit upon the soul and all the blessed realities of salvation, why these are not like the airy mists of time. These are not vapours that spring idly out of earth only to return back unto it. These are enduring and eternal, "an inheritance incorruptible, and undefiled, and that fadeth not away, reserved in heaven for you," (1Pet. 1:4).

31st

"My counsel shall stand, and I will do all my pleasure." Isaiah 46:10

There is one grand idea running through the whole of Scripture from Genesis to Revelation. This one grand idea runs through every part of the sacred page, and, like a golden band, unites the whole together. What is this one grand thought?

God has many thoughts as well as we, for he tells us that the thoughts of his heart stand to all generations, (Psa. 33:11). We read in the same verse of the counsel of the Lord which standeth forever, and the apostle tells us also of his working "all things after the counsel of his own will," (Eph. 1:11). Thus in the mind of God, as well as in the mode of his subsistence, there is unity and variety. There is his one thought, and his many thoughts, for though his thoughts are many, his counsel is but one, and is the exaltation and glorification of his dear Son.

It may be as well briefly to trace this unity of thought and the variety of its expression. We see it first in the creation of man, when God made him in his own image and after his own likeness, (Gen. 1:26). Therein was the expression of God's one thought, for the first Adam was created as a type of the second Adam. As Christ was by lineal descent "the son of Adam," (Luke 3), there was a foreview in the creation of the first man of the incarnation of God's dear Son, who is the brightness of his glory and the express image of his Person.

Next, observe how all things were put under Adam's feet, and how he was thus made the visible head of creation. Read this exaltation of Adam in the light of Psalm 8, and you will see how the inspired

Psalmist, as interpreted by the Apostle, (Heb. 2:7-9), viewed Adam, in having all things put under his feet, as a type of Christ. "What is man, that thou art mindful of him? Or the son of man, that thou visitest him? Thou madest him a little lower than the angels; thou crownedst him with glory and honour, and didst set him over the works of thy hands. Thou hast put all things in subjection under his feet."

Now read the first promise given after the fall, that the seed of the woman should bruise the serpent's head, (Gen. 3:15). God's one thought is again there expressed, his dominant counsel in the incarnation of his dear Son, as the seed of the woman to bruise Satan's head. Look at Noah preserved in the ark with his family when the rest of the world was swept away by the deluge, that from the loins of Adam might come the promised seed.

Take the case of Abraham, called by a special calling, that in him and his seed all the nations of the earth might be blessed. Here we have again God's one thought. Take, again, the whole of the Levitical dispensation. Every rite, every sacrifice, every type, every ordinance, all still bear the same stamp of God's one thought, and indeed every part of Scripture is but an exposition of this one thought of God's heart, of this one counsel of his eternal will.

The word of God is a total mystery to us, and we can see no beauty or harmony in the various books of either the Old or the New Testaments until we see the mind of God in it, until we gather up God's thoughts, and especially that grand thought which I have spoken of as binding the whole together. That thought, the exaltation of his dear Son to his own right hand as the promised reward of his sufferings and death, and the glorious result of his resurrection and ascension up to the courts of bliss, is the golden thread which winds its way through every page from Genesis to Revelation.

Scripture Index

Scripture Reference	Occurrences	Daily Reading
Acts 14:22	1	4th January
16:5	1	27th July
20:24	1	9th July
20:28	1	1st March
20:32	1	28th December
Amos 4:7	1	15th May
6:1	1	4th February
1 Chronicles 4:10	2	27th February
4:10	2	28th February
2 Chronicles 6:29	1	17th July
20:12	1	20th April
Colossians 1:18	1	24th August
2:3	1	5th September
2:6-7	1	20th June
2:9	1	22nd January
3:2	1	17th December
3:3	1	16th October
3:4	1	3rd August
1 Corinthians 1:9	1	3rd September
1:18	1	29th December
1:22-23	1	2nd July
1:30-31	1	21st April
2:4	2	11th September
2:4	2	12th September
2:5	1	2nd April
3:11	1	26th November
3:13	2	28th January
3:13	2	10th June
3:22	1	27th October
3:23	1	28th October
6:11	1	2nd November
2 Corinthians 1:7	1	11th July
1:9	1	19th November
3:17	1	20th February
3:18	1	7th April
4:4	1	21st March
4:6	1	20th May

Reference		Date
2 Corinthians 4:7	1	8th November
4:8	2	30th June
4:8	2	19th August
4:9	1	6th October
4:10	2	24th January
4:10	2	25th January
4:11	1	3rd March
4:13	1	26th April
4:17	1	15th December
Daniel 4:37	1	6th July
Deuteronomy 8:3	1	23rd September
32:2	1	15th October
32:10	1	22nd June
32:39	1	21st February
33:27	2	30th March
33:27	2	2nd August
Ecclesiastes 3:3	1	15th June
3:4	1	5th November
12:7	1	9th December
Ephesians 1:3	1	14th September
1:4-5	1	1st December
1:13	1	3rd June
1:14	1	8th October
1:19-20	1	5th March
2:4-6	1	24th July
2:5	1	31st October
2:6	1	25th July
2:10	1	29th August
2:19	1	16th March
2:20	1	29th June
2:21	1	16th May
3:17	1	13th June
3:19	1	20th December
4:15	1	18th February
4:21	1	12th April
5:13	1	15th April
5:25-26	1	27th May
5:27	1	28th May
6:18	1	8th April
Exodus 25:22	1	17th February

Ezekiel 21:27	1	30th November
36:25	1	18th January
36:26	1	13th August
47:12	1	5th July
Galatians 2:20	1	15th August
5:17	1	31st May
5:18	1	11th November
6:14	1	3rd July
Genesis 5:24	1	13th September
18:14	1	27th March
32:26	1	9th November
49:22-24	1	16th September
Hebrews 1:4	1	27th August
2:8	1	1st September
2:9	1	4th April
2:14	1	23rd February
2:15	1	13th November
2:17	1	1st May
4:3	1	9th June
4:12	1	10th February
4:15	1	8th May
5:7	2	25th March
5:7	2	26th March
6:9	1	18th June
6:18	1	28th April
6:20	1	4th October
7:15-16	1	18th November
8:1-2	1	13th July
9:13-14	1	12th August
10:12	1	9th September
10:14	1	29th March
10:19	1	5th June
10:39	1	24th November
11:1	1	26th December
12:1	1	30th January
12:6	1	5th December
12:11	1	22nd July
Hosea 2:19	1	19th May
6:3	2	5th May
6:3	2	24th September
11:4	1	12th February

Hosea 11:7	1	30th October
11:9	1	8th June
13:9	1	1st April
Isaiah 2:11	1	1st October
4:2	2	3rd May
4:2	2	4th May
4:5	2	6th February
4:5	2	7th February
6:5	1	25th April
7:14	1	11th April
27:13	1	17th June
33:2	1	8th March
33:6	1	7th August
35:4	2	28th September
35:4	2	29th September
40:4	1	8th September
40:29	1	31st August
40:31	2	11th June
40:31	2	27th December
45:3	1	7th September
45:22	1	9th February
45:24	2	24th May
45:24	2	23rd October
46:10	1	31st December
53:6	1	11th October
54:5	1	20th November
64:8	1	17th August
James 1:4	2	18th August
1:4	2	22nd December
1:18	1	18th April
Jeremiah 2:13	1	5th February
2:17	1	19th October
2:2	2	24th February
2:2	2	6th June
8:22	1	14th March
15:12	1	16th April
17:9	1	9th October
31:9	1	11th August
45:5	2	3rd October
45:5	2	21st October
50:5	2	2nd February
50:5	2	23rd August

50:6	1	7th November
50:20	1	16th June
Job 23:10	1	13th March
28:7	1	25th November
John 1:12	1	19th June
1:14	1	22nd October
3:6	1	19th March
4:10	1	14th February
6:29	1	18th October
6:37	1	2nd June
:32	1	16th August
8:35	1	5th April
10:1	1	10th April
10:28	1	7th July
10:29	1	15th November
10:30	1	17th March
11:25	2	25th August
11:25	2	26th August
14:6	1	8th August
14:16-17	1	8th January
14:19	1	24th April
14:26	1	13th October
15:3	1	14th April
15:5	1	10th July
15:8	1	11th May
15:26	1	22nd February
16:13	1	31st January
17:3	1	5th August
17:17	1	26th May
17:19	1	8th February
17:24	1	22nd September
1 John 1:9	1	3rd December
2:2	1	28th June
2:27	1	21st September
3:2	1	22nd April
4:7	2	29th July
4:7	2	4th November
4:13	1	18th May
4:16	1	4th September
5:7	1	27th April
5:10	1	14th December
5:20	1	25th October

Jude 1	1	11th January
20	1	14th July
21	1	15th July
Lamentations 3:26	1	3rd November
3:39	1	5th October
:41	1	7th January
5:21	1	23rd July
Luke 1:74-75	1	23rd May
1:78-79	1	5th January
18:7	1	6th April
22:28	1	12th May
22:29	1	13th May
24:21	1	22nd November
Malachi 4:2	1	2nd September
Mark 4:28	1	15th September
Matthew 1:23	1	9th May
5:3	1	26th June
5:6	1	30th September
5:16	1	9th April
5:20	1	24th October
9:12	1	29th October
11:5	1	26th February
11:25	1	7th October
12:20	1	21st August
14:33	1	12th July
26:41	2	2nd May
26:41	2	6th November
28:5	1	10th August
Micah 7:19	1	12th November
Nehemiah 5:15	1	11th December
Numbers 6:24	2	13th January
6:24	2	14th January
6:25	2	15th January
6:25	2	16th January
6:26	1	17th January
1 Peter 1:2	2	22nd March

1 Peter 1:2	2	17th October
2:4	1	30th December
2:24	1	21st May
3:16	1	14th November
5:10	2	29th April
5:10	2	4th August
2 Peter 1:1	1	17th November
1:2	1	2nd October
1:10-11	1	20th August
1:19	1	18th March
1:20-21	1	9th January
3:18	1	2nd January
Philippians 1:27	1	26th July
2:6-7	1	25th December
3:12	1	11th February
3:13-14	1	6th May
3:9	1	14th October
4:6	1	16th November
4:19	1	30th May
Proverbs 8:20-21	1	12th December
10:21	1	13th April
15:6	1	3rd April
16:15	1	10th November
16:32	1	6th August
17:17	1	23rd April
19:21	1	2nd March
22:15	1	15th March
27:7	1	28th August
Psalm 3:3	1	28th November
4:6	1	14th May
12:5	1	30th July
16:10	1	28th March
17:5	1	1st January
19:8	1	17th May
23:4	1	21st December
25:4	1	16th February
25:5	1	17th April
39:7	1	10th May
39:8	1	21st November
42:1	1	1st July
42:2	1	10th December

Psalm 43:3	1	22nd August
46:1	1	19th December
48:2	1	7th March
51:17	1	3rd February
55:19	1	19th July
63:1	1	6th January
63:2	1	6th September
84:5-6	1	23rd June
4:7	2	24th June
84:7	2	25th June
84:11	3	19th January
84:11	3	23rd March
84:11	3	26th September
84:12	1	6th December
89:1	1	3rd January
90:16	1	1st August
90:17	1	23rd December
91:14	1	8th July
91:16	1	12th October
91:7	1	21st January
103:1	1	10th January
104:27	1	26th October
107:6	1	31st July
107:7	1	24th March
107:10	1	12th March
107:39	1	14th June
109:22	1	4th December
112:4	1	9th August
115:1	1	16th December
118:27	2	4th March
118:27	2	18th December
119:17	1	20th July
119:31	1	22nd May
119:41-42	1	11th March
119:105	1	21st June
119:130	1	1st November
119:175	1	29th February
132:15	1	12th June
138:2	1	14th August
139:23-24	1	16th July
141:8	1	28th July
145:15	1	27th January
145:16	1	19th February
Revelation 12:10	1	15th February

Revelation 12:11	1	30th August
21:7	2	7th December
21:7	2	8th December
Romans 1:16	1	10th March
3:23	1	4th June
3:24-25	1	27th September
3:26	1	2nd December
4:16	1	6th March
4:18	1	23rd November
5:5	1	10th October
6:11	1	25th September
6:17	1	9th March
7:9	1	30th April
8:6	1	7th May
8:10	1	27th November
8:17	1	1st February
8:26	1	18th July
8:29	1	20th March
8:34	1	1st June
8:37	1	10th September
9:16	1	21st July
10:11	1	4th July
12:1	1	17th September
12:2	3	18th September
12:2	3	19th September
12:2	3	20th September
1 Samuel 1:15	1	19th April
2 Samuel 14:14	1	31st March
Song of Solomon 4:16	1	25th May
1 Thessalonians 1:3	1	27th June
2 Thessalonians 1:4-5	1	23rd January
2:13	1	12th January
1 Timothy 1:18-19	1	29th November
1:19	1	29th May
2:5	1	26th January
6:12	1	29th January
2 Timothy 2:3	1	20th October

2 Timothy 2:11-12	1	25th February
3:16-17	1	20th January
Titus 2:14	1	13th February
3:5	1	24th December
Zechariah 3:1	1	13th December
3:8	1	7th June

Printed in Great Britain
by Amazon